Connect and Divide

Connect and Divide

The Practice Turn in Media Studies

Edited by
Erhard Schüttpelz, Ulrike Bergermann,
Monika Dommann, Jeremy Stolow, Nadine Taha

DIAPHANES

Gedruckt und organisiert mit freundlicher Unterstützung der DFG.

1st edition
ISBN 978-3-0358-0051-7
© DIAPHANES, Zurich 2021

Layout: 2edit, Zurich
Printed in Germany

www.diaphanes.com

Table of Contents

Connect and Divide:
The Practice Turn in Media Studies

Media divide and connect simultaneously: they act as intermediaries between otherwise disconnected entities, and as a *middle* that mediates, but also shields different entities from each other. This ambiguity gives rise to conflicting interpretations, and it evokes all those figures that give a first clue about this Janus-faced relationship of *connect and divide*: gatekeeper and parasite, amongst others. And if we give accounts of media before and after their mediated action, we refer to persons and organizations, automatisms and artifacts, signals and inscriptions, and we seem to find it easy to refer to their distinct potentials and dis/abilities. But within the interaction, the *middle* of media itself seems to be distributed right across the mix of material, semiotic and personal entities involved, and the location of agency is hard to pin down. In case of breakdown we have to disentangle the mix; in case of smooth operations action becomes all the more distributed and potentially untraceable—which makes its attribution a matter of the simultaneously occurring distribution of (official and unofficial) knowledge, labor and power. The empirical and historical investigation of this two-faced relationship of *connect and divide* has thus resulted in what may be called a veritable *practice turn in media studies*. This book will discuss four aspects of the practice turn in media studies:

Section 1: Media History from a Praxeological Perspective

Since its origins in Toronto or Freiburg, media studies has developed what might be called strong narratives of history, identifying causes and origins and often bordering on the teleological; sometimes even making quite specific media both the telos and cause of fundamental historical changes. The challenge of these sometimes mythical narratives has inspired a host of corrections, revisions and reservations from professional historians, who are devoted to a cult of the archives (Lorraine Daston) and used to accounting for which evidence they can use or not use: "How can I know what I want to propose?" (in Marc Bloch's famous words). This skeptical question leads historians and media historians alike to a double focus on media practices: their own and those they have to study. Historians developed media studies *avant la lettre* by making the medium the message in their *Quellenkritik*, by making the production, distribution and reception of texts and artifacts both the topic and resource of historical work. How do we reconstruct and deconstruct the media practices of the past? Which practice theories are helpful for historians, who are used to going against the grain of their sources and their contemporaries alike? Which new questions might arise when a traditional discipline like history and undisciplined fields, like science and technology studies and media studies, exchange their theories and tools?

Section 2: Religion Is as Religion Does: The Practice Turn in Religion and Media Studies

In recent years, the study of religion has expanded dramatically, commensurate with the rising public visibility of diverse organizations, movements, and events that constitute the religious field. Scholars have begun to challenge the longstanding theoretical framework in which religions were defined as systems of ideas to which believers assented, and in which religious meaning and action was understood to reside primarily in (relatively fixed) sacred texts, symbols, and ritual dramas. *Religion and media* as a field of study has attended instead to religious affiliations, sensibilities, and ways of knowing and doing as they are found *in medias res*: in other words, as they are embedded within existing social solidarities, power relations, and embodied practices of mediation, encompassing the material affordances, disciplinary techniques, rules of exchange, and logistical orderings of space and time that make diverse forms of religious communication and experience possible in the first place. However, within this field of study, the agency ascribed to *media* remains a matter of considerable confusion. For some, media are understood simply as instruments at the disposal of religious actors in the service of diverse spiritual and/or theological goals; for others, media operate according to their own, independent logic, imposing new constraints and demands on religious actors who struggle for recognition and legitimacy. The chapters in this section explore and confront this terminological ambiguity, and so contribute to the larger aims of this book to shed new light on the concept of *practice* within media studies.

Section 3: Connecting and Dividing Media Theories: Gender, Post-Colonial, and Other Agencies

Mediated practices of connecting and dividing resonate with senses of belonging and desire, negotiating hegemonies, exclusions, subaltern people and their im/possible agencies, in moving constellations. Taking into account networks and subjects, cultural, gender and post-colonial studies consider the constitutive role of certain "Others" in shaping our concepts of representation, authenticity, or translation, and look at the agencies and performativities of those said to be non-agents. "Doing media," then, comprises diasporas, post-colonies, gendered and racialized subjectivities as places of knowledge production. "Situated knowledge"[1] (Haraway) holds true for "the knowledge of media" as well, while technologies elicit new temporal conceptualizations of precedence and antecedence,

---

[1]   Donna Haraway, "Situated Knowledges: The Science Question in Feminism and the Privilege of Partial Perspective," in *Feminist Studies*, Vol. 14, No. 3. (Autumn, 1988): pp. 575–599.

including both humans and non-humans. The respective connections and divisions will be discussed in this section, focusing on the uses of mass media, art, popular culture, and their Kulturtechniken—and the ways they incite media theory.

Section 4: The Current Relationship (After a Longer Non-Relationship) of Media Theory and Practice Theory

Not long ago, it seems, media theory and practice theory went their separate ways. The original "practice turn" in the social sciences didn't seem to concern media studies, though it partly originated from science and technology studies (Schatzki/Knorr Cetina/ von Savigny).[2] And some of the seminal topics of science and technology studies were media topics from the start, like the technological *systems building* and in the less obvious guise of laboratory instruments, two topics that German media research has continued to investigate. But the practice turn in the social sciences originated from questions of *social agency* and its socio-technical entanglements—with controversial consequences, especially in the *posthumanist* versions of practice theory, where the agency of humans and cyborgs is being discussed. It took some time for media theory to join this discussion. Classical media theory tended to see *the state of the media* as the independent variable to be established first, and to treat media practices as *messages*. Research on the "use" of media first appeared to be one of the manifestations of this asymmetrical distinction, until such research slowly transformed into an all-pervading exercise in symmetry: How to derive media from their practices, and how to characterize social practices in their dependence on media? And the challenge is here to stay: If media theory and practice theory started with their backs to one another, how will they proceed in the future? And if we re-assess the *posthumanist* trajectory in which social theory and media technology first met, does the practice turn itself have a specific media historical setting?

---

[2]   Karin Knorr Cetina, Theodore R. Schatzki, Eike von Savigny, *The Practice Turn in Contemporary Theory* (London: Routledge, 2001).

Monika Dommann

Introduction:
Unobservable Practices? Methodologies
of Media History

If there was ever a practice turn, then it took place around 1980. One of the disciplines challenged by it was the history and philosophy of science. Science and technology studies disconnected anthropology from its ties to the *primitive* or the *prescientific* belief system and directed it towards the *modern, technical* and *scientific* world. Participant observation was the new method of choice; going native the great methodological promise. Studying scientific practices implied looking at the everyday practices of scientists in the laboratories, and not just reading their textbooks. Bruno Latour and Steve Woolgar spoke about "an effort both to penetrate the mystique of science and to provide a reflexive understanding of the detailed activities of working scientists."[1] The practical involved a methodology to look behind the self-stylization of organizations and institutions, to unveil the false promises of scientific evidence and universal truth.

Since the 1970s, cultural anthropology had been a means to criticize modernization theory. In the 1980s, cultural history developed a new concern for practices. Nathalie Zemon Davis, the great historian of the everyday life of rural farmers in sixteenth century France, was well aware of the methodological difficulties historians face when she read books written by anthropologists and their accounts of the living experiences of people and attempts to flesh out the smell, taste, postures, and gestures of everyday life. This was a world that remained hidden to historians, she argued: "Many of the things our documents don't reveal to us can be observed by an anthropologist working in the field."[2] It was during that time that Nathalie Zemon Davis became interested in filmmaking. She served as a historical advisor for *Le Retour de Martin Guerre*, directed by Daniel Vigne in 1982. Her move towards cinema went far beyond the hope to have significance for a

---

[1] Bruno Latour and Steve Woolgar, *Laboratory Life. The Social Construction of Scientific Facts* (Princeton: Princeton University Press, 1986), p. 18.

[2] Natalie Zemon Davis, *The Return of Martin Guerre* (Cambridge MA and London: Harvard University Press, 1983); Ed Benson, "Martin Guerre, the Historian and the Filmmakers: An Interview with Natalie Zemon Davies," *Film & History: An Interdisciplinary Journal of Film and Television Studies* 13/3 (1983): pp. 49–65, here p. 50.

group other than university people. Davis was looking for ways to visualize the peasants she was studying: "Your eye would choose from what's being experienced and then you could retell it very economically by images."[3] But she had also a methodological interest in filmmaking. Davis discovered that historians could get a sort of feedback that normally only anthropologists working in the field are capable of receiving. She was interested in the dialectical relation at work between the past and the present when directors work together with farmers, as for example the French director René Allio did. He went to a village in Normandy, not far from the village where Pierre Rivière had murdered his mother and sisters back in the nineteenth century, when he was shooting *Moi, Pierre Rivìere*, drawn from a text edited by Michel Foucault and his students in 1973.[4] The dialogues in the film directed by Allio came from the confession of the young nineteenth century murderer. But the interpretation grew from an interplay between the villagers of the present, the director René Allio, and the text edited by Michel Foucault and his students.[5] Cinematographic reenactment was for Allio and Davis a method to overcome the obstacle of a missing link to the mentalities and practices of the dead persons: "The anthropologist can bounce her account off live subjects. Here the subjects were dead, but you had someone else in their stead, and that someone else wasn't another scholarly historian who would read." [6]

This use of filmmaking and reenactment as a methodological tool for history is one way to deal with the problem that most of the practices remain silent in historical documents and therefore unobservable for historians. The study of the production, distribution, storage, and destruction of media is another. Already Bruno Latour and Steve Woolgar pointed towards inscription devices and inscriptions as sets of procedures used by scientists in and outside the laboratory.[7] These inscriptions, which are flat, mobile, and reproducible, are able to bridge distances in time and space, and—and this is their value for historians—can be kept and stored in archives.

Drawing on Harold Innis, John Durham Peters has argued that historians, like communication scholars, are dealing with communication problems: "Both fields face the methodological problem of how to interpret under conditions of remoteness and estrangements."[8] Recordings and transmissions, the overcoming of time and space, are central themes to both fields. Like media scholars, historians are often more interested in the medium (the paper, the seals, the binding, the ink; in short, the materiality of a text, etc.) than in its message. And they are well aware that the records are incomplete and biased; that they are

---

[3]   Ibid.

[4]   Michel Foucault et al., eds., *Moi, Pierre Rivière, ayant égorgé ma mère, ma soeur et mon frère ...: Un cas de parricide au XIXe siècle*, Collection Archives 49 (Paris 1973).

[5]   Benson, "Martin Guerre," p. 51.

[6]   Ibid.

[7]   Latour and Woolgar, *Laboratory Life*, p. 89; Bruno Latour, "Drawing Things Together," in *Representation in Scientific Practice*, ed. Michael Lynch and Steve Woolgar (Cambridge MA: MIT Press, 1990), pp. 19–68.

[8]   John Durham Peters, "History as a Communication Problem," in *Explorations in Communication and History*, ed. Barbie Zelizer (London and New York: Routledge, 2008), pp. 19–34, here p. 20.

just partial and inherently fallible testimonies of the past. Records are neither produced for posterity, nor for historians. They often distort or hide intentions, interactions, and practices of the past rather than making them visible for the present. With the revolution in visual and audio technologies since the nineteenth century (such as photography, phonography, or cinematography) writing lost its longstanding monopoly on the cultural stage. But the methodological problems of source criticism remained or became even more complicated. Historians actually still encounter difficulties in dealing with cultural techniques beyond writing and even struggle to develop a potentially new methodology of source criticism for the audio-visual or digital age.

This is where media historians, with their awareness of silent and discrete routines, their expertise in formats, and their capabilities in observing practices under technical conditions can step in. The studies in this section are historical in nature and deal with issues such as accounting, coordination, writing, designing, and appropriation practices. All of them share a preference for the micro-perspective and a bottom-up methodology. All these case studies show that media standards and formats are deeply rooted in their historical and social environments and still bear fragments of past craftsmanship, routines, rituals, or older media within themselves. The authors share the approach of often reading their documents sideways. They are all skeptical of anthropocentric views but are nevertheless concerned with the role of human agency under the conditions of technology. Practices are, as the following case studies show, shaped but not fully determined by media. But it is only via media that historians are able to study the past. Media historians often look at documents which were neglected by other scholars before them. Sometimes they are dealing with materials that have been looked at a million times before, "but maybe with a different temperament," as Lisa Gitelman points out in the interview at the end of the section. Currently, the archival situations are changing dramatically. Both media scholars and historians will have to face this epistemic break and think about its methodological implications, as Gitelman argues: "We have to think ahead to things. I'm thinking about Wikileaks or Snowden, and these big disclosures, these big leaks where, or the Panama Papers now, where what really has to happen is data mining of vast corpora of leaked documents. And that's a kind of history, you and I are not prepared to do that kind, but it's coming down the road."

Sebastian Giessmann

How to Coordinate Digital Accounting?
Infrastructuring Payment and Credit with the Eurocard[1]

What do bankers do? How does a credit card come into being? Which skillful media practices need to be learned and performed in creating a digital international payment system? How do payment practices, sociotechnical infrastructures, and histories of capitalism interrelate? If the *practice turn* can be rendered productive within media history, questions like these must be taken into account. On another note, the practice turn revitalizes micro-historical approaches,[2] especially if it deals with highly localized and situated action in a globalized world.[3] Besides a reflexive return to the classics of micro-historical work,[4] the recent liaison between science and technology studies, history, and media studies has shed new light on the pioneering science and technology studies histories of the 1980s.[5] Still, the limits of praxeographical historiography are a question of material and method, since a lucky combination of singular case and abductive writing is actually a rather unlikely event. On a methodological level, this also means getting back to approaches to writing

---

[1] Parts of this text have also been published in slightly revised form as Sebastian Gießmann, "'Ein weiteres gemeinsames Medium zur Banken-Kooperation'. Der Fall der Eurocard," in *Materialität der Kooperation*, ed. Sebastian Gießmann, Tobias Röhl and Ronja Trischler (Wiesbaden: Springer VS, 2019), pp. 169–198.

[2] Adrian Johns, *Piracy. The Intellectual Property Wars from Gutenberg to Gates* (Chicago: University of Chicago Press, 2009); Pamela H. Smith, "Science on the Move. Recent Trends in the History of Early Modern Science," *Renaissance Quarterly* 62 (2009): pp. 345–375. See also the Germanophone discussion on "Historical Praxeology" in *Historische Praxeologie. Dimensionen vergangenen Handelns*, ed. Lucas Haasis and Constantin Rieske (Paderborn: Schöningh, 2015).

[3] Hans Medick, "Turning Global? Microhistory in Extension," *Historische Anthropologie* 24/2 (2016): pp. 241–253.

[4] See for example Carlo Ginzburg, *The Cheese and the Worms. The Cosmos of a Sixteenth-Century Miller* (Baltimore: Johns Hopkins University Press, 1980); Arlette Farge, *The Allure of the Archives*, The Lewis Walpole Series in Eighteenth-Century Culture and History (New Haven: Yale University Press, 2013).

[5] Paul N. Edwards et al., "American Historical Review Conversation: Historical Perspectives on the Circulation of Information," *American Historical Review* 116 (2011): pp. 1393–1435; Tarleton Gillespie et al., eds., *Media Technologies. Essays on Communication, Materiality, and Society* (Cambridge MA and London: MIT Press, 2014).

history that—like the 1980s science and technology studies-based histories—do not treat theoretical and narrative issues as separate entities.[6] Within the following case study of the Eurocard as an early digital medium of monetary exchange, I therefore tack back-and-forth between close-up micro-historical situations,[7] larger contexts in the history of payment systems,[8] and a grounded way of tackling theoretical questions.

If media practices are a key conceptual element of the practice turn, how can they be understood out of their material remains, for example archival materials that still bear the imprint of work and usage practices? Following the media practices of a tightly knit group of European bankers inevitably means dealing with a *managerial bias* of the sources for the Eurocard.[9] Working documents of a social elite have their own limitations, but at the same time they represent what a closed social world could actually do in practice. Admittedly, the dramatis personae of the following production study mainly consist of male white bankers. In doing my own fieldwork between folders,[10] I have decided to use this given limitation as an actual strength of the material. The given traces of office practices primarily document coordinative work, delegative practices, and an ongoing effort to register and identify both banking actors and actions. Besides regular meetings and considerable monetary resources, a bureaucratic paper trail is all that the bankers had at hand to coordinate digital accounting and to build a European payment system.

Via these administrative trajectories, I would like to propose three interrelated categories to grasp how media practices unfold. While this text concentrates on media

---

[6] Cf. Monika Dommann's introduction to this section, "Unobservable Practices? Methodologies of Media History," the interview with Lisa Gitelman, "From Documentary Practices to WikiLeaks," by Monika Dommann and Erhard Schüttpelz, "Media Theory Before and After the Practice Turn," in this volume.

[7] "Tacking back-and-forth" is a grounded theory terminology that I take from the works of Susan Leigh Star. See Susan Leigh Star, "Living Grounded Theory. Cognitive and Emotional Forms of Pragmatism," in *The SAGE Handbook of Grounded Theory*, ed. Anthony Bryant and Kathy Charmaz (Thousand Oaks CA, London and New Delhi: Sage, 2007), pp. 75–94.

[8] Barbara Bonhage, "Befreit im Netz. Bankdienstleistungen im Spannungsfeld zwischen Kunden und Computern," in *Vernetzte Steuerung. Soziale Prozesse im Zeitalter technischer Netzwerke*, ed. Stefan Kaufmann. (Zurich: Chronos, 2007), pp. 95–108.

[9] Historisches Institut der Deutschen Bank (HIDB), Frankfurt am Main. I am tremendously grateful to the team at HIDB, especially Dr. Martin Müller and Reinhard Frost. Dr. Ulrich Weiss and Hubert Leitermann have shared their insights from working at Deutsche Bank in an oral history interview conducted in Frankfurt, August 11, 2016. The files in question belong to a *Vorstandsbüro*, an office of the executive manager for retail banking on the board of directors, Dr. Eckart van Hooven (1925–2010). In 2011, the records and papers of the everyday business of van Hooven were transferred to the bank's Historical Institute. They have a work in progress character, assembling drafts in German, English, and French, handwritten notes, protocols, letters, telexes, travel arrangements, bills, credit card designs, advertising campaign proposals, publicity leaflets, and the international press documentation van Hooven's office used to work with.

[10] Patrice Ladwig et al., "Fieldwork Between Folders. Fragments, Traces, and the Ruins of Colonial Archives," *Max Planck Institute for Social Anthropology Working Papers* 141 (2012): pp. 1–26.

practices of *coordination*, it also briefly introduces the corresponding media practices of *delegation* and *registration/identification*. Their interrelations should be understood as a 3D model which can be turned in every direction: up and down, left and right, rotated through 360 degrees.[11] Choosing coordinating, delegating, registering and identifying as media practices is based on a *longue durée* assumption in media history[12] and on a specific media-theoretical choice in dealing with long-term continuities of payment practices.[13] It relates *media* and *practice* to the bureaucratic and administrative character of infrastructural media, namely to the *invisible work* of everyday infrastructuring and managing of accounts and payments.[14] Coordination, delegation, and registration/identification thus serve as analytic categories based on actors' practices in the Eurocard case. Partly, these were also explicitly formed as actors' categories, which in turn account for an indexical and reflexive reference to actors' understanding of their own practices. My interest relates to tensions within this back-and-forth between practices, actors' categories, and the following three analytical categories.

Media Practices of Coordination, Delegation and Registration/Identification

1. *Media practices of coordination* concern and integrate work processes that aggregate, compute, and circulate information in a collectively distributed manner. They are embodied by everyday usage of protocols, forms and labels, tables, files, formulas, databases, algorithms, maps, atlases, diagrams, worksheets, timelines, software packages and mobile apps. *Information* in this case refers less to a historical-epistemological understanding like the one found in *information theory*, than to the coordinative agency an object develops while being used in cooperative data processing. Susan Leigh Star has called these objects *boundary objects*, since they are used to mediate between different viewpoints

---

[11] I would like to express my gratitude to Anna Echterhölter who pointed out the 3D character of the media practice categories at the DFG symposium "Connect and Divide: The Practice Turn in Media Studies," August 2015. For a similar open model of media practices see Nick Couldry, *Media, Society, World. Social Theory and Digital Media Practice* (Cambridge and Malden MA: Polity Press, 2012), pp. 33–58.

[12] For media-historiographical purposes, Fernand Braudel's classic stratification of the *longue durée* should be used in a slightly modified manner. In this case, it describes continuities in administrative practice, which have been significant for infrastructural media at least since the nineteenth century. In Braudel's terminology this can be related to a "less short" time of long-term economic developments and transformations that might comprise several centuries. See Fernand Braudel, "Histoire et sciences sociales: la longue durée," *Annales. Histoire, Sciences Sociales* 13/4 (1958): pp. 725–753, here p. 748.

[13] It is also a preliminary result of the discussions with Erhard Schüttpelz, Jörg Potthast, Christian Henrich-Franke and the *Lecture and Workshop Series on Practice Theory* at Siegen University's collaborative research center "Media of Cooperation," to which I am heavily indebted.

[14] This focus has also recently been emphasized by other media researchers looking at payment systems. See Bill Maurer and Lana Swartz, eds., *Paid. Tales of Dongles, Checks, and Other Money Stuff* (Cambridge MA and London: MIT Press, 2017).

and heterogeneous actors in work practices.[15] They are interpretatively flexible, thereby allowing visions of different actors to be aggregated. If boundary objects are being used in a non-consensual pragmatic manner, they work as coordination devices.[16] Their mediating qualities are rather subtle, and methodologically require an insider's or institutional point of view to be understood.

Coordination might be conceived as the ongoing mutual establishment and control of conditions for cooperation. It should be understood less as a top-down process than as a stabilization of micro-coordinative actions that have proven themselves useful in work practices. These ways of acting should be teachable, learnable, and intelligible.[17] Boundary objects must allow for changes in scale between local appropriation and global robustness of coordinative action. A form or an instrument can be generalized from local coordinative usage. Even if it is globally standardized, it remains flexible for situated use. Media practices at work process information in an interpretively flexible way, therefore establishing "communities of practice."[18] Coordinative solutions that are found while communicating with boundary objects can be provisional or "ill-structured solutions."[19] They are continually adapted to administrative, technical, and economic changes. Over time, micro-coordinative practices become a part of more stabilized "boundary infrastructures,"[20] which tend to bypass the interactional character of boundary objects in favor of irreversibilities, and a larger scale and scope.

---

[15] Susan Leigh Star, "The Structure of Ill-Structured Solutions. Boundary Objects and Heterogeneous Distributed Problem Solving," in *Distributed Artificial Intelligence*, ed. Les Gasser and Michael N. Huhns, Research Notes in Artificial Intelligence 2 (London: Pitman; San Mateo CA: Morgan Kaufmann, 1989), pp. 37–54; Susan Leigh Star and James R. Griesemer, "Institutional Ecology, 'Translations' and Boundary Objects: Amateurs and Professionals in Berkeley's Museum of Vertebrate Zoology, 1907–39," *Social Studies of Science* 19/3 (1989): pp. 387–420; Susan Leigh Star, "This Is Not a Boundary Object. Reflections on the Origin of a Concept," *Science, Technology, & Human Values* 35/5 (2010): pp. 601–617.

[16] Erhard Schüttpelz, "Elemente einer Akteur-Medien-Theorie," in *Akteur-Medien-Theorie*, ed. Tristan Thielmann and Erhard Schüttpelz (Bielefeld: transcript, 2013), pp. 9–67. See Kjeld Schmidt and Carla Simone, "Coordination Mechanisms: Towards a Conceptual Foundation of CSCW Systems Design," *Computer Supported Cooperative Work (CSCW)* 5/2 (1996): pp. 155–200.

[17] Jon Hindmarsh and Christian Heath, "Sharing the Tools of the Trade. The Interactional Constitution of Workplace Objects," *Journal of Contemporary Ethnography* 29/5 (2000): pp. 523–562.

[18] Jean Lave and Etienne Wenger, *Situated Learning. Legitimate Peripheral Participation* (Cambridge: Cambridge University Press, 1991).

[19] Susan Leigh Star, "The Structure of Ill-Structured Solutions"; Sebastian Gießmann and Gabriele Schabacher, "Umwege und Umnutzung oder: Was bewirkt ein Workaround?" *Diagonal. Zeitschrift der Universität Siegen – Alte Sachen, Neue Zwecke* 35 (2014): pp. 13–26.

[20] Geoffrey Bowker and Susan Leigh Star, *Sorting Things Out. Classification and Its Consequences* (Cambridge MA and London: MIT Press, 1999), pp. 313–314.

2. *Media practices of delegation* begin with the arrangement of *co-operational chains*, including the most elementary forms of tool and instrument usage.[21] They imply the training of specific skills that serve as a foundation for media practices.[22] The complexity of skillfully learned action programs and their tacit, non-propositional knowledge begins with learning them. Teachable techniques of the body are the basis for all forms of delegation, even in institutions and sociotechnical networks. Media practices of delegation specifically underscore the intercorporeal and interactional character of practices—concerning all constellations of delegated actions between persons, persons and objects, persons and signs.

Delegation begins with cooperative practices that involve small groups of actors in defining the rules of common procedure.[23] Once delegations are being coordinated, divisions of labor emerge—both on the micro- and the macro-level, reaching from informal agreements to rather rigid scripts, organizational processes, semi-automated and automated action.[24] This is true for infrastructural and public media, with both relying on the concatenation of delegated actions in specific organizational forms.

3. *Media practices of registration and identification* primarily address the traceability of a given action, and relate to the filing and documentation of both coordinative and delegative practices. They also begin in mutual interaction, for example in gestural and linguistic practices of indexical showing and demonstration *(deixis)*. Using registering and identifying media transforms, scales, and modifies an interactional situation. This finding not only relates to the well-established data technologies of governmental registration and identification.[25] Rather, registration and identification also refer to everyday logistical media practices: addressing, processing, recognizing, finding, accounting, and tracking of a message, an object, or a person. Technologies of registration and identification allow both for a reference to single persons or objects, and to localizable and datable

---

[21] Erhard Schüttpelz, "Der Punkt des Archimedes. Einige Schwierigkeiten des Denkens in Operationsketten," in *Bruno Latours Kollektive. Kontroversen zur Entgrenzung des Sozialen*, ed. Georg Kneer et al. (Frankfurt am Main: Suhrkamp, 2008), pp. 234–258; Christoph Borbach and Tristan Thielmann, "Über das Denken in Ko-Operationsketten. Arbeiten am Luftlagebild," in *Materialität der Kooperation*, ed. Sebastian Gießmann et al. (Wiesbaden: Springer VS, 2019), pp. 115–167.

[22] Tim Ingold, *Making. Anthropology, Archaeology, Art and Architecture* (London: Routledge, 2013); Shaun Moores, "Digital Orientations: 'Ways of the Hand' and Practical Knowing in Media Uses and Other Manual Activities," *Mobile Media & Communication* 2/2 (2014): pp. 196–208.

[23] Harold Garfinkel, *Studies in Ethnomethodology* (Englewood Cliffs NJ: Prentice Hall, 1967), p. 33.

[24] Lucy A. Suchman, *Plans and Situated Action. The Problem of Human-Machine Communications* (Cambridge and New York: Cambridge University Press, 1987); Antoine Hennion and Cécile Méadel, "Dans les laboratoires du désir. Le travail des gens de Publicité," *Réseaux. Communication – Technologie – Société* 6/28 (1988): pp. 7–54.

[25] Michel Foucault, *Surveiller et punir. La naissance de la Prison* (Paris: Gallimard, 1975); Theodore M. Porter, *Trust in Numbers. The Pursuit of Objectivity in Science and Public Life* (Princeton: Princeton University Press, 1995); Alain Desrosières, *La politique des grands nombres – Histoire de la raison statistique*, 2nd ed. (Paris: La Découverte, 2000); Lisa Gitelman, ed., *Raw Data Is an Oxymoron* (Cambridge MA and London: MIT Press, 2013).

transmissions. Practices of registration and identification are generally being used to make actions, signs/data, goods, knowledge, and services *accountable*.

So how do these interconnected analytic categories help us in understanding the ways in which media practices unfold historically? And how do historical cases, including their actors' categories, translate and transform the theoretical heuristics? After all, a practice turn in media studies needs to take actors' accounts and their practical reflexivity as seriously as the socio-materiality of any infrastructure: There is no such thing as (a monetary) medium without its formation in interaction.

A Turned Down Invitation, 1983

In August 1983, Deutsche Bank's retail section received a spectacular, diplomatically risky, and indecent invitation. In a letter addressed to Eckart van Hooven, the president of Visa, Dee Ward Hock, invited van Hooven and his wife to join the forthcoming Visa member congress in Kyoto, Japan as honorary guests.[26] In a world where every bank to decide between offering credit cards either from MasterCard or Visa, this was an unlikely offer. Since Deutsche Bank had since 1977 strategically positioned its own Eurocard independently, but close to the American Interbank Card Association (which turned into the MasterCard/Master Charge system in 1979), Dee Hock's letter instantly received the diplomatic attention of van Hooven's office.[27] It is dated August 1, 1983, and the internal postal stamp of Deutsche Bank marks the reception date as August 3. The letter was typed out in German, with the oddly spelled *San Franzisko* as spatial reference. A pencil mark annotates this diplomatic gesture: *deutsch!*, thus creating a first level of commentary for all internal readers (see Figures 1a and 1b).

With the letter, Dee Hock himself suggested that opening the closed congress to external *leading personalities* (*Führende Persönlichkeiten*) was exceptional. His invitation to van Hooven literally came with a first-class ticket: all expenses would have been covered. In the end, Hock concluded with a personal remark of extraordinary gravity in elegant German: "Although our paths took different directions in the past, I was always impressed by your personal qualities, inspired by our verbal disputes, and intrigued by our enjoyable short personal encounters."[28]

Along with this letter, a brief note with the personal sign of van Hooven was attached. It also served as a short delegative letter form, since it was meant to be used for personal

---

[26] HIDB, V19/0258.

[27] It also sticks out in the archival order, because letters with Master Charge and Interbank heads are to be found often, while Visa letters present an absolute rarity.

[28] "Obwohl in der Vergangenheit unsere Wege in verschiedene Richtungen liefen, fand ich doch immer ihre persönlichen Eigenschaften beeindruckend, unsere verbalen Gefechte inspirierend und unsere kurzen persönlichen Begegnungen einen Genuß." One of these meetings was at the Payment Systems Conference of the European Financial Marketing Association (EFMA) in Monte Carlo, March 11–14, 1980. Cf. HIDB V19/0251/2. All translations of non-English language sources in this text are those of the author.

3. 08. 83

Dee Ward Hock
President

San Franzisko, den 1. August 1983

deutsch!

Herrn
Dr. Eckart van Hooven
Deutsche Bank A.G.
Große Gallusstraße 10-14
6000 Frankfurt am Main
West Germany

Sehr geehrter Dr. van Hooven,

Jedes Jahr veranstaltet Visa International, immer in einem
anderen Land, einen Mitglieds-Kongreß, dem regionale Aufsichts-
ratsversammlungen vorausgehen und dem eine Sitzung des
Internationalen Aufsichtrates folgt. Über 200 Vorstandsvor-
sitzende und Vorstandsmitglieder von Banken aus der ganzen Welt
sind anwesend. Der sechstägige Kongreß ist eine einmalige
Gelegenheit, die Funktionsweise des Visa Systems zu erleben;
alle Teilnehmer sind nämlich nicht nur bei den allgemeinen
Sitzungen und dem geselligen Beisammensein willkommen, sondern
können auch als Beobachter der Aufsichtsratsitzung beiwohnen.
Die Versammlungen bleiben der Presse verschlossen und waren in
der Vergangenheit nur für Vorstandsmitglieder der Mitgliedsbanken
zugänglich.

vom 8. – 14.9.83

Dieses Jahr, zum ersten Mal, laden wir ebenfalls eine exklusive
Gruppe führender Persönlichkeiten aus dem Bereich der Bank-
Zahlungssysteme ein. Es würde uns sehr freuen, wenn Sie und
Ihre Gattin die Einladung annehmen würden, als Ehrengäste zu
unserem September-Treffen in Kyoto, Japan, zu kommen. Ich bin
überzeugt, daß Sie diese ungewöhnliche Verbindung von geschäft-
lichen, kulturellen und gesellschaftlichen Ereignissen einzig-
artig finden werden. Alle Auslagen für Reisekosten erster
Klasse, Unterkunft, Verpflegung und sonstige Unkosten werden von
uns übernommen. Obwohl in der Vergangenheit unsere Wege in
verschiedene Richtungen liefen, fand ich doch immer Ihre persönlichen Errungenschaften beeindruckend, unsere verbalen Gefechte
inspirierend und unsere kurzen persönlichen Begegnungen einen
Genuß.

Es wäre für Visa eine Ehre und für mich persönlich eine Freude,
wenn Sie unserer Einladung nachkommen könnten.

Mit freundlichen Grüßen,

DWH:mk

P.S. Ich habe es mir erlaubt, Information über den
     Kongreß beizufügen.

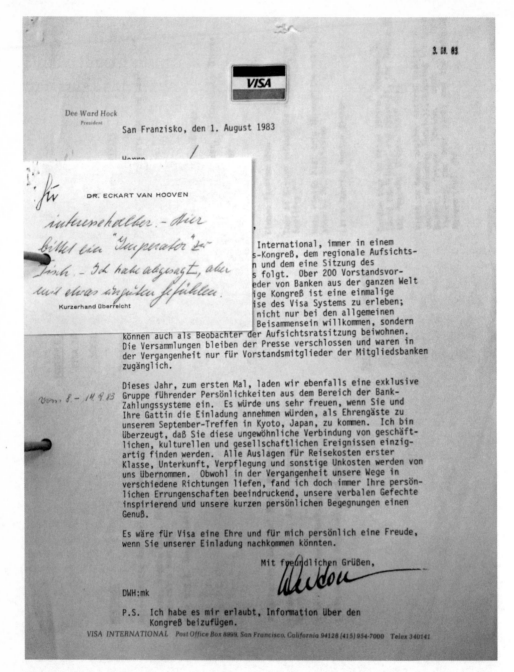

VISA

3. 08. 83

Dee Ward Hock
President

San Franzisko, den 1. August 1983

Herrn

DR. ECKART VAN HOOVEN

*interessehalter. - hier
bittet ein "Imperator" z-
Tisch. - Ich habe abgesagt, aber
uns etwas ungeheu gefühlen.*

Kurzerhand überreicht

... International, immer in einem
...-Kongreß, dem regionale Aufsichts-
... und dem eine Sitzung des
... folgt. Über 200 Vorstandsvor-
... der von Banken aus der ganzen Welt
... ige Kongreß ist eine einmalige
... ise des Visa Systems zu erleben;
... nicht nur bei den allgemeinen
... Beisammensein willkommen, sondern
können auch als Beobachter der Aufsichtsratsitzung beiwohnen.
Die Versammlungen bleiben der Presse verschlossen und waren in
der Vergangenheit nur für Vorstandsmitglieder der Mitgliedsbanken
zugänglich.

Dieses Jahr, zum ersten Mal, laden wir ebenfalls eine exklusive
Gruppe führender Persönlichkeiten aus dem Bereich der Bank-
Zahlungssysteme ein. Es würde uns sehr freuen, wenn Sie und
Ihre Gattin die Einladung annehmen würden, als Ehrengäste zu
unserem September-Treffen in Kyoto, Japan, zu kommen. Ich bin
überzeugt, daß Sie diese ungewöhnliche Verbindung von geschäft-
lichen, kulturellen und gesellschaftlichen Ereignissen einzig-
artig finden werden. Alle Auslagen für Reisekosten erster
Klasse, Unterkunft, Verpflegung und sonstige Unkosten werden von
uns übernommen. Obwohl in der Vergangenheit unsere Wege in
verschiedene Richtungen liefen, fand ich doch immer Ihre persönlichen Errungenschaften beeindruckend, unsere verbalen Gefechte
inspirierend und unsere kurzen persönlichen Begegnungen einen
Genuß.

Vom 8. - 14.9.83

Es wäre für Visa eine Ehre und für mich persönlich eine Freude,
wenn Sie unserer Einladung nachkommen könnten.

Mit freundlichen Grüßen,

DWH:mk

P.S. Ich habe es mir erlaubt, Information über den
       Kongreß beizufügen.

VISA INTERNATIONAL   Post Office Box 8999, San Francisco, California 94128 (415) 954-7000   Telex 340141

Fig. 1a and 1b: Invitation letter from Dee Ward Hock (Visa) to Eckart van Hooven (Deutsche Bank),
with handwritten commentary. August 1 and 3, 1983. HIDB V19/0258.

dedications of a member of the board to someone else (*Kurzerhand* überreicht). Yet this time, van Hooven's office staff used it to notify him first: "*[F]ür Dr. Eckart van Hooven.*" Van Hooven himself did inform another member of the board in a handwritten note, since he decided not to accept the invitation.[29] "*Interessehalber.—Hier bittet ein 'Imperator' zu Tisch.—Ich habe abgesagt, aber mit etwas unguten Gefühlen.*" (see Figures 1a and 1b)[30]

"For your information.—An 'Emperor' has sent an invitation to dinner.—I have declined, but with somehow uneasy feelings" is likely to have denoted a message for the internal records, confirming a decision after a conversation about turning down the invitation. It certainly involved a justification to comply with corporate accountability, since responding might also have created business opportunities. Labelling Hock as *Imperator* does not come as a surprise here, though. The Visa president had an industry-wide reputation as a die-hard manager, which he had gained through his organizational and business skills in digitizing payment operations in the 1970s.[31]

This letter presented the 1983 situation of the consumer credit card industry in a nutshell: Visa and MasterCard found themselves in tight global competition for making the credit card a consumer product in retail banking, while American Express and Diners Club still provided a luxury product for an exclusive clientele. The Eurocard, which had been advertised as a European credit card since 1977, was still struggling to find a place between the American high-class *travel & entertainment* cards and the strategy of Visa to attract the Western European middle class. Although the company had proven to be profitable by the end of the 1970s, it always followed the market lead of its American competitors, with 326,000 international cards issued all over Europe by mid-1979, 663,000 by mid-1981 and 1.5 million by mid-1984.[32]

Within the German banking system, American style credit cards for the masses had been regarded with skepticism and downright refusal since the 1960s. In actual banking practice, private banks like Deutsche Bank had slowly started to open their business for everyday customers in the 1950s. Besides the offer of small credits, this involved new forms of accounting. Private and cooperative bank accounts were offered as a *giro* account[33] for everyday transactions like salaries and rent payments, which was considered a substantial business innovation.[34] Relating one person to one account was the organizational ratio

---

[29] Dr. Ulrich Weiss and Hubert Leitermann have confirmed this in an oral history interview, explaining it as part of internal bureaucratic procedure. Frankfurt, August 11, 2016.

[30] Italics denote handwritten parts.

[31] See David L. Stearns, *Electronic Value Exchange. Origins of the VISA Payment System*, History of Computing (London: Springer, 2011), pp. 29–51.

[32] In Germany: 73,000 cards by mid-1979, 173,000 by mid-1981, 258,000 by mid-1984. Eurocard's internal statistics usually listed American Express's slightly higher numbers for comparison.

[33] The German *Girokonto* translates both into *current account* (UK) and *checking account* (US).

[34] Karl Weisser, *Bargeldlose Lohn- und Gehaltszahlung. Ihre Durchführung in der Praxis* (Wiesbaden: Springer Fachmedien, 1959); Reinhard Frost, *Wünsche werden Wirklichkeit. Die Deutsche Bank und ihr Privatkundengeschäft*, ed. Historische Gesellschaft der Deutschen Bank e.V. (Munich: Piper, 2009); Sophia Booz, "Von der Schalterhalle zum Erlebnisbanking. Eine kulturwissenschaftliche

of registration/identification that was upheld once the transatlantic transfer of credit card business models became a hotly debated issue for the German banks.[35]

In an article written for the magazine *Bank-Betrieb* in 1970, Deutsche Bank retail banker Ulrich Weiss strictly argued against the multiplication of accounts, which came as a necessity once credit cards were issued.[36] Instead of going the way of the American Bankers Association (ABA), which had pursued a swift standardization of credit cards and digitization of payment and accounting procedures since 1965,[37] Ulrich Weiss wrote:

> The question of this article is as follows: Does the credit card inflation also get to us? After balancing out benefits and disadvantages of credit and check cards we would like to change this question into 'Do we want the credit card inflation to get to us?' The answer to this question can only be NO, integrating the interests of all stakeholders: those of the customers, the retailers and of the banks themselves. If the German commercial banks would introduce one or more credit cards, they would start a project that is not being asked for by the public. It would only create disadvantages, both for retailers and banks.[38]

Weiss' statement was not only a criticism of *foreign* (*ausländische*) credit card systems. Since it also promoted Deutsche Bank's alternative medium of exchange, the Eurocheque, which was introduced in 1968, it made the case for a specifically European way of handling payments. This was part of a larger conflict between European and American approaches towards banking, whose cultural tensions have aptly been named as a *Kulturkampf*—a

---

Perspektive auf die Veränderung des Bankwesens durch den Bankautomaten," in *Kultur der Ökonomie. Zur Materialität und Performanz des Wirtschaftlichen*, ed. Inga Klein and Sonja Windmüller (Bielefeld: transcript, 2014), pp. 81–95, here p. 82; Simon Gonser, *Der Kapitalismus entdeckt das Volk. Wie die Deutschen Großbanken in den 1950er und 1960er Jahren zu ihrer privaten Kundschaft kamen*, Schriftenreihe der Vierteljahrshefte für Zeitgeschichte 108 (Munich: De Gruyter Oldenbourg, 2014).

[35] Multiple accounts were handled with a differentiation between "Stammdaten" (standing data, master file data) and account data.

[36] This is also a trope that is often found in memorial accounts of the Eurocheque project.

[37] See Bernardo Bátiz-Laszlo, Thomas Haigh and David L. Stearns, "How the Future Shaped the Past: The Case of the Cashless Society," *Enterprise & Society* 15/1 (2014): pp. 103–131, here p. 115. Sebastian Gießmann, "Money, Credit, and Digital Payment 1971/2014: From the Credit Card to Apple Pay," *Administration & Society* 50/9 (2018): pp. 1259–1279.

[38] "Die Fragestellung dieses Artikels lautet 'Kommt die Kreditkarteninflation auch zu uns?' Nach Abwägung der Vor- und Nachteile von Kredit- und Scheckkarte möchten wir diese Fragestellung ändern in 'Wollen wir die Kreditkarteninflation auch bei uns?' Die Antwort auf diese Frage kann nur NEIN heißen, und zwar unter Berücksichtigung der Interessenlagen aller Beteiligten: der Kunden, des Einzelhandels und der Kreditinstitute selbst. Die deutschen Kreditinstitute würden sich mit der Einführung ein oder mehrerer Kreditkarten in ein Projekt begeben, für das beim Publikum kein Bedarf besteht und das den Kreditinstituten, besonders aber dem Einzelhandel große Nachteile im Vergleich zur Scheckkarte brächte." Ulrich Weiss, "Kommt die Kreditkarteninflation auch zu uns?" *Bank-Betrieb* 6 (1970): pp. 1–6.

clash of different business mentalities—by Werner Abelshauser.[39] So instead of opting for the American credit card approach, the paper-based system of the Eurocheque was conceptualized to be Europe's mobile international medium of monetary exchange for touristic purposes. With its introduction, van Hooven, Weiss, and other skeptical European bankers had made a temporary decision against the *mass credit card*. Due to this decision, the building of computerized special purpose digital payment infrastructures was partly postponed, at least until 1973, when the cooperative SWIFT network started to be built.[40] Yet the exclusive market of *travel and entertainment* cards like Diners Club and American Express remained attractive for retail bankers.

Conventional narratives of the Eurocard usually start with its early establishment by the Swedish Wallenberg bank in 1964, take note of the significant transformation in 1992 (in which the check, debit, and credit card businesses were merged into the Europay company), and end with its takeover by MasterCard in 2002/2003.[41] The following account, however, mainly relates to the inception of Eurocard as a pan-European product and a quasi-currency, which from 1977 was offered to customers by Deutsche Bank and other European licensing banks. In fact, this re-organization as a European company with a Brussels headquarters almost represented a start from scratch, in which all organizational, infrastructural, and marketing activities had to be set up anew. For this, coordination was the key activity to establish common procedures of delegation (who is responsible for what?) and all related questions of registering actual business practices and identifying payment transactions. Institutionally, all of these practices were part of distributed western European accomplishments. These brought with them questions of actual coordination, which in turn led to considerable tensions, for instance in the case of establishing joint computing centers. Where and under which terms should the clearing and settlement of accounts take place? This key infrastructural question is where Eurocard International decided to build a different system than its American competitors—one that was tailored to the coordinative specifics of digital exchange between a multitude of European currencies.

Coordinating Actors and Accounts: Establishing a European Clearing Centre, 1979–1981

The practices of organizational coordination within Eurocard's corporate structure and within the files of its work processes were consistently bureaucratic, as well as highly diplomatic. This is significant even for the first years after 1977, when the company's working procedures had to be established anew in working groups and committees. Primary formats

---

39 Werner Abelshauser, *Kulturkampf. Der deutsche Weg in die neue Wirtschaft und die amerikanische Herausforderung* (Berlin: Kadmos, 2003).

40 Susan V. Scott and Markos Zachariadis, *The Society for Worldwide Interbank Financial Telecommunication (SWIFT). Cooperative Governance for Network Innovation, Standards, and Community*, Routledge Global Institutions Series 83 (London and New York: Routledge, 2014).

41 The brand name is now being used by Scandinavian banks only. See *http://www.eurocardinternational.com.* (last accessed April 10, 2019).

of coordination consisted of board and committee meetings all over Europe, which were meticulously prepared by the cooperating European banks, handling problematic issues in advance. Van Hooven's office added a micro-coordinative handling of report drafts to deal with the subtleties of pan-European communication. This involved a culture of note taking and annotating documents that were about to be circulated. Reports and protocols of meetings were checked for references, especially when it came to the part taken by van Hooven himself. Most of the handwriting was done by office secretary Ms. Radtke, office clerk Hubert Leitermann, and the general manager (*Prokurist*) Norbert Massfeller.

Throughout the protocols of the Eurocard board meetings, notes like "You have been quoted"[42] indicated the important interventions of van Hooven himself throughout the gatherings.[43] Within these practices of micro-coordination, sensitive and possibly controversial points on the agenda were registered and identified in advance. One example for this procedure can be found in several memoranda written for van Hooven by Norbert Massfeller. They served as a preparatory measure for the *5th meeting of the Executive Committee to be held at Deutsche Bank, Frankfurt (Main) on January 10, 1979*, which brought together the members of the Executive Committee Carl Martin, Bent Carlsen, Norbert Massfeller, Jean Pierre Peronnet, Peter Stewart, and Björn Wahlgren.[44] Micro-coordination in advance did serve a double purpose here: apart from the diplomatic effort, it also set up a future division of labor between the company's board and its executive committee.

While drafting the agenda and preparing a business dinner,[45] the general manager Norbert Massfeller also informed van Hooven about the specifics of the executive committee, which was meant to relieve the members of the board from "detail work"[46] and to support the managing director of Eurocard in coordinating the overall corporate network.[47] Massfeller also suggested that van Hooven to addresses the working mandate of the executive committee: "Efficiency of the Executive Committee must be measured by its success in taking up national initiatives, and filtering out the decisive parameters to integrate national initiatives into the European frame (concrete example: cash advance)."[48]

---

42   In German: *Sie sind quotiert.*
43   Memorandum from 78th Board Meeting in Château Sainte-Anne, rue du Vieux Moulin 103, 1160 Brussels (December 9, 1981). HIDB V19/0240.
44   Franco de Bartolomeo (Eurocard Italiana) is mentioned under "Apologies for absence," because all flights from Italy had been cancelled due to weather conditions. Martin, Stewart, and Wahlgren had to be accommodated at the Deutsche Bank guesthouse, because all other hotels were booked out, due to a parallel fair. Job affiliations were the following: Carl Martin, Managing Director Eurocard International, Brussels; Bent Carlsen, Eurocard Danmark, Copenhagen; Norbert Massfeller, Deutsche Bank, Frankfurt; Jean Pierre Peronnet, Crédit Agricole, Paris; Peter Stewart, Access, London; Björn Wahlgren, Eurocard Nord, Stockholm.
45   Massfeller and his wife Claudia also invited the committee members to an evening cheese fondue at their home.
46   In German: *Detail-Arbeit.*
47   In German: *Gesamtverbund.*
48   "Effizienz des Executive Committees muss sich daran messen lassen, ob es ihm gelingt, nationale Initiativen aufzugreifen und die entscheidenden Eckwerte herauszufiltern, um nationale Initiativen

As part of micro-coordinative practice, Massfeller's memoranda always related to the position of other actors in the field, for example whether they could support a measure like saying *no* to a unified Master Charge Card,[49] or how a joint Clearing Centre was likely to be regarded both by other companies and within the Eurocard network.[50] The issue of a European Clearing Centre actually developed into a central discussion point for a meeting on January 10, 1979. Already the first of the drafts for the agenda did put it on top of the list, with an additional handwritten and crossed out *European Clearing Centre?* scribble. A detailed memorandum by Massfeller in German, dated January 9, 1979 Frankfurt a.M., explained the stakes for a centralized European Clearing Centre. Massfeller identified two companies' computing centers as being capable of unifying both clearing and settling of payments: Crédit Agricole (Paris) and Access (a UK-based credit card company with online connection to the USA). Instead of opting for just one, he sketched out a compromise, which involved using Crédit Agricole's infrastructure for European transactions, and that of Access for payments from Europe to the US.

The *Minutes of the 5th meeting of the Executive Committee held on January 10, 1979, in Frankfurt (Main), at 10.00 am* indicate that "[t]he committee thoroughly discussed the proposals," declared participation in the Centre as mandatory, opted for a start on July 1, 1979 but "did not agree on a joint recommendation to the Board." On the annotated agenda of the following meeting, *The 6th meeting of the Executive Committee to be held at the office of Eurocard International, Brussels, on March 6, at 9:30 a.m.*, a handwritten pencil note hints at a decisive infrastructural decision. It proposed *Wählleitungen statt Bänder – dial-up lines instead of tapes* – for the European Clearing Centre, which also meant daily clearing, as opposed to doing it on a weekly basis.[51] Yet this important technical detail did not become part of the minutes, which simply denoted a report by the chairman Carl Martin on the planned structure, and a move of the start-up date to August 1, 1979.

Martin also emphasized the mandatory participation of all companies in the Clearing Centre, thus enforcing its coordinative function. This was at least a partially controversial issue, since it was questioned by the Italian Franco de Bartolomeo, both in Brussels and during the next meeting on May 22, 1979 in Dubrovnik.[52] Since the company's board of directors had been following the executive committee's recommendation, which had been given while de Bartolomeo was absent, this coordinative standardization was put in

---

in einen europäischen Gesamtrahmen einzubinden (konkretes Beispiel: Bargeldbevorschussung)." Norbert Massfeller, Memorandum for Eckart van Hooven, Mittagessen mit Executive Committee am 10.1.1979, HIDB V19/0251/1.

[49] Norbert Massfeller, Untitled memorandum for Eckart van Hooven, January 9, 1979, p. 2. HIDB V19/0251/1.

[50] Ibid., pp. 4–6.

[51] *The 6th meeting of the Executive Committee to be held at the office of Eurocard International, Brussels, on March 6, at 9:30 a.m.*: "Present: Carl Martin (in the Chair), Franco de Bartolomeo, Bent Carlsen, Norbert Massfeller, Jean Pierre Peronnet, Peter Stewart, Björn Wahlgren." HIDB V19/0251/1.

[52] *Minutes of the 7th Meeting of the Executive Committee held on May 22, 1979 in Dubrovnik, Yugoslavia*, HIDB V19/0251/2.

action by a bottom-up committee proposal and a top-down board decision. Throughout the minutes, tensions between the cooperating banks on the question of localizing the Clearing Centre are present. In the end, an agreement was achieved that kept bidding for this infrastructural center of coordination open for one bank per card-issuing country.[53]

Competition between Crédit Agricole and Access was resolved by a diplomatic agreement off the protocol, which was prepared by mutual letters. While the French were eager to win the bid for the Clearing Centre, the British were considered competent to handle the center for authorizing both European and transatlantic payments. In a letter to Carl Martin, the head of Crédit Agricole's International Division Serge Robert emphasized his company's clearing competence in a rather blunt manner, while recognizing Access's capacities in authorization:

> For organization of the European Clearing Centre, Crédit Agricole and Cedi have extended particularly favorable financial terms and have allocated substantial staff and material resources thereto, in order to satisfy the requirements of Interbank and Eurocard [...]. Crédit Agricole Mutuel would find it hard to understand a failure to take its viewpoints and its efforts into account when the net settlement decisions are made.[54]

Within the enclosures for the same Stockholm meeting on September 13, the European Clearing Centre is officially declared "ready to start and will do so on August 28" with Belgium, France, Germany, and Israel as the first connected countries.[55] This optimism, however, was not mutually shared, since the American Interbank association was also introducing new procedures for settling accounts in their INET system between member banks.[56] Hence, in a statement by Bruno Paternostre at the 9th meeting of the executive committee, smooth operations were expected as late as February 1980. The minutes also documented ongoing discussions about dial-up lines vs. mailed tapes: "The possibility of having direct lines within Europe was discussed; this service is given by Visa but would be very expensive if not shared with other groups such as the Eurocheque."[57] Parts of the October 10, 1980 board meeting were prepared with an internal memorandum for van Hooven and Massfeller at Deutsche Bank. It included a down-to-earth summary of how the settlement system of Cedi had been working since the beginning of September 1979:

---

[53] *Minutes of the 8th Meeting of the Executive Committee held on June 19, 1979 at the Offices of Eurocard International, Brussels*, p. 3. HIDB V19/0251/2.

[54] *The 9th meeting of the Executive Committee to be held in the offices of Eurocard Nord, Stockholm, on September 13, 1979, at 9:00 a.m., Process to appoint a suitable bank, enclosure 5*. Typescript based on a Telex, dated August 1, 1979, p. 1. HIDB V19/0251/2.

[55] Ibid., enclosure 4.

[56] This was enacted through its Operations Bulletin that distributed up-to-date information on how to coordinate digital accounting.

[57] *Minutes of the 9th Meeting of the Executive Committee held on September 13, 1979 at the offices of Eurocard Nord*, Stockholm, p. 3. HIDB V19/0251/2.

The current smooth operation of the system—apart from some minor start-up problems—lets us expect that a fully automated data exchange of international transactions in the Eurocard domain once a week, starting with February/March, is going to be a routine procedure. For this, data transmission has been designed to be feasible both
– via exchange of magnetic tapes, and
– via online connection (leased or dial-up line).[58]

Once the handling of authorization and clearing of account data had been stabilized, it was supposed to be used for the clearing of payments, that is, for registration and identification of all transactions. On top of this infrastructure, a *net settlement system* was expected to deal with the European multi-currency problem. Norbert Massfeller had been leading the ad hoc research group on net settlement, and his proposal to have a German bank handle the net settlement articulated another tension in the coordinative endeavor.[59]

At least three computational coordination devices were needed to make the Eurocard work outside of paper-, telephone- and telex-based transactions. Computing—as Michael Sean Mahoney and Kjeld Schmidt have put it—is a protean technology, which is forged in practice.[60] If coordination can be understood as the ongoing mutual establishment and control of conditions for cooperation, it certainly relies on the stabilization and upkeep of coordination devices. Clearing technologies were thus inseparable from the micro-coordinative writing practices in the management offices of the Eurocard banks and in actual retail banking branches. This was where local delegation and delegation between European bank offices did establish an institutional ecology for building computing infrastructure.[61] In fact, both the Eurocheque and the Eurocard delegated established institutional sociotechnical scripts of accounting and monetary exchange into new payment infrastructures and, in the case of the credit card, new digital infrastructures.

---

[58] "Das bisherige – bis auf unbedeutende, schnell behebbare Anfangsschwierigkeiten – reibungslose Funktionieren des Systems läßt erwarten, daß etwa ab Februar/März zunächst einmal die Woche der vollautomatische Austausch sämtlicher Daten der grenzüberschreitenden Transaktionen im Eurocard-Bereich zu einem Routinevorgang geworden ist. Dabei ist die Datenübertragung so ausgelegt, daß sie sowohl mittels Magnetbandaustausch als auch über online-Verbindung (Stand bzw. dial-up-Leitung) erfolgen kann." *Eurocard International. Zum Stand des Aufbaus eines automatisierten internationalen Verrechnungssystems*, p. 3. Attached to the *Minutes of the 69th Board Meeting held on Wednesday, October 10, 1980 at the offices of Caisse Nationale de Crédit Agricole*, Paris. HIDB V19/0239/1.

[59] Ibid., p. 5.

[60] Michael Sean Mahoney, *Histories of Computing*, ed. Thomas Haigh (Cambridge MA: Harvard University Press, 2011); Kjeld Schmidt, "Of Humble Origins. The Practice Roots of Interactive and Collaborative Computing," *Zeitschrift für Medienwissenschaft* 1 (2015), http://www.zfmedienwissen-schaft.de/online/humble-origins (accessed April 10, 2019). Cf. the interview with Thomas Haigh "Practice in the History of Computing," by Erhard Schüttpelz, in this volume.

[61] See Ben Peters, *How Not to Network a Nation. The Uneasy History of the Soviet Internet* (Cambridge MA and London: MIT Press, 2016), pp. 125–129, 183–185, 202–206 on relations between networks and institutions.

Registering the Values: Digital Accounting and Currency Conversion, 1982–1984

Already while coordinating the Eurocard company—and also in commemorative narrations—the involved bankers were emphasizing the European dimension of what they wanted to achieve. Building a proud European company "without politicians" was a recurring emotional phrase, which was also translated into marketing campaign slogans like "We Europeans all have our pride."[62] (See Figure 2)

The overall situation was paradoxical, since economic competition and sociotechnical developments were influenced by American market leaders like American Express and Visa. In fact, Eurocard International was supposed to be organized in a cooperative structure, like the one the American Interbank network had developed in the 1960s. Just like Interbank, and its follow-ups Master Charge and MasterCard, the Brussels headquarters of Eurocard was expected to fulfill mostly coordinative, standardizing, and compliance-related tasks. Keeping it as *lean* as possible, with only a few paid positions, became a standard trope within the founding protocols since 1977, although the question of a larger corporate workforce occasionally turned into an issue of concern. While the European mindset of the participants was not tied to official infrastructural policies, it resembled and paralleled the evolving political networking style of the European Union.[63]

US-American dominance in payments remained a constantly debated topic, even within the frame of cooperation that existed with the global Interbank Card Association. In a typical 1978 letter from Tage Andersen, the Managing Director of Danske Bank, to G.A. Gilhespy of the UK-based Joint Credit Card Company[64], this ongoing tension was articulated along the question of European board membership in the Interbank Card Association:

> The fact remains, however, that the Americans will retain their overall majority and I am well aware that this may be a natural unavoidable pre-condition—at least in the short term. On the other hand, this also emphasizes the necessity of some form of European independence in order that the Americans shall not outvote us at their pleasure, but how this may be brought about or constructed is another question. […] Apparently, the Americans have not shown much appreciation of this point of view [which suggested that Eurocard could run the European business of Interbank, SG], and as a matter of fact—to put it bluntly—I find their rejection of it not only rather un-cooperative and unfriendly, but also somewhat unwise. If the Americans would allow

---

62   A clipping of the advertisement is documented in HIDB V19/0239/2.
63   Jean-Marc Offner, "Are There Such Things as Small Networks?" in *The Governance of Large Technical Systems*, ed. Olivier Coutard, Routledge Studies in Business Organzations and Networks 13 (London and New York: Routledge, 1999), pp. 217–238; Barry Andrew, *Political Machines. Governing a Technological Society* (London and New York: Athlone Press, 2001); Erik van der Vleuten and Arne Kaijser, eds., *Networking Europe. Transnational Infrastructures and the Shaping of Europe, 1850–2000* (Sagamore Beach MA: Science History Publications, 2006). On European monetary policy see Emmanuel Mourlon-Druol, *A Europe Made of Money. The Emergence of the European Monetary System*, Cornell Studies in Money (Ithaca NY: Cornell University Press, 2012).
64   The Joint Credit Card Company was offering the Access credit card.

Fig. 2: Eurocard Advertising Campaign, published May 12, 1980. HIDB V19/0239/02.

business aspects and common sense to prevail instead of empty prestige and self-asserting considerations, they would be able to perceive the manifest advantages to themselves of a strong, well-organized <u>European</u> set-up (Eurocard International), and would refrain from attempts to establish a remote-controlled branch of their own outfit whose efficiency none of us have found impressive in the first place.[65]

A copy of this letter from September 11, 1978 found its way into the Eurocard files at Deutsche Bank, along with a note of Norbert Massfeller that reads: "This is exactly our opinion"[66] added three days later. Interbank's proposal of a world-wide unified Master Charge card was also dismissed by other Eurocard bankers, since it represented "ongoing US dominance."[67]

Articulating a *European consciousness* as business identity was particularly difficult in a market in which substantial coordinative inventions both in organization and computing were still being made on the other side of the Atlantic. This was felt quite literally in complaints about slow payments processing for Eurocard customers in the USA. When it came to the technical handling of net settlement, the Interbank approach was still acknowledged as superior to the European payment technologies. Yet in a preparatory

---

[65] Letter from Tage Andersen to G.A. Gilhespy, September 11, 1978. HIDB V19/0255/2.

[66] In German: *Das trifft genau auch unsere Meinung.*

[67] In German: *weiterhin US-Dominanz. Gespräch mit Herr Lars* Ölander *am 9.10.1978*, p. 3: This relates to the proposal of a world-wide unified Master Charge card. HIDB V19/0257.

memorandum for the Board of Directors Meeting on November 22, 1982, on a *Future Eurocard data communication system*, the already built-up infrastructure was considered to be "excellent and leading."[68]

The tension between French, British, and German ambitions of running computing centers had been resolved diplomatically throughout 1980 and 1981. It created a division of labor, which involved clearing in Paris, authorization in England (via connection to MasterCard's global authorization center in St. Louis), and internal accounting for the service provision with a fee per transaction. Clearing and net settlement was still taking place via magnetic tapes brought by special couriers, a practice "built on an installed base"[69] that lasted at least until 1984. Since this was collectively felt to be insufficient, even interim solutions were acceptable, as long as they would abandon the tape and mail principle.[70] This physical infrastructure even suffered from a severe breakdown at the end of 1983, when the Cedi computing center in Paris was not able to process a number of tapes with clearing data because the tape headers had been damaged.[71]

Yet the solution of such technical problems and nuisances was never just a matter of software programming and system updates, but a socio-organizational challenge of translation between heterogeneous European actors and currencies. The Eurocard International management, while delivering another *Memorandum on the Future Eurocard Communication System* on November 3, 1982, emphasized this elegantly: "The Eurocard system does not try to erase national differences but rather to use them, synergetically. And it can do so, because it is designed with those differences in mind."[72]

There was even one part of the sociotechnical infrastructure that literally served as a nexus for coordinating many-to-many translations[73] in networked accounting—the multi-currency net settlement system called ENESS (see Figure 3).

It was in operation in Brussels since October 2, 1981,[74] thus adding another computing center in proximity to the Paris clearing center at Cedi. Ideally, both settlement and currency conversion were meant to be frictionless automations of payment identification

---

[68] *Future Eurocard Data Communication Center*, HIDB V19/0241.

[69] Susan Leigh Star and Karen Ruhleder, "Steps Toward an Ecology of Infrastructure. Design and Access for Large Information Spaces," *Information Systems Research* 7/1 (1996): pp.111–134, here p. 113.

[70] "In response to a strong demand from members to switch from the time-consuming courier transmission, to telecommunication, the provision of an interim solution for teletransmission of clearing data has been planned, since a final solution cannot be accommodated before January 1984. This interim solution could be made operational in less than three months after decision." *Future Eurocard Data Communication System, Memorandum from ECI Management to the Board of Directors*, October 27, 1982, p. 3. HIDB V19/0241.

[71] *88th Meeting of the Board*, May 4, 1985, Frankfurt, Enclosure 8. HIDB V19/244/1.

[72] *Future Eurocard Data Communication System, Memorandum from ECI Management to the Board of Directors*, November 3, 1982, p. 2, 22. HIDB V19/0241. The memorandum also argues for a hardware-based standardization for the network, usage of X.25 as standard protocol, and national Post, Telegraph and Telephone Service (PTT) packet switched networks as providers.

[73] See Star and Griesemer, "Institutional Ecology," p. 390.

[74] *Projects according to the ECI budget 1981/1982*, p. 4. HIDB V19/0240.

Functionning of ENESS

The same procedure
as given in the
practical example
applies for all members

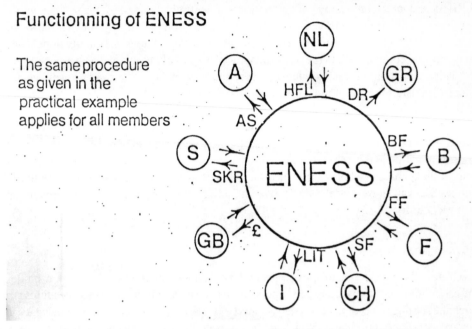

Fig. 3: Scheme of currency conversion within the Eurocard Net Settlement System (ENESS), November 1979. HIDB V19/0252.

and registration. An explanatory manual on *The Eurocard Interchange System* described the complex operations as simple procedures:

> The heart of Eurocard Interchange is the Eurocard Net Settlement System (ENESS). This system is the only multicurrency net settlement system which exists in the entire credit card world. […] It works as follows: the aggregate amounts payable and receivable per country are communicated from ECC (Eurocard Clearing Centre) to ENESS. Then these payables, which are still in varying amounts and currencies, are converted into the card's issuer's currency at the Brussels foreign exchange market mid-rates. Thus, one amount for all payables per Eurocard company is established in its own currency. This amount is then netted off against the sum to be received and the difference is either to be paid or received by the Eurocard company concerned. Eurocard International then arranges—via a Brussels based settlement bank—to execute the actual foreign exchange market deals for the net amounts, and the company's accounts with this bank are either credited or debited. The national Eurocard companies are immediately informed of settlements made, enabling them to make the necessary transfers or withdrawals to and from their settlement account. The main objective is to reduce costs.[75]

---

[75]　*The Eurocard Interchange System,* Typescript, part "Eurocard Net Settlement," p. 1. Brussels, May 4, 1982. HIDB V19/0241.

Hence, double conversions of currencies were entirely avoided by the system, while settlement and currency conversion could be realized from one day to the next between Paris and Brussels (see Figure 4). And, "[f]inally, these operations are mainly done automatically by computer dialogue, thus manpower is virtually eliminated."[76]

This managerial promise to delegate accounting work into networked machines neglected the significant amount of software- and hardware-related work, which was an actual part of every technical proposal and annual budget plan at Eurocard International. Relations between capital, work, and computing have been regularly biased towards rationalization only, while they have in fact created new tensions and manual work as part of industrialization and computerization movements. The banking industry was an integral part of this paradox of both digitization and globalization, where a staggering amount of money was put into new infrastructures without creating a corresponding improvement of productivity.[77]

Practices to Turn to

Seen from the perspective of a *less short* understanding of the *longue durée*,[78] new modes of accounting and transacting rely upon relatively stable administrative procedures. In fact, the settling of accounts consisted of intertwined practices of coordination, delegation, and registration/identification which already existed in early nineteenth century banking. Within Charles Babbage's *Economy of Machinery and Manufacture* (1832) chapter on "Money as Medium of Exchange," the London banker's practices of exchanging paper checks figured quite prominently as an assemblage of embodied media practices. Instead of delivering every single check by messenger to every single bank, the settlement of accounts was done by representation and impersonation of every bank at *The Clearing House* on Lombard Street (established in the early 1800s). All that was needed for this were bank clerks as human computers and the calculation of mutual payments via bookkeeping:

> At five o'clock the Inspector takes his seat; when each clerk, who has upon the result of all the transactions a balance to pay to various other houses, pays it to the inspector, who gives a ticket for the amount. The clerks of those houses to whom money is due, then receive the several sums from the inspector, who takes from them a ticket for the amount. Thus, the whole of these payments are made by a double system of balance, a very small amount of bank-notes passing from hand to hand, and scarcely any coin.[79]

---

76 Ibid.
77 Paul N. Edwards, "From 'Impact' to Social Process. Computers in Society and Culture," in *Handbook of Science and Technology Studies*, ed. Sheila Jasanoff et al. (Thousand Oaks CA, London and New Delhi: Sage, 1995), pp. 257–285.
78 See also note 12 and Braudel, "Histoire et sciences sociales: la longue durée," p. 748.
79 Charles Babbage, *The Works of Charles Babbage*. Volume 8, The Economy of Machinery and Manufactures, ed. Martin Campbell-Kelly (London: William Pickering, 1989), p. 90.

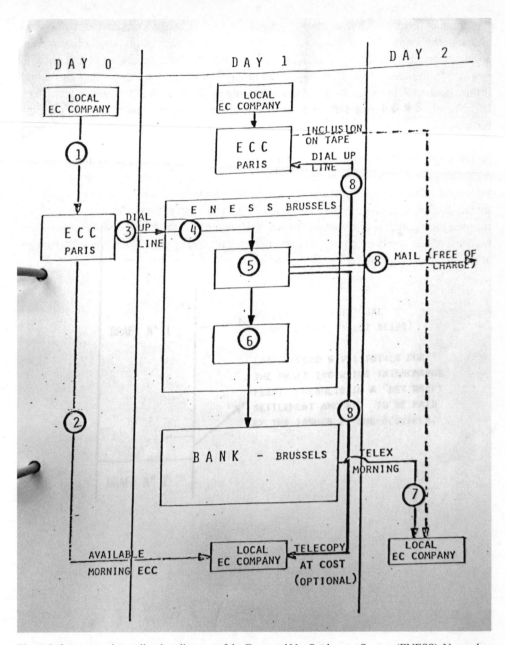

Fig. 4: Infrastructural coordination diagram of the Eurocard Net Settlement System (ENESS), November 1979. HIDB V19/0252.

Payment practices seem to have bypassed any harsh change from analogue to digital, although the materiality of architectures, message processing, institutional organization, and computation has changed significantly throughout the digitization of the banking world.[80] In the case of the Eurocard, even newly built paper-based, plastic, and digital infrastructures kept their close ties to accounting practices that dated, at the least, back to the beginning of the nineteenth century. The mutual agreement of the associated European bankers—how should settling and clearing practice be dealt with?—was based on their shared enskilment in bookkeeping and their ability to form a close-knit European community of practice. A *practice turn* in media history must take such administrative continuities into account, as well as explain the *longue durée* of related practices such as coordination, delegation, registration, and identification. Even in the most significant material-semiotic changes—like the replacement of physical money movement by institutional arrangements and networked accounting—all infrastructural stabilizations and business routines rely on constant innovation, repair, and upkeep. They are only manageable, usable, and accountable for by practice.

---

[80] See Martin Campbell-Kelly, "Victorian Data Processing. Reflections on the First Payment Systems," *Communications of the ACM* 53/10 (2010): pp. 19–21; Stearns, *Electronic Value Exchange*.

Fabian Grütter

On Practices and Other Paper Tigers.
Surfaces, Office Work, and Media Studies 1920–2000

It is pretty safe to say that whoever picked up Janet Ward's *Weimar Surfaces* in 2001 was in for a bit of a surprise. While the subtitle of her new book promised insights into *Urban Visual Culture in 1920s Germany*, the introduction's title indicated quite the historical detour: Instead of the Swinging 1920s, it was the era of *Postmodern Simulation* which was, at least during the course of the introduction, on the agenda.[1] But as is usually the case with detours, Ward's side trip into the last third of the twentieth century was inevitable, since understanding this period "of the copy without original, that is, of the 'simulacrum' or the 'hyperreal'" was the chief reason for venturing into the long-gone days of interwar Germany in the first place:[2] "I find enormous value in examining the tangible perceptual ways in which the modern era is still part of our own."[3] And: "In our condition as postmodern epigones we are still inevitably responding to the heritage of Weimar urban culture."[4] For Ward, then, Weimar's appeal lay in the fact that it was back then that postmodern *façadism* as a decidedly visual culture started to take shape.[5] In other words, she considered the historical roots of a Debordian "society of the spectacle" or a Baudrillardian *hyperreality* as firmly grounded in interwar Berlin.[6]

More specifically, Ward maintained, postmodern visuality was primarily rooted in four distinct dispositifs: the functionalist façade of Weimar architecture, advertising, the cinema, and the display window[7]—dispositifs which by now, of course, have become synonymous with Weimar (visual) culture. The reason for this is that Ward was not the only one examining these peculiar visual artifacts populating the metropolitan 1920s. One area which fits the mold of Weimar surfaces perfectly, but only plays a tangential role in Ward's narrative, is modernist typography; that is, the New Typography of such

---

[1] See Janet Ward, *Weimar Surfaces. Urban Visual Culture in 1920s Germany* (Berkeley: University of California Press, 2001), pp. 1–43.

[2] Ibid., p. 2.

[3] Ibid., p. 2.

[4] Ibid., p. 41.

[5] Ibid., p. 43.

[6] Ibid., pp. 3–5.

[7] Ibid., p. 10.

acclaimed practitioners as Jan Tschichold, Herbert Bayer, or László Moholy-Nagy, whose work Ward described as "smooth-surfaced"[8]—very much in line with her general thesis, of course. Frederic J. Schwartz dealt quite extensively with the New Typographers. In his paper titled "The Eye of the Expert" (also published in 2001, a pre-publication to his 2005 book *Blind Spots*), modernist typography came to "represent [...] and explore [...] the conditions in which perception and therefore visual communication had come to take place."[9] Schwartz demonstrated how "the typographers of the avant garde [sic] played the part of experts in the realm of visual attention,"[10] placing their products in the midst of what Ward, in the same year, would dub Weimar surfaces.

The realm of the visual's importance notwithstanding, modernist typography was accompanied by, and, more importantly, interacted with a discourse in media theory on how artifacts influence manual practices, and vice versa. (In the case at hand, these were related to office work.) During the first two decades of the twentieth century, the German physicist Otto Wiener developed a media theory elaborating on the role practical artifacts play in human evolution. Intrigued by Wiener's musings on tools, instruments, and media—*extensions* (*Erweiterungen*) of the human *physis*, as he called them[11]—Walter Porstmann, a former student of Wiener's, picked up his reflections as they promised to open up a way of accessing human behavior. Through designing office equipment, Porstmann hoped to engineer the manual tasks of office clerks, and partake in the forging of the *Neuen Menschen*. By means of his interest in all things connected to office work, Porstmann unwittingly brokered Wiener's media theory to the New Typographers. Although they marketed themselves as experts of the visual, these designers of Weimar surfaces were, in fact, perfectly aware that their (typo-)graphical products are, first and foremost, manually handled. As indicated by this story, Weimar surfaces thus cannot be grasped without acknowledging their counterparts: three dimensional artifacts with which to perform manual tasks. As the surfaces' flipside, they attracted just as much attention.

This interrelation between typographers, an office equipment dealer, and a media theoretician asks for, I would argue, a slight adjustment of the question of what media history, from a praxeological perspective, could look like. This constellation rather raises the question of what the history of debates about everyday practices reveals about the circumstances in which media theories flourish or become acute. Based on the set-up just outlined, I will argue that praxeological reflections gain momentum whenever the human fear of being supplanted by novel media(-technologies) becomes urgent (the case of 1920s typography mainly points to the "office reform"[12] which turned the cozy *Schreibstube* into

---

[8]   Ibid., p. 28.

[9]   Frederic J. Schwartz, "The Eye of the Expert: Walter Benjamin and the Avant Garde," *Art History* 24/3 (2001): pp. 401–444, here p. 405.

[10] Ibid., p. 409.

[11] Otto Wiener, *Die Erweiterung unserer Sinne. Akademische Antrittsvorlesung* (Leipzig: Johann Ambrosius Barth, 1900), p. 5.

[12] Markus Krajewski, *Paper Machines. About Cards & Catalogs, 1548–1929* (Cambridge MA: MIT Press, 2011), p. 124.

the mechanized office); a claim I will substantiate by secondly looking at c. 2000, when office work again turned problematic. In the face of the widespread ramblings regarding the paperless office due to networked PCs, practices connected to paper attracted not only the attention of cognitive psychologists, but of media scholars, too. Both these groups of paper specialists will, finally, be linked to c. 1980, when in light of the surge of so-called video display terminals (VDTs), cognitive psychology remodeled cognition "as situated, tacit, and embodied."[13] Needless to say, this was also the time when science was being discovered as something in action; and, just as importantly, as something happening on paper. Juxtaposing these three historical snapshots therefore suggests that reflections of media theory or investigations into media history have a *built-in practice turn*. That is, they communicate with mundane practical problems of their time, raised by novel media. Presently calling for such a turn, then, might be less indicative of methodological short-comings regarding the historiography of media than it is indicative of certain shortcomings regarding the historiography of media studies itself.

c. 1920

> It is significant that one of the best new books on speech, type, and orthography has been written not by an artist or a philologist but by an engineer: *Sprache und Schrift* (Speech and Writing) by Dr. W. Porstmann. Anyone interested in these problems will find this essential reading.[14]

This somewhat startled recommendation from a 1928 book called *The New Typography* came from none other than Jan Tschichold, the German master-typographer in the making. However, this was not even the first time Tschichold made this point: In *Elementare Typographie*, his acclaimed manifesto on modernist typography from 1952, Tschichold had referenced Dr. Porstmann several times.[15] Apparently, the latter had published works on three crucial postulations Tschichold now made in his own programmatic texts: the exclusive use of lowercase letters in the German language and, thus, typography; the need to standardize paper formats, and the importance of using standardized preprints (see Figure 5). Indeed, according to the stylist of modernist typography himself, these three characteristics, defining the look of *The New Typography* from the 1920s, harked back to Walter Porstmann – a person not even interested in aesthetics, let alone involved in typography or graphic design. Nevertheless, Tschichold was very responsive to Porst-

---

13 Max Stadler, "Man not a machine: Models, minds, and mental labor, c. 1980," in *Vital Models. The Making and Use of Models in the Brain Sciences*, ed. Tara Mahfoud et al. (Cambridge MA: Academic Press, 2017), pp. 73–96, here p. 75.

14 Jan Tschichold, *The New Typography. A Handbook for Modern Designers* (Berkeley: University of California Press, 1998), p. 81.

15 See Jan Tschichold, ed., *Elementare Typographie*, Typographische Mitteilungen 22 (Leipzig: Bildungsverband der deutschen Buchdrucker, 1925), pp. 198, 200.

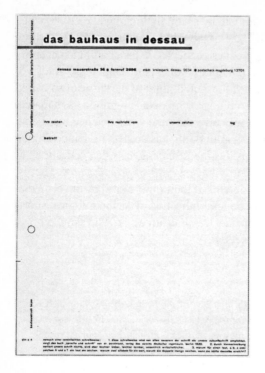

Fig. 5: A Letterhead by Herbert Bayer for the Bauhaus Dessau (1925), from Jan Tschichold, *The New Typography. A Handbook for Modern Designers* (Berkeley: University of California Press, 1998), p. 124.

mann, who was not concerned with matters regarding visuality at all, but, instead, devoted himself to the material office culture of his time, hoping to engineer practices connected to such artifacts such as paper, office furniture, or writing tools.

Walter Porstmann was born in Geyersdorf, a small town in the German Ore Mountains, in 1886.[16] However, he soon left the countryside to pursue his interest in mathematics and physics. Aside from a detour to Erlangen and Kiel, Porstmann stayed in Leipzig, where he studied with the German physicist Otto Wiener, an acquaintance who would affect his professional life permanently.[17] Wiener had acquired some renown through his studies of light waves.[18] However, it was not so much the physicist's research into the nature of light waves that caught Porstmann's attention. On May 19, 1900, Wiener had held his inaugural lecture at the University of Leipzig entitled *Erweiterung der Sinne* (*On the Extension of the Senses*).[19] In it, he described media, which in Wiener's broad notion

---

[16] See Walter Porstmann, *Technische Andachten* (Hamburg and Berlin: fabriknorm, 1956), p. 127.

[17] See Porstmann, *Technische Andachten*, p. 127.

[18] See Otto Wiener, "Stehende Lichtwellen und die Schwingungsrichtung polarisirten Lichtes Stehende Lichtwellen und die Schwingungsrichtung polarisirten Lichtes," in *Annalen der Physik* 276/6 (1890): pp. 203–243.

[19] Wiener has been somewhat neglected by media studies. The only two major publications he is mentioned in are Christoph Hoffmann's *Unter Beobachtung* and Friedrich Kittler's *Grammophon*

meant instruments and tools of all sorts, as quasi natural, external advancements of our deficient senses—a theory he based on Herbert Spencer's *The Principles of Psychology* from 1855: "Thus, all observing instruments, all weights, measures, scales, micrometers, verniers, microscopes, thermometers, barometers, &c., are artificial extensions of the senses; and all levers, screws, hammers, wedges, wheels, lathes, &c., are artificial extensions of the limbs."[20] Wiener slightly altered Spencer's concept by giving it a distinctively social Darwinist twist, emphasizing the fact that he considered extensions of the senses as supporting humans in their struggle to survive.[21] Consequently, innovation in terms of media meant progress in terms of human evolution. This was the central idea which Porstmann adopted from his professor.

Of particular importance regarding this exchange of ideas was the year 1917, when Porstmann drafted his Ph.D. thesis on measuring systems while stationed on the Western front as a meteorologist. In his meteorological study, supervised by Wiener,[22] Porstmann asked for a standardization of measuring systems because as the scientist's and the engineer's key tools, they were far from being perfectly in tune with the practical needs of those professionals. Three years later, Porstmann followed up on this Wienerian line of thinking: according to an exchange of letters between the two, Porstmann conceived of his new book *Sprache und Schrift* (1920)—that is, the one crucial to Tschichold and (typo-) graphical modernism in general—as yet another application of Wiener's program, this time to language and writing.[23] In the meantime, Porstmann had obviously read Wiener's 1919 publication *Physik und Kulturentwicklung durch technische und wissenschaftliche Erweiterung der menschlichen Naturanlagen* (*Physics and Cultural Development through Technical and Scientific Extension of the Human Senses*), which constituted the climactic endpoint of his musings in media theory. Porstmann professed to Wiener that he modeled his *Sprache und Schrift* after *Physik und Kulturentwicklung*, arguing that both spoken and written German hampered the betterment of man: as tools, they were not perfectly adapted for their respective applications as means of communication.[24]

Film Typewriter. See Christoph Hoffmann, *Unter Beobachtung. Naturforschung in der Zeit der Sinnesapparate* (Göttingen: Wallstein, 2006), p. 268; Friedrich Kittler, *Grammophon Film Typewriter* (Berlin: Brinkmann & Bose, 1986), pp. 121–122.

20 Herbert Spencer, *The Principles of Psychology* (London: Longman, Brown, Green, and Longmans, 1855), p. 461.

21 See Hoffmann, *Unter Beobachtung. Naturforschung in der Zeit der Sinnesapparate*, p. 268.

22 See Walter Porstmann, *Untersuchungen über Aufbau und Zusammenschluß der Maßsysteme* (Berlin: Normenausschuß der deutschen Industrie, 1918), p. 2.

23 See Walter Porstmann to Otto Wiener, letter, June 12, 1920, Nachlass Otto Wiener, Universitätsbibliothek Leipzig.

24 On Porstmann's notion of language as a tool, see Walter Porstmann, "Knechtung der Sprache," in *Prometheus. Illustrierte Wochenschrift über die Fortschritte in Gewerbe, Industrie und Wissenschaft* 30/1554 (1919): p. 358; on his notion of writing as a tool, see Walter Porstmann, *Sprache und Schrift* (Berlin: Verlag des Vereins Deutscher Ingenieure, 1920), pp. 63–69.

On the surface, the adjustments modernist typographers made in accordance with Porstmann's *Sprache und Schrift* had predominantly aesthetic consequences. However, there was more to the story. In Porstmann's view, the German use of uppercase letters as well as its tricky orthography were particularly disruptive. In this spirit, he proposed the following rule: one sound, one sign ("ain laut—ain zeichen").[25] As it is impossible to distinguish between minuscule and majuscule in speech, for uppercase letters, this would have meant the end. And it would have also implied the introduction of a quasi-phonetic orthography. While in the long run neither revision stuck, when it came to modernist typography, Porstmann's demand was widely implemented—be it by Tschichold, Moholy-Nagy, or Bayer.[26] These typographers would often cite advantages with regard to visual perception as their reason for applying the Porstmann-rule.[27] Nevertheless, these changes in writing were directly linked to debates regarding media practices, too—especially the use of the typewriter. In other words, the typographical revolution of the 1920s as adopted by the New Typography was one means of trying to positively influence—at the time, this meant making more economical—typewriting.

As part of the *Medienverbund* taking over the *Schreibstuben* and transforming them into offices, working with typewriters occupied the mind of many a psychotechnician.[28] These experts on work efficiency, however, did not only busy themselves with typewriters.[29] With the steep increase in number as well as size of business and public administrations, office equipment in general became a prime subject of organizational efforts emanating from psychotechnics.[30] For Porstmann, these developments signified an opportunity to convert Wiener's media theory into money. After all, his theoretical expertise regarding the interaction between men and material was unquestionable. And, by now, so was his practical know-how: Around 1920, Porstmann had a brief but impactful stint with the German standards organization *Normenausschuß der deutschen Industrie* (NDI), which had called upon him regarding a series of standard paper sizes he had developed and now was trying to introduce on a large scale.[31] He had had his first encounter with standard paper sizes while working for the German chemist Wilhelm Ostwald, who had developed

---

25 Porstmann, "Knechtung der Sprache," p. 70.
26 See Robin Kinross, *Modern Typography. An Essay in Critical History* (London: Hyphen Press, 2010), p. 112; Walter Scheiffele, *Bauhaus, Junkers, Sozialdemokratie: ein Kraftfeld der Moderne* (Berlin: Form + Zweck, 2003), pp. 57–62.
27 See Kinross, *Modern Typography*, p. 111.
28 See for example Erich A. Klockenberg, "Rationalisierung der Schreibmaschine und ihrer Bedienung," *Bücher der industriellen Psychotechnik*, 2 (Berlin: Julius Springer, 1926).
29 On psychotechnics in Weimar Germany, see Andreas Killen, "Weimar Psychotechnics between Americanism and Fascism," in *Osiris* 22/1 (2007): pp. 48–71; Mary Nolan, *Visions of Modernity. American Business and the Modernization of Germany* (Oxford: Oxford University Press, 1994).
30 See for example Irene M. Witte et al., *Psychotechnik der Organisation in Fertigung, (Büro-)Verwaltung, Werbung* (Halle: Carl Marhold Verlagsbuchhandlung, 1930), pp. 287–344.
31 See Markus Krajewski, *Restlosigkeit. Weltprojekte um 1900* (Frankfurt am Main: Fischer, 2006), pp. 126–127.

a series of standardized paper formats himself. Porstmann slightly changed Ostwald's version, and in the end, successfully pitched his formats to the NDI.[32] (These standard formats, which are still in use today, are widely considered as Porstmann's legacy.) By the end of the 1910s, his interest in standardization, which, of course, also showed in his Ph.D. thesis on measuring systems, had translated into something much more material: paper formats. While they, of course, are very different in nature from measuring and writing systems, to Porstmann they were just another instrument or tool for practitioners to work with.

While at first, Porstmann primarily had technical drafters in mind as the main customers of his new standard paper sizes,[33] it soon became clear that the booming offices constituted a much more lucrative market. In 1923, Porstmann thus started to run a company called *Fabriknorm*,[34] the aim of which was, on the one hand, to sell the NDI standards; on the other hand, to produce and sell office furniture in line with the NDI standards—from desks to folders to card catalogues (see Figure 6). From Porstmann's perspective as a pupil of Wiener's as well as a cunning businessman, it was the office which constituted the engineer's new site of influence. While Porstmann regarded the mechanization of production as largely concluded, the office was in the midst of replacing the *Schreibstuben*. Hence, now was the time to mold the practices performed in this new work environment. And having been Wiener's student, this obviously meant shaping the media—that is, office equipment of all sorts—on which office work relied. Similar to the innovations proposed by Porstmann with regards to writing, his venture to shape office work by means of standardized office equipment fell on fertile ground with modernist typographers.

In his 1928 book *The New Typography*, Tschichold included an extensive section on standardization, again referencing Porstmann's standard paper formats.[35] What is of interest regarding the topic at hand is the fact that Tschichold asked for typographers to use Porstmann's paper formats for the benefit of office workers. As the NDI sizes' main *users*, their handling of paper would become much easier, Tschichold maintained: "The storing of all printed matter will be easier and more practical."[36] And Tschichold was not the only modernist graphic designer relating his work to practical matters regarding office tasks. Preprints by the New Typographers started to include *built-in manuals* such as punch-holes, fold-marks or endpoints, which signal to the typist that she is running out of paper (see Figure 5). The exact placement of such marks was, of course, specified by NDI standards, which, in turn, related to other NDI standards specifying the exact form and format of paper containers (from folders to files to filing cabinets).[37] In matching their

---

[32] On how Porstmann took over the standard paper formats from Wilhelm Ostwald, see Krajewski, *Restlosigkeit*, pp. 120–130.

[33] See Walter Porstmann, "Wie ich zu den Formaten kam," in *DIN 1917-1927*, ed. Deutscher Normenausschuß. (Berlin: Beuth, 1927), p. 53.

[34] See Walter Porstmann, *Typoscript "Lebenslauf,"* (DIN-Archiv: undated): p. 6.

[35] See Tschichold, *The New Typography*, pp. 96–106.

[36] Ibid., p. 97.

[37] See Walter Porstmann, *Normformate*, Dinbuch (Berlin: Beuth, 1930).

Fig. 6: An illustration of the nested office structure based on standard paper sizes, from Walter Porstmann, *Normformate*, Dinbuch (Berlin: Beuth, 1930), p. 106.

products with the standardized office environment pushed by the NDI and sold, among others, by Porstmann, typographers sought to take part in creating a *nested structure* (see Figure 6),[38] thus engineering practical tasks regarding this new work environment called the office.

Interestingly enough, then, the New Typography as one of the hotbeds for the production of Weimar surfaces (that is, a world withdrawing itself from men onto surfaces, thus creating a distance between the two) was, in fact, deeply concerned with tactile questions of handling. Far from being drivers of an *oberflächliche* world only, modernist typographers were very well aware of the fact that the alleged surfaces they designed were three-dimensional objects which are manually handled by office workers. What the affiliation between Porstmann and Tschichold implies, then, is that the *oberflächliche* interwar period and the very tangible, haptic world of office work, in a way, were two sides of the same coin. This case study suggests, then, that almost in a dialectical volte-face, questions of

---

[38] According to Susan Leigh Star and Martha Lampland, standards are nested, meaning that "they fit inside one another, somewhat like a set of Russian dolls (maitruska)." Martha Lampland and Susan Leigh Star, "Reckoning with Standards," in *Standards and their Stories. How Quantifying, Classifying, and Formalizing Practices Shape Everyday Life*, ed. Martha Lampland and Susan Leigh Star (Ithaca NY and London: Cornell University Press, 2009), pp. 5–6.

materiality and practices came into play at a point in history when the world threatened to become, to cite the title of Kasimir Malevich's 1927 book, a *Non-Objective World*.[39]

c. 2000

Approximately 70 years later, at the dawn of the new millennium, a similar turn to the non-objective appeared to be in full swing. Thanks to "a fairly simple markup language called HTML," the World Wide Web seemed able to tap its full potential: "any desktop computer linked to the telephone network [can now] read and display any other computer's documents," contemporaries reportedly marveled.[40] The paperless office finally seemed in reach. However, Abigail J. Sellen, a cognitive psychologist, and Richard H. R. Harper, a sociologist-turned-computer-scientist, did not buy it: "It seems that the promised 'paperless office' is as much a mythical ideal today as it was thirty years ago," the two laconically surmised in the introduction to their *The Myth of the Paperless Office*, published in 2002.[41] Despite being "exposed to more of the latest technological gadgets than most people,"[42] (Sellen at the time worked at Hewlett-Packard Laboratories in Bristol, UK while Harper was Principal Researcher in Socio-Digital Systems at Microsoft Research in Cambridge, UK), the two former Xerox employees just could not find any evidence for the widely perceivable claim that the paperless office was looming. Indeed, their examination of work environments pointed in the opposite direction: "The bottom line is that no slowdown in office paper consumption appears on the horizon. In fact, if we look at the figures for worldwide consumption, the trend is a steady, steep increase."[43]

To account for their unexpected finding, they called on James J. Gibson's 1979 book *The Ecological Approach to Visual Perception*. By introducing the concept of *affordance*, the psychologist known for his work on the psychology of perception seemed to provide a useful means to explain Sellen and Harper's empirical anomaly: "An affordance refers to the fact that the physical properties of an object make possible different functions for the person perceiving or using that object," they paraphrased a section titled "TOOLS."[44] Gibson had described the evolution of tools starting with the unworked stone missile (bear in mind, it was 1979 and Cold War tensions were growing rapidly).[45] Subsequently, hunters allegedly developed "striking tools, edged tools, and pointed tools."[46] Crucial to

---

[39] In German, the book was entitled *Die gegenstandslose Welt*. See Kasimir Malewitsch, *Die gegen-standslose Welt* (Munich: Albert Langen, 1927).

[40] Abigail J. Sellen and Richard H. R. Harper, *The Myth of the Paperless Office* (Cambridge MA: MIT Press, 2002), p. 7.

[41] Sellen and Harper, *The Myth of the Paperless Office*, p. 1.

[42] Ibid., pp. 1–2.

[43] Ibid., pp. 11–12.

[44] Ibid., p. 17.

[45] See James J. Gibson, *The Ecological Approach to Visual Perception* (Boston MA: Houghton Mifflin Company, 1979), pp. 40–41.

[46] Gibson, *The Ecological Approach to Visual Perception*, p. 40.

Sellen and Harper's argument, however, was not so much Gibson's history of military equipment, but his claim that every tool—as an "extension of the hand"[47]—affords being used in a certain manner. In this light, artifacts always suggest a way of most effectively using them, interlocking users with their environment; the philosophical consequence (to which we shall return in the next section) being "that the absolute duality of 'objective' and 'subjective' is false."[48] Or as Sellen and Harper would put it: "Without these bits of paper ready to hand, it is as if the writing, and more especially the thinking, could not take place in earnest."[49]

This statement's somewhat provocative overtone becomes clear when bringing to mind the wider context of Sellen and Harper's book: their studies on the use of paper in office work were undertaken in the midst of heated discussions on the knowledge society and knowledge work.[50] Of course, the imagined worker working in the paperless office was exclusively using his cognitive capacities along with the latest technological innovations, finally freeing work from any bodily and, above all, material inhibitions stemming from old-fashioned media(-technologies). This vision, however, could not have been any further from reality. According to Sellen and Harper, "it is easy to see who is engaged in intensive knowledge work: it is the person whose desk is strewn with paper."[51] (Figure 7) Or to put it differently, knowledge work, against all assertions, was never going to be performed exclusively by dis-embodied workers staring at the screens of networked desktop computers; instead, it will remain an embodied practice interacting with a palpable material office environment which is always going to be interlaced with seemingly outdated, or, more positively phrased, anachronistic artifacts. That paper—out of all of these *outdated* artifacts—was the one garnering the most attention around 2000 becomes clear when scrutinizing another scholarly field.

In 1998, visitors to the Landesgalerie am Oberösterreichischen Landesmuseum Francisco-Carolinum were presented with an exhibition entitled *Work & Culture. Büro: Inszenierung von Arbeit* (*Office: Mise-en-Scène of Labor*). For its catalogue, the young media theorist Gloria Meynen wrote a piece discussing—apart from the inevitable rocket—Porstmann's standard paper sizes.[52] In 2000, Cornelia Vismann published the original German version of *Files: Law and Media Technology*—and she too took an interest in Porst-

---

47   Ibid., p. 41.
48   Ibid.
49   Sellen and Harper, *The Myth of the Paperless Office*, p. 1.
50   In Germany, for example, CDU politician Jürgen Rüttgers had just published his ardent and rather naïve eulogy on the *Wissensgesellschaft*, with the year 2000 as important a date as 1453, when the Gutenberg Galaxy started. See Jürgen Rüttgers, *Zeitenwende – Wendezeiten. Das Jahr-2000-Projekt: Die Wissensgesellschaft* (Berlin: Siedler, 1999).
51   Sellen and Harper, *The Myth of the Paperless Office*, p. 72.
52   See Gloria Meynen, "Büroformate – von DIN A4 zu Apollo 11," in *Work & Culture: Büro. Inszenierung von Arbeit*, ed. Herbert Lachmayer and Eleonora Louis (Klagenfurt: Ritter, 1998), pp. 80–90.

Fig. 7: A knowledge worker's workplace as encountered by Sellen and Harper during their fieldwork, from Abigail J. Sellen and Richard H. R. Harper, *The Myth of the Paperless Office* (Cambridge, MA: MIT Press, 2002), p. 24.

mann's DIN formats.[53] The same applied to Anke te Heesen, who followed suit in 2002 with her first major publication on newspaper clippings, a catalogue for the exhibition *Cut and Paste um 1900* presented at the Max-Planck-Institut für Wissenschaftsgeschichte in Berlin (te Heesen's interest went even further as she also wrote on the New Typography).[54] And in the same year, Markus Krajewski released the original German version of *Paper Machines. About Cards & Catalogs, 1548-1929*, following up with *World Projects: Global Information before World War I* in 2006, which contains the most in-depth research yet on the standard paper sizes' originator Walter Portsmann.[55] In short, media scholars—very much in tandem with occupational psychologists such as Sellen—started to systematically dedicate themselves to *paper studies*. Since the turn of the millennium, the corpus of works on a plethora of paper artifacts has grown to an impressive size, with scholars such as Lisa Gitelman, Matthew S. Hull, Monika Dommann, Bernhard Siegert or Ben Kafka adding to the, admittedly, incomplete and highly random list[56]—a shortcoming due in part to my omitting historians of science (I am aware of the coarse division this implies, especially

---

53 See Cornelia Vismann, *Akten. Medientechnik und Recht*, 3rd ed. (Frankfurt am Main: Fischer, 2011), pp. 27–276.

54 See Anke te Heesen, ed., *Cut and Paste um 1900. Der Zeitungsausschnitt in den Wissenschaften*, Kaleidoskopien (Berlin: Vice Versa, 2002); for her remarks on the New Typography, see Anke te Heesen, *Der Zeitungsausschnitt. Ein Papierobjekt der Moderne* (Frankfurt am Main: Fischer, 2006), p. 271.

55 See Markus Krajewski, *Zettelwirtschaft. Die Geburt der Kartei aus dem Geiste der Bibliothek* (Berlin: Kadmos, 2002); on the relation between Portsmann and Ostwald, see Krajewski, *Restlosigkeit*, pp. 120–130.

56 See Lisa Gitelman, *Paper Knowledge. Toward a Media History of Documents* (Durham NC: Duke University Press, 2014); Matthew S. Hull, *Government of Paper. The Materiality of Bureaucracy in Urban Pakistan* (Berkeley: University of California Press, 2016); Monika Dommann, *Autoren und Apparate. Die Geschichte des Copyrights im Medienwandel* (Frankfurt am Main: Fischer, 2014); Bernhard Siegert, *Passagiere und Papiere. Schreibakte auf der Schwelle zwischen Spanien und Amerika* (Munich: Fink, 2006); Ben Kafka, *The Demon of Writing. Powers and Failures of Paperwork* (New York: Zone Books, 2012).

in light of the fact that many of the scholars invoked above have studied the history of science). However, the history of science can under no circumstances be excluded from the—pardon the expression—*paper turn* of the 2000s.

Peter Becker and William Clark in 2001 co-edited *Little Tools of Knowledge*, a collection of essays focusing on the role of paper objects in the history of science. More importantly with regards to the story at hand, however, Becker and Clark hinted at a possible reason for the *paper turn*: in the face of the digital workspace/the paperless office, the *self-evident nature* of ordinary paper objects had suddenly become something not-so-self-evident.[57] Put a bit pompously, at the turn of the millennium, paper came to be seen as the lover about to leave, inciting the one in fear of being left to reflect on what they had taken for granted. In their introduction, Becker and Clark refrained from blatantly proclaiming what they felt was at stake. In hindsight, however, academic courtesy cannot obfuscate their motivation for zooming in on paper and the manual practices related to it: Namely, counterbalancing what they perceived as a rather lopsided analysis of the role of paper in the history of science.

Not without a grain of criticism, the two established that the "visual empire of illustrations, charts, diagrams, tables, and graphs stretches far and wide today."[58] And they made it rather clear who—at least in the realm of historiography—they perceived as being largely responsible for this visual bias: "Historians of science have brought the fabrication of the observer onto center stage…"[59] In Becker and Clark's eyes, even Bruno Latour, who around 1980, along with Steve Woolgar and Karin Knorr-Cetina, had convincingly shown that scientific work is always bureaucratic work, too, had a penchant for "visualization."[60] And in *Leviathan and the Air-Pump* from 1989 we are told by Becker and Clark that Steven Shapin and Simon Shaffer also displayed a slight condition of "ocularcentrism" (Martin Jay).[61] After all, they were concerned with virtual witnessing, "a technique creating in the mind's eye the sense of virtually partaking of an observation or experiment."[62] In short, for the editors of *Little Tools of Knowledge*, it was discernible by means of the history of science as well as science and technology studies that visual culture studies had become quite—or maybe a little bit too—fashionable by the dawn of the 2000s. Thus, they felt it was time to prioritize paper practices.

---

[57] Peter Becker and William Clark, "Introduction," in *Little Tools of Knowledge. Historical Essays on Academic and Bureaucratic Practices*, ed. Peter Becker and William Clark (Ann Arbor: The University of Michigan Press, 2001), p. 1.

[58] Becker and Clark, "Introduction," p. 17.

[59] Ibid., p. 22.

[60] Ibid., p. 18.

[61] Ibid.

[62] Ibid.

c. 1980

In the eyes of Becker and Clark, the early Latour might have been the opponent. Structurally speaking, however, his research—as representative of late 1970s/early 1980s science and technology studies in general—was actually quite akin to what was going on in media studies, the history of science or cognitive psychology around the year 2000. Take Latour's eminent essay "Visualisation and Cognition: Thinking with Eyes and Hands," which he prepared for a conference at École des *Mines* for the Centre national de la recherche scientifique (CNRS), December 12, 13 and 14, 1983 and published in English in 1986.[63] It is hard to argue with Clark and Becker regarding their claim that Latour was interested in visuality—after all, it says so in the title. But the vehicle for the visual processes Latour was concerned with was, first and foremost, paper. "This is precisely the paradox. By working on papers alone, on fragile inscriptions which are immensely less than the things from which they are extracted, it is still possible to dominate all things, and all people."[64] In other words, no matter how important and potent the eyes, Latour's research indicated that paper was the basic, most powerful tool regarding cognition—an insight, as I have argued above, echoed by Sellen and Harper twenty years later.

And just as the paper turn of the 2000s responded to the threat of the physical world disappearing into a network of screens, Latour's praxeology with its paper-bias can, to some degree, be seen against the backdrop of the desktop computers' slowly but surely taking over the office. In 1984, one year after Latour had given his paper on paperwork, Jonathan Crary cautioned his reader that "the VDT imposes a highly articulated, coercive apparatus, a prescriptive mode of activity and corporal regimentation."[65] In other words, with the spread of desktop computers, alienation was looming, as workers were clamped into a techno-material dispositif; at the same time, however, they were constantly being kept at a distance from the material world, only really being able to access it by means of vision. It might have been nothing more than a historical contingency that the German version of Malevich's *The Non-Objective World* was re-printed in 1980—but it sure was a fitting one; after all, the material world seemed to be disappearing into the prototypical *Weimar surface* of the 1980s: flickering CRT monitors.

But just like the original Weimar surfaces, their postmodern simulacra had, of course, a material flipside: a fact that at least to office workers as well as to "the fledgling communities of 'computer ergonomists' and allied specialists" was evident.[66] Those who, instead of philosophically reflecting on VDTs, actually had to do with them as tools of work were perfectly well aware of the fact that they still very much meant physical labor.

---

[63] Bruno Latour, "Visualisation and Cognition: Drawing Things Together," in *Knowledge and Society. Studies in the Sociology of Culture Past and Present*, ed. Elizabeth Long and Henrika Kucklick (Greenwich CT: Jai Press, 1986), p. 30.

[64] Ibid., p. 30.

[65] Jonathan Crary, "Eclipse of the Spectacle," in *Art after Modernism: Rethinking Representation*, ed., Brian Wallis (New York: The Museum of Contemporary Art, 1984), p. 293.

[66] Stadler, "Man not a Machine," p. 88.

How else could one account for the multiple ailments associated with the novel technology ("migraines, eyesore, blurred vision, double vision, visual flicker, dizziness, diminished intellectual functioning, irritability, skin rashes, and a host of other conditions"[67])? One scientist crucial to the somatic flipside of postindustrial labor and cognition was none other than Sellen's Ph.D. adviser Don Norman. Around 1980, just like Gibson, the Xerox consultant and head of the Cognitive Science Department at UC San Diego was campaigning against mentalist models of cognition.[68] Instead, he championed interactionist approaches, stressing the role of material environments to cognition. It should now be clear why Sellen referenced one of her adviser's kindred spirits of the time. Just like Norman, Gibson had a predilection for examining the material flipside of the postindustrial surface-culture. In this sense, they were both representative of a cognitivist practice turn. And so, one could argue, was Latour (maybe because, as Max Stadler has pointed out, the Science Study department in San Diego was only 200 meters away from Norman's institute[69]), as he did not grow tired of stressing the importance of paper. At one point, he even went as far as to suggest that computers, too, were made from paper: referencing Tracy Kidder's 1981 *The Soul of a New Machine*, which recounts Data General's development of their computer codenamed Eagle, he claimed that they are really just "a pile of paper…"[70]

The fact, then, that Latour was picked up by Becker and Clark—even if in a distancing gesture—or Gibson by Sellen and Harper should, by now, be quite comprehensible. Their respective research suggested—even though it has become Latour's catchphrase—a collapsing of "the absolute duality of 'objective' and 'subjective'"[71] to cite Gibson again. In times when VDTs seemed to separate humans and the world, cognition found its way back out of the mind and into a body situated in and interacting with its material environment. Or as Stadler has put it: the computer metaphor, which "dominated neurological and psychological theorizing in the early post-WW2 era, came apart during the 1970s and 1980s; and […] it was, step by step, replaced by a set of model entities more closely in tune with the significance that was now discerned in certain kinds of 'everyday practical action' as the ultimate manifestation of the human mind."[72] That it was not only Latour's thinking which can be looked at against the backdrop of an allegedly dematerializing world retracting into the screen, but also Gibson's, becomes obvious when considering what follows the section on tools in *The Ecological Approach to Visual Perception*: after a few remarks on "OTHER ANIMALS," Gibson goes on to discuss "HUMAN DISPLAYS."[73] Even though he claimed to refer "to all the surfaces of the environment that bear writ-

---

67   Ibid., p. 86.
68   See Ibid., p. 94.
69   See Max Stadler, "Der Geist des Users. Oder: vom Ende des 'Boole'schen Traums'," in *Nach Feier-abend – Digital Humanities*, ed. Caspar Hirschi and Michael Hagner (Zurich and Berlin: Diaphanes, 2013), p. 72.
70   Latour, "Visualisation and Cognition: Drawing Things Together," p. 26.
71   Gibson, *The Ecological Approach to Visual Perception*, p. 41.
72   Stadler, "Man not a Machine," p. 75.
73   See Gibson, *The Ecological Approach to Visual Perception*, p. 42.

ing," it should now be evident that his frame of reference was deeply embedded in his own time, since the surfaces Gibson had in mind "exhibit information for more than just the surface itself."[74]

Conclusion

With regards to all the historical snapshots I have looked at, be it the 1920s, the 1980s, or the 2000s, surfaces have played a crucial role—both as historical phenomena and as historiography's poster children. In the 1920s, it was advertisements, neon signs, photography, cinema, or shop windows which seemed to banish the material world into two-dimensional Weimar surfaces. In the 1980s, similar worries expressed themselves in light of VDTs. And in the 2000s, the networked infrastructure of PCs finally seemed to finish off outdated office equipment, most prominently paper. What I have tried to show is that in all three instances, practices and artifacts managed to garner a lot of attention—be it in Wiener's media theory, Tschichold's typography, or Porstmann's office standardization; in Gibson's perceptual psychology, Norman's notion of cognition, or Latour's science studies; or in Sellen and Harper's ethnography of office workers, and, of course, media studies' *paper turn* of the 2000s. Materiality, along with the practices connected to it, thus seems to flash up whenever new media technologies fan the fear that they will devour the world as we know it.

With regards to the proclamation of a practice turn in media studies, this raises some questions. First off, it would seem that proclaiming a practice turn in the sense of breaking out into a *new direction* really only makes sense when having a quite narrow notion of media studies as a point of reference—that is, its Freiburg implementation with its alleged media determinism. The appeal of breaking away from this particular way of doing media studies, which was time and again voiced during the symposium with reference to Nick Couldry's 2004 paper "Theorising Media as Practice,"[75] could be interpreted as an attempt at reassuring a humanistic position: that is, that in the light of all this talk about new media technologies supplanting the human, we would be well advised to look at actual instances of people using media. For then we could see that the power of media is constantly being subverted by what Michel de Certeau has called "tactics,"[76] expressing themselves in praxis. When deepening the historical focus, however, one cannot shed the impression that practices have always played a role in media theorists' considerations—that is, as a central pole in triangulating the workings of media. The history of reflections on practices, even if they were spelled out in fields other than ethnomethodology, sociology, or science and technology studies, is a promising starting point for writing a history of media studies itself. Because of what else is the present proclamation of a practice turn

---

[74] Ibid.

[75] See Nick Couldry, "Theorising Media as Practice," in *Social Semiotics* 14/2 (2004): pp. 115–132.

[76] Michel de Certeau, *The Practice of Everyday Life* (Berkeley: University of California Press, 1984), p. xix.

indicative of if not of a need for exactly that? And since it has become very clear during the symposium that it is the Freiburg school which is mainly being wrestled with, it might well be an appropriate place to start—beyond the received narrative of Pink Floyd, Silicon Valley, military equipment, and hackers.[77] Such an endeavor, I suspect, might turn out to be much more productive in addressing the Freiburg elephant in the room than rashly confronting it with what might just turn out to be a meek paper tiger.

---

[77] Claus Pias, as is well known, asked for such a historicization in April 2015, just four months before the symposium; see Claus Pias, "Friedrich Kittler und der 'Mißbrauch von Heeresgerät'. Zur Situation eines Denkbildes 1964 – 1984 – 2014," *Merkur. Deutsche Zeitschrift für europäisches Denken* 69/791 (2015): pp. 31–44.

Philipp Goll

"I like the Beach Boys!" Literary Covering in Uwe Nettelbeck's *Die Republik*

Play

"Uwe Nettelbeck is back"—the alternative leftist mail order magazine *Zweitausendeins* announced in its catalog *Merkheft* in 1976.[1] In the late 1960s, Nettelbeck had been causing some stir with his articles, critiques, and reportages in the liberal weekly newspaper *DIE ZEIT* and in left-wing cultural magazines like *Filmkritik* and *konkret*.[2] At the end of the decade, he had disappeared from journalism almost entirely. In 1976, his distributor could proudly present the return of the famous whizz kid among its offers of LPs, magazines, and books.

When Nettelbeck re-emerged, he did so first with his book *Mainz wie es singt und lacht* [*Mainz how it sings and how it laughs*],[3] which was published by the newly founded independent publishing house Verlag Petra Nettelbeck.[4] The book is structured in seven chapters and consists of texts of various kinds, such as satirical assaults against journalists and writers, letters from editors and publishers who had refused to publish the book, and montages of newspaper articles or other texts. The book was followed by a magazine called *Die Republik*, with its first issue appearing in the same year.[5] On its cover, one finds the note "edited by Uwe Nettelbeck" and the contents of the issue. Inside the magazine, however, there is no reference to the authors of the texts. Like the book, the magazine mostly consists of montages of texts by others, polemical attacks against the establishment, reproductions of newspaper articles or transcriptions of radio and TV shows, sometimes with the addition of satirical comments.

---

[1] *Das Merkheft* 20 (1976), np.

[2] See Uwe Nettelbeck, *Keine Ahnung von Kunst und wenig vom Geschäft. Filmkritik 1962-1968*, ed. Sandra Nettelbeck (Hamburg: Philo Fine Arts, 2011); Uwe Nettelbeck, *Prozesse. Gerichtsberichte 1967-1969*, ed. Petra Nettelbeck (Berlin: Suhrkamp, 2015).

[3] The translations in brackets are intended as an aid in comprehension. All translations are mine, if not quoted from a translated source.

[4] Uwe Nettelbeck, *Mainz wie es singt und lacht* (Salzhausen-Luhmühlen: Petra Nettelbeck, 1976).

[5] From nos. 55–60 (3 June 1982) to the last issue (nos. 123–125, 7 January 2008), *Die Republik* was co-edited by Petra and Uwe Nettelbeck. For nos. 86–91 (3 May 1991), D.E. Sattler also was a co-editor.

When *Mainz wie es singt und lacht* appeared, some critics lamented the lack of Nettelbeck's "own texts"[6]. Others saw in *Die Republik* an inauthentic twin of Karl Kraus's magazine *Die Fackel* (1899-1936), since Nettelbeck had imitated the way Kraus strongly criticized Vienna's journalistic and literary establishment of the early twentieth century—mainly through satirical quotes and polemical comments. According to a critique from Nettelbeck's time, *Die Republik* "resembles" Karl Kraus's project both "in outlook and concept."[7] Another critic wrote: "Die Republik appears in the format of Fackel, is printed in the Fackel fonts, uses the same font size, the Fackel sentence structure, the citation method of the Fackel"—in short: Nettelbeck "wants to do what Karl Kraus did."[8] Nettelbeck, they seem to say, does not write himself, but transcribes—and he transcribes as Karl Kraus used to transcribe. Literary historical research based on damning reviews came to the conclusion that Nettelbeck's writing will never achieve a "similar impact"[9] as that of the legendary Kraus. It could be one of the reasons why Uwe Nettelbeck appears to be merely a footnote in the history of German literature today.

These critical approaches, pitting Nettelbeck's literary production against a concept of genuine creation, abide by a Romantic aesthetic of genius that still haunts literary critics today.[10] The criticism leveled at the author Uwe Nettelbeck offers an ideal occasion for literary studies to emphasize how texts are always a "tissue of quotations"[11] as Roland Barthes wrote in his influential article about the "The Death of the Author." The rare defenses of Nettelbeck's writing come from a position similar to Barthes: critique of the Romantic genius concept of authorship, and allusion to the dependence of all literature on pre-existing texts. From this perspective, to some critics, Uwe Nettelbeck's literary production seems to be a dismissal of the concept of "authorship as originality."[12] According to others, his writing is just an honorable expression of the universal principle of literature, stating that a writer never invents, because "the Alphabet does not belong to him, he didn't shape the words, he did not come up with the sayings and the images."[13]

[6]   Hellmuth Karasek, "Eine Scherbenwelt aus Zitaten," *Der Spiegel*, 19 April 1976, pp. 172–174, here p. 174.
[7]   Wilhelm Bittorf, "Karl Kraus, klein geschrieben," *Der Spiegel*, 11 October 1976, pp. 226–228, here p. 228.
[8]   Hermann L. Gremliza, "Nettelbeck," *konkret*, October 1976, p. 48.
[9]   Volker Hage, *Collagen in der deutschen Literatur. Zur Praxis und Theorie eines Schreibverfahrens*. (Frankfurt am Main: Peter Lang, 1984), p. 61.
[10] In 2013 a critic wrote: "he did not write." See Willi Winkler, "Einsame Spitze," *Süddeutsche Zeitung*, 21 October 2013, p. 12.
[11] Roland Barthes, "The Death of the Author [1968]," in Roland Barthes, *Image–Music–Text*, ed. and trans. Stephen Heath (New York: Hill and Wang, 1977), pp. 142–148, here p. 146.
[12] Brigitte Weingart, "Flüchtiges Lesen: TV-Transkripte (Goetz, Kempowski, Nettelbeck)," in *Transkribieren – Medien/Lektüre*, ed. Ludwig Jäger and Georg Stanitzek (Munich: Fink, 2002), pp. 91–114, here p. 104.
[13] Stefan Ripplinger, "Return to Sender. Über Uwe Nettelbecks Zitatmontagen," *Kultur & Gespenster* 7, (Fall 2008): pp. 73–97, here p. 74.

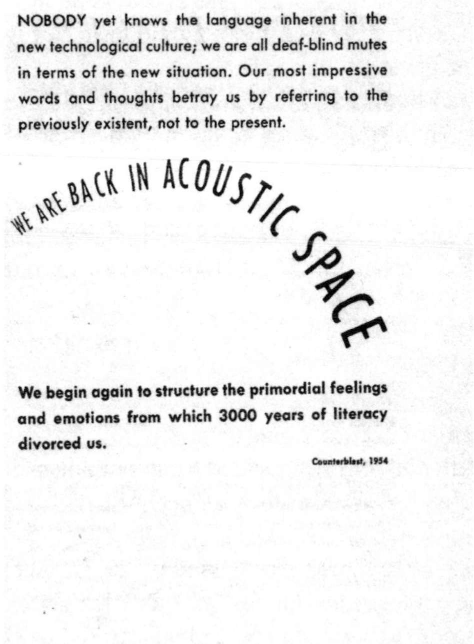

NOBODY yet knows the language inherent in the new technological culture; we are all deaf-blind mutes in terms of the new situation. Our most impressive words and thoughts betray us by referring to the previously existent, not to the present.

WE ARE BACK IN ACOUSTIC SPACE

We begin again to structure the primordial feelings and emotions from which 3000 years of literacy divorced us.

Counterblast, 1954

Fig. 8: Marshall McLuhan, *Verbi–Voco– Visual Explorations* (New York and Frankfurt: Something Else Press Inc., 1967), np.

Rewind

This article should not be misunderstood as an attempt to belatedly canonize a writer. I will not claim that *Die Republik,* through reproduction and montage of found materials, is basically a swan song of the poetic voice of a godlike author. But I will not use the aesthetic of production as a test case for discussing a universal concept of literature either. Instead of invoking these kinds of grand narratives, I will propose an approach that tentatively investigates practices belonging to a certain *region of intensities*, where expressions and actions are constituted in a rhizomatic interplay rather than seen as related to "exterior or transcendent ends."[14] Subsequently, I will describe practices such as writing or reading as performances that are not dependent on identifiable, categorically fixed patterns but rather carried out technically, socially, locally, and situatively.[15] In avoiding disciplinary

---

[14] Gilles Deleuze and Félix Guattari, *A Thousand Plateus. Capitalism and Schizophrenia*, trans. Brian Massumi (Minneapolis and London: University of Minnesota Press, 1987), p. 2.

[15] For a seminal program for the practice turn in literary studies, see Philipp Löffler, "Was ist eine literarische Epoche? Literaturgeschichte, literarischer Wandel und der Praxisbegriff in den Geistes- und Sozialwissenschaften," in *Praxeologie. Beiträge zur interdisziplinären Reichweite praxistheoretischer Ansätze in den Geistes- und Sozialwissenschaften*, ed. Friederike Elias et al. (Berlin and Boston MA: de Gruyter, 2015), pp. 73–96.

preconceptions that read phenomena through universal or functional categories, I shall open up a space in which practices like writing and reading are not necessarily bound to what we call *literature*. Through this approach, aesthetic categories of literature, and even definitions of what literature might be, become questionable.

My interest addresses not only the overlap between practices of appropriation in popular music and literature. I will also focus on how practices of consumption and of production of literature are tuned by media technologies, especially by new modes of experience available in electronic music. I therefore propose to look at—or rather listen to—what came into play in the 1960s when media theorist Marshall McLuhan wrote: "The Age of Writing has passed. We must invent a NEW METAPHOR, restructure our thoughts and feelings."[16]

Replay

"Uwe Nettelbeck is back"—the alternative leftist mail order magazine *Zweitausendeins* announced in its catalog *Merkheft* in 1976.[17] After having disappeared from journalism at the end of the sixties, from 1970 to 1974 Nettelbeck worked as the producer of Krautrock band Faust.[18]

"Krautrock"—a term coined by the British press—was proclaimed as the German version of American Progressive Rock's sonic explorations. On the one hand, Krautrock mimicked the soundscapes assembled in the studio experiments carried out by producers such as Brian Wilson (Beach Boys) and George Martin (The Beatles). On the other hand, it was also inspired by the avantgarde experiments of artists such as John Cage, Karlheinz Stockhausen, Andy Warhol, and Frank Zappa, and by their use of existing materials.

Along with the conceptualist of German Krautrock Rolf Ulrich Kaiser, who co-organized the legendary Internationale Essener Songtage 1968 [Essen International Song Days], and who produced for his label Ohr [Ear] bands like Tangerine Dream, Guru Guru and Ash Ra Tempel, Nettelbeck is considered the other big influencer of the German Krautrock scene.[19]

What Faust's first label Polydor was supposedly looking for, when approaching Nettelbeck, was the German Beatles.[20] They got something different. In listening to the first track "Why Don't You Eat Carrots" in Faust's eponymous debut album from 1971, it becomes

---

[16] Marshall McLuhan, *Counterblast*, designed by Harley Parker (London: Rapp & Whiting Limited, 1969), p. 14.

[17] *Das Merkheft*, 20 (1976), np.

[18] Between 1970 and 1974 Nettelbeck produces four albums of Faust, as well of Anthony Moore, Slapp Happy and Tony Conrad. For more details see Julian Cope, *Krautrocksampler. One Head's Guide to the Great Kosmische Musik – 1968 Onwards* (Yatesbury: Head Heritage, 1995), pp. 21–27.

[19] See Julian Cope, *Krautrocksampler*, pp. 17–20. For a detailed depiction, see Andy Wilson, *Faust. Stretch Out Time 1970-1975* (London: Unkant, 2006).

[20] David Stubbs, *Future Days: Krautrock and the Building of Modern Germany* (London: Faber & Faber, 2014), p. 215.

apparent where it was going: the track starts with distorted samples from the Rolling Stones ("Satisfaction") and The Beatles ("All You Need is Love"), which ultimately blend in a march rhythm, in some piano and horn tunes, and in a Zappaesque montage of sounds. Krautrock historian Julian Cope wrote that the band used western music as "a mythical and ancient currency to be plundered."[21] Among Krautrock heads, it is an accepted credo that this sound is a synesthetic experience that takes the listener "into the most inventive editing territory Rock'n'Roll has seen."[22] Thus, Faust tried to establish an entirely new German cosmology for popular music and bands.[23]

Underscoring the role of Uwe Nettelbeck as the producer and artistic director of Faust does not mean to undermine the artistic importance of Faust's musicians or of their sound engineer Kurt Graupner. But as much as the musicians and Graupner may have had autonomous creativity as their goal, there are no doubts that Nettelbeck engaged conceptually in the band's output. As drummer Arnulf Meifert pointed out, when comparing Nettelbeck to The Beatles' George Martin, "Uwe Nettelbeck wanted us—and we wanted that too—to hand in a concept album that would be comparable to 'Sgt. Pepper,' that had adventurous sonic invention and radicalness."[24] References of this kind and the fact that Uwe Nettelbeck presented himself as a music producer who positioned himself within a specific tradition, emphatically acknowledging it—"I like the Beach Boys"![25]—were not in themselves a reason for criticism in the community of Progressive Rock. Comparisons with other mavericks of music production can be read as evidence of the authentication of his production skills; Nettelbeck was said to be the "Teutonic Tony Wilson or Malcolm McLaren."[26]

I will not try here to determine whether or not this comparison is a valid one. Instead, I will focus on performance practices in the studio and examine how this environment prepared the ground for new artistic self-perceptions and new artistic practices. With the development of multitrack recording and the establishment of music studios, the producer had acquired an entirely new role. Former divisions between technicians and artists were turned upside down.[27] The producer claimed rights as an artist (and the other way around). The production phase, with the selection of pre-existing, pre-recorded materials, the assembling and the mastering, gained an unprecedented weight. With multi-track recording, separately recorded

---

21   Julian Cope, *Krautrocksampler*, p. 42.

22   Ibid., pp. 22–23.

23   Arne Koch and Sel Harris, "The Sound of Yourself Listening: Faust and the Politics of the Unpolitical," *Popular Music and Society* 32/5 (2009): pp. 579–594.

24   Martin Büsser, "'Internationalität als Generallinie'. Im Gespräch mit Arnulf Meifert (Ex Faust)," in Martin Büsser, *Antipop* (Mainz: Ventil Verlag, 2002), pp. 75–103, here p. 85.

25   Ulrich Adelt, *Krautrock. German Music in the Seventies* (Ann Arbor: University of Michigan, 2016), p. 63.

26   Andy Wilson, *Faust*, p. 20.

27   Edward Kealy, "From Craft to Art: The Case of Sound Mixers and Popular Music," in *On Record: Rock, Pop and the Written Word*, ed. Simon Frith and Andrew Goodwin (London: Routledge, 1990), pp. 207–220.

takes were modified and then blended together in a single track at the end. It was there that the final outcome was shaped. For the working process of the producer, this meant that reception and production coincided as forms of creative consumption: "choosing rather than making has come to mediate the creation of music [...]: choose and judge by *listening, as consumers*"[28] as the musician Chris Cutler, who worked with Faust, put it.

What is decisive is that, from the point of view of the practices under those technical conditions, artistic creation was no longer bound to creation *ex nihilo*, but understood as a combination of choice, arrangement, and mastering of material. When speaking of the Beatles' 1966 album *Revolver*, Uwe Nettelbeck describes the emergence of these appropriation practices that treat pre-existing materials as a resource, regardless of an original authorship or any claim of originality:

> The Beatles steal more eagerly and skillfully than ever before, not in order to add cultural value to their pieces, but simply because they steal everything and make a montage of it in their pieces [...] also foreign musical elements, even when they have a venerable tradition. They go for it insofar as those elements are not deemed private property that nobody should put their hands on but are simply seen as material that is lying there, around them, and that anybody could use as they pleased.[29]

Uwe Nettelbeck too, as the producer of Faust, seems to rely on this practice, at least if we take his word for it when he declares that "we try to make an amalgam from all the material which comes to us to form something which goes beyond quotations."[30]

The moment sounds could be recorded and mastered, a new mode of production of music was born. "Rock music," writes musician and anthropologist H. Stith Bennett, "takes its shape as a finished product because of controls over sound that take effect *after* performers have relinquished their control over what and how they play."[31] The ability of people other than the original creators to manipulate sounds is one of the crucial aspects of electronically produced music.[32] Stories of producers who are "notorious for making musicians' performances unrecognizable to their originators" are well known—just as

---

[28] Chris Cutler (who worked with Uwe Nettelbeck) in Steven Jones, *Rock Formation. Music, Technology, and Mass Communication* (Newbury Park CA: Sage, 1992), p. 193.

[29] "Die Beatles klauen eifriger und geschickter als früher, aber nicht, um ihren Titeln etwas Kultur beizumengen, sondern nur, weil sie alles klauen und in ihre Titel montieren, ... auch fremde musikalische Elemente, selbst wenn die eine ehrwürdige Tradition haben. Sie machen sich über sie her, weil diese Elemente für sie keine Besitztitel sind, an denen man sich nicht zu vergreifen hat, sondern einfach Materialien, die vorliegen und an denen jedermann auf seine Weise sein Vergnügen haben kann." Uwe Nettelbeck, "Die neue Schallplatte," *Die Zeit*, 23 September 1966, p. 21.

[30] Carl Dallas, "Faust and Foremost. Interview with Uwe Nettelbeck," *Melody Maker*, 2 June 1973, p. 36.

[31] H. Stith Bennett, *On Becoming a Rock Musician* (Amherst MA: University of Massachusetts Press, 1980), p. 117.

[32] Ibid., p. 125.

those of editors of written texts "mangling the literary constructions of authors."[33] The fundamental difference between musical and literary production consists in the fact that in the former, none of those involved would question the artistic sovereignty of those manipulating the materials of others. The producer may be a poorly skilled person, but he is nevertheless acknowledged as occupying a legitimate place in the artistic process. These observations on the practices of electronic music production have hopefully indicated how the analysis of Nettelbeck's literary production from the standpoint of extra-literary elements can be insightful.

The rare poetological statements by Nettelbeck carry the echo of his musical critics from the end of the 1960s, when he was putting much emphasis on montage techniques like those of the Beatles, and on working with existing materials. In a radio interview from 1972, dedicated to an upcoming book eventually published as *Mainz wie es singt und lacht*, he said: "I didn't want to write, but I wanted to collect everything [...], all the junk that makes its way to me, you see?"[34] What is clearly stated here is a crossover in the practices of musical production and the production of literature. It all culminates in "choosing"[35] the material, as Nettelbeck said in an interview about his literary debut, explaining the challenge of being a writer.

Instead of criticizing the lack of his *own essays* or the imitative technique, as the reviewers did for Nettelbeck's literary work, I shall speak of writing under the condition of a *recording consciousness*. This condition is characterized by "an intimate relationship between [...] the studio environment and the mental creation,"[36] and can suggest describing Nettelbeck's writing as "making tracks," or literature in studio style.[37] Originality has to be understood not as writing original texts in the sense of a creation *ex nihilo*, but as versioning and mastering material by others. To understand Nettelbeck's production values, it is worth looking at the fine print in his book and in his magazine. Here it becomes

---

[33] Ibid., p. 126.

[34] Uwe Nettelbeck in the radio show "Ein Hörspiel und sein Autor" ["A radio play and its author"], directed by Peter Michel Ladiges, Südwestrundfunk, 2 May 1971. It is worth noticing from that standpoint that Nettelbeck describes his literary practices of textual modifications in musical terms as "modulation"; compare "Notizen," *Die Republik*, ed. Petra and Uwe Nettelbeck, nos. 98–108, 12 December 1999, pp. 1–64, here p. 13. Compare to the cited poetological statement Nettelbeck's remarks on Frank Zappa's contribution to The Mothers of Invention's album *Absolutely Free* (1967): "Zappa's collages out of [...] voices, distorted voices [...], in which he [...] mixes everything at once, and that he then recombines in larger units where one finds the musical trash from the last couple of decades of American music [...], this overshadows everything else I've heard so far about collages." Uwe Nettelbeck, "Beat," *konkret* 11, 1967, pp. 46–47, here p. 47.

[35] Uwe Nettelbeck in the radio show "Ein Hörspiel und sein Autor," directed by Peter Michel Ladiges, Südwestrundfunk, 2 May 1971.

[36] H. Stith Bennett, *On Becoming a Rock Musician*, p. 128.

[37] Friedrich Kittler sees an interrelation of styles of writing and media technology. See Friedrich Kittler, "Im Telegrammstil," in *Stil. Geschichten und Funktionen eines kulturwissenschaftlichen Diskurselements*, ed. Hans Ulrich Gumbrecht and K. Ludwig Pfeiffer (Frankfurt am Main: Suhrkamp, 1986), pp. 358–370, here p. 358.

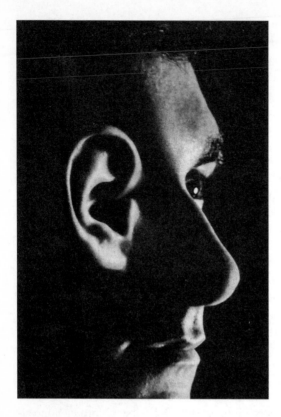

Fig. 9: Marshall McLuhan and Quentin Fiore, *The Medium is the Massage. An Inventory of Effects*, co-ordinated by Jerome Agel (London: Allan Lane and Penguin, 1967), p. 121.

apparent that creation is carried out by intervening in the material, through arrangement and high-end copy-editing: "Foreign texts are not necessarily italicized, but italicized texts are always foreign; typos are left uncorrected where they do facilitate comprehension. In case of doubt it has to be assumed that *Die Republik* is more carefully edited than the texts it uses."[38]

Looking at the aesthetic of production of electronic music from the specific standpoint of music producers, a new concept of authorship emerges, one which does not imply so much the refusal of authorship, in Roland Barthes's sense, as rather a kind of "profane creativity"[39] that draws on recorded resources, and that replaces the inventions of a transcendental genius. What kind of practice writing is, as I hope to have clarified, always

---

[38] "Fremde Texte sind nicht ausnahmslos kursiv gesetzt, kursiv gesetzte aber ausnahmslos fremde; Schreib- und Druckfehler in diesen wo sie dem Verständnis dienen unberichtigt geblieben. In Zweifelsfällen ist anzunehmen, daß Die Republik sorgfältiger redigiert ist, als es die Texte sind, derer sie sich unter beliebiger Wahrung der vorgefundenen Flüchtigkeiten bedient."

[39] Paul Willis, *Profane Culture* (London: Routledge & Kegan Paul, 1978).

depends on "who[m] we are describing and when."[40] In a community that is "literally wired for sound,"[41] one has to take into account the subliminal transformations in the practices of production.

Sensing Literature

It was not just an empty pun when, earlier in the text, I declared it was my intention to *listen to*—rather than look at—what was happening in those days when media theorist Marshall McLuhan wrote: "The Age of Writing has passed. We must invent a NEW METAPHOR, restructure our thoughts and feelings."[42] In order to grasp the literary phenomenon in question in all its sensory dimensions, I shall take Marshall McLuhan at his words and try to restructure my faculties of perception by tuning myself into a historical situation. If what Susan Sontag observed in the Sixties is true, namely that the impact of electronic media across all genres of art leads to an entirely different form of experience, which she summarized as "adventures in sensation,"[43] then I, too, have to pay attention to new kinds of sensual experience. I have proposed listening as a way to explore the affective and tactile encounters with Nettelbeck's literary work. I will try to grasp the perception of Nettelbeck's book *Mainz wie es singt und lacht* by paying attention to the vibrations of the reader's metaphoric description triggered by that encounter.

The predominance of music in specific communities has changed not just the practices of production, but the practices of consumption, too. When literature was produced in *studio style*, the experience of it was compared with music. Jürgen Frey wrote in the music magazine *Sounds*: "Sometimes I still feel *thrills* and *kicks*, when I stumble upon a certain book. I think it must be a similar feeling to what Jörg has when he discovers a totally *awesome* new LP. Last month it has happened four times with new books. [...] Uwe Nettelbeck's hodgepodge of texts [is] the big negative kick of the month."[44]

Even Nettelbeck's harshest critics, who wind up with emotional virulence against his polemical statements, acknowledge a reading experience that appears to interrupt the linear perceptual habits of the Gutenberg Galaxy, and that resembles Marshall McLuhan's characterization of the "acoustic space" introduced by electronic media.[45] Michael Zeller, in the newspaper *Frankfurter Allgemeine Zeitung*, saw himself enveloped by an out of

---

[40] Nick Couldry, "Theorising Media as Practice," in *Social Semiotics* 14/2 (2004): pp. 115–132, here p. 125.

[41] H. Stith Bennett, *On Becoming a Rock Musician*, p. 114.

[42] Marshall McLuhan, *Counterblast*, p. 14.

[43] Susan Sontag, "the basic unit of contemporary art is not the idea, but the analysis of and extension of sensations," in *McLuhan: Hot & Cool. A Primer for the Understanding of & a Critical Symposium with a Rebuttal by McLuhan*, ed. Gerald E. Stern (New York: The New American Library, 1967), pp. 249–258, here p. 259.

[44] Jürgen Frey, "Wer spinnt hier eigentlich?," *Sounds* 5 (1976): p. 40.

[45] Marshall McLuhan and Quentin Fiore, *The Medium is the Massage. An Inventory of Effects*, co-ordinated by Jerome Agel (London: Allan Lane and Penguin, 1967), p. 111.

the ordinary medial environment: "from the outside package, a delightful rarity [...]: the light font in a calming grey makes one eager to read; one doesn't feel the pressure to go on reading because the page numbers are missing."[46]

A text by Carl Weissner in the distributor's catalogue *Merkheft* was very different in the evaluation of Nettelbeck's polemical attacks against the establishment. That his text is likely meant to be a recommendation should not mislead us as to his peculiar practice of reading and writing. Weissner, as German translator of cut-up literature by William S. Burroughs, is literally informed by the reading of experimental texts. His review begins with the disclaimer that instead of writing about his current favorite LP he will write about his current favorite book. But while other reviews follow the schematic structure of a literary review-author's biography, with comparisons to other writers and aesthetic judgements, Weissner's approach is completely different. His text is not written in a continuous style but divided into paragraphs by blank lines. First, his review is structured as if he were reading the selected chapters of the book always anew, the way one would move a needle on a record to listen again to certain tracks. Second, his text is reminiscent of a sympathetic report rather than of a detached review. His metaphorical depiction describes tactile encounters with the book. One chapter is experienced as a "heavy hammer" (the montage of letters of the editors who refused to publish the book), another as a "resting period" (a montage of newspaper articles about balloon flights). On the whole, he seems to positively enjoy the sentiment of the book against the establishment and its hypocrisy: "It's sickening."[47]

Another reviewer in the magazine *Der Spiegel*, Hellmuth Karasek, is perplexed by the breach of etiquette of Nettelbeck's move to publish what is habitually concealed (the letters of the editors). He experiences it as "distortions" triggered by the montage. Moreover, Karasek expresses his fear of being potentially a victim of Nettelbeck's critique as a member of the cultural establishment writing in a mainstream magazine, declaring: "like [Karl] Kraus, Nettelbeck knows how to use quotations against their original creators."[48]

The different perceptions of *Mainz wie es singt und lacht* prove that one cannot speak of a transcendental essence of literature. What is thought of as being literature and how it is evaluated is a result of practices of interpretation carried out in "interpretative communities"[49] each with their own rules. These practices of interpretation are based on an incorporated know-how shared by a certain community.

In Weissner's review it becomes apparent how the practices of reading and writing are in fact informed by shared experiences and tuned senses that are part of a certain "aesthetic

---

46 Michael Zeller, "Das Weltgewissen von Luhmühlen," *Frankfurter Allgemeine Zeitung*, November 16, 1976, p. 2.

47 Carl Weissner, in *Das Merkheft* 21 (1976), np.

48 Hellmuth Karasek, "Eine Scherbenwelt aus Zitaten," *Der Spiegel*, 19 April 1976, pp. 172–174, here p. 172.

49 Stanley Fish, *Is there a Text in this Class? The Authority of Interpretive Communities* (Cambridge MA and London: Harvard University Press, 1980).

formation."[50] In emphatically embracing Nettelbeck's book and without questioning his literary practice it also becomes apparent that Weissner belongs to a different "literary community"[51] with a distinct self-understanding.

Especially in the contradictory affective perceptions of the readers it becomes clear that the crucial skill of the writer-turned-producer is to mediate ideas, that is to say, to manage how one object's or person's "vibrations can influence those of others."[52] These artists should be seen against this backdrop as "intermediaries" between production and consumption, who "produce the worlds that they want to make work for them."[53]

Literary Appropriation

The reframing of the literary practice of Uwe Nettelbeck in terms of a *recording consciousness* helps to adequately grasp his practices of production. It shows that under these conditions an artistic self-understanding occurs, which explicitly draws on resources created by others instead of pretending to create out of nothing in a godlike manner. This applies to conceptual work as well. It is well known that producers such as Brian Wilson (Beach Boys) and George Martin (The Beatles) entered a head-to-head competition for the most virtuoso studio production, and it is no secret that Wilson's production of *Pet Sounds* (1966) was remarkably influential for *Sgt. Pepper's Lonely Hearts Club Band* produced by Martin (1967). The point here is not only the appropriation of pre-existing material, but the skillful appropriation of a certain style, too. This is generally true, and more strongly so in the practice of covering: the key to understanding twentieth century rock music culture.[54]

The practice of covering a performance or appropriating pre-existing materials is not concerned with the notion of authenticity based on the Romantic concept of genuine creation. Appropriation in this sense means to validate one's own authenticity through embedding oneself in a tradition. In Blues music, for example, appropriation of a style

---

50 Birgit Meyer, "Introduction. From Imagined Communities to Aesthetic Formations: Religious Mediations, Sensational Forms, and Styles of Bindung," in *Aesthetic Formation. Media, Religion, and the Senses*, ed. Birgit Meyer (New York: Palgrave Macmillan, 2009), pp. 1–28.

51 Subsequently to Stanley Fish's notion of the "interpretative community," Philipp Löffler develops the concept of the literary community in "Was ist eine literarische Epoche? Literaturgeschichte, literarischer Wandel und der Praxisbegriff in den Geistes- und Sozialwissenschaften," in Friederike Elias et al., *Praxeologie. Beiträge zur interdisziplinären Reichweite praxistheoretischer Ansätze in den Geistes- und Sozialwissenschaften* (Berlin and Boston MA: de Gruyter, 2015), pp. 73–96, here p. 87.

52 Antoine Hennion, "An Intermediary Between Production and Consumption: The Producer of Popular Music," in *Science, Technology & Human Values* 14/4 (1989): pp. 400–424, here p. 402.

53 Ibid., p. 402.

54 Deena Weinstein, "The History of Rock's Past through Rock Covers," in *Mapping the Beat: Popular Music and Contemporary Theory*, ed. Thom Swiss, John Sloop and Andrew Herman (Malden MA: Blackwell, 1998), pp. 137–151.

served as a means to acquire a supposedly authentic mode of expression from Black musicians. Authenticity, from this standpoint, is "a matter of interpretation"[55] carried out and fought for from within a community. It is hence important to ask "who," rather than "what," is being authenticated.[56]

In the 1960s and 1970s, one can find racist constructions of ethnic authenticity in transnational countercultures leading to expressions of "Afroamericanophilia."[57] Here, White and wealthy groups for the most part identified themselves not just with African American music, but with the civil rights movement in the US in general. At the same time, a similar form of self-stigmatization took place through the identification with postcolonial liberation battles in the *Third World*. The constructed authenticity of an oppressed minority had been appropriated as counter-project to the dominant social order.

The appropriation of Blues can be observed among the radical wing of the extra-parliamentary opposition in the Federal Republic of Germany gathered in the Bewegung 2. Juni (2 June Movement). The constructed authenticity of Blues, rooted in the struggle against White supremacy, became in Europe a stylistic device to prove one's authenticity against the authorities. A leaflet by Bewegung 2. Juni declares:

> Blues was first the songs of Black slaves in America, later a musical form that could be played almost only by Black people: they felt that the roots of Blues, acquired so to say with the mother's milk, had to do with the reality of living a shitty life. Living in chains, running from guards, getting locked up and then—then maybe cleaning up supermarkets or avenging a dead brother: 'Watch out, Mr. Jones, we are alive' […] Maybe it's good, to find first your own Blues […] Let's not bury our Blues under the constant smirks of a Mister Jones or a Mister Schmidt. The Blues goes on—our war against the establishment will be different from their wars.[58]

---

[55] Allan Moore, "Authenticity as authentication," in *Popular Music* 21.2 (2002): pp. 209–223, here p. 210.

[56] Ibid., p. 220.

[57] See Moritz Ege, "Becoming-Black. Patterns and Politics of West-German 'Afroamericanophilia' in the 1960s and 1970s," July 2015, *PORTAL. Journal of Multidisciplinary International Studies* 12/2, https://epress.lib.uts.edu.au/journals/index.php/portal/article/view/4395/5000 (accessed 10 April, 2019).

[58] "Der Blues—das war zuerst der Gesang amerikanischer Negersklaven, später eine Musikrichtung, die fast nur von schwarzen ausgeübt werden konnte: Denn sie hatten das feeling, das die Grundlage des Blues bildete, ja praktische mit der Muttermilch reingekriegt: Zu leben auch in der größten Scheiße. Zu leben mit Ketten; vor den Gewehrläufen, hinter Knastgittern und hin und wieder Supermarkt ausräumen oder einen der ermordeten Brüder rächen: ,Sieh dich vor, Mr. Jones, wir leben!' […] Vielleicht ist es gut, zuerstmal seinen eigenen Blues zu finden… Begraben wir nicht unseren Blues unter dem Dauergrinsen von Mister Jones und Mister Schmidt. Der Blues geht weiter—unser Krieg gegen die Alten wird anders sein als ihre Kriege je waren." Anonymous author, "Was ist der Blues heute?," in *Der Blues: Gesammelte Texte der Bewegung 2. Juni* (Berlin: anonymous publisher, c. 1980), p. 137.

Although far from its original context in the racial conflicts of American culture, the appropriation of African American culture and music reflects an effort to "actualize the 'minority' experience of bodies, community and rebellion."[59] The appropriation of a perspective from within a situation of oppression can be understood as a "technique of the self"[60] that shaped the self-perception of counterculture groups in the German Federal Republic.

Hopefully, this digression will unravel the confusion created by Uwe Nettelbeck's magazine *Die Republik*. The widespread criticism against Uwe Nettelbeck as a slavish imitator of Karl Kraus appears trapped in a paradigm of originality as genuine creation that is unable to account for the ways a tradition is appropriated. It is a truism that Nettelbeck's *Die Republik* resembles Kraus's *Die Fackel* "in outlook and concept,"[61] as a critic wrote. But in the context of the practice of appropriation it seems that through appropriating Karl Kraus's literary performance as a formidable critic and sovereign editor of his own magazine, Nettelbeck tried to acquire a mode of expression that would serve as a means to authenticate his own practice. This phenomenon is describable as "third person authenticity," and it arises when a performer conveys the impression of "accurately representing the ideas of another, embedded in a tradition of performance."[62] One could hence say that Nettelbeck found his Blues in Karl Kraus's war against the Viennese cultural establishment of the early twentieth century—the touchstone of skillful appropriation being the execution of literary techniques hinging on "mastering the material."[63]

That Nettelbeck managed to convey the impression of representing Kraus's sovereign attitude towards the establishment and executed the device of mere transcribing and quoting, is attested by his readers. Even though Kraus's way of exposing others through mere quotation requires hard practice and "must be learned only slowly,"[64] as some readers conceded, Nettelbeck successfully appropriated the performance of Karl Kraus—as expressed not only in Hellmuth Karasek's fear of getting exposed by him.

---

59   Moritz Ege, "Das 'spezifisch Negroide' und seine weißen Freunde: Anmerkungen zur Soul-Rezeption in der Bundesrepublik," in *Kuckuck: Notizen zur Alltagskultur*, 2 (2006): pp. 58–64, here p. 62.

60   Michel Foucault, *The Use of Pleasure: The History of Sexuality* vol. 2 [1984], trans. Robert Hurley (New York: Vintage Books, 1990), pp. 10–11.

61   Wilhelm Bittorf, "Karl Kraus, klein geschrieben," *Der Spiegel*, 11 October 1976, pp. 226–228, here p. 228.

62   Allan Moore, "Authenticity as Authentication," in *Popular Music* 21/2 (2002): pp. 209–223, here p. 218 [emphasis in the original].

63   "Materialbeherrschung" [Mastering of material] so comments Juliane Vogel with regard to the editing practice of Karl Kraus: "The mastering of text of Die Fackel can be described first of all as mastering of the material… Only in the subordination of the material to the imperatives of Die Fackel, with its cuts, abbreviations, interruptions, the authority of the journal…is established." Juliane Vogel, "Materialbeherrschung und Sperrgewalt. Der Herausgeber Karl Kraus," in *Die Souveränität der Literatur. Zum Totalitären der Klassischen Moderne 1900–1933*, ed. Uwe Hebekus and Ingo Stöckmann (Munich: Fink, 2008), pp. 459–471, here p. 469.

64   Jörg Schröder, "The Making of Pornography (4)," 2 August 2006, http://blogs.taz.de/blog/2006/08/02/the-making-of-pornography-4/ (accessed 10 April, 2019).

Fig. 10 and 11: Covers from *Die Republik* and *Die Fackel*

In proposing a reading that emphasizes the overlap of music and literary production in terms of appropriation, I am not claiming, as mentioned, to belatedly justify the literary project of Uwe Nettelbeck. Like the readings by others, mine is also based on conclusions drawn from within a specific "interpretative community." My observations and theoretical conclusions are the outcome of reading sessions together with peers who are as experienced in making and listening to popular music as in theorizing about this very practice.[65] Nevertheless, the appreciation of appropriation as a legitimate practice paved the way past the Romantic conceptions of genuine creation towards a "NEW METAPHOR," as McLuhan called for. I would suggest speaking of *Die Republik* as—literally—a literary cover of *Die Fackel*.

Translation: Elena Fabietti

---

[65] Without the responses of Erhard Schüttpelz, musician (Kosmonautentraum) and media scholar (University of Siegen), I would have come to a different and less musical interpretation.

Anna Echterhölter

(Dis-)manufacturing Bonds. Rural Measuring Practices as Media of Exchange

"To all astronomers, surveyors, measurers of tapestry, barrels and other things, to all mintmasters and merchants good luck!"[1] This optimistic dedication addresses special-ists working with their hands. Nevertheless, the pamphlet quoted here uses theoreti-cally advanced decimal fractions for the first time in print. As Edgar Zilsel—an Austrian scientist forced into migration—emphasized: There is a co-development of science and craftsmanship. But the knowledge of compass-makers, miners, navigators, and military engineers did not easily trespass the social barrier. The practical arts were considered lowly occupations—much to the impediment of the natural sciences. And this decisive relation between the social fabric and its units of measure will be investigated here. Zilsel's example points to the fact that advances in quantification can easily remain unnoticed. They occur throughout the separate realms of administration, economics, and science, where everything is transcribed into numbers, abbreviations and units.

This paper discusses unit formation in a rural setting. Unit formation is a particularly good test case for a historical media praxeology, since virtually no discourse exists around this basic cultural technique. One has to resort to the practices, routines, and even rituals surrounding quantification to gauge its political potential.

The case studies are taken from two authors who engaged intensely with the uniting and dividing forces of weights and measures. After a methodological clarification, I will present the classical account of agrarian metrology. It was published in 1970 by Witold Kula, an internationally renowned economic historian from Poland. Then I turn to a far less known list of weighting practices, compiled and commented on by Jacob Grimm. In sum, the material arranged by the older of the two brothers amounts to a critical theory of the metric system.

Both accounts of rural quantification are unique treatments in that they include social practices in their analysis of measurement. Metrology—the science of weights and mea-

---

[1]   Edgar Zilsel, "The Sociological Roots of Science," in *The American Journal of Sociology* 47/4 (1942): pp. 544–562, here p. 547, quoting a pamphlet by the pioneer of mathematics and mechanics Simon Stevin (Leyden, 1585). Edgar Zilsel wrote his classic article with a Rockefeller Foundation grant from the *Committee in Aid of Displaced Foreign Scholars*.

sures —reveals its capacity as a guide through uncharted regions of the history of the monetary sphere and shows its potential to assemble non-modern narrations of quantification.

Units and Method

In light of the current concern around the politics of data, the history of quantification is an important branch at the crossroads of historical epistemology and media historiography. It focusses on practices of mediation which form the backbone of bureaucracy, economy, and science alike.[2] My particular angle is informed by the auxiliary sciences, because of their proficiency in the materiality of governance. Genealogies, sigils, and coins, for example, are in their respective way objects of statehood. While excellent research has been dedicated to the social medium of money, the economic and social relevance of measures and units remains underexplored. Only a few specialists wrote about metrology.[3] Karl Polanyi sees metrology as a communication system in its own right alongside money and language. Most certainly weights and measures help to build the *monetary sphere*.[4] Gabriel Tarde even sees an inter-spiritual bond in measures, uniting the nation.[5] This testifies to a spatial dimension, and indeed metrology is at times subsumed to the ensemble of infrastructure.[6] This opens perspectives, even if units of measurement are not simply "matter that enables the movement of other matter," as Brian Larkin described infrastructure.[7] But they certainly shape goods in a way that facilitates logistics and circulation. Infrastructures build public space and structural encounters. It is vital to remember that Susan Leigh Star called for an "ethnography of infrastructure"[8] to capture the influence exerted by units of

---

[2] Theodore M. Porter, "The Promotion of Mining and the Advancement of Science. The Chemical Revolution of Mineralogy," in *Annals of Science* 38/5 (1981): pp. 543–570; Elena Aronova, Christine von Oertzen, and David Sepkoski, eds., "Data Histories," *Osiris* 32 (2017).

[3] Metrology refers to present scientific advances. It has and used to have an institutional side which is often referred to as legal metrology. Especially in German speaking countries *Historical Metrology* emerges as a distinct sub-discipline of the auxiliary sciences (such as numismatics, diplomatics, heraldry, papyrology, sigilography etc.) in the mid-eighteenth century.

[4] Karl Polanyi, "Money Objects and Money Uses," in *The Livelihood of Man*, ed. Karl Polanyi (New York: Academic Press, 1977), pp. 97–121; Karl Polanyi, "Über den Stellenwert wirtschaftlicher Institutionen in der Antike am Beispiel Athen, Mykene und Alalakh," in Ökonomie und Gesellschaft, trans. Heinrich Jelinek (Frankfurt am Main: Suhrkamp Taschenbuch,1979), pp. 387–413, here p. 392.

[5] Gabriel Tarde, *Psychologie économique*. 2 vols. (Paris: F. Alcan, 1902), vol 1, p. 221.

[6] Gabriele Schabacher, "Medium Infrastruktur. Trajektorien soziotechnischer Netzwerke in der ANT," in *Zeitschrift für Medien- und Kulturforschung* 2 (2013): pp. 129–148; Bruno Latour, *Science in Action. How to Follow Scientists and Engineers through Society* (Cambridge MA: Harvard University Press, 1987), p. 251.

[7] Brian Larkin, "The Politics and Poetics of Infrastructure," in *Annual Review of Anthropology* (2013): pp. 327–343, here p. 329.

[8] Susan Leigh Star, *Grenzobjekte und Medienforschung*, ed. Sebastian Gießmann and Nadine Taha (Bielefeld: transcript, 2016); Susan Leigh Star, "The Ethnography of Infrastructure," in *American Behavioral Scientist* 43 (1999): pp. 377–391.

measurement. Most prominently, units appear to be neutral. This unquestionable status is probably one of the most artful economic materials. Albeit the vast efforts necessary to arrive at global standards and albeit the tremendous costs of gauging, the mediating influence of standards and units almost invisible—from foodstuffs to weapons, from the glass eye industry to the digital representation of different alphabets and scripts.

Simon Schaffer has recently shown that this particular medium of exchange could gain from a historical perspective, since it is vital to decode its apparent neutrality. What he suggests is the analysis of "cérémonies de la mesure"—of practices in their historical context and perceived capacity to establish equivalence.[9] Since the formation of units through measurement involves symbolic labor and transcribes matter, it is possible to address measurements as cultural techniques of numeracy.[10] Other cues are taken from research in media praxeology[11] and economic practices,[12] as well as the history of standardization.[13] All perspectives

---

[9]   Simon Schaffer, "Les cérémonies de la mesure. Repenser l'histoire mondiale des sciences," in *Annales. Histoire, Sciences Sociales* 2/70 (2015): pp. 409–435.

[10] Helen Verran, "Number as Inventive Frontier in Knowing and Working Australia's Water Resources," in *Anthropological Theory* 10 (2010): pp. 171–178; Harun Maye, "Was ist eine Kulturtechnik?," in *Zeitschrift für Medien- und Kulturforschung* 1.1 (2010): pp. 121–135; Moritz Wedell, "Vom Kerbholz zum Kalkül. Wortgeschichtliche Annäherung an die Kulturtechnik Zahl," in *Grenzfälle. Transformationen von Bild, Schrift und Zahl*, ed. Moritz Wedell and Pablo Schneider (Weimar: Verlag und Datenbank für Geisteswissenschaft, 2004), pp. 65–100.

[11] Andreas Wolfsteiner and Markus Rautzenberg, "Trial-and-Error-Szenarien. Zum Umgang mit Zukünften," in *Trial and Error. Szenarien medialen Handelns*, ed. Andreas Wolfsteiner and Markus Rautzenberg (Munich: Fink, 2014), pp. 7–33.

[12] Monika Dommann, Christof Dejung and Daniel Speich, "Wissen und Wirtschaften," in *Werkstatt-Geschichte* 58 (2012): pp. 3–7; Laurence Fontaine, "Bemerkungen zum Kaufen als sozialer Praxis. Feilschen, Preise festlegen und Güter ersteigern im frühneuzeitlichen Europa," in *Historische Anthropologie* 14/3 (2006): pp. 334–348; Anna Echterhölter, "Ökonomische Praktiken," in *ilinx* 3 (2013): pp. 7–20; Aashish Velkar, *Markets and Measurements in Nineteenth-Century Britain* (Cambridge: Cambridge University Press, 2012).

[13] Ken Alder, "Making Things the Same. Representation, Tolerance and the End of the Ancien Régime in France," in *Social Studies of Science* 28/4 (1998): pp. 499–545; Tore Frangsmyr, John Lewis Heilbron and Robin E. Rider, eds., *The Quantifying Spirit in the Eighteenth Century* (Berkeley: University of California Press, 1990); Oliver Schlaudt, *Messung als konkrete Handlung. Eine kritische Untersuchung über die Grundlagen der Bildung quantitativer Begriffe in den Naturwissenschaften* (Heidelberg: Königshausen & Neumann, 2009); Heinz Otto Sibum, "Les gestes de la mesure. Joule, les pratiques de la brasserie et la science, in *Annales. Histoire, Sciences Sociales* 4-5 (1998): pp. 745–774; Simon Schaffer, "Metrology, Metrication, and Victorian Values," in *Victorian Science in Context,* ed. Bernard Lightman (Chicago: University of Chicago Press, 1997); Theodore M. Porter, "The Culture of Quantification and the History of Public Reason," in *Journal of the History of Economic Thought* 26/2 (2004): p. 165; Laurence Moulinier et al., eds., *La juste mesure. Quantifier, évaluer, mesurer entre Orient et Occident (VIIIe–XVIIIe siècles)* (Saint-Denis: Presses Universitaires de Vincennes, 2005); Hector Vera, "Economic Rationalization, Money and Measures: A Weberian Perspective," in *Max Weber Matters: Interweaving Past and Present*, ed. David Chalcraft et al. (London: Ashgate, 2008), pp. 135–147. On quantification and money see also Jane I. Guyer,

highlight the necessity to arrive at an archive of movements and capacities, as projected by André-Georges Haudricourt.[14]

Working Units

Pre-metric measures are "expressive of man and his work" according to Witold Kula.[15] A block of salt hewn in the Wieliczka mines near Krakow is a standard unit formed by three forces: It is as large as possible, to keep it stable and most of it shielded from dirt during shipping. But it is not too large, to keep it transportable, and finally it is shaped by customs regulations.[16] Historians of weights and measures agree that all over the world pre-metric units were limited by performance.[17] For craftsmen—those working with their hands—it was evident what a *charretée* would signify: The unit from medieval France stood for the load that two oxen could pull.[18] Afghanistan even kept the *donkey load* when it introduced the metric system in 1926.[19] In Arab countries, the *harwar* differed according to the strength of the carrying animal, be it camel, mule, or horse.[20] Richard K. Pankhurst adds a distinction common to Ethiopian measurement systems, which is "expressed in the

Marginal gains. Monetary Transactions in Atlantic Africa (Chicago: University of Chicago Press, 2004); Frank Engster, *Das Geld als Maß, Mittel und Methode. Das Rechnen mit der Identität der Zeit* (Berlin: Neofelis, 2014).

[14] André-Georges Haudricourt, "Technologie als Humanwissenschaft," in *Zeitschrift für Medien und Kulturforschung* 1 (2010): pp. 79–87. "...die Menge der traditionellen und technisch wirksamen muskulären Bewegungen," p. 79; "Nun haben wir aber noch keine Notation die sich durchgesetzt hätte, um die Bewegungen zu notieren, die der Mensch bei seiner technischen Aktivität ausführt," p. 80.

[15] Witold Kula, *Measures and Men*, trans. Richard Szreter (Princeton: Princeton University Press, 1986), p. 123. Originally published as *Miary i ludzie* (Warsaw, 1970); Witold Kula, "Historical Metrology," in *The Problems and Methods of Economic History* (1963), trans. Simon and Richard Szreter (Aldershot: Ashgate, 2001), pp. 338–364; Bernard Garnier and Krzystof Pomian, eds., "Les Mesures et l'Histoire. Table ronde Witold Kula 1984," in *Cahiers de Métrologie* (1984): pp. 37–53; Douglass North, "Kula, Witold: Measures and Men. Review," in *The Journal of Economic History* 47/2 (1987): pp. 593–595; Jean-Michel Servet, "Note de lecture," in *Revue économique* 1 (1989): pp. 111–118.

[16] Kula, *Measures and Men*, p. 7.

[17] Stephen Gudeman, *Economics as Culture; Models and Metaphors of Livelihood* (London: Routledge & Kegan Paul, 1986); Harald Witthöft, *Umrisse einer historischen Metrologie zum Nutzen der wirtschafts- und sozialgeschichtlichen Forschung: Mass u. Gewicht in Stadt u. Land Lüneburg, im Hanseraum u. im Kurfürstentum/Königreich Hannover vom 13. bis zum 19. Jh.*, 2 (Göttingen: Vandenhoeck und Ruprecht, 1979).

[18] Jean-Claude Hocquet, Bernhard Garnier and Denis Woronoff, eds., "Introduction à la Metrologie Historique," in *Metrologie Historique* (Paris: Economica, 1989), p. 90.

[19] BArch R 1519/549 (Bundesarchiv Berlin/Physikalisch-Technische Reichsanstalt/Ausland), Abschrift II 12909, VM 2934, Blatt pp. 2–5. (1923 to other sources)

[20] Walther Hinz, *Islamische Maße und Gewichte. Umgerechnet ins Metrische System* (Leiden: E.J. Brill, 1955), p. 9.

Amharic term [...] *cĕnāt*, i.e. the amount carried by a beast of burden, and the [...] *sĕkem*, the amount carried on human shoulders."[21]

What these pre-metric measures have in common is that the units are almost indexical traces of working conditions. Rural measurements are silent brokers mediating between animals and locations, between people and substances, lending themselves to an archaeology of efforts. And what is more, they convey the conditions of production: Circular measures of land, for example, can only be conceived of where space is ample and imagined as a void. And indeed, they occur in the colonial setting of New Spain.[22] From Portugal to Russia, the European surface measures indicate either land ploughed in one morning or day, or the amount of seed needed for the area. In an agrarian setting, these types of measurements prove superior to a mere linear measurement. They are precise on another level, since the most interesting dimension of a field is not its extension. In a subsistence context, it may be more important to know its yield and the size of the possible crop. The amount of workforce or seed employed is in a sense economically more telling, because they both differ with the quality of the soil, with its steepness or flatness or fecundity. Yield is the most important information for those reduced to subsistence as well as for those planning to extract a toll or a tenth. Kula presents rural quantification as a superior system for practical use, which is why he uses the term *representational measures*.[23]

Units Against the Sovereign

The metric system, on the contrary, Kula presents as a mere convention. It loosens the representational link between persons and things and divides the units from the procedure of work. This makes them conventional, idealized, neutral, but by no means less communicative: Metric measures connect although their mode of representation suggests disentanglement. Multiple are the forces behind this transformation. During the first decades of its introduction the metric system is the carrier of a revolutionary rationalism. In the *Cahiers de doléances* strong claims for metric reform are voiced ("One King, One Law,

---

[21] Richard Pankhurst, "A Preliminary History of Ethiopian Measures, Weights and Values – (Part 3)," in *Journal of Ethiopian Studies* 8/1 (1970): pp. 45–85, here p. 45. (Richard Keir Pankhurst was son to Sylvia and grandchild to Emmeline Pankhurst, the famous Suffragettes.)

[22] Kula, *Measures and Men*, p. 29; Manuel Carrera Stampa, "The Evolution of Weights and Measures in New Spain," in *Hispanic American Historical Review* 39 (1949): pp. 2–24.

[23] The Polish original is "znaczeniowy," an adapted adjective from "znaczenie" which translates as "meaning" or "significance" (Kula, p. 3). Szreter translates this with "representational measures," in a later article with "functional measures" and uses "anthroprometric" when the connection to the body is stressed, although he admits to the danger of confusion: The measures Kula refers to take the human body as an etalon, not as an object that is being measured by laymen and scientists with a racist motivation for data collection. Compare Gert Thiele, ed., *Anthropometrie. Zur Vorgeschichte des Menschen nach Maß* (Munich: Fink, 2005). With emphasis on Poland and France Kula describes these measurements as a European phenomenon. For example, the *Morgen,* the *journée, or the giornata* estimate the *productivity* of a unit of land in different languages.

One Weight, One Measure!").[24] Expectations were high to augment justice, transparency and equality in taxation and trade alike. Kula traces the shattering of these plans, and hints at the fact that the metric system mirrors a different layer of economic functionality compared to the agrarian measures. At the same time, when the word *market* gains an abstract meaning[25] and trade is largely internationalized, the practices of quantification lose their rural functionality and adapt to the now dominant economic relations: book-keeping and comparability.[26] A measure is still a measure, but overall the units mediate entirely different settings. In this they are seismographic markers of a shift in economic relations.

A historical perspective on media praxeology can even do more. Not only are the systems of measurement telling of work procedures, they are indicators of juridical powers at play. This dimension was not lost on political economists of the nineteenth century such as Gustav Schmoller and Gustav von Below, who debated over the question of whether the right to define the standards for local weights and measures proved the sovereignty of medieval cities.[27] Kula sees one striking advantage of the meter and the kilogram compared to the pre-metric polyphony of measures. He classifies the right to define weights and measures not only as attributes of authority but describes it as a *resource* of power typical to feudal governments. When it came to taxation, they could demand the same number of units, but enlarge the volume of the units themselves. And what is more, this increased revenue is not in fluctuation, as a price might be. It becomes part of the law, because legal metrology was a prerogative of the lower gentry. Setting the standards for everyone's weights and measures constituted a sovereign resource to augment one's income: "Thus everything conspired to produce conflict about measures."[28]

This particular form of *metrological advantage* over the people is very similar to the kind of benefits generated by reducing the metal value of a country's coinage. This automatically augmented the seigniorage—the value to be gained because the coin is more valuable

---

[24] Kula, *Measures and Men*, p. 185; James C. Scott, *Seeing Like a State*: How Certain Schemes to Improve the Human Condition Have Failed (New Haven: Yale University Press, 1998), p. 31.

[25] Monika Dommann, "Markttabu," in *Auf der Suche nach der Ökonomie. Historische Annäherungen*, ed. Christof Dejung, Monika Dommann and Daniel Speich Chassé (Tübingen: Mohr Siebeck, 2014), pp. 183–207, here p. 188.

[26] "The measure given to it is unrelated to its maker or its user. The mass production of commodities is intended for vast, remote, and diverse markets. Each of them will have a measure of its own. Commodities cannot bear the measure of the country of origin if it be unintelligible to the buyers, nor of the country of destination, for those will be many and varied. The dimensions of such a product cannot be expressed in any measure that *belongs* to some particular locality or nation. No measure can enjoy favoured treatment in a market situation. Each must be abstract, just as market value is—or rather, conform to the abstract character of the market." Kula, *Measures and Men*, p. 123.

[27] Gustav Schmoller, "Die Verwaltung des Maß- und Gewichtswesens im Mittelalter," in *Schmollers Jahrbuch/Jahrbuch für Gesetzgebung* 17 (1893): pp. 287–309; Gustav von Below, „Die Entstehung der deutschen Stadtverfassung," *Historische Zeitschrift* 58.2 (1887): pp. 193–244 and 59.2 (1889): pp. 193–247; R. Hoeninger, *Gustav von Belows Detailpolemik. Ein Nachwort zu dessen Arbeiten über städtische Verfassungsgeschichte* (Berlin: Walther, 1892).

[28] Kula, *Measures and Men*, p. 16.

than the metal it consists of. Practices like this, which depend on numismatic metrology, are very much in favor of those in charge. Joseph Vogl made currency manipulations an important example of what he calls the *sovereignty effect (Souveränitätseffekt)*.[29] These effects bend the rules of law towards the establishment of new sources of revenue, which are only accessible for the few and typically negotiated between financial and political elites. The right to determine the local standards of measure, although no device of high finance, but of the feudal order, certainly shows the dynamics conceptualized by Vogl.

Remarkably, Kula credits the metric system of the French Revolution with closing precisely this space beyond the law, where metric standards were defined. At least, it was no longer to the deliberation of local authorities to change the system in their favor. But this huge gain and achievement came at a price, in Kula's analysis. In one respect he deplores the demise of the representational units: Rural quantification had its precision. It lay with the measurement of yield, performance, and lived time as opposed to the comparably arbitrary metric units of extension, surface, or gravity.

All in all, rural measures prove to be a medium influencing the distribution of value in societies. In their *representational* format before metrication they echo the working conditions of craftsmen. But at the same time, they are a contractual format organizing and mediating social hierarchies effectively without words.

It is very rare to come by descriptions that acknowledge quantification's potential for governance. This makes Jacob Grimm's account of the same transition, from rural measurements to the metric system that Kula described, a valuable source. In Grimm's account, the process of transition of Central European measuring routines is less historical fact than polemic. The rural measures are credited with a higher degree of rationality and democratic fitting than the revolutionary metric system. Although one does not necessarily have to follow Grimm's opinion, his treatment of quantification brings to the fore that for measures to work as a social medium, a high degree of codification is necessary.

Open Units of Negotiation

The question of quantification reoccurs in the historical rural law codes which Jacob Grimm commented on in his *Deutsche Rechtsalterthümer*. Grimm writes almost entirely through quotations from rural law decrees and the codes of conduct of different villages—all of which he secured though travels and his extensive correspondence network. His critique of modern metric practices entirely rests on these so-called *Weistümer*, which he later published in a source edition of no less than seven volumes. But although it is indubidtably based on historical documents from German law,[30] Grimm's theory of measurement needs a very cautious reading, because it is an implicit political polemic.

---

[29] Joseph Vogl, *Der Souveränitätseffekt* (Zurich and Berlin: diaphanes, 2015), pp. 69–70.

[30] This term denotes different types of codified law from Central Europe, as opposed to Romanic law. For Grimm Germanic or German designates a family of languages. The term includes the larger part of middle and northern Europe, England and Scandinavia. France is excluded, although ironically,

He quotes, for example, from a code of an agrarian field cooperative, or *Markgenos-senschaft*. The communal rules set limits upon when wood can be cut:

> It is further our ancient law and our old freewill, that a *markgenosse* on this side of the river is not allowed to hew any oak or beech wood that is still so green, that a hawk likes to eat beneath it in mid-summer.[31]

Crucial amounts are created by minute descriptions. Everything depends on the leaves; their shadow's expansion gives an approximate size in relation to the hawk's body. Thus, they form a rough measure, in keeping with the changing seasons and the growth of the plants. Grimm extols the poetry of this passage: "How beautifully is the size of the branch—which is forbidden to be cut down—determined by the leaves that grant shadow to the hawk eating his food."[32]

According to Alain Testart, comparison is the main feature of measurement that distinguishes measuring from mere counting. While counting relies on numbers of already visible pieces, measurement requires an ideal object or a third unit of reference: "there is no measurement without a standard."[33] The relation of the leaves to the hawk's body form such a model unit. And although usually quantification requires numbers, the examples Grimm gives stay altogether in the more physical dimension of relations and units of comparison. The rural law decree mentioned above can thus be said to comply at least with a minimum definition of ethnometrology—expanding the notion of measurement beyond the idea of instrument, number, and spatial exactitude. Remarkably, not only the capacity of the tree to yield wood at a particular time is included in the unit, but the *interest* of the environment is measured against the interests of the members of the cooperative. Compared to Kula, Grimm's examples are less work-centered, but use natural processes as rules for everyone's share of the common good. In an early article, Grimm describes the particular intimacy between things, animals, and persons that the juridical rules are

---

the only thorough follow up study to Grimm's *Deutsche Rechtsalterthümer* shows similar relations in France. See Jules Michelet, *Origines du droit français cherchées dans les symboles et formules du droit universel* (1837) (Cergy: Pagala, 2009). For an overview of research on Grimm's juridical studies, see Kaspar Renner, "Archäologie des Rechts. Zur Geschichte einer vergessenen Disziplin zwischen Jacob Grimm, Karl von Amira und Michel Foucault," in *Literatur der Archäologie: Materialität und Rhetorik im 18. und 19. Jahrhundert*, ed. Jörn Lang and Jan Broch (Munich: Fink, 2012), pp. 75–105.

[31] Jacob Grimm in a letter to Savigny, Kassel, February 4, 1816, in *Briefe der Brüder Grimm an Savigny*, ed. Wilhelm Schoof (Berlin: Schmidt, 1953), p. 230. Grimm gives the "Willkür von Ostbevern" (1339) as source.

[32] Ibid.

[33] Alain Testart, "Préface," in *Poids et mesures en Asie du Sud-Est. Systèmes métrologiques et sociétés. Asie du Sud-Est austronésienne et ses marches* 1, ed. Pierre Le Roux, Bernard Sellato and Jacques Ivanoff (Paris: École française d'Extrême-Orient, 2004), pp. 9–20, here p. 10.

expressive of as a *poetic* element of the law.[34] Here he clearly surpasses the functional or relative measurements confirmed by historians of metrology and economic history. What gives measures the power to connect and divide lies within the setting or the particular performance of the practice.

Thus, I argue that it would be a misunderstanding to see the poetic measures as qualitative units which could be expected of a Romantic thinker. Grimm's intellectual labor lies in the subversion—or a new rendering—of the dichotomy of the quantitative and the qualitative. He tackles the notion of quantification, as will be shown by outlining his argument. It begins with the insight that Grimm also sees a liberating tendency in these agrarian units and the ways they are translated into rules:

> Finally, I have to count as a proof of the poetry that [resides] in the old law the light-heartedness of the latter: by this I understand the tendency not to pin down each and every thing and to prescribe fixed measurements for people.[35]

Qualities, relations, and sizes serve as approximate measures. They give no fixed amounts that could serve as recipes for action but leave things open and thus induce negotiation. Sizes, rough amounts, even numbers are incomplete without further decisions of local actors.

One rural decree on the regulation of water shows this openness more closely. It stipulates the level to which a millstream may be dammed. This example was frequently quoted by Grimm, and applied in a fertile region north of Frankfurt am Main, the Wetterau:

> The water shall be adjusted to a level and the miller shall not raise his weir above [a point] that a bee [landing] on a nail's head, that is right in the middle of the pole, [is able to] support itself and drink and enjoy the water [with its] feet and wings unharmed and un-moistened.[36]

Evoking the natural milieu of a small insect, this decree creates precision through vivid description. A shifting, precarious zone between the bee's leg and the waterline indicates a narrow range of tolerance for the miller wishing to augment his main source of energy. The mode of description may be easy to memorize, even though it offers neither decisive amounts nor measures. The pole's length and the nail's location remain subject to negotiations beyond the law. Grimm characterizes the procedural measurements as *poetic* in a way that he discerns from mere poetical language. Contrary to all preconceived notions, this *poetic* kind of practice resides in measurement:

---

34   Jacob Grimm,"Von der Poesie im Recht [1815]," in *Jacob und Wilhelm Grimm. Werke*, ed. Ludwig Erich Schmitt, Abteilung I, Bd. 6, Rezensionen und vermischte Aufsätze 1 (Hildesheim: Olms, 1991), pp. 152–191.

35   Grimm, "Von der Poesie im Recht," p. 189.

36   Edmund Stengel, ed., *Private und amtliche Beziehungen der Brüder Grimm zu Hessen. Eine Sammlung von Briefen und Actenstücken als Festschrift zum hundertsten Geburtstag Wilhelm Grimms den 24. Februar 1886*. 3, 1 (Marburg: Elwert, 1886–1910), p. 109.

Poetic regulations are found first and foremost in the imaginations of space and time when it has to be determined how far something is supposed to reach and how long it is supposed to last.[37]

These regulations entrust bodies, actions, and things with determining sizes, borders, and effective dates. According to Grimm,[38] ancient rules shun numbers, in favor of simple procedures. For example, conventionally known measures such as *ell* or *foot* are mentioned in the poetic descriptions, but the issue to be determined by them is never fully elaborated. The model unit consists of an image or scene that serves as a frame for further agreement. The main issue—for example, millstream water levels—is under-determined while minor elements—the situation of the bee—are highly detailed. Grimm suggests that the dysfunctionality of such measures, their vagueness, is their virtue and refers again to *light-heartedness* [*Vergnügtheit*]:

> Above all the old German law prefers a light-hearted approach when it comes to bestowals and easements, which grants more room to the free play of rough estimation than to dry words. The dues, which are described in detail in the most sensual and detailed way, remain ambiguous when it comes to the main contract.[39]

Practical mediation of matter thus triggers a whole different behavior, compared to a precise measurement in numbers. It is their ambiguity that makes these measurements valuable for Grimm, since the key issues are left for local actors to decide. The crucial addendum to qualitative or *poetic* quantification is thus an element of decision or judgment. At this point it becomes necessary to describe rural measurement as a part of the larger argument Grimm has in mind.

Units in 1848

Grimm's rural measurement procedures were deployed against the metric system, which was introduced as a part of the *Code Civil* in all the German areas conquered by Napoleon. In the new model states, such as, the short-lived kingdom of Westphalia, this legal code reformed weights and measures at the same time as disentangling political power and the system of jurisdiction, which were one during feudalism.[40] It was in Westphalia that Grimm reluctantly served as librarian to Napoleon's younger brother Jérôme. Since Grimm parallels metric measures and the character of the new, centralized law as a politi-

---

[37] Grimm, "Von der Poesie im Recht," p. 169.

[38] Jacob Grimm, *Deutsche Rechtsalterthümer [1828],* in *Jacob und Wilhelm Grimm. Werke,* ed. Ludwig Erich Schmitt, Abteilung I, 17 and 18. Reprint of the 4th edition, 1899. (Hildesheim: Olms, 1991), p. 103.

[39] Grimm, "Von der Poesie im Recht," p. 174.

[40] Françoise Knopper, "La Westphalie, un laboratorie des idées napoléoniennes," in *L'Allemagne face au ' modèle' Français de 1789 à 1815,* ed. Françoise Knopper and Jean Mondot (Toulouse: Mirail, 2008), pp. 181–196.

cal protest, his suggestions fall in line with the general direction of the *German Historical School of Jurisprudence*, especially the fraction of the *Germanists* who would counter the centralization of the Prussian king, and the unification and egalitarianism of the French Revolution, by inventing and stressing the tradition of German communal self-rule.[41] Some developed rights to collective use in the tradition of the commons (*Genossenschaftsrecht*) against the strong emphasis of the newly introduced Roman law, with its acute provisions for private property. The fatal reception of many reoccurring motives of the *Germanists* in the twentieth century cannot be denied, although in the nineteenth century they served as arguments in the political upheavals of 1848. Progressive and conservative forces countered administrative reform by campaigning against codification.

To all these issues the discovery of the *jus commune*, the customary law of the people, lent itself graciously: Contracts were much closer to action, and even oral negotiations took on a much more practical format.[42] It is a well-established fact that performative and symbolic dimensions were discovered during that time in all kinds of non-codified law.[43] The influential jurist Carl von Savigny could thus identify formalized actions (*förmliche Handlungen*) as the *grammar of law*,[44] which is in keeping with modern research on non-codified jurisdictive cultures.

It is on this gestural level, where measurements prove themselves as social media of economic relations, that many measuring acts from Grimm's list can be interpreted as performative in the true sense, since they anchor contracts and agreed upon regulations in public space. This is the case, for example, when bowshots in a circular direction determine where to build the moat around a city.[45] The space is irrevocably altered by the practice and there is no need for words to accompany the rule. In one instance, Grimm even compares the practical and physical demarcation of the landscape with a notarization.[46] Measurement establishes borders, rights to use, and property. Thus, as in Kula, the measurement procedures indicate wordless disputes over possession. Aiming at the times before feudalism, Grimm collects material to invoke autonomous peripheral zones, self-governed by the people, where symbolic actions and measurements took on the form of a visible contract. Additionally, the very format of rural law decree invited this

---

[41] Gerhard Dilcher and Rüdiger Kern, "Die juristische Germanistik des 19. Jahrhunderts und die Fachtradition der Deutschen Rechtsgeschichte," in *Zeitschrift der Savigny-Stiftung für Rechtsgeschichte, Germanistische Abteilung* no. 101 (1984): pp. 1–46, here p.7; Erich Rothacker, "Savigny, Grimm, Ranke. Ein Beitrag zur Frage nach dem Zusammenhang der historischen Rechtsschule," *Historische Zeitschrift* 128 (1923): pp. 415–445, here p. 423.

[42] Even codified procedures do not necessarily exclude oral traditions: Marcus Twellmann, "Mündliche Rede. Auch ein Medium der Bürokratie," in *Archiv für Mediengeschichte* 16 (2016): pp. 29–39.

[43] Michelet, *Origines du droit français*; Paul Girard, *Manuel élémentaire de droit romain* (1918) (Paris: Dalloz, 2003).

[44] Friedrich Carl von Savigny, *Vom Beruf unserer Zeit für Gesetzgebung und Rechtswissenschaft* (Heidelberg: Mohr und Zimmer, 1814), p. 10.

[45] Grimm, "Von der Poesie im Recht," p. 173.

[46] Ibid., p. 179.

kind of political reading, since the rules were rendered in the form of a dialogue between village people and authority. Grimm develops his arguments closely from sources and documents, but critiques of Grimm's evaluation of the democratic nature of the *Weistümer* were audible from the start.[47]

Pre-eminence for Grimm lay with the political argument within the discussions of his day. In 1848, he became an elect member of the Frankfurt National Assembly. Although Grimm did turn his studies on ancient law into a political argument in the quest for more democratic rights,[48] it is not quite the French egalitarianism, unification, and civic codes he supports. And it is in this refusal that Grimm's intellectual contribution to the history of quantification lies. He does not subscribe to the inevitable association of measurement and rationality but develops a counter myth where less quantified practices can summon more rationality, in the sense of judgment and personal deliberation. Grimm denies many of the claims that quantification gained during the Enlightenment. Balancing his reflective measurements between antagonistic and consensual modes is probably one of his strongest strategic moves. Negotiation is situated between aggressive confrontation and compromise amongst equals; between established claims and granted fairness; and between personal interest and justice. Grimm's space of negotiation is not a place where equivalents meet and come to terms. It is open to hierarchical and asymmetric relations. Just as in his special brand of textual criticism, which once was aptly termed *wild philology*,[49] there is an almost postmodern element to his thinking about units.

---

[47] Dieter Werkmüller, *Über Aufkommen und Verbreitung der Weistümer. Nach der Sammlung von Jacob Grimm* (Berlin: Schmidt, 1972), p. 67. Evidence from several local courts in the Swiss midlands from the thirteenth to the fifteenth centuries fully supports the opposite view to Grimm and sustains the aristocratic bias of the juridical genre. Simon Teuscher, *Erzähltes Recht. Lokale Herrschaft, Verschriftlichung und Traditionsbildung im Spätmittelalter* 68 (Frankfurt am Main: Campus Historische Studien 44, 2007). While this is supported by evidence, documents from other regions investigated by Gadi Algazi suggest considerable agency for the side of the peasants. Gadi Algazi, "Lords Ask, Peasants Answer. Making Traditions in Late-Medieval Village Assemblies," in *Between History and Histories: The Making of Silences and Commemorations*, ed. Gerald M. Sider and Gavin A. Smith (Toronto: University of Toronto Press, 1997), pp. 199–229, here p. 202. "Being involved in the making of tradition had serious implications for peasants. In the case of the Weisung, *tradition* did not stand for the unofficial refuge of subjects excluded from the making of *real* law: it was itself the law, and peasants took an active part in transmitting and reshaping it. In this respect, peasant participation in the work of tradition was a resource that at least some of them could deploy and impose constraint on the lords' freedom of action, a point stressed notably by Max Weber."

[48] Though once progressive, many motives of this juridical movement received a fatal reception during the Third Reich. The ideas and documents furnished by the German faction of the historical school of law, to which Grimm belonged, played a crucial role for the nationalist and racist agenda of Nazi-Germany.

[49] Ulrich Wyss, *Die wilde Philologie. Jacob Grimm und der Historismus* (Munich: Beck, 1979), p. 289.

Concluding Remarks

The narrations of rural measurement in Kula's and in Grimm's accounts converge and differ. Both present weights and measures in the context of law. Quantitative practices are thus part of a fixed behavioral pattern or guideline. Both authors maintain that measurement takes place in times of conflict over possession or rights of use. Measures mediate between parties and can thus be said to connect people as well as things through their capacity to connect subject matter to commensuration. For Kula, this capacity to compare idealized simplifications, this *investment in form*,[50] develops out of working procedures. Compared to the metric strategies of measurement, which emphasize exact extension, gravity, or surface, the methods of rural measurement are less numerical, but more exact in economic terms. They measure yield or performance, approximate values or revenue. Metric measures, on the other hand, divide procedures from visibility and put them out of reach for estimation. Although this distancing effect by no means changes the capacity of measures to mediate, neutrality becomes to define measurements as such. The metric system is conceived of as a neutral, rational, and universal system divided from social issues. Grimm, on the other hand, develops a thorough strategy to discredit the revolutionary rationalism of the metric system. For this he remarkably subverts the dichotomy of the qualitative and the quantitative. Aligning measuring procedures with local practices of the *jus commune* imbues them with a sense of personal freedom and the right to defend oneself. The emphatic identification of equal units and equality before the law, which belongs to the metric system, is disentangled and unmasked as a means of centralization. For Grimm, building equivalents is never a *matter of fact*, but a crucial scene of possible connections or divisions, hierarchies and losses—an incalculable game of material and interests, bodies and chance, sizes and shapes. Despite their wordlessness and due to their affinity to numbers, measuring practices prove to be an important communication system. It falls short of a gestural language, but is a very practical means of exchange, a shorthand for consensus that sometimes remains mute to its disadvantage.

---

[50] Wendy Nelson Espeland and Michael M. Sauder, "Rankings and Reactivity. How Public Measures Recreate Social Worlds," *American Journal of Sociology* 113 (2007): pp. 1–40, here p. 17.

From Documentary Practices to WikiLeaks

Interview with Lisa Gitelman, by Monika Dommann[1]

MD: Media scholars have many different disciplinary backgrounds. I've read that you come from the history of literature and was wondering how you became a media historian?

LG: Yes, I did my doctoral work in literature. And it's really a story of an accidental set of failures. I failed to get a teaching job when I finished my degree, and instead, I got a job working for the Papers of Thomas Edison, which is a scholarly research project that still exists. (The project was and is researching, editing, and publishing the papers of the American inventor.) Working in the history of technology made some sense, because my dissertation had been about narrative in scientific writing. It was also a moment when science and technology studies was exploding and becoming itself, with canonical works by Steven Shapin and Simon Schaffer, Bruno Latour, etc. And then, I found the Edison Papers to be a very congenial place to think and to work. I was based at an archive, so I developed a completely new expertise. It was an expertise in the giant mountain of paper, because over many years (I was there for eight or nine years), I learned the collections there, and that was a very empowering thing. And it also gave me something of a documentary sensibility. Even though I'm not a trained historian, in other words, I developed an aptitude for archivally-driven arguments and explanations.

MD: Was science and technology studies a topic at the university where you studied?

LG: It wasn't.

MD: How… was the first encounter with science and technology studies? Do you still remember—which scholar, or which book?

LG: I don't remember why I started reading it, but I started reading *ISIS*, the History of Science Society journal. I remember reading Latour's *Laboratory Life*, and…

---

[1] This text is a slightly revised version of an interview at the IKKM in Weimar on June 6, 2016. Many thanks to Julia Engelschalt for the transcripts.

MD: *Science in Action*?

LG: Not *Science in Action*; the classic article… "Drawing Things Together," when it first came out in English. I definitely remember *Leviathan and the Air-Pump*. These were books that friends of mine and I read and talked about. They weren't taught in our classes, but they were cutting-edge. It was the moment of High Theory or its passing; hard to say. This just seemed a way to step aside from that *agon* and think about interesting things, and also —particularly because of Latour's notion of inscription—to think about writing in ways that exceeded the literary. I have to confess that I've moved beyond the literary as such. Though I still think of myself as a literary scholar, I still perform readings in some sense, I have lost much of my interest in literature, or literary history *per se*.

MD: When you looked at the Papers of Edison, was it the gaze of science and technology studies already, or was it the gaze of the literary scholar you brought in?

LG: Well, it was the gaze of science and technology studies already. I think everybody else who had been in that archive to that point was more of a straight historian of technology. What happened on the laboratory table top? How did the machine work? And nobody had looked at it from a science and technology studies perspective. About inscriptions. About the kinds of things that *could* be written down, that *could* occur on paper, that *weren't* writing, that might be *like* writing, that might be allies mobilized in an argument about a patent dispute or the operational workings of a machine. That was really fun to look at the stuff that had been looked at a million times before, but maybe with a different temperament.

MD: But, you know, in science and technology studies the big thing was constructivism. And in literary theory, it was deconstruction.

LG: Yeah.

MD: How did you deal with that?

LG: No, I just kind of left the literary behind. I left it. And I mean, there are other developments in the academy that are concurrent with science and technology studies. Media studies of one kind or another was contemporaneous with science and technology studies and overlaps with it. But there were area studies and ethnic studies in the same moment. So, there were plenty of other ways to move beyond the literary object, toward a more contextual, a more networked approach.

MD: You told me now that you left your old field completely. Would you say that you never came back?

LG: In some ways I've come full circle. The way I now engage with literature is really in a kind of bibliographical register. Bibliography is centuries old. It's an honored discipline, but it has a bad reputation in most of the academy. Dry, dull, old-fashioned. And yet, in the current moment, I think in a large measure because of digital technology, bibliography is back. It's an exciting way to develop a precise language for textuality. So, to the extent that I've always been interested in texts, bibliography, a bibliographical sensibility is kind of a nice way to operate. Largely in the interest of precision, I would say, so that you can say what something is, so you can describe it critically, get it to speak.

MD: I think there's a similar movement going on in history at the moment. We realize that marginalized, so-called *Hilfswissenschaften* are the core of the historical method.

LG: I think that's right. All of those old, you know, specialties like paleography which are incredibly highly developed disciplines. I have nothing but respect for the people who are real experts there. Under the sign of the digital we're sort of able to re-see. I have the sense that we are able to see things about textuality, and in particular about books, about formats, the codex form, and about different print technologies, because of the ongoing development in digital technology. It's just like, we lived in this past and we couldn't even see it. And every day it becomes richer and richer because of the world we actually live in today.

MD: I read in one of your interviews that you are looking for what is missing in the digital editions and what is disappearing in the process of becoming a digital object.

LG: I am interested in what is lost and what is gained.

MD: Tell me more about this.

LG: Well I'm now thinking in particular about digitization projects, and certainly, there's plenty to be gained by digitizing historical sources. Access is a big gain. And I think it's also very interesting to think about what's lost. It's also interesting to think about gain and loss as an ongoing dynamic that changes over time and that has different episodes in it. A lot of the digitized sources that my colleagues and I use in the United States have been digitized from microfilm. So, even before the gain and loss of digitization, there's the gain and loss of microfilming. And so, to try and think about the gain and loss of digitization is to also think about that gain and loss, and there's kind of a telescoping effect, and that's something I'm very interested in.

MD: Why are you interested in history? What's history for you?

LG: I have to confess that I think of myself as something of an antiquarian. Part of me is interested in history for its own sake, as kind of an enthusiast. And I guess I joke all the time that we've finally lived long enough that antiquarians have become hipsters, and hipsters have become antiquarians. It's kind of fashionable now to use a typewriter, say—in some parts of Brooklyn, at least. But to be honest and a little less glib, I think you can't have an interest in history apart from the present. So, we all, whatever we say, have interests in the past because of the present.

MD: At the moment, one can observe that the history of science, science and technology studies, media studies are more or less converging. Would you say it's one field now, or are there differences you can name?

LG: I think there are real differences among those fields. I do think that we are at a very exciting and productive moment, when there is a large territory of overlap. In other words, that there is an intellectual terrain where the inquiries share a great deal. I think my department at New York University, in particular, is kind of prospering, where science and technology studies and media studies overlap. That shouldn't deny real differences though, and there are people who have kind of far more training in science studies, say, or science and technology studies, or media studies. There are different places to come from, and each have different intellectual and institutional histories. I think it's important for all of us to have some kind of an account of how the inquiries we're engaged with have developed over time. I think German media studies is particularly adept at thinking about its past, its origins, and the kind of confluence of questions that come together in German media studies. In the U.S., we may not be as good at it, but it certainly is important work to do, to think about how media studies is, and is not, born of a legacy of communication studies, say. Or the kind of hermeneutic disciplines that would do readings of films, television, and things like that. That's not a big part of media studies as I do it, or as I see it connected to science and technology studies, but it is part of media studies the way some people do it. And I think we do have to be kind of attentive to all those confluences, to think about the inquiry that we are engaged in, because these inquiries are dynamic, and they're also, of course, institutionally grounded. And media studies is certainly an inquiry that is institutionally very heteromorphic, it's very differently shaped across, and located in different institutions.

MD: You already told me that you learned from science and technology studies going to the lab, looking at what's going on, looking at the inscriptions and the inscription devices. Could you name other things you learned from, for example, the history of technology or the history of science?

LG: Well, I'm really interested in the history of technology, again, in a kind of antiquarian, gee-whizzery kind of way, but also became interested in questions of innovation. Where does innovation come from? How do we recognize innovation? How is that in itself a kind of bounded construct that's dynamic, culturally and historically, across time? That's the question around new media as we've been saying it all along, and why not use the history of technology, which has been wrangling with similar questions for just as long?

MD: In your writings I found an awesome awareness of the context. Of the social world, of economic structures. How do you get to the context? Is the context a thing you have in mind when you write?

LG: It seems to me, as I proceed, that I focus on something, and part of my focus is to see more and more and more context, as if the context needs to be kind of painstakingly discovered in an ongoing way. One of the devices, I guess, that I have used methodologically to aid in this, is to work with case studies. This has obvious pros and cons. By constraining my inquiry to a small chronological window, I'm able to see a lot of context. There's a very rich context—but it has certain limits, right? Because I've cut it off from the world. It's a little terrarium, or a fish-bowl. And then, you know, you build some other fish-bowls. And what you get, you could say, it's just a collection of fish-bowls, but it also, at least at a speculative level, lets you see sort of broader framing conditions—conditions of change, conditions of continuity—that, you know, are kind of interesting and important to pick out.

MD: You have already mentioned a methodological interest in *formats*. And at our summer school we were discussing the relevance of practices in media studies. Is format a relevant concept for you? And what about practices?

LG: Well, certainly, I've been influenced by Jonathan Sterne's work on the .mp3 as a format, and his articulation of format as a productive site of inquiry in media studies, rather than the media form, meaning a kind of hunk of technology in this really kind of isolated way, you know, "*the* book" or "*the* phonograph." Thinking about forms, plural, is a help. Thinking about formats is a new and productive way to go. And thinking, you know, from literary studies, or from bibliography, *format* has a slightly different cast to it. I've always been—again, this is coming out of literature, maybe I haven't escaped it entirely—interested in a triad of terms. So, medium, format, and genre. It seems to me that there are a lot of terms missing there, among the three, but the three are themselves really interesting and really capacious. They're used in all kinds of different ways. Format is used to mean all kinds of different things. But so is medium, and so is genre, interestingly enough. So, I'm interested in those terms. Practices... I mean, practices, in one sense, are sort of crystallized as media formats or genres. I've most recently been studying documentary practices.

MD: Can you tell me more about that?

LG: Sure. This is the recent book, *Paper Knowledge*, which is about documents, and it again uses a kind of case-study approach, and each case has to do with a particular medium. So, without saying that documentary practices are fully determined by media,

I am trying to show that dynamic, that epistemic practices of documentation and documentary presentation have a lot to do with the ongoing development and apprehension of new media forms.

MD: The German media tradition has a big interest in case studies, but also an interest in strong narratives about long periods, using the telescope rather than the microscope. Are these strong narratives productive, epistemologically?

LG: Well, definitely. I think for all media studies, the strong narrative out there tends to be one of rupture, right? Of revolution. And it's still enormously productive to think with that narrative, and against it. I think that all of us have more and more become committed to seeing continuity as well as change. We're all living in the same kind of post-Foucauldian moment where epistemic rupture is just part of the story, and I think that the most productive questions for me now turn on questions of historical epistemology. And so, they can be more gradualist and less about rupture. But it's still kind of the same set of big-picture questions. What do you think?

MD: I'm also interested in evolution, because the revolutions or ruptures are quite infrequent. I think the normal case is evolution. And this is also the more interesting case. But it's the difficult case, because you need a lot of patience to study it, and it's not such a strong narrative to write a book about it. And we face the problem, especially in the history of science, that we have a lot of case studies now describing evolutions. And on the way, we are losing the big questions.

LG: I see.

MD: The current history of science and the history of knowledge lost contact with the philosophy.

LG: Interesting, yes.

MD: …we've lost contact with the science and technology studies scholars.

LG: There's a kind of similar problem in media history. If we're not careful, it becomes a kind of perpetual account of the triumph of modernity. And I think that there is a real danger in that. Among other things, I think it's an extremely Western way to think about things. It enforces a certain, probably a narrower epistemology than we might want. And so, trying to think against that in interesting ways, I think, is an important goal for the future. It's not anything that I've done enough of myself, but I have colleagues thinking in these ways, and we need to pay more attention to that. It's less a question of evolution or revolution, and more of how is the inquiry, as we have received it from our predecessors, continuing to be limited in ways that we might counteract?

MD: You told me at the beginning that the 1980s were the decade of the theories. And I think all these interesting fields that you were talking about were driven by a lot of theory work. What's theory now for you… in 2016?

LG: I've never thought of myself as a theorist. I think only historians have ever called me a theorist, and of course, theorists call me a historian. I've found that a very productive place to be, under the radar. Nobody can see you. But that's not to deny that we are all living in a post-Foucauldian world. It's in the groundwater. I think that, to a certain extent, deconstruction might have its day in media studies, to the extent that we could say that, you know, in a sense, McLuhan is the first media studies professor in a certain way, but we might look again tomorrow and see that Derrida is the first media studies professor in a different way. That's kind of new, no? I don't think people have been saying that for all that long. But I'm not a trend spotter any more than I'm a theorist.

MD: You told me now that you're interested in epistemological questions. I'm really interested now in historicizing the 1980s, the epistemic decade.

LG: Really? I don't think I'm ever going to be interested in the 1980s…

MD: No?

LG: …having lived through it. So maybe I'm blindly interested in only that. But to the extent that I'm interested in epistemology, I should be clear: I'm interested in historical epistemology. What are historically specific ways of knowing? And at any one time, there are many different ways of knowing available, right? So, how does the repertoire of ways of knowing at any particular time evolve from the repertoire before it? Those are questions really interesting to me, and they're kind of connected to media forms and media practices. So, I don't know where I'm going to take that kind of questioning next exactly.

MD: For a long time, history was based on your object of study: paper. Historians followed the paperwork of other periods. But this has changed now. We have a lot of records and tapes, for example sources produced by huge oral history projects.

LG: Well, yes, if you think about the records that you and I are going to leave, they're going to be digital. You know, 98 per cent of them. And I think that we are just beginning to think about what this means for future historians. Again, I think that a bibliographical as well as a documentary sensibility is really what we need to cultivate. One of the reasons I got interested in documentary is because I think that the Web itself is, even at a kind of popular level, helping to produce a kind of documentary sensibility. So that, even though files are shared kind of indiscriminately, people have new questions about documents, about different digital objects. So, I'm not completely pessimistic about the future, or the future historian, but we still really are just beginning to see what that looks like.

MD: Many historians argue that we don't get anything new we don't already know from the written sources. On the one hand, that's true, but on the other hand, there is more in the sources than just the message.

LG: We learn lots that we didn't know before from tapes and other kinds of sources. You know, and then we have to think about recent things like…

MD: What can we learn from phonographic records, from tapes? The sources you've studied for such a long time.

LG: Well, I haven't made use of those sources myself. But I think there are lots of things that we don't know about what happened behind closed doors, as much as we might think we did, that will be revealed when things come into the open. And I think, even more than kind of analogue, archival media sources, we have to think ahead to things. I'm thinking about Wikileaks or Snowden, and these big disclosures, these big leaks where, or the Panama Papers now, where what really has to happen is data mining of vast corpora of leaked documents. And that's a kind of history, you and I are not prepared to do that kind, but it's coming down the road.

MD: Yes, definitely. But still, at the beginning, there must be some smart questions.

LG: It's true, I mean, and we can help think…

MD: A heuristic.

LG: Exactly.

MD: Yeah, and that's what I think the Digital Humanities are more or less missing at the moment.

LG: Well, but it's really exciting to think about how inquiry itself, ways of knowing, have to dynamically engage the sources available.

Jeremy Stolow

Introduction: Religion Is as Religion Does

What can the notion *media practice* offer for the study of religion and media? How might a turn to practice shed new light on the work of religious mediation? Do the specific characteristics of religious (as opposed to some other category of) actors, actions, and fields of activity pose unique problems for the study of media practices? I propose that religious media do indeed present a significant challenge for media research and for the very prospect of a practice turn. At stake are fundamental questions about what sorts of actors and actions can be admitted for analysis, including—for religious practice, perhaps most importantly—agents and activities that in different ways defy ordinary human experience and challenge established consensus about the natural order of things. What are often identified as examples of *religious media*—such as print publications, radio emissions, or smart phone applications —are best understood as instances of a more capacious process of *religious mediation*: a term that encompasses not only the contents of linguistic, visual, and auditory communications, but also their material and technological infrastructures, the embodied sensoria of human actors, and their coordinated interactions with a wide range of nonhuman agents, from clothing to architecture to money to animals and body parts, both living and dead. But sooner or later, students of religion and media must contend with the existence of yet other classes of actors and types of activity whose ontological status remains controversial within the larger enterprise of media studies. What indeed are we supposed to do with all the deities, angels, spirits, demons, magical spells, astral bodies, curses, and miracles that serve as the key focal points of religious mediation? Ought we accord such things the ontological status of *real* actors? Should we presume they somehow belong *within* the networks, assemblages, and entanglements that provide the conditions of possibility for religious communication and performance? Or are we better off sticking to a well-trodden path in the history of social-scientific inquiry that denies the reality of the transcendent entities, forces and events reportedly at work in the religious field: stripping them of their *external* existence and relocating them in the twists and turns of the collective social imaginary, the individual unconscious, or even the neural networks of human brains? What else might a god be if it is not a shared figure of discourse, a cathected object of desire, or a cognitive algorithm designed to enact an inherited survival mechanism? But do we even need to ascertain the ontological status of that god in order to study the media practices that accrue around it?

Answers to these questions are far from straightforward, not least given the ambivalent legacy of *religion* as an object of scholarly inquiry. Since its inception in the nineteenth century, the scientific study of religion has been dominated by an ideational definition of religion, one that posits symbols, dogmas, beliefs, emotions, and experiences as the central pillars of the religious field, and that relies upon textual hermeneutics, philology, semiotics, and other reading strategies to elucidate their meaning and function. Of course, at least since Marx, religion has also been understood as a system of social power, possessing distinctive institutional and organizational features, and working in the service of particular interests, political, economic, and sexual. But whether committed to the study of symbolic meaning, disciplinary practice, or institutional structure, scholars of religion have generally assumed a position of methodological agnosticism, according to which their tools of critical analysis are presumed to exist entirely independently from the faith commitments or communal adherences of the researchers themselves. Among other things, this separation of the study of religion from religious performance and practice has helped ensure that whatever enterprise aspires to adopt the name *scientific* or *scholarly* or *academic* study of religion must first make its peace with all the other sciences that establish the conditions of possibility for *naturally* occurring events. To avoid the charge of theological promulgation, students of religion must work to ensure their accounts of transcendent, magical, or supernatural occurrences, entities, or forces remain within the strict boundaries of scientific consensus.[1] A comparable strategy of containment and segregation can be noted in the way media studies has tended to treat supernatural and enchanted forces and presences within mediated technologies and practices; such magical creatures and operations can easily be granted admission to analysis if they are understood as figures of discourse or allegories for the workings of human perception or technological infrastructure, or as a way to describe the consequences of media storage and transmission for human efforts to communicate with absent others across space and time.[2] But this is a far cry from suggesting that spirits *really exist* or that magical gestures *really work*.

---

[1]   Compare Danièle Hervieu-Léger's brilliant treatment of the semantic and ontological stakes in early equivocations whether the field should be called *sociology of religion* or *religious sociology*. See for example Danièle Hervieu-Léger, *La Religion pour Mémoire* (Paris: Éditions du Cerf, 1993).

[2]   It is well known that German media studies enjoys a long history of interest in ghostly and supernatural forces and presences, from Friedrich Kittler's *Draculas Vermächtnis* (1993) and Wolfgang Hagen's *Radio Schreber* (1993) to more recent work, for example Moritz Bassler et al., eds., *Gespenster: Erscheinungen, Medien, Theorien* (Würzburg: Königshausen & Neumann, 2005); Michael Gamper and Peter Schnyder, eds., *Kollektive Gespenster: Die Masse, der Zeitgeist und andere unfassbare Körper* (Freiburg: Rombach, 2006); Marcus Hahn and Erhard Schüttpelz, eds., *Trancemedien und Neue Medien um 1900: Ein anderer Blick auf die Moderne* (Bielefeld: Transcript Verlag, 2009). There are different ways to account for this thematic focus, but it is notable that its growth in the 1990s mirrored a broader international engagement with the magic and ghostliness of modernity itself, as reflected in widely circulating books such as Jacques Derrida's *Spectres de Marx* (1993), Avery Gordon's *Ghostly Matters* (1997), and Michael Taussig's *The Magic of the State* (1997).

Here I am invoking, in crude shorthand, a much longer tradition from which the modern social sciences themselves have been born: as one of the key upshots of the reordering of the cosmos that Bruno Latour (1993) has described as occidental modernity's Great Divide, a sundering of nature and culture, the commensurate monopolization of the natural sciences over the physical world, and the reduction of all cosmic entities unknown to science to the symbolic terrain of culture. But why should a practice-oriented study of religion and media remain committed to this tradition? What would be the alternative? If, for instance, as students of religious mediation, we choose to take seriously—as many religious actors themselves seem to do—the presence of spirits, souls, demons, and gods, how exactly are such presences supposed to work their way into our analyses? What exactly does it mean to take a transcendent presence *seriously*?

This is not the place to review the long and vexed history of the term *religion* as a conceptual category. Suffice it to note that in both scholarly and popular discourse, it is rather difficult to avoid coming across the nominalist error of presupposing the existence of a universally distributed yet locally differentiated body of precepts, doctrines, affective dispositions, and modes of social affinity that all can be captured in the singular word *religion*. As argued by a growing chorus of scholars, the very idea that in every society there exists a phenomenon called religion is rooted in a specifically post-Reformation Christian theological distinction between, on the one hand, the internal, timeless, private experience of faith and belief and, on the other hand, the external, temporal, public domains of politics, science, social habit, and cultural expression.[3] The consequences of that distinction have been far-reaching, among other things having buttressed the colonial and Orientalist legacy of the study of comparative religion, whereby European Christian intellectuals sought to make sense of the ideas, rituals, and habits of non-European, non-Christian peoples, drawing comparisons and evaluating differences through the lens of their own understanding of what religions are made of. Patterns of practice *discovered* in every corner of the colonized world were thereby transformed into species of the universal category of religion, regardless of whether such a category made any sense in the local idioms or contexts where it was put to use, as occurred in the case of many great nineteenth century anthropological and philological inventions such as Hinduism and animism.[4]

I raise these points in order to lay some groundwork for thinking about religion and media from the vantage point of practice theory, and in particular the latter's promise to liberate research agendas from the prison-house of text-centrism and functionalism. What would a practice turn in religion and media look like and what makes such a turn worth our while? Whereas most researchers on religion and media have relied on some version

---

[3] See for example Talal Asad, *Genealogies of Religion: Discipline and Reasons of Power in Christianity and Islam* (Baltimore: Johns Hopkins University Press, 1993); Guy G. Stroumsa, *A New Science: The Discovery of Religion in the Age of Reason* (Cambridge MA: Harvard University Press, 2010).

[4] Tomoko Masuzawa, *The Invention of World Religions* (Chicago: University of Chicago Press, 2005); David Chidester, *Empire of Religion: Imperialism and Comparative Religion* (Chicago: University of Chicago Press, 2014).

of the assumption that there must exist something called *religion* separate from and prior to its conditions of mediation—such that one can study, for instance, the impact of digital technologies on the formation of religious communities or the *religious motivations* of particular kinds of media practices—a growing minority of researchers proposes instead that the objects, actors, and situations that constitute the study of religion and media can only be approached *in media res*. From this perspective, the mandate of religion and media studies is to observe religious phenomena only as they make themselves visible within existing social solidarities, power relations, embodied techniques and repertoires of action, material affordances, rules of exchange, and logistical orderings of space and time—in short, all the *media* that make religious communication and experience possible in the first place.[5] The virtue of such an approach is that the researcher is under no obligation to articulate or defend a substantive definition of religion *per se*, although this is not to suggest that anyone has escaped from the problems of ontological specificity that plague this topic from start to finish (as I shall try to clarify presently).

Here is the point of convergence, I think, with the tradition of practice theory. In his pioneering 2004 article, "Theorising Media as Practice," Nick Couldry decries the longstanding research focus on media texts as surfaces of meaning that somehow—mysteriously—engender their social effects, an approach Couldry charges with the crimes of functionalism and arbitrariness. Couldry invites media scholars to pursue instead a research agenda organized around a simple but more fruitful question: "What are people *doing* in relation to media across a whole range of situations and contexts?"[6] In this formulation, the work of media is understood to be available to direct observation and critical scrutiny, in the form of concrete actions undertaken by humans in particular material circumstances.[7] On these terms, Couldry's vision of media studies can be aligned with a longer history of practice theory that seeks to negotiate between the *objectivism* of social structure and material infrastructure, on the one hand, and the *subjectivism* of volitional human agency and meaning-making, on the other. Pierre Bourdieu famously elaborated his notions of habitus and field as the crucial mediating elements in the ongoing production, but also the dynamic reconstruction and contestation, of social life, its modes of power, and its uneven

---

[5]   Hent de Vries and Samuel Weber, eds., *Religion and Media* (Stanford CA: Stanford University Press, 2001); Jeremy Stolow, "Religion and/as Media," *Theory, Culture, & Society* 22/4 (2005): pp. 119–145; Jeremy Stolow, ed., *Deus in Machina: Religion, Technology, and the Things in Between* (New York: Fordham University Press, 2013); Birgit Meyer, *Mediation and the Genesis of Presence: Towards a Material Approach to Religion [Inaugural Address]* (Utrecht: Utrecht University, 2012); David Morgan, *The Embodied Eye: Religious Visual Culture and the Social Life of Feeling* (Berkeley: University of California Press, 2012); Sally M. Promey, ed., *Sensational Religion: Sensory Cultures in Material Practice* (New Haven: Yale University Press, 2014).

[6]   Nick Couldry, "Theorising Media as Practice," *Social Semiotics* 14/2 (2004): pp. 115–132, here p. 119.

[7]   This approach also undergirds Couldry's own contribution to the field of religion and media: the study of *media rituals* as instruments of power. See for example Nick Couldry, *Media Rituals: A Critical Approach* (London: Routledge, 2003).

distribution of scarce resources.[8] By synthesizing the phenomenological study of human action with the analysis of institutional structure, practice theory, as it has developed since Bourdieu, offers a robust elaboration of Couldry's deceptively simple question, locating the *doing* of human actors in a complex and dynamic web of structure and agency.[9] Working out of this tradition, Couldry's call for direct observation of media practice suggests a fruitful shift in focus for media researchers, and it is arguably one of the central goals of the present collection to move such an agenda forward through empirical analysis as well as theoretical engagement with practice theory's key notions and assumptions.

But whereas practice theory promises to resolve the longstanding debate about how to negotiate between individual human agency and social structure, other problems haunt its project. In particular, we must come to terms with practice theory's commitment (sometimes unwitting, sometimes unapologetic) to an anthropocentric research focus, reserving for human creatures the unique properties of agency, intention, purpose, and knowledge. Baldly stated, the privilege that practice theory accords to (individual as well as collective) human actors flies in the face of longstanding traditions of critical inquiry that have directly challenged many of the key assumptions about *the human subject* and *human agency* as unified, coherent, and intentional sources of action and meaning-making. In the late nineteenth and early twentieth centuries, Marx, Nietzsche, and Freud—the three "masters of suspicion"[10]—pioneered this assault on the long-cherished image of a volitional human subject. In the 1930s and 1940s, new voices were added, such as those of the behaviorist B. F. Skinner and the paleontologist Leroi-Gourhan. In the 1960s and 1970s, new critiques emerged from the vantage point of structuralist linguistics, Lacanian psychoanalysis, deconstruction, and Foucaultian genealogy. In more recent years, yet other challengers have emerged, including advocates of Deleuzian assemblage theory, Latourian actor network theory, media archaeology, cognitive science, and so-called *new materialist* philosophy, among other intellectual trends addressed elsewhere in this book. Despite their many points of disagreement, these theoretical frameworks share a common, anti-anthropocentric impulse: to extend the notions of action and actor beyond their normal application to conscious, self-directing humans, in order make room for new actors, from language games to scientific instruments, from computer algorithms to recorded sounds and images, from built environments to bacteria. One of the great challenges for practice theory might thus be framed as a question about the locus and role of human actors in relation to all these nonhuman agents that traffic with human minds and bodies. What indeed legitimates a privileged focus on human, as opposed to nonhuman, actors and how is that very divide constructed in the first place?

---

8   Pierre Bourdieu, *Outline of a Theory of Practice* (Cambridge: Cambridge University Press, 1977).

9   Sherry B. Ortner, *Anthropology and Social Theory: Culture, Power and the Acting Subject* (Durham NC: Duke University Press, 2006); Theodore R. Schatzki, *Social Practices: A Wittgensteinian Approach to Human Activity and the Social* (Cambridge: Cambridge University Press, 1996); Theodore R. Schatzki et al., eds., *The Practice Turn in Contemporary Theory* (London: Routledge, 2001).

10   Paul Ricoeur, *Freud and Philosophy* (New Haven: Yale University Press, 1970).

Such questions become particularly complicated when it comes to the sorts of nonhuman actors abounding in the religious field. Are the gods to make their appearance within media analyses only as figures of discourse, symbols, or visual and auditory hallucinations? Or can they be accorded some sort of reality within the frame of critical analysis? Does this very choice oblige us to revisit ingrained assumptions about the degree and manner by which *secular* sciences, such as physics, biology, or statistics, have already adjudicated the reality of the cosmos? Is there room for consideration of other strata of actors and action whose very postulation is hostile to modern scientific structures of knowledge? What do we believe we will gain or lose if we give credence to the kinds of nonhuman actors that religious agents have long accepted at face value?

The chapters gathered in this section offer various points of entry into these questions, offering distinct takes on the prospects of a practice-focused agenda of research in the field of religion and media. In my interview with John Durham Peters, we entertain (among other things) William James's pragmatism as a framework for addressing the ontological ambiguity that abounds in religious fields of practice.[11] Especially in his later writings, James elaborated the notion of radical empiricism, grounded on the metaphysical principle of *pure experience* that precedes all efforts to divide the cosmos into subject psychology, on the one hand, and objective reality, on the other. This version of pragmatism posits an ontologically and epistemologically neutral field of infinite possibilities that precedes all dual constitutions and distinctions—such as body and soul, subject and object, or consciousness and content—in and through which humans may be said to construct themselves and their world. Most importantly, for our purposes here, James's pragmatic approach treats all experiential relations as real in the simple sense that they occur and are made present within the interiority of experience itself. In James's words: "Everything real must be experienced, and every kind of thing experienced must somewhere be real."[12] Among other things, this approach afforded James considerable latitude to take seriously a whole range of phenomena as valid candidates for admission to the order of reality, including things that remained highly controversial from the perspective of the evolving natural sciences, as was the case with the sorts of *paranormal* phenomena, occurrences, and states that drew James into a longstanding commitment to the enterprise of psychical research.[13] Treating paranormal phenomena as real, on an ontologically level playing field in comparison with normal things, not only offers a rejoinder to the prerogatives of the natural sciences but also to the assumption that the objects proper to the field of *religion* can only exist as symbols in the minds of their believers, an argument that has been pur-

---

[11]   William James, *Pragmatism: A New Name for Some Old Ways of Thinking* (New York: Longmans, Green & Co, 1907).

[12]   William James, "The Experience of Activity," *Psychological Review* 12/1 (1905): p. 3.

[13]   See for example William James, "Address of the President before the Society for Psychical Research," *Science,* New Series 3/77 (1896): pp. 881–888.

sued in more recent years by a growing number of scholars of paranormal phenomena and their challenges to both the natural and human sciences.[14]

The other chapters of this section introduce instructive case material for the elaboration of practice theory as an analytical mode of media research. In Anthony Enns's examination of spiritualist uses of sound technologies, he argues that in the late nineteenth and early twentieth centuries, new media technologies intersected with spiritualist practices to the extent that both were based on new ways of separating voices from bodies, and thus mounting a significant challenge to the longstanding assumption that the human voice serves as a marker of interiority and the self.

Anderson Blanton explores the notion of the healing power of touch via electronic mediation, a process in which, for evangelical Christian radio preachers, most famously the 1950s American broadcaster Oral Roberts, a circuit is formed between preacher and supplicant through the medium of the radio set itself. Through the establishment of a *point of contact*, by placing their hands directly on their radio receivers, audience members could overcome the problem of distance in order to partake directly in the miraculous, healing powers of Roberts's spoken words. In this way, as Blanton describes it, "the agency of the radio apparatus itself opened up or extended the senses, allowing the hand to become an organ of audition."[15] *Pace* our differences of focus and theoretical interest, a common thread tying together the exchange between Stolow and Peters, and the chapters by Enns and Blanton that precede it, is an ebbing confidence that, I dare say, we all share in the power of reductionism to resolve once and for all the inscrutable presence of the supernatural, magic, the ghostly, the wondrous, or the holy in those practices, technologies, objects, and experiences that constitute media and the work of mediation. The easy path, as I have argued here, consists of *reducing* religious phenomena to a more familiar ground of social interest and power, or to cognitive structures of perception and interpretation; to do otherwise, some have argued, would court "the end of the human sciences as we know them."[16] The more rewarding path, I propose, refuses to bow to such a threat.

---

[14] For example Jeffrey J. Kripal, *Authors of the Impossible: The Paranormal and the Sacred* (Chicago: University of Chicago Press, 2010).

[15] Blanton, in this volume, p. 109.

[16] Russel McCutcheon, "It's a Lie. There's no Truth to it! It's a sin! On the Limits of the Humanistic Study of Religion and the Costs of Saving Others from Themselves." *Journal of the American Academy of Religion* 74/3 (2006): p. 720–750, here p. 736.

ANDERSON BLANTON

The Mass Miracle: Healing Touch and Other "Special Effects" of Radio Prayer

As one of the most influential charismatic Christian revivals in American history swept through the country in the 1950s, Oral Roberts, a famous healing evangelist from Oklahoma, described a new form of divine intervention that he termed *The Mass Miracle*. Both theological concept *and* ritual healing practice, the mass miracle marked that therapeutic moment when the flow of power from the hand of the healer into the body of the patient would be replicated on a mass scale through the mediation of technologies such as radio and television. With an intense, enthusiastic voice, Roberts elaborated upon this theologico-technical term during one of his sermons broadcast over the radio:

> What do I mean by 'The Mass Miracle'? I mean that at one time, in one single, explosive moment, the healing power of Christ will come upon a multitude of people and heal them all. They may be either in one crowd assembled in a public place such as a church, or our big [revival] tent, or they may be at home listening to a particular broadcast, or watching a television program such as ours. In the flash of a second the power of God shall sweep like a wind over the vast audience and heal them all, from the crowns of their heads to the soles of their feet. That's what I call the mass miracle.[1]

This essay focuses on a popular ritual of mass mediated healing prayer—and the visceral qualities of tactility, embodiment, and sensory transformation that are implicated in such techniques of ecstasy—in order to evaluate the recent *theorizing media as practice* turn in media studies. Through a demonstration of the specific ways in which the material affordances, or transductions[2], of the radio apparatus influence the ritual form, my essay suggests that a robust *media as practice* framework must not only struggle with "what people are *doing* in relation to media across a whole range of situations and contexts," but

---

[1]   Oral Roberts, *The Oral Roberts Reader* (New York: Zenith Books, 1958), p. 20.

[2]   In this analysis, the term *transduction* refers to the technical process whereby sound is converted into something else and that something else is translated back into sound. For more on this concept, see Jonathan Sterne, *The Audible Past: Cultural Origins of Sound Reproduction* (Durham NC and London: Duke University Press, 2003). I would like to thank the ethnomusicologist David Novak for his helpful insights regarding the concept of transduction (personal communication).

what media *do* to people.[3] More specifically, the media as practice turn must also engage with the specific media effects, or sensory environments and attunements, that emerge through the process of mediation. This is not merely an infusion of the old psychoana-lytic account of the cinematic apparatus and its imprints upon the passive faculties of the spectator, but an attempt to theorize *media practice* in that strange, and perhaps ecstatic, space between the capacities of the material medium and the potentialities of the *human* sensorium. In order to flesh out these more theoretical claims, let us return to Oral Roberts and his mass miracle.

Every Sunday throughout the 1950s, millions of listeners tuned in their radios to hear Oral Roberts' *Healing Waters Broadcast*. During the "prayer time" of the broadcast, Roberts would instruct the audience to "put your hand upon the radio cabinet as a point of contact" to facilitate the mass miracle and its communication of healing power. In addition to an extensive network of radio stations within the United States, this charismatic faith healing program encircled the globe through powerful transmitters strategically located in Europe, Africa, and India. The point of contact has now become a key descriptive phrase *and* technique of prayer within global charismatic Christian and Pentecostal faith healing movements. Several recent studies of Pentecostalism in religious studies and the anthro-pology of media, moreover, have made reference to the global prevalence of this phrase.[4]

The most important segment of the *Healing Waters Broadcast* occurred toward the end of the thirty-minute program, when after several songs, some testimonies of miraculous healing by faith, and a brief sermon, Oral Roberts delivered the healing prayer during the prayer time of the program. As a specific technique of prayer, the prayer time of the broadcast was structured around what Roberts termed "the point of contact." In the early days of his ministry, Roberts developed this faith healing technique specifically in rela-tion to the radio apparatus. According to Roberts, the radio as a point of contact allowed the patient to "turn loose" or "unleash" a standing reserve of faith that resided within the interior of the religious subject. Through numerous printed tracts, magazines, books and comics, the faith healer described how the point of contact focused the attention of the patient, allowing him or her to experience the presence of that which, under everyday sensory regimes, would persist undetected (see Figure 12).

---

3   Nick Couldry, "Theorizing Media as Practice," *Social Semiotics* 14 (2004): pp. 115–132, here p. 119.
4   For other descriptions of the global performance of the point of contact, see Lucas Bessire, "'We Go Above': Media Metaphysics and Making Moral Life on Ayoreo Two-Way Radio," in *Radio Fields: Anthropology and Wireless Sound in the 21st Century*, ed. Lucas Bessire and Daniel Fisher (New York: New York University Press, 2012), pp. 197–214; Candy Gunther Brown, ed., *Global Pente-costal and Charismatic Healing* (Oxford: Oxford University Press, 2011), p. 93; Marleen de Witte, "The Electric Touch Machine Miracle Scam: Body, Technology, and the (Dis)authentication of the Pentecostal Supernatural," in *Deus in Machina*, ed. Jeremy Stolow (New York: Fordham University Press, 2012), pp. 65, 71, 74; J. Kwabena Asamoah-Gayadu, "Anointing through the Screen: Neo-Pentecostalism and Televised Christianity in Ghana," *Studies in World Christianity* 11/1 (2005): pp. 9–28, here p. 20.

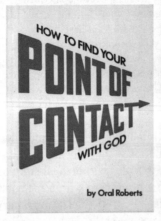

Fig. 12: Mass circulated booklets explaining the Point of Contact.

Roberts often used technological metaphors to explain this charismatic technique of prayer, comparing the point of contact to an electric light switch that, when actuated through a manual gesture upon the object, allowed divine healing power to flow through the body of the patient.[5]

It is not mere coincidence that Roberts was constantly invoking metaphors of technology to describe the point of contact, as the first explicit formulation of this new prayer-gesture emerged within the context of his popular radio broadcast. In an article entitled "The Story Behind Healing Waters," published in the mass-circulated *Healing Waters Magazine*, Roberts explains the basic ideas behind the radio as point of contact:

---

[5]   For more on the flow of anointed power and its relation to technology in the Pentecostal tradition, see Bruno Reinhardt, "Soaking in Tapes: The Haptic Voice of Global Pentecostal Pedagogy in Ghana," *Journal of the Royal Anthropological Institute* 20/2 (2014): pp. 315–336. Recent contributions to the study of religious radio within the fields of anthropology and religious studies include Lucas Bessire, "'We Go Above'"; Anderson Blanton, "Appalachian Radio Prayers: The Prosthesis of the Holy Ghost and the Drive to Tactility" in *Radio Fields: Anthropology and Wireless Sound in the 21st Century*, ed. Lucas Bessire and Daniel Fisher (New York: New York University Press, 2012), pp. 215–232; Tona J. Hangen, *Redeeming the Dial: Radio, Religion, and Popular Culture in America* (Chapel Hill NC: University of North Carolina Press, 2002); Brian Larkin, *Signal and Noise: Media, Infrastructure, and Urban Culture in Nigeria* (Durham NC: Duke University Press, 2008); Pamela E. Klassen, "Radio Mind: Protestant Experimentalists on the Frontiers of Healing," *Journal of the American Academy of Religion* 75/3 (2007): pp. 651–683; Dorothea Schulz, "Reconsidering Muslim Authority: Female 'Preachers' and the Ambiguity of Radio-Mediated Sermonizing in Mali," in *Radio Fields: Anthropology and Wireless Sound in the 21st Century*, ed. Lucas Bessire and Daniel Fisher (New York: New York University Press, 2012), pp. 108–123; Isaac Weiner, *Religion Out Loud: Religious Sound, Public Space, and American Pluralism* (New York, New York University Press, 2013).

I conceived the idea of placing my hand over the microphone while people put their hands on the radio cabinet and by these two actions forming a double point of contact. From the very beginning of the *Healing Waters Broadcast*, I have felt led to offer a healing prayer at the close of each Program. [...] At this time, people gather around their radios and place their hands on their radio cabinets while I place mine over the microphone as a point of contact in lieu of placing my hands upon them [...]. It has been amazing how many thousands of people have caught on to this idea and have turned their faith loose. Some very powerful miracles have been wrought through the broadcast and still even greater miracles are being wrought from week to week.[6]

Although Roberts claimed that the point of contact technique was divinely inspired when he fell into a deep trance-like state during his early ministry, it is interesting to consider earlier formations of this idea within the history of evangelical Christianity. The phrase *point of contact* became prominent within the context of late-nineteenth century debates about the proper pedagogical methods for primary and beginner classes within the Sunday school. This phrase entered the debates in religious pedagogy full-force with the 1896 publication *The Point of Contact in Teaching,* by the prominent advocate of progressive Sunday school education and editor of the *Sunday School Times*, Patterson Du Bois. Heavily influenced by the training methods of the Swiss educational reformer Johann Pestalozzi, Du Bois insisted that new methods of religious instruction in the Sunday school must begin with the immediate sensory experience of material objects that are "close at hand" for the child. Criticizing established catechistical memo techniques that required children to retain and recite abstract theological concepts far removed from the child's developmental plane of experience, Du Bois proposed *object lessons* that would mobilize things of everyday life as a point of contact between the immediate sensory experiences of the child and the pedagogical development of more abstract concepts. In the methodological section of his work entitled *"Applying the Principle,"* Du Bois recounts a story of how the point of contact was used to instruct a group of mischievous young boys who refused to pay attention to their Sunday school lesson on the Golden Rule. When it became painfully obvious to Du Bois, in his position of substitute teacher, that the usual methods of *scripture readings* or *ethical abstractions* would not quell the boisterous Sunday school mob, he mobilized the pedagogical strategy of the object lesson:

In less time than it takes place to tell it, I said to myself, 'Get your point of contact; address them through their senses; get on to the plane of their common activity.' I immediately drew an ivory foot-rule out of my pocket and asked what it was. Silence and attention were immediate. Some called it a 'ruler,' some a 'measure,' and one finally said it was a 'rule.' My next inquiry was to ascertain what it was made of. Some said ivory, some said bone. The class was in full control. It was easy then to lead them on to an imaginary rule, though keeping them in a certain suspense of meaning, until we had reached the Golden Rule. Questioning then drew from them the relative value of ivory and gold, and of rules made from them—real or figurative. It is unnecessary to follow this process in more detail, but the class was conquered, for that day at least, and their disgraceful hubbub was turned into an exemplary discussion of eternal truth. Golden

---

6   *Healing Waters Magazine* (June 1952): p. 15 (my italics).

texts, theological doctrines, ethical abstractions from the Catechism or the Epistles, taken in themselves, would have been hurled at these bright minds in vain; but the contact with a single tangible object such as a boy would use, or, at all events, enjoys handling, was the successful point of departure for his spiritual instruction.[7]

It is important to note that the point of contact, as elaborated by Du Bois, was not merely a method that thematized the *raw* empirical data experienced by the child. The point of contact and its associated object lessons were designed to *train* the sensory faculties through exercises in observation and manual work. Thus, in his introduction to another influential treatise on religious pedagogy, Milton Littlefield's *Handwork in the Sunday School* (1908), Du Bois emphasizes that the education of the child's developing sensory faculties and motor energies is best achieved through a manual pedagogical method known as handwork.

Describing the manual techniques of coloring with crayons, sewing with thread, caressing the contour lines of a relief map of biblical geography, or playing finger games, he states: "Give a boy a mode of Bible study which so *vivifies* the sacred page as to beget a love of it—as only manual methods can—and, in an otherwise Christian atmosphere, you have gone far toward making a Bible lover of him."[8] Prefiguring the insights of Marcel Mauss's famous lecture on body techniques, Du Bois quotes a missionary from the coast of Labrador saying: "There is only one way to reach the soul, and that is through the body."[9] As an educational method, the point of contact cannot be limited to a pedagogical exercise that highlighted certain empirical phenomena that had *given* themselves to immediate sense perception, but can be seen as a pious technique of the body that attuned the sense faculties and *vivified* the moral and spiritual character through a process of manual training.[10]

By the late teens of the twentieth century, the point of contact concept had become so ubiquitous within American Christian religious education that it was often mentioned as a key selling point in advertising catalogues issued by massive Sunday school printing factories such as the David C. Cook Publishing Company. Although I cannot go into more detail here, it might be a fruitful avenue of future research to consider how the pedagogical strategies of the point of contact and concomitant object lesson became closely articulated with the emergence of massive evangelical Christian Sunday school factories and their promotion of pious paraphernalia such as the Bible lesson picture card. With these earlier pedagogical resonances in mind, let us return to the point of contact within the context

---

[7]   Patterson Du Bois, *The Point of Contact in Teaching* (Philadelphia: J.D. Wattles & Co., 1896), p. 48.

[8]   Milton Littlefield, *Handwork in the Sunday School* (Philadelphia: The Sunday School Times Company, 1908), p. xii (introduction by Patterson Du Bois).

[9]   Ibid., p. xi.

[10] For Mauss's classic text on techniques of the body, see Marcel Mauss, "Techniques of the Body," in *Techniques, Technology and Civilization*, ed. Nathan Schlanger (New York: Durkheim Press, 2006), pp. 77–96.

of mass mediated rituals of faith healing, with an actual transcription of prayer from the *Healing Waters Broadcast*.[11]

Healing Waters Broadcast, March 15, 1953
[Translation Note: In an attempt to convey some of the sonic and poetic intensities that were sounded through Roberts' prayer, I have utilized the textual devices of italics and bold, capitalized words. The italics are meant to convey to the reader a moment when the sound of the enunciation is characterized by an importunate urgency of the voice, while the bold capitals signal the percussive, visceral enunciation of a word during crucial moments of the healing prayer.]

[23:33] And now comes that wonderful moment of prayer in the Healing Waters Broadcast when something like two million people this time each week gather around their radio cabinets for my healing prayer. You come too, unsaved man, unsaved woman. You sick people come. Some kneel, some raise their hands, *some touch their radio cabinets as a point of contact*. But I'm going to pray for God to save ya, for God to heal ya. Believe now. Just after they sing "Only Believe" I'm going to pray.

[24:07] song "Only Believe"
Only believe, only believe,
All things are possible, only believe.
Only believe, only believe,
All things are possible, only believe.

[24:32] Now Heavenly father, thousands and thousands of people are gathered around their radio cabinets for this healing prayer, for thy salvation, for thy healing, for thy deliverance. Grant me the miracle of their salvation. Grant me the miracle of their souls being transformed from sin, saved by thy power. And now father grant me the miracle of healing for the mortal bodies of every man, woman, and child who is looking to thee right now with faith in God. Here, father, is a man who's been sick for years, a woman who's been bedfast, a little child who is crippled and afflicted. Hear my prayer, and grant their healing in the name of Jesus. Thou foul tormenting sickness, thou foul affliction and disease, I come against you in the name of the savior. In the name of Jesus of Nazareth, not by my name, but by the name and power of the son of God. And I take authority over you in the name of Jesus; and I charge you loose them. LOOSE THEM! COME OUT! COME OUT in the name of Jesus of Nazareth! And now neighbor, be thou made whole.

---

[11]   I would like to thank Steve Weiss and the archival technicians of the Southern Folklife Collection on the campus of the University of North Carolina at Chapel Hill for their generous assistance in helping me to digitize several rare radio transcription discs of the *Healing Waters Broadcast*. These rare radio discs are now archived within the Southern Folklife Collection and are accessible to researchers.

Be thou made WHOLE! In the name of Jesus, be thou LOOSED from thy AFFLICTIONS! Rise and praise God and be made whole. Amen, and amen. Believe now with all your heart.

[26:02] song "Only Believe"
Only believe, only believe,
All things are possible, only believe.
Only believe, only believe,
All things are possible, only believe. (see Figure 13)

Since the beginning of the *Healing Waters Broadcast* in 1947, hundreds of thousands of letters have been sent to the Oral Roberts headquarters in Tulsa, Oklahoma, by listeners claiming to have been miraculously healed during the prayer time of the program. Many of these testimonies were reproduced in Roberts' popular *Healing Waters Magazine*, and were intended to help cultivate a sense of belief in the reading audience. Indeed, these mass circulated testimonies helped to reinforce and replicate this technical gesture of prayer. The following testimonies have been selected from the healing magazine and are representative of the general spirit of the curative narration and its relation to the radio as point of contact.

PLACES HAND ON RADIO AND HEARS AGAIN
Dear Brother Roberts,
During your healing campaign in Jacksonville I was listening to your radio program. As you prayed for the sick I laid my hand and head upon the radio, and was healed of deafness in my left ear, which I had not heard out of in thirty years. I do praise God for what he has done for me. You may use this testimony in any way that others might believe God still hears.
L.D. Lowery,
3019 Dillon St.,
Jacksonville, Fla.[12]

NAZARENE MINISTER HEALED THROUGH BROADCAST
Dear Brother Roberts:
For years I have been bothered with bad tonsils. I had been holding a revival near Mineral Wells, Texas and had developed a serious case of tonsillitis. I had been taking Sulfa drug but to no avail. My fever was high, pulse irregular and my throat was swelled so inside until I could hardly swallow.
I was driving home that night after services and was suffering considerably. Brother Roberts' program was coming over my car radio and when he asked those in radioland to lay their hand on the radio if they wanted healing, I did so. As he prayed, I

---

[12] *Healing Waters Magazine* 2/9 (August 1949): p. 9.

Fig. 13: Cartoon illustration of the Point of Contact from the widely-circulated treatise, If You Need Healing Do These Things.

prayed, and suddenly it seemed that something turned loose in my throat, and I swallowed and found the swelling was all gone. My temperature was normal and my pulse was regular. That has been nearly four years ago, and I have never had a sore throat since that time. Praise God for his healing power!

Rev. J. Royce Thomason

Nazarene Minister

Eldorado, Oklahoma.[13]

The Objectile *Dimension of Prayer*

In terms of the therapeutic efficacy organized through this technique of mass mediated healing prayer, it is interesting to note how the curative procedure is bracketed by what Mauss and Hubert termed a rite of entry and exit.[14] More specifically, at precisely the same moment that the ritual performance must be supplemented by a material apparatus (the point of contact), there is a repetitive disavowal of the very material conduit that allowed faith to be *turned loose*. In this instance of healing prayer, the point of contact is insulated by a repetitious insistence on belief itself: *Only Believe*. At the very heart of the curative technique, this performance of revelation and concealment discloses the *objectile* dimension of prayer. The objectile of Pentecostal prayer connotes an irreducible

---

[13]   *Healing Waters Magazine* (November 1952): p. 9.

[14]   Henri Hubert and Marcel Mauss, *Sacrifice: Its Nature and Function* (New York: Cohen & West, 1964).

materiality that is necessary for the appearance of faith, yet denied or disavowed during the ritual enactment of healing (hence the term objectile also resonates with the words projectile and abject). As the crucial performative and experiential dimension of prayer, the objectile can neither be attributed to a Pentecostal hypocrisy or anxiety in the face of *things of this world*, nor to an instrumental interpretation that describes the way credulous audience members are duped through the technological artifice of the healer. Instead of these typical explanations, the objectile of prayer suggests that the force or efficacy of the ritual hinges upon this simultaneous revelation and concealment of the material medium.[15] In other words, the objectile is not some anxious appendage or qualification to the performance of prayer, but intrinsic to the organization of ritual efficacy itself.

The concept of ritual efficacy is here limited to a description of the opening or organization of specific experiential frameworks in-and-through the performance of prayer. In this way, the efficacy of prayer emerges from its specific attunements of the senses. This organization of somatic experience, in turn, "heals" or enframes bodily experience, the classification of suffering, and the structures of everyday life in a profoundly different register. The proscriptions that characterize the objectile of prayer prepare the religious subject to experience the ritual environment—an environment that emerges, or is structured by material objects and media technologies—in a particularly compelling, perhaps even shocking, way. To deny or dismiss the very medium that is structuring an appearance of sacred presence amplifies the basic sensory experience of technological mediation with an even greater immediacy and actuality.[16] This is not simply a logic of oscillation between two poles, of explicit awareness of the material infrastructure of healing on the one hand, or forgetting on the other, but a doubled awareness, that, like the objectile itself, experiences an excessive presence through the material medium precisely because it is a reproduction.[17] In this ritual milieu, presence becomes doubled—simultaneously immediate and actual within the private space of the home or automobile, yet emerging from a displaced space *somewhere else*. The objectile of prayer thematizes this doubled

---

[15] This notion of revelation and concealment within the healing performance is inspired by Michael Taussig, "Viscerality, Faith and Skepticism: Another Theory of Magic," in *Magic and Modernity: Interfaces of Revelation and Concealment*, ed. Birgit Meyer and Peter Pels (Stanford CA: Stanford University Press, 2003), pp. 272–306.

[16] For some recent accounts of the relation between mediation and immediacy in the anthropology of media, see, among others, Patrick Eisenlohr, "Technologies of the Spirit: Devotional Islam, Sound Reproduction, and the Dialectics of Mediation and Immediacy in Mauritius," *Anthropological Theory* 9 (2009): pp. 273–296; and "What is a Medium: Theologies, Technologies and Aspirations," *Social Anthropology* 19 (2011). Birgit Meyer has written extensively on this question of the production of immediacy through a material process of mediation. For a useful introduction to her influential body of work, see for instance "Mediation and Immediacy: Sensational Forms, Semiotic Ideologies and the Question of the Medium," *Social Anthropology* 19 (2011): pp. 23–39.

[17] For more on the *doubled awareness* of radio audition and an analysis of media technology through the ancient divinatory art of physiognomy, see Theodor W. Adorno, *Current of Music: Elements of a Radio Theory* (Frankfurt am Main: Suhrkamp Verlag, 2006).

awareness of the material infrastructure, and through this ritual performance organizes new structures of awareness and embodiment.[18]

There is No Distance in Prayer

Intimately related to the theological-technical term *point of contact*, the healing campaigns of Oral Roberts also helped to solidify the phrase *there is no distance in prayer* within the vernacular language of global charismatic Christianity. Pentecostals often invoke the saying *there is no distance in prayer* to describe the collapsing of physical distance through the performance of prayer. Roberts popularized this phrase on a mass scale during the 1950s to explain the way that patients could be cured through his performances of healing prayer despite the fact that his actual physical presence remained unavailable to the dispersed magazine, radio, and television audience. On the one hand, this key descriptive phrase is based on the idea that *God is everywhere; therefore, there is no distance in prayer*. This overt theological claim, however, elides the specific circumstances of technological mediation from which this descriptive phrase emerged. Roberts' description of this concept within his widely-circulated healing magazine is revealing and worth quoting at length:

> A woman seriously ill in Norway heard my voice over Radio Luxembourg, the most powerful station in Europe. She couldn't understand a word of English. Two words stuck in her mind: my name, Oral Roberts. However, she later testified, that there was a power in my voice. Suddenly she sensed I was praying. She felt impelled to rush over to her radio and place her hands upon it. As my voice continued to utter prayer, she felt the surging of God's power enter her body, and in the flash of a second—she was healed! [...] I prayed in Tulsa, Oklahoma. This prayer was put on Radio Luxembourg in Europe. A woman in Norway, who couldn't understand a word I was saying, felt God's power in my voice and was instantly and completely healed. There is no distance in prayer. God was with me in Tulsa when I prayed, was in Luxembourg in Europe when the program was released, was in Norway with the woman who couldn't understand English. God is everywhere; therefore, there is no distance in prayer.[19]

As described by many practitioners of Pentecostal prayer, the negation of physical space between two distanced religious subjects and the concomitant unleashing of healing power is actuated by faith. During these performances of prayer, it is faith that bridges the distance between both the sacred and the everyday, and the patient and healer. This faith, in turn, requires a physical point of contact to enliven the efficacy of the prayer—what Roberts called *turning your faith loose*. Like the objectile of prayer previously described, this key component to the curative technique re-inscribes the material supplement in the selfsame moment it claims *no* distance in prayer. In other words, a forceful aspect of the

---

[18] For a fascinating account of another disavowed object in the Protestant practice of prayer, see the description of the "pebble-prayer" in Matthew Engelke, "Sticky Subjects and Sticky Objects: The Substance of African Christian Healing," in *Materiality*, ed. Daniel Miller (Durham NC: Duke University Press, 2005), pp. 118–139.

[19] *America's Healing Magazine* (January 1955): p. 2.

therapeutic rite is organized around an overt denial of the very material medium that allows for an experience of sacred presence to be sensed by the patient. To be sure, there is *no* distance in prayer; *yet* faith itself makes its appearance, or becomes sensible, through a structure of mediation that is contingent upon a material point of contact.

The ubiquitous phrase *there is no distance in prayer* is thus an implicit commentary on prayer and on the production of presence in an age of tele-technology. More specifically, Roberts employed this phrase to describe the millions of written testimonies that claimed to have experienced the *presence* of Roberts himself in their private domestic spaces through the mediation of radio, television, and magazine. As in the account of the Norwegian woman healed through radio prayer, this experience of ritual presence often reverberates before or beneath the circuitry of representation. Here the radio is not merely a passive medium for the transmission of a discrete religious message, but an apparatus of faith that enlivens the voice with a presence in excess of any stable semantic content. Even more than this, the machinations of the radio *loudspeaker* allow the religious subject to experience the vibrations of prayer entering through the hand and resounding throughout the body. In an age of mass mediated healing, the performative language of the evangelical faith-cure becomes inextricably bound up with the specific capacities enabled through media technologies such as the radio loudspeaker. As a crucial objectile in the technological history of prayer, the radio apparatus was interfaced with the healing performance and a new form of ritual efficacy was organized.

Conclusion: Prayer and the Apparatus of Belief

Like Christ in the *Book of Mark* putting his finger into the deaf man's ear and exclaiming "Be opened!," radio as point of contact marks a new aesthetic formation in the history of charismatic healing prayer.[20] The vibrating electromagnetic diaphragm of the radio loudspeaker allowed for a new experience of the *prayer of faith*, one that collapsed the gesture of manual imposition and the enunciation of prayer into a single sensation of tactility. With eyes closed and hand upon the apparatus, the patient could sense the prayer not as a meaningful articulation of words, but as a non-representational resonance that, like glossolalia, signaled that the body had been quickened by an ecstatic presence from elsewhere. The agency of the radio apparatus itself opened up or extended the senses, allowing the hand to become an organ of audition. This special effect produced through the transductions of the radio loudspeaker organized a new sensational form that interfaced classic prayer techniques from the evangelical Christian tradition of the *faith cure* and pedagogical methods in the Sunday school with the materiality of the radio apparatus.[21]

---

[20] *Bible*, King James Version: Mark 7.34.

[21] For a more in-depth account of Birgit Meyer's notion of the *sensational form*, see her "Religious Sensations: Why Media, Aesthetics and Power Matter in the Contemporary Study of Religion," http://www.fsw.vu.nl/nl/Images/Oratietekst%20Birgit%20Meyer_tcm30-36764.pdf (accessed 8 May, 2016), and Birgit Meyer, *Aesthetic Formations: Media, Religion, and the Senses* (New York: Palgrave, 2009). For an in-depth and useful analysis of the early history of the evangelical faith

In this way, the embodied practice of charismatic mediation was inextricably linked to the material agency of this specific medium of communication.

Within the context of charismatic healing prayer and its concomitant rituals of manual imposition (the laying on of hands), the transduction of sound through the mouth of the radio loudspeaker organized new performative and somatic possibilities. The transductions of the radio apparatus amplified the poetic inflections of Roberts' prayer—those crucial moments within the ritual form when the healer voices words with a visceral, almost violent intensity—arming words to strike the illness-causing demons within the patient with a percussive force. This is meant to work not merely on a metaphorical register, but through a reverberation of religious language that was *heard* through the palm of the listener like a hand placed upon the surface of a drum or the warm, fleshly contours of the throat. Sounding what might be called a healing poetics of percussion, the ritual of faith-cure was transduced through the radio apparatus.[22] Through this technical translation, the boisterously voiced words "COME OUT!," "LOOSE!" and "WHOLE!" struck the distanced patient with visceral, palpable force. Like so many instances within the history of charismatic Christianity, the belief organized through this interfacing of prayer with a technical apparatus reverberates within the body with a sonic presence in excess of the mere semantic content of the word—as do speaking in tongues, rhythmic liturgical schema that open upon an ecstatic soundscape of unintelligible cacophony, tambourines, the guttural grunts of the preacher that signal the poetic anointing of the Holy Ghost, clapping, etc. Through the transductions of an apparatus such as the radio, there are instances of religious language when the praying voice of the loudspeaker usurps the function of the manually imposed hand—literally touching, pressing, and palpating the patient with a haptic presence.

Older forms of materialized prayer within the Pentecostal tradition, such as the anointed handkerchief (prayer cloth), relied on exchanges of hand, postal economies, and physical movement to produce an experience of belief through a temporal articulation characterized by delay and deferral.[23] The special effect of the radio, however, shifted away from this logic of circulation, organizing a new tactile attunement through the mechanical reproduction of the organs of hearing and vocalization. Belief became structured through a new form of immediacy that maintained a parasitical dependence upon the technical capacities of the radio as a specific medium of communication. Here the term *communication* should also resound with connotations of flow and hapticity that are foregrounded in performances of religious language such as the prayer gesture of radio tactility. Oral Roberts constantly evoked this apparatus of belief thorough his popular charismatic phrase, "get a point of contact and *turn your faith loose!*"

---

cure, see Heather D. Curtis, *Faith in the Great Physician: Suffering and Divine Healing in American Culture, 1860-1900* (Baltimore: Johns Hopkins University Press, 2007).

[22] Rodney Needham, "Percussion and Transition," *Man* (New Series) 2 (1967).

[23] Michel de Certeau, "What We Do When We Believe," in *On Signs*, ed. Marshall Blonsky (Baltimore: Johns Hopkins University Press, 1985), pp. 192–202.

In conclusion, I would like to suggest how, as a concept, the apparatus of belief at once recalls earlier developments in the history of anthropology, while also gesturing toward a new direction in the study of prayer.[24] Following the work of Mauss and Hubert on magic, the efficacy of the healing technique often subsists upon a "moment of prestidigitation" wherein the artifice of the healer actuates a transformation in the patient.[25] The radio as a point of contact and other modes of mass-mediated healing prayer can be seen as just such artificial moments, when the patient's experience of illness and pain is re-organized through a therapeutic technique that tricks or outbids the established sensory regimes. Healing prayer and the laying on of hands in an age of mass media subsist upon an aesthetic of shock or sensory-disjuncture that enframes suffering in a new experiential register. And like Christ putting his finger in the ear of the deaf-mute, the technique of healing prayer must performatively numb one sense so that others may be opened anew.

In our contemporary time, new religious movements continue to proliferate through media channels, while millions of charismatic Christians around the globe practice the point of contact in expectation of the mass miracle. As the practice turn in media studies attends to these new communities of belief and religious experience, it must account for not only what people are doing in relation to media, but what media does to people. This is not merely a return to a deterministic model, but an attempt to describe the specific ways in which the media is itself imbricated in the appearance of a culturally specific experiential boundary *from the crowns of their heads to the soles of their feet.*

---

[24] Sections of this paper were presented at the Capstone conference of the Social Science Research Council's New Directions in the Study of Prayer (NDSP) research initiative (February 6-7, 2015; Italian Academy, Columbia University). I am grateful to the Social Science Research Council and the NDSP for funding a two-year research project that explored the *Materiality of Prayer* in the Pentecostal tradition. More contemporary ethnographic descriptions of the radio as point of contact within the context of American Pentecostalism can be found in Anderson Blanton, *Hittin' the Prayer Bones: Materiality of Spirit in the Pentecostal South,* Series in American Religion (Chapel Hill NC: University of North Carolina Press, 2015).

[25] Henri Hubert and Marcel Mauss, *A General Theory of Magic* (New York: Cohen & West, 1964).

Anthony Enns

Auditory Revelations: Spiritualism, Technology, and Sound

Since the early twentieth century, the study of religion has largely been divided into two approaches. The first approach is perhaps best exemplified by the work of French sociologist Émile Durkheim, who conceived of religion as a set of beliefs and practices that produce a communal bond between the participants.[1] The second approach is most prominently represented by the work of American psychologist William James, who was more concerned with the varieties of individual religious experience, which serve "a permanent function" in the present regardless as to whether they are "true or false."[2] While the former approach has dominated the field for many years, scholars are now becoming more interested in the religious significance of unusual experiences, such as hallucinations, trance states, occult manifestations, and psychic phenomena. While these experiences do not necessarily constitute a religion in the traditional sense, historians like Thomas Laqueur argue that they should still be understood as religious:

> The occult generally, and the esoteric in particular, [...] need to be understood not just as a response to social and cultural dislocation or to the making of modern subjectivity but to the desire to have a relationship with the divine even if it is not one mediated through the institutions of a church [...]. It self-consciously appropriates some of the language of the modern world to address the thinly veiled, pre-modern—perhaps timeless—anxieties that are at the heart of religion: what is death? Does the universe have meaning?[3]

Ann Taves similarly emphasizes the value of studying *special, unusual,* or *anomalous* experiences, which are not part of any religious system but still "provide the fundamental raw material that people use to construct 'religions.'"[4] Jeffrey Kripal correspondingly describes psychic phenomena as encounters with the sacred, and he argues that the exist-

---

[1]   Émile Durkheim, *The Elementary Forms of Religious Life*, trans. Joseph Ward Swain (London: George Allen & Unwin, 1915), p. 47.

[2]   William James, *The Varieties of Religious Experience* (London: Longmans, Green & Co., 1903), p. 507.

[3]   Thomas Laqueur, "Why the Margins Matter: Occultism and the Making of Modernity," *Modern Intellectual History* 3/1 (April 2006): pp. 111–135, here p. 131.

[4]   Ann Taves, *Religious Experience Reconsidered: A Building-Block Approach to the Study of Religion and Other Special Things* (Princeton: Princeton University Press, 2009), p. 26.

ing methodologies in the study of religion, inspired by Karl Marx and Michel Foucault, are not sufficient to explain them.[5] Like Taves, Kripal also urges scholars not simply to dismiss such phenomena as fraudulent, but rather to see them as highly individualized encounters with the divine. The study of paranormal phenomena thus represents an attempt to acknowledge the significance of individual religious experiences and to reconcile these experiences with the idea of religion as a social formation. While these experiences often produce a communal bond between the participants, they are not necessarily related to any particular religious doctrine.

In recent years, historians have also recognized that religion and technology are becoming increasingly difficult to separate. In his introduction to the recent anthology *Deus in Machina: Religion, Technology, and the Things in Between*, for example, Jeremy Stolow outlines the recent *media turn* in the study of religion, which examines "the many ways religious practice and imagination are inextricably bound up with the materialities of media and the labor of mediation—not just textual or iconographic systems of representation, but also a much broader terrain of sensorial techniques, tools, material artifacts, and systems of coordinated action."[6] Stolow notes that historians of technology have also "placed a new premium on technology's sacral and/or magical dimensions," as "modern technologies have […] come to be understood as possessing transcendent or uncanny features, the encounter with which is phenomenologically comparable with the performative techniques of prayer, ritual action, or magic, or with the 'religious' experiences of ecstasy and awe."[7] The parallels between religion and technology thus appear to be at least partly inspired by the recent trend toward the study of paranormal phenomena, as Stolow suggests that the effects of technological mediation are comparable to special, unusual, or anomalous religious experiences.

One of Stolow's primary examples, which will also be the subject of this paper, is the rise of Modern Spiritualism—a nineteenth-century religious movement that was based on a belief in the possibility of technological communication with the dead. Some historians describe this movement as an attempt to preserve a traditional, spiritually-based sense of community in the face of unsettling social conditions, such as the sudden influx of immigrants and the accelerating rate of industrialization,[8] while others argue that it reflects a growing dissatisfaction with Christianity and a decline in the authority of the church.[9]

---

[5]   Jeffrey J. Kripal, *Authors of the Impossible: The Paranormal and the Sacred* (Chicago: University of Chicago Press, 2010), p. 254.

[6]   Jeremy Stolow, "Introduction," *Deus in Machina: Religion, Technology, and the Things in Between*, ed. Jeremy Stolow (New York: Fordham University Press, 2012), pp. 1–24, here p. 4.

[7]   Ibid., p. 5.

[8]   See for example Geoffrey K. Nelson, *Spiritualism and Society* (New York: Schocken Books, 1969) and Werner Sollors, "Dr. Benjamin Franklin's Celestial Telegraph, or Indian Blessings to Gas-Lit American Drawing Rooms," *American Quarterly* 35/5 (1983): pp. 459–480.

[9]   See for example R. Laurence Moore, "Spiritualism and Science: Reflections on the First Decade of the Spirit Rappings," *American Quarterly* 24/4 (October 1972): pp. 474–500; Janet Oppenheim, *The Other World: Spiritualism and Psychical Research in England, 1850-1914* (Cambridge: Cambridge

Richard Noakes argues, for example, that Spiritualists "embraced late-nineteenth century machine cultures," as "they saw technology as a symbol of social progress."[10] Steven Connor similarly notes that Spiritualists employed modern scientific methods and that "the séance was seen […] as a kind of laboratory for the investigation of the spirit world."[11] Erhard Schüttpelz even describes Spiritualism as part of the prehistory of modern media theory.[12] Historians thus disagree as to whether Spiritualism represented an attempt to resist or embrace the forces of modernity, as there is ample evidence to support either of these interpretations. On the one hand, Spiritualist practices clearly reflected a desire to experience the sacred, and it would therefore be wrong to conclude that Spiritualists simply accepted scientific materialism. In a practical manual on Spiritualist séances, for example, Hudson Tuttle emphasized the religious nature of these events: "The members of the circle should […] feel the sacredness of the hour, the place and the purpose. I use the word sacred with full thoughtfulness of its meaning, for what can be more sacred than the presence of the so-called dead?"[13] On the other hand, however, Spiritualists did not attempt to formulate any unified doctrine,[14] and their beliefs were strictly dependent on material evidence and verifiable tests. These contradictions were also apparent at the time, as critics often warned that the Spiritualists' attempts to procure scientific and technological explanations for spirit manifestations would ultimately bankrupt their religious values.[15]

Contemporary interpretations of Spiritualism thus remain somewhat limited, as they tend to privilege one of these aspects over the other, and this limitation is a result of their dependence on sociological explanations, which typically ignore the significance of individual religious experiences. Theodore Schatzki argues, however, that a practice-based

---

University Press, 1985); Logie Barrow, *Independent Spirits: Spiritualism and English Plebeians, 1850-1910* (London: Routledge, 1986); Alex Owen, *The Darkened Room: Women, Power and Spiritualism in late Victorian England* (London: Virago Press, 1989); and Jose Harris, *Private Lives, Public Spirits: A Social History of Britain 1870-1914* (Oxford: Oxford University Press, 1993).

10 Richard Noakes, "'Instruments to Lay Hold of Spirits': Technologizing the Bodies of Victorian Spiritualism," in *Bodies/Machines*, ed. Iwan Rhys Morus (London: Berg, 2002), pp. 125–164, here p. 126.

11 Steven Connor, "Voice, Technology and the Victorian Ear," in *Transactions and Encounters: Science and Culture in the Nineteenth Century*, ed. Roger Luckhurst and Josephine McDonagh (Manchester: Manchester University Press, 2002), pp. 16–29, here p. 23.

12 Erhard Schüttpelz, "Trance Mediums and New Media: The Heritage of a European Term," in *Trance Mediums and New Media: Spirit Possession in the Age of Technical Reproduction*, ed. Heike Behrend, Anja Dreschke, and Martin Zillinger (New York: Fordham University Press, 2014), pp. 56–76, here p. 66.

13 Hudson Tuttle, *Mediumship and Its Laws: Its Conditions and Cultivation* (Chicago: Progressive Thinker, 1900), p. 114.

14 Spiritualism clearly would not be considered a religion according to Durkheim's definition, despite the fact that its tremendous popularity inspired Theodore Parker to predict that it would eventually become "the religion of America." John Weiss, ed., *Life and Correspondence of Theodore Parker* 1 (London: Longmans, Green & Co., 1863), p. 428.

15 For example, American psychologist George Beard warned that "a religion proved, dies as a religion, and becomes a scientific fact." George Beard, "The Psychology of Spiritism," *North American Review* 129 (July 1879): pp. 65–80, here p. 65.

approach is more useful for understanding such experiences, as it is able to negotiate seemingly contradictory ideas by "abandoning the traditional conception of reason as an innate mental faculty and reconceptualizing it as a practice phenomenon."[16] In this sense, a practice can refer to a wide array of actions that are linked by shared understandings, emotions, goals, and beliefs, yet these rules or discourses are not necessarily prescriptive; rather, rules and discourses can also be understood as being anchored in the practices themselves—that is, in the experiences of individual practitioners.[17] An analysis of Spiritualist practices would thus focus on the actions performed during séances and how these actions were understood by the participants (that is, the emotions, goals, and beliefs that informed their understanding of their own and each other's actions). The following paper will employ such an approach by examining not only the truth claims of Spiritualists, but also the significance of their practices as media rituals—that is, as religious rituals that incorporate the use of media technologies.[18] An analysis of Spiritualist practices as media rituals helps to overcome the limitations of earlier sociological theories by addressing both the intentions as well as the effects of their actions, and it will particularly focus on the following three aspects:

1. Spiritualism encouraged the formation of micro-communities that were united by a common belief in the survival of human personality after death. This belief not only allowed them to formulate a comparative approach to the study of religion (as survival theory was considered to be the common foundation of all world religions), but it was also seen as deeply democratic by encompassing differences in opinions between individual believers. These common understandings could also be adjusted and modified depending on the immediate context of an individual's experience.[19]

2. The Spiritualists' challenge to religious authority was fundamentally rooted in a medial shift, as their practices were indelibly linked to the development of new media technologies that threatened both the dominance of traditional religious institutions as well as the cultural centrality of print.

---

[16]   Theodore R. Schatzki, "Introduction: Practice Theory," in *The Practice Turn in Contemporary Theory*, ed. Theodore R. Schatzki et al. (London: Routledge, 2001), pp. 1–14, here p. 14.

[17]   Theodore R. Schatzki, "Practice Mind-ed Orders," in Schatzki et al., eds., *The Practice Turn in Contemporary Theory*, pp. 60–61.

[18]   While the study of media rituals tends to focus on mediated rituals (such as televangelism) and media pilgrimages (such as encounters with celebrities or visits to media locations), Ronald Grimes points out that media not only "contain" or "mediate" ritual but that ritual may 'contain' media and media devices." Ronald L. Grimes, "Ritual and the Media," in *Practicing Religion in the Age of the Media: Explorations in Media, Religion and Culture*, ed. Stewart Hoover and Lynn Schofield Clark (New York: Columbia University Press, 2002), pp. 219–234, here p. 222.

[19]   The Spiritualist movement thus exemplifies what Leigh Eric Schmidt refers to as the "modern privatization and fragmentation of religious authority."

3. By incorporating new media technologies into their religious rituals and endowing them with a profoundly spiritual significance, Spiritualist practices effectively blurred the boundaries between tradition and modernity or between the sacred and the secular.

A practice-based approach thus reconciles the two opposing views of Spiritualism by revealing how this movement was an attempt to integrate religious and scientific world-views. In other words, Spiritualist practices were neither anti-modern nor modern, but rather something in-between, as they satisfied the desire for religious experiences while at the same time grounding these experiences in a materialist understanding of nature. In Stolow's words, "Spiritualism cannot readily be contained within the tidy binarisms of religious/secular, modern/primitive, erudite/popular, or scientific/magical."[20]

The Spiritualists' use of sound is particularly significant in this context, as the distinction between writing and speech was deeply intertwined with religious ideas and practices. While religious doctrines were largely dependent on written texts for their preservation and dissemination, religious rituals were more often tied to oral performances that made the written word come alive. This idea can be traced back to Plato's *Phaedrus*, in which speech was described as the "living word of knowledge which has a soul."[21] Aristotle similarly argued that writing cannot be equated with speech because a voice is produced through the agency of a soul, which "animates the vocal organs."[22] In the late twentieth century a number of scholars attempted to expand this philosophical distinction between writing and speech into a broader distinction between literacy and orality.[23] The foremost theorist in this field was Walter J. Ong, a Jesuit priest who identified four key qualities of speech based on the unique characteristics of sound:

1. Sound is evanescent, so speech is grounded in the experience of the immediate present.
2. Sound is dependent on resonant bodies, so speech represents the manifestation of an interior.
3. Sound is immersive, so speech allows people to share and inhabit each other's interiorities.

---

20 Jeremy Stolow, "Salvation by Electricity," in *Religion: Beyond a Concept*, ed. Hent de Vries (New York: Fordham University Press, 2008), pp. 668–686, here p. 673.
21 Plato, "Phaedrus," *The Dialogues of Plato*, Vol. 1, trans. Benjamin Jowett (Oxford: Clarendon Press, 1892), p. 485.
22 Aristotle, *De Anima*, trans. R. D. Hicks (Cambridge: Cambridge University Press), p. 89.
23 See Albert B. Lord, *The Singer of Tales* (Cambridge MA: Harvard University Press, 1960); Eric A. Havelock, *Preface to Plato* (Cambridge MA: Harvard University Press, 1963); Marshall McLuhan, *Understanding Media: The Extensions of Man* (New York: McGraw-Hill, 1964); and Adam Parry, ed., *The Making of Homeric Verse: The Collected Papers of Milman Parry* (Oxford: Clarendon Press, 1971).

4. Sound is social, as speech signals involvement and participation in the present and the act of listening serves to unite sounds and to move towards harmony.[24]

Like Plato, therefore, Ong described speech as the "vehicle of the living word," which was essential for the formation of community.

Ong also claimed that the rise of new sound technologies, like the phonograph and the tape recorder, produced a "renewed orality," as they resonorized and reanimated language: "Voice, muted by script and print, has come newly alive."[25] This argument was based on the *liveness* of the electronic voice, which seemed to convey a genuine sense of presence and participation:

> The sense of presence and of participation results […] from the ability of electronic media to deal with verbalization as sound. Sound, bound to the present time by the fact that it exists only at the instant when it is going out of existence, advertises presentness. It heightens presence in the sense of the existential relationship of person to person (I am in your presence; you are present to me), with which our concept of present time (as against past and future) connects: present time is related to us as is a person whose presence we experience. It is "here." It envelops us. Even the voice of one dead, played from a recording, envelops us with his presence as no picture can.[26]

In other words, Ong claimed that sound technologies are capable of recuperating the sense of presence that is lost in writing, and this theory was largely derived from his religious beliefs. As a practicing priest, Ong found "the question of the sensorium in the Christian economy of revelation […] particularly fascinating because of the primacy which this economy accords to the word of God and thus in some mysterious way to sound itself."[27] Ong's primary goal was thus to understand how the shift from orality to literacy resulted in the silencing of God and how the rise of new sound technologies could potentially inspire a revival of religious experience.

Ong's equation of voice and presence has often been subject to criticism,[28] yet I would argue that his theologically-informed distinction between literacy and orality remains relevant to the study of Spiritualist sound practices, as it provides a particularly apt description of the religious significance of the disembodied voices that manifested during séances. Ong's claim that electronic voices are capable of conveying a sense of presence also provides a useful description of the Spiritualists' hopes for new sound technologies, which they saw as spiritual devices that could effectively resonorize and reanimate the

---

24 Walter J. Ong, *The Presence of the Word: Some Prolegomena for Cultural and Religious History* (New Haven: Yale University Press, 1967), pp. 111–138.

25 Ibid., p. 88.

26 Ibid., p. 101.

27 Ibid., p. 12.

28 See Jacques Derrida, "The Voice That Keeps Silence," in *Speech and Phenomena*, trans. David Allison (Evanston IL: Northwestern University Press, 1973), pp. 70–87; Schmidt, *Hearing Things*, pp. 1–22; Jonathan Sterne, "The Theology of Sound: A Critique of Orality," *Canadian Journal of Communication* 36 (2011): pp. 207–225.

dead. As this paper will demonstrate, Spiritualist sound practices not only illustrate their shared belief in the equation of voice and presence, but also reveal how this equation of voice and presence was part of the experience of listening to technologically mediated voices, which explains why Spiritualists conceived of their practices as emulating the effects of new sound technologies. In other words, the history of Spiritualist sound practices represents the development of an *electrical theology of sound*, which was based on their belief in the voice as a marker of presence as well as their belief that sound technologies could potentially reactivate this sense of presence by facilitating a form of mediated immediacy.

In order to understand the significance of Spiritualist sound practices as media rituals, it is important to consider the historical context in which they first emerged. Spiritualist sound practices were largely inspired by those of earlier religious movements, such as Swedenborgianism—a movement that was based on the writings of Swedish theologian Emanuel Swedenborg, who claimed to have heard messages spoken by spirits and angels. In his major work, *Arcana Coelestia* (1749-1756), Swedenborg explained that these auditory revelations were common during biblical times, but they gradually disappeared due to a loss of faith:

> It is known from the Word of the Lord that many persons formerly spoke with spirits and angels [...] but that afterwards heaven was as it were shut, insomuch that at the present day the existence of spirits and angels is scarcely credited, and still less that any one can speak with them; for men regard it as impossible to speak with the unseen, and with those whose existence they in their hearts deny.[29]

Swedenborg thus claimed that his auditory revelations represented a modern resurgence of divine miracles, which signaled the birth of a new spiritual revival. He also explained the mechanics of spirit communication as follows: "Their speech [...] fell into my interior speech, and thence into the corresponding organs. [...] Hence their speech was heard by me as sonorously as the speech of man."[30] In other words, he believed that spirits did not produce sonic vibrations in the atmosphere, but rather communicated through a form of internal thought transference. Nevertheless, their voices were still perceived by the auditory nerve as sound, so the only essential difference between spirit communication and terrestrial communication was that the perception of spirit voices was restricted to an exclusive group of believers who had been chosen by God.[31]

Although these claims were regarded with skepticism by the religious establishment, auditory revelations became increasingly popular during the nineteenth century. American

---

[29]   Emanuel Swedenborg, *Arcana Coelestia: The Heavenly Arcana Contained in the Holy Scripture or Word of the Lord Unfolded Beginning with the Book of Genesis Together with Wonderful Things Seen in the World of Spirits and in the Heaven of Angels*, Vol. 2, trans. John Faulkner Potts (New York: Swedenborg Foundation, 1938), p. 264.

[30]   Ibid., Vol. 6, p. 332.

[31]   Ibid.

biblical scholar George Bush described Swedenborg's work as "an exposé of the law of spiritual acoustics," which proves that "all of sensation […] which man enjoys here he enjoys also in the other world, only in a more exquisite degree."[32] Swedenborg's ideas were also embraced by American Spiritualist Andrew Jackson Davis, who developed his own form of *psychophonetics*, which he defined as the ability to hear "soul-sounds" that are "inaudible to the physical ear."[33] Like Swedenborg's "spiritual acoustics," therefore, Davis' *psychophonetics* also represented a form of heightened perception that allowed a select few to experience auditory revelations from the spirit world. Schmidt also notes that these practices were seen by the religious establishment as a potential threat and that they were widely dismissed using the language of "hallucination, credulity, sympathetic imitation, and fanaticism."[34]

The practice of *spiritual acoustics* and *psychophonetics* set the stage for the emergence of Modern Spiritualism. The origin of this movement is often identified as the famous *Hydesville rappings*, which took place in a small town near Rochester, New York, in 1848. This was the first public occasion when Margaret and Kate Fox allegedly channeled spirits, who answered questions using *rapping* or *knocking* sounds to indicate affirmative and negative responses—a practice that was clearly inspired by the invention of the electrical telegraph.[35] Over time, the spirits gradually relinquished the need for telegraphic codes and began to speak directly to the séance participants. Unlike Swedenborg's *spiritual acoustics* and Davis' *psychophonetics*, however, the acoustic manifestations that occurred during séances were understood as real vibrations in the atmosphere, and they were believed to be authentic because they were understood as emanating from the invisible yet material bodies of the spirits themselves. For example, British Spiritualist Florence Marryat claimed that spirits were capable of materializing their own vocal organs, as they "speak to you with a thorax and gullet of their own."[36] British Spiritualist J. Arthur Findlay provided a vivid description of such a materialization in his account of a séance with the Scottish direct voice medium John Sloan:

> [The spirit] forms a rough mask in the likeness of a mouth, throat, larynx, lungs, etc. This, when
> finished, is placed in the most suitable part of the room, often in the centre of the circle. The spirit
> wishing to speak then presses into this mask, slow in vibration, and with it clothes or covers his

---

[32] George Bush, *Mesmer and Swedenborg; or, the Relation of the Developments of Mesmerism to the Doctrines and Disclosures of Swedenborg* (New York: John Allen, 1847), p. 143.

[33] Andrew Jackson Davis, *Views of Our Heavenly Home* (Boston MA: Colby and Rich, 1878), pp. 15–16.

[34] Schmidt, *Hearing Things*, p. 233.

[35] See for example Friedrich Kittler, *Gramophone Film Typewriter*, trans. Geoffrey Winthrop-Young and Michael Wutz (Stanford CA: Stanford University Press, 1999), p. 12; John Durham Peters, *Speaking into the Air: A History of the Idea of Communication* (Chicago: University of Chicago Press, 2000), p. 94; Jeffrey Sconce, *Haunted Media: Electronic Presence from Telegraphy to Television* (Durham NC: Duke University Press, 2000), p. 12; and Barbara Weisberg, *Talking to the Dead: Kate and Maggie Fox and the Rise of Spiritualism* (New York: Harper Collins, 2004), p. 102.

[36] Florence Marryat, *The Spirit World* (London: F. W. White, 1894), p. 138.

own vocal organs, and absorbs this substance into his own organs of speech. These organs then take on a thicker or heavier condition, the tongue requires more exertion to move, but with a little practice it all becomes possible.[37]

This ectoplasmic mask appears to resemble a kind of spiritual automaton that recalls Wolfgang von Kempelen's *Speaking Machine* and Joseph Faber's *Euphonia*. Unlike these machines, however, spirit voices were understood as autonomous, living entities.[38] According to American Spiritualist Edward C. Randall, who published several books on his séances with the American direct voice medium Emily French, spirits often claimed that there was no difference between the physical presence of the sitters and the acoustic presence of the spirits: "I am for the moment really an inhabitant of your world [...]. In the conditions prevailing at this moment, there is no line of demarcation between the so-called two worlds; we are both in the same room [...] and each hears the other's words."[39]
The "direct voice" was thus understood as a tangible, physical, and embodied presence that could be perceived by anyone in the immediate vicinity of the phenomenon.[40]
These acoustic manifestations were also seen as reliable because of the content of the messages received, which reportedly provided proof of the genuine identity of the spirits. For example, the American direct voice medium Maina Tafe argued that "*it is what the voice says* and the little peculiarities of character that manifest which comprise the all-important factor in the Direct Voice séance."[41] Some participants also claimed that even if the spirit voices were produced through the use of ventriloquism they would still be impressed by the content of what was said, as the voices relayed information that would not have been available to the medium herself. For example, American Spiritualist Florizel von Reuter argued that a fraudulent direct voice medium "would not only have to be a ventriloquist, but also a phenomenal mind-reader, capable of digging information out of the subconsciousness of all present."[42] Other participants claimed that it was the presence

---

[37] J. Arthur Findlay, *An Investigation into Psychic Phenomena: A Record of a Series of Sittings with Mr. John C. Sloan, the Glasgow Trance and Direct Voice Medium* (Glasgow: Society for Psychical Research, 1924), p. 36.

[38] The idea that spirits spoke through ectoplasmic masks was also used to explain why their voices tended to sound different than they did while they were alive. See for example Maina L. Tafe, "Conversing in Different Tongues," *The Direct-Voice: A Magazine Devoted to the Direct Voice and Other Phases of Psychic Phenomena* 1/5 (September 1930): pp. 152–153, here p. 153.

[39] Edward C. Randall, *The Dead Have Never Died* (New York: Knopf, 1917), p. 67.

[40] Steven Connor also argues that the ectoplasmic larynx represents "a phantasmal displacement and intensification" of the "process of impressing speech into wax." This argument is compelling, yet spiritualists more often conceived of spirit voices as markers of physical presence rather than indexical recordings or traces of sonic events. Steven Connor, *Dumbstruck: A Cultural History of Ventriloquism* (Oxford: Oxford University Press, 2000), p. 385.

[41] Tafe, "Conversing in Different Tongues," p. 153.

[42] Florizel von Reuter, "Mediums I Have Known and Experimented With," *The Direct-Voice: A Magazine Devoted to the Direct Voice and Other Phases of Psychic Phenomena* 1/3 (July 1930): pp. 71–74, here p. 73.

of the voice that provided the most convincing proof of the phenomenon, regardless of the content of the messages conveyed. In his account of a séance with the American direct voice medium Mina "Margery" Crandon, for example, American Spiritualist J. Malcolm Bird reported that he was

> wholly satisfied of the genuineness of this voice, as an independent phenomenon in space, outside the physical organism of the psychic. [...] I give no hypothesis whatever as to the *modus faciendi* of these sounds; I am discussing only the question of their genuine occurrence. That the two tests of which I quote the record actually present examples of genuine independent voice, produced in space and without the agency of any human vocal apparatus and without any other tangible physical agency, I am obliged to believe. They were produced by nobody properly present; nobody was improperly present; and oblique suggestions like wireless and speaking tubes and phonographs are inapplicable.[43]

According to Bird, therefore, the presence of the voices was far more significant than any information they might convey. Some Spiritualists also noted that the voices rarely provided any information at all, other than confirming their identity and reassuring their loved ones that they still loved them. After conveying this message there was often little else to say, and some spirits reportedly passed the time humming tunes requested by the sitters.[44]

Belief in the reliability of Spiritualist sound practices continued to increase as the importance of the role played by spiritual mediums decreased. While mediums were initially conceived as conduits or channels that facilitated communication with the dead, spirit voices were gradually seen as independent, as they were often heard in different parts of the room or the house.[45] The voices also tended to be mobile, although the mediums always remained fixed in particular locations (often inside cabinets). Mediums were also expected to remain silent in order to show that the voices were not produced through the use of ventriloquism. At a sitting with Crandon in 1924, for example, a spirit voice was reportedly heard by all of the sitters while one of the participants kept his hand tightly clasped over the medium's mouth and every other sitter's mouth was covered by the hand of a neighbor.[46] When preparing to channel the voice of Walter (her deceased brother and spirit control), Crandon also agreed to be hooked up to a *Voice Control Machine* that forced her to hold her mouth over a nipple that kept afloat in a U-shaped tube filled with water at a constant level. Witnesses confirmed that "under these conditions (the water remaining at a constant level in the U-tube), whisperings, voices, and whistling were heard as distinctly as before."[47] Unlike earlier Spiritualist practices, spirit voices could also manifest in broad

---

[43]   J. Malcolm Bird, *'Margery' the Medium* (Boston MA: Small, Maynard & Co., 1925), pp. 299–302.

[44]   See von Reuter, "Mediums I Have Known and Experimented With," p. 75.

[45]   Some spiritualists even referred to these manifestations as "independent voice phenomena." See Hereward Carrington, *The Story of Psychic Science* (London: Rider, 1930), pp. 151–154.

[46]   Bird, *'Margery' the Medium*, pp. 299–302.

[47]   Carrington, *The Story of Psychic Science*, pp. 153–154.

daylight, when it was possible to see that the medium's throat muscles were not moving. The voices were thus seen as independent of the actions of the medium, and ensuring the silence of the medium helped to make such phenomena seem more reliable. As British Spiritualist W. Usborne Moore argued in his account of the American direct voice medium Etta Wriedt: "The direct voice is the highest spiritistic phenomenon yet discovered [...] because the possibility of fraud is removed one stage further off than it is in any other phase of manifestation; and, in the case of the independent voice [...] it is entirely eliminated."[48] In other words, Spiritualist sound practices were seen as more reliable than other forms of spirit communication because they allegedly facilitated direct, unmediated access to the spirit world, which effectively decentered the authority of the medium.

Steven Connor also argues that Spiritualist sound practices were "undoubtedly encouraged by the development of acoustic technologies," which seemed to offer "explanations for the new manifestations."[49] Indeed, spiritual mediums were often described as technical devices that conveyed acoustic information without any conscious mediation. For example, Randall described direct voice mediums as "instruments by the aid of which communication is established between the two worlds,"[50] and some direct voice mediums, like Richard Zenor, were described as "telephones" capable of facilitating "direct communication between worlds."[51] Moore similarly described Etta Wriedt as "a machine through which spirit people found they could carry conviction of their presence,"[52] and sitters even compared the voices produced during her séances to the voices heard over the telephone, as seen in Edith Harper's description of the voice of William T. Stead following his death aboard the Titanic in 1912: "His voice sounded much as it did when he spoke in a great hurry through a long-distance telephone, as I have heard it so often, when, for instance, he telephoned to his office in Mowbray House, Norfolk Street, Strand, from Hayling Island, seventy miles away."[53] British Spiritualist James Coates also referred to Wriedt as a "psychophone" because "the manifestations in Mrs. Wriedt's presence are analogous to telephonic messages."[54] The experience of listening to distant voices had clearly become commonplace due to the invention of the telephone, yet it would be wrong to conclude that the practice of channeling spirit voices was simply inspired by the development of new sound technologies. As Coates himself pointed out, such practices actually prefigured the rise of telephony: "In these days of scientific discovery great advances have been made, and the Intelligences in the Invisible are evidently keeping up to date. In advance, indeed, for long before telephonic communication was deemed possible on earth, voice phenomenon [sic] was reported in séance-rooms."[55] Coates also recognized that this

---

48   W. Usborne Moore, *The Voices* (London: Watts & Co., 1913), pp. 422–423.
49   Connor, *Dumbstruck*, pp. 365–366.
50   Randall, *The Dead Have Never Died*, p. vii.
51   James Crenshaw, *Telephone Between Worlds* (Los Angeles: De Vorss & Co., 1950), p. 2.
52   Moore, *The Voices*, p. 174.
53   Ibid., p. 334.
54   Ibid., p. 372.
55   Ibid., p. 373.

practice exceeded the capabilities of the telephone, as it was primarily understood as a broadcast technology: "As a rule, a telephone message is only heard by the user; but not so with the psychophonic messages. They are not only heard by the person most interested, but are heard by all privileged to be present."[56] This explains why some mediums, like Tafe, preferred to use the radio as a metaphor to describe direct voice phenomena.[57]

Not only were direct voice mediums compared to new sound technologies, but Spiritualists also developed their own technical devices that could be used to channel spirit voices in the absence of a medium. For example, the practice of *trumpet manifestations* involved the use of megaphonic instruments to amplify the voices of spirits, thus enabling the automation of direct voice phenomena. As Connor points out, "the spiritualist use of the trumpet was probably first suggested by the use of speaking trumpets for the deaf […] rather than by the characteristic amplifying horn of the phonograph," but "the technique of making spiritual voices audible comes increasingly to cohere with the technological means of amplification."[58] Spiritualist trumpets not only resembled phonograph horns, but they were also understood as an electrical form of sound amplification. One of the most famous direct voice mediums, Mrs. Cecil M. Cook, not only marketed her own brand of aluminum trumpets, which supposedly allowed people to converse with spirits in the privacy of their own homes, but also claimed that "the voices seem to come clearer when the trumpets are moist" because "there is something about the forces that resembles electrical energy."[59] W. W. Aber's *Guide to Mediumship* provides similar instructions for producing trumpet manifestations without a medium: "Use a tin or aluminum trumpet, about three feet in length, six inches in diameter at the large end and about one-half inch in diameter at the small end. Place the trumpet in a basin of water in the center of the floor; form a circle around it. […] You may sit many times […] but after [the spirits] begin to speak through the trumpet, the progress will be very rapid."[60] In some cases, the connection to phonography was even more explicit, as some séance-goers reportedly brought their own phonograph horns for use by the spirits, which once again illustrates the technological displacement of the medium.[61]

In the early twentieth century, trumpet manifestations were gradually replaced by the development of *spirit telephones*. In 1915, for example, *The Daily Chronicle* reported that a British inventor had constructed a telephone capable of receiving messages from the spirit world.[62] In 1920, American inventor Thomas Alva Edison announced that he

---

[56] Ibid.

[57] Maina L. Tafe, "Development of Mediumship," *The Direct-Voice: A Magazine Devoted to the Direct Voice and Other Phases of Psychic Phenomena* 1/1 (April 1930): p. 30.

[58] Connor, *Dumbstruck*, p. 365.

[59] Mrs. Cecil M. Cook, *How I Discovered My Mediumship* (Chicago: William T. Stead Memorial Center, 1919), p. 34.

[60] W. W. Aber, *A Guide to Mediumship Given by a Delegation from the Star Circle of the Spirit World* (Kansas City MO: Aber, 1906), p. 22.

[61] Moore, *The Voices*, p. 319.

[62] Harold Begbie, "Ghosts on the Telephone," *The Daily Chronicle*, December 7, 1915, p. 6.

was also attempting to construct a telephone to facilitate spirit communication, as he was convinced that "the units of life which compose an individual's memory hold together after that individual's 'death,'" and it should therefore be possible to construct a sensitive instrument capable of amplifying the voices of these material yet invisible entities.[63] Edison thus predicted that spirit communication would be perfected by engineers, which would eliminate the need for spiritual mediums: "If this is ever accomplished it will be accomplished, not by any occult, mystifying, mysterious, or weird means, such as are employed by so-called *mediums*, but by scientific methods."[64] While Edison never patented this invention, a British Spiritualist named F. R. Melton claimed to have successfully built such a device in 1921.[65] Melton's apparatus consisted of a 23 inch long aluminum trumpet that was 3 inches in diameter at one end and 8 inches in diameter at the other. A microphone was placed at the smaller end, which was attached to an amplifier and a telephone headset. Melton's *psychic telephone* thus represented the integration of spirit trumpets and telephones, although he later replaced the trumpet with an inflated balloon covered by a netting that was connected to a telephone receiver.[66] Melton was reportedly able to receive messages from deceased friends and relatives using this device, as the air in the balloon was thought to contain material yet invisible spirits whose voices were amplified by the receiver. Melton also claimed that he had "built his psychic telephone with the intention that anyone could use it successfully,"[67] and he predicted that "soon communication with the other life will be quite a common thing."[68] Schmidt argues that Spiritualists were drawn to the telephone because of its ability to "make present the voice of the absent," which he describes as a "sacramental effect."[69] In other words, the tele-

---

[63] B. C. Forbes, "Edison Working on How to Communicate with the Next World," *American Magazine* 90 (1920): p. 85. See also Douglas Kahn, "Death in Light of the Phonograph," *Wireless Imagination: Sound, Radio, and the Avant-Garde*, ed. Douglas Kahn and Gregory Whitehead (Cambridge MA: MIT Press, 1992), pp. 97–98; Jeffrey Sconce, "The Voice from the Void: Wireless, Modernity and the Distant Dead," *International Journal of Cultural Studies* 1 (1998): pp. 228–229; Anthony Enns, "Voices of the Dead," *Culture, Theory and Critique* 46/1 (2005): pp. 18–19; and George Noory and Rosemary Ellen Guiley, *Talking to the Dead* (New York: Tom Doherty Associates, 2011), pp. 85–97.

[64] Ibid., p. 10.

[65] F. R. Melton, *A Psychic Telephone: Its Construction, the Laws and Conditions that Govern Its Use* (Nottingham: E. Brown & Co., 1921). See also Anabela Cardoso, *Electronic Voices: Contact with Another Dimension* (Winchester: O-Books, 2010), p. 28.

[66] Carrington, *The Story of Psychic Science*, p. 233.

[67] Noory and Guiley, *Talking to the Dead*, p. 95.

[68] F. R. Melton, Letter to Harry Price, 12 May 1932, Psychical Research Files, Harry Price Library, University of London. Harry Price was a psychical researcher who tested Melton's invention at the National Laboratory of Psychical Research and concluded that it did not work. See J. Gordon Melton, ed., *Encyclopedia of Occultism and Parapsychology* (Detroit: Gale Group, 2001), p. 2: 1255; Mary Roach, *Spook: Science Tackles the Afterlife* (New York: W. W. Norton & Co., 2005), p. 181; and Raymond Buckland, *The Spirit Book: The Encyclopedia of Clairvoyance, Channeling, and Spirit Communication* (Detroit: Visible Ink Press, 2005), p. 329.

[69] Schmidt, *Hearing Things*, p. 241.

phone's ability to bridge vast distances already seemed to represent an auditory revelation that was comparable to spirit communication. The key difference between direct voice mediumship and spirit telephones, however, is that everyone could supposedly use these devices, and some Spiritualists even predicted that spirit communication would become as commonplace as telephonic communication.

Historians like Connor often describe the history of Spiritualist sound practices as an attempt to resist the disembodying effects of new sound technologies: "The direct voice of spiritualism restores to vocality the substantiality and the sense of living presence which were in danger of being stripped away by contemporary technologies."[70] This is certainly a compelling argument, yet it seems to obscure the religious significance of these practices as well as the degree to which Spiritualists embraced and celebrated the effects of new sound technologies. Instead of reflecting an underlying fear or anxiety with regard to these technologies, Spiritualist sound practices more often reinforced the idea that technological advances were contributing to a revival of religious experience. Randall claimed, for example, that spirit voices were just as real as those produced by new sound technologies, which were also experienced as miraculous when they first appeared:

> Two or three generations since, the idea that a cable would one day be laid under the sea and that messages would be transmitted under the waters and over the waters from continent to continent, was laughed at as a chimera.[71]

Like Melton, Randall also predicted that technological advances would eventually extend into the spirit realm: "Who shall now say that it is not possible to send thoughts, words, sentences, voices even, and messages, out into the ether of the spirit world, there to be heard, recorded, and answered? Has man reached the end of his possibilities; will all progression stop with Marconi's achievements and telephoning without wires?"[72] Spiritualists like Randall were thus convinced that spirit communication represented the next logical step in the development of sound technologies. It would therefore be wrong to conclude that Spiritualists perceived these technologies as a potential threat because they *stripped away* the *sense of living presence* associated with the voice. On the contrary, an analysis of the Spiritualists' understanding of their own practices reveals that their encounters with spirits and technologies were both informed by a belief in the equation of voice and presence. Like Ong, in other words, Spiritualists did not fear the disembodying effects of new sound technologies; rather, they privileged the voice as the primary marker of human presence and they were firmly committed to the idea that this sense of presence could be facilitated by electronic communication.[73]

---

[70] Connor, *Dumbstruck*, p. 392.
[71] Randall, *The Dead Have Never Died*, pp. 19–20.
[72] Ibid.
[73] Marleen de Witte similarly points out that technological and spiritual communication are linked by a common concern with liveness, presence, and immediacy: "When the mystery of new communication technologies meets the mystery of religion, the intersection of religious and media ideologies of

These parallels between Spiritualist sound practices and the effects of new sound technologies clearly show how Spiritualists were attempting to incorporate scientific materialism into their religious worldview by conceiving of technological communication as facilitating religious experiences. What makes this fusion of religion and technology so complex is that its underlying principles simultaneously confirmed and challenged traditional religious doctrine. For example, Spiritualists like Moore argued that these acoustic manifestations confirmed "the precepts, though not the literal text, of the Bible."[74] However, he also argued that "the time has come [...] when the Almighty has thought fit to permit the veil to be slightly lifted, and to allow us to meet the growing materialism of the day with evidences of the senses—not alone by faith, which is inadequate; and to let us know that the phenomena recorded in the Bible did not cease with the mission of the Apostles."[75] Moore thus described this phenomena as a continuation of the auditory revelations described in the Bible, like Swedenborg, yet he also claimed that they satisfied the "materialism" of the modern era, in which people require scientific evidence rather than "faith." While he did not want "to decry any religion," he was quick to add that Christian teachings are "not meat for the strong man who jealously guards his own individuality, who is true to himself, and is temporarily stunned by some crushing sorrow." Such a man requires "assurance that his dead are alive," and "if he searches diligently for it, he will find that there is a way of communing with those he has lost; and in spiritism he finds peace."[76] For Moore, therefore, Spiritualist sound practices seemed to confirm Christian beliefs while simultaneously offering a more sincere form of spiritual consolation, and he urged churches to incorporate such practices in order to remain relevant: "Spiritism is a Divine institution permitted by the Almighty to meet the growing materialism of the age, and [...] sooner or later the Church will have to come into line with it. If it does not, so much the worse for the Church."[77] Moore thus promoted Spiritualism as a more enlightened alternative to orthodox religion, and he predicted that it would lead to either religious reform or the decline of faith.

American Spiritualist Edwin F. Bowers similarly recognized that Spiritualist sound practices represented a potential threat to the religious establishment:

Our religious teachers assert that the *only* channel through which knowledge of the spirit *should* come is by way of *accepted authority*—or church sanction. The church, obviously, cannot sanction the tenets of spiritualistic philosophy, because these contradict the accepted teachings of churchianity. Hence the vitriolic opposition of orthodox churches to the spread of a belief that

---

liveness, presence, and immediacy may generate experiences of being in touch with a spirit power." However, she fails to mention that these shared concerns are based on the fundamental equation of voice and presence. Marleen de Witte, "The Electric Touch Machine Miracle Scam: Body, Technology, and the (Dis)authentication of the Pentecostal Supernatural," in Stolow, ed., *Deus in Machina,* p. 81.

[74] Moore, *The Voices,* p. 431.
[75] Ibid., p. 128.
[76] Ibid., pp. 419–420.
[77] Ibid., p. 431.

teaches immortality, irrespective of morality; that gives us daily proof, *out of the mouths* [...] of the supposed dead, that the redemption of man is always possible.[78]

Like Moore, Bowers similarly argued that Spiritualist sound practices provided scientific evidence of the survival of human personality after death and that this evidence challenged traditional religious doctrine by discrediting the idea that moral judgments were made in the afterlife: "If every man and woman in the world [...] could hear the voices of his beloved dead [...] or speak with these dead, in their materialized form, as I have done on scores of occasions, he would know that the truth concerning survival after death is taught in very few churchs [sic] today."[79]

Spiritualism was thus informed by a set of goals and desires that were shared by orthodox religions, such as a desire to understand the nature of life and the universe, to ameliorate people's suffering, and to make the world a better place. However, Spiritualism also represented a potential rival to orthodox religions, as it offered a more scientific, rational, and non-dogmatic belief system. Participants were also seen as independently-minded thinkers, who were free to interpret their experiences without any interference from recognized religious authorities. In other words, Spiritualists were not attempting to either accept or reject a secular worldview; rather, it would be more accurate to understand their practices as an attempt to negotiate the competing demands of tradition and modernity by reconciling these contradictory impulses. While the participants clearly believed that their practices were facilitating encounters with the sacred and contributing to the creation of a better world, they were not aligned with any particular religious system and they refused to construct an alternative religious doctrine by codifying and policing the rules governing their own practices. While Spiritualists published numerous instruction manuals, which provided guidelines on how to produce direct voice phenomena, their practices remained extremely fluid, as there were no recognized leaders and séance conditions were easily modified by individual members, who were openly encouraged to perform these practices on their own.

The question of individual agency is particularly complex due to the ambiguous nature of the spirits themselves. The presence of spirits during séances was clearly contingent on the actions performed by the mediums and the sitters, as spirit voices could only be generated under certain conditions that were determined by a set of shared techniques and instruments. The structure of these performances thus suggests that Spiritualists saw spirits as objects that were to a certain extent under their control. However, accounts of Spiritualist séances also show that spirits were considered to be autonomous living entities that possessed a greater degree of agency than the subjects who allegedly brought them into their existence. Taves notes, for example, that people often attribute agency to an invisible presence if they believe this presence causes anomalous events to occur:

---

[78]   Edwin F. Bowers, "Scoffing Spirit Survival," *The Direct-Voice: A Magazine Devoted to the Direct Voice and Other Phases of Psychic Phenomena* 1/5 (September 1930): pp. 154–156, here p. 155.
[79]   Ibid.

Although some people might view the experience as (say) a hallucination, we can assume that in many cases the *feeling* of presence (the intimations of agency) will be attributed to the *actual* presence of an invisible agent. [...] When people interpret feelings, perceptions, or sensations that are suggestive of agency as evidence of the presence of an actual agent, they attribute the experience to an external source. Thus [...] we can say that people *ascribe* intentionality to things, thus creating agents; they then can attribute *causality* to the agent, assuming that the agent *caused* the experience in question.[80]

According to Taves, therefore, shared feelings, perceptions, or sensations can give rise to a collective belief in the agency of invisible operators. It is evident from the accounts of Spiritualist séances that sitters similarly perceived spirits as possessing a will of their own, as their presence often modified the goals and intentions of those around them. It is also important to note that séances were both individual and collective experiences, as spirits could address individual sitters as well as an entire group as a whole. In doing so, the spirits effectively became participants in the actions of the séance-goers by bringing sitters together in constantly shifting configurations or relations. In this sense, the spirits can be understood literally as *operators* or *controls* through which sitters were constituted as either individual subjects or communities who shared similar emotions, goals, and beliefs. On the one hand, this phenomenon clearly illustrates Durkheim's claim that the social function of religion is to produce a communal bond. On the other hand, however, it also illustrates James' understanding of religion as a personal experience that is real in so far as it produces real effects in the world. Spirits can thus be understood as active agents that facilitate both individual and collective religious experiences, which reinforces Ong's notion of the voice as the manifestation of an interiority as well as his claim that sound is fundamentally social, as it signals involvement and participation in the present.

A practice-based approach is particularly useful when studying the auditory revelations that occurred during Spiritualist séances, as these paranormal phenomena involved not the passive reception of ideologically informed texts, but rather the active production of invisible agents that were seemingly capable of facilitating special, unusual, or anomalous experiences. While it is easy to dismiss these experiences as fraudulent or to reject the Spiritualists' belief in technological communication with the dead as hopelessly naïve and misguided, it is far more useful to consider the function of their practices as media rituals that served to construct an intermediate space between the subject and the object, the individual and the collective, and the sacred and the secular. Such an approach can thus help scholars to devise new strategies that open up other modes of engagement beyond ideology critique.

---

[80] Taves, *Religious Experience Reconsidered*, p. 41.

Religion, Media, and the Practice Turn

INTERVIEW WITH JOHN DURHAM PETERS, BY JEREMY STOLOW

PART ONE: On The Practice Turn

JS: What comes to mind when you hear the term *practice turn*? What are the prospects of such a turn? What are its aims? Its assumptions?

JDP: When I hear the word *turn* in an academic context, at first, I smell a branding exercise. In the German scene, the practice turn seems in part a compensation for the anti-humanist pose that Kittler liked to cultivate. You can see a turn against that in Bernhard Siegert's interest in ontology-making *Kulturtechniken*. With others, such as Erhard Schüttpelz's interest in ethnomethodology, practice is more than the return of the repressed, it's a full-fledged program. The *anthropoi* are finally back! It's hard for me to tell if the practice turn is a re-inscription of the human within media studies or a convergent evolution with a long interest in Anglo-American media studies in what audiences do with media. For instance, Herta Herzog in the early 1940s, during her long stay in the US, led interview studies of women listening to day-time radio serials.[1] What were women doing with these shows? They're avoiding housework, they're fantasizing a better world, they're projecting their hostilities in a kind of Freudian way. Or take Bernard Berelson's famous piece, "What 'Missing the Newspaper' Means"[2]. There's a strike in New York in 1945, and the newspaper doesn't get delivered for three weeks. Berelson's underlying question is, "What do people do with newspapers?" It turns out that people use newspapers for finding what's scheduled on the radio, as a kind of oral pleasure, as a daily ritual, and as a preparation for conversation. This *uses and gratifications* tradition later gets transmogrified in British cultural studies in a much hipper way because the focus is often subcultural, on subversive decoding. In terms of media studies, it's hard for me to understand what a practice turn is because, at least as far as Anglo-American media studies are concerned, it seems like the core of media studies has always been anthropocentric, by focusing on what audiences do with media texts.

---

[1] Herta Herzog, "What Do We Really Know about Daytime Serial Listeners?," *Radio Research* (1943): pp. 3–33.

[2] Bernard Berelson, "What 'Missing the Newspaper' Means," in *Communication Research,* ed. P. F. Lazarsfeld and F. N. Stanton (New York: Duell, Sloan, and Pearce, 1949).

JS: It is interesting that these older traditions of audience research get so little mention in contemporary discussions about what ails media studies and what would be the best remedies. They don't have much bearing, for instance, on the way Nick Couldry sets out his own program for practice-focused media research.[3] Instead, Couldry presents *practice* as a needed innovation: a correction to what he perceives as a dominant problem in Anglophone media studies, namely its overly narrow (or overly central) focus on the symbolic contents of media products, at the expense of gaining a clear picture of how media are produced and used in local contexts of activity. Hoping to free media research from the grips of text-centrism, Couldry thus raises the specter of Durkheimian functionalism. Without recourse to a fine-grained understanding of how media are put to work within particular contexts of production, management, and reception, Couldry warns us, media researchers will have no means to defend themselves from unpersuasive and speculative claims about the power of media texts and the roles they play in social life. Couldry's compellingly simple answer to this problem is to have media researchers become better ethnographers. Start your analysis in the field; go see what is actually happening. Of course, depending on what decade or what national context we are talking about, it might not sound particularly innovative to suggest that media researchers ought to privilege empirical investigation and inductive reasoning, to bring us back to your examples of Herzog and Berelson. Might it be important, then, to situate a given call for a *practice* (or any other) *turn* historically and geographically, within its distinct national or language-based traditions of research and scholarly discussion?

JDP: In the American context, which is traditionally so practical and so utilitarian, I think the practice turn is something we perhaps ought to resist because practice is already the constant gravitational pull as application or implementation.

JS: What about the etymology of the term *practice*? What clues might we find there about what is at stake in a turn to practice?

JDP: The word *practice* is related to *pragma*, which in Greek means thing or affair. It is very much in the Latourian sense of how a thing is also a council or a parliament, something that is constituted by collective deliberative labor.[4] In Kant, *pragmatisch* and *praktisch* are very different kinds of words; the latter always implies a kind of ethical dimension. *Praxis*, of course, is an Aristotelian category. The term *practice theory*, which seems at first blush an oxymoron, actually makes sense in the Aristotelian tradition with all the so-called *sciences* that end with *-ics* such as *poetics* and *politics* and *ethics* and *aesthetics* and *rhetoric*. None of these can be reduced to categorical imperatives. There is no general

---

3   Nick Couldry, "Theorising Media as Practice," *Social Semiotics* 14/2 (2004): pp. 115–132.
4   Bruno Latour, ed., *Making Things Public: Atmospheres of Democracy* (Cambridge MA: MIT Press, 2005).

maxim that you can follow to say, *this is beautiful* or *this is ethical* or *this is proper*. There is a kind of prudence—*phronêsis*, as the Greeks called it—that seriously informs the idea of a praxis theory. Perhaps it would make more sense if we called it a *return to Aristotle*.

JS: Could we not push this etymological exercise even further? The Greek *praxis* is a substantive based on the verb, *prassō, to do, to act, to effect, or to accomplish*, which, depending on context, might refer to either a transitive or an intransitive action. To my mind, this brings us back to the *how* questions, and the *how*—the intermediary—makes the topic of practice perfect territory for media studies, of course. We're back in the middle.

JDP: Leo Spitzer talks about Aristotle's notion of *to periekhon*: *peri* means *surrounding* and *ekhon* means, essentially, *having*.[5] The German *Umwelt* and French-derived term *environment* both continue the sense of surrounding.

JS: Yes, the *doing, acting, effecting*, and *accomplishing* work of practice must be located somehow. So, presumably one thing that proponents of the practice turn must also demand is that we can identify a given practice's environmental conditions. What surrounds us when we act and how does that surrounding have bearing on our action? Who, for that matter, is the *we* that undertakes action, and where and how should we draw the line separating the subjectivity of the actor from their outside environment? And how should researchers who wish to study practice proceed? Is there an Archimedean vantage point from which one can observe practice unfold? Or are we always, as Heidegger would put it, thrown (*geworfen*) into its milieu? Maybe that would suggest that to make good on its promises, the practice turn would have to become something like a phenomenological turn.

JDP: Or why don't we go back to pragmatism, which is often very close (in James, at least) to phenomenology?

JS: That's interesting because it suggests that, intellectual trends in nomenclature notwithstanding, it remains the task of media studies to start the analysis *in medias res*, because, after all, media and mediation are always already happening. I have in mind something not unlike Foucault's famous call upon historians to abandon the quest for *essentia* or prime causes and focus instead on *how* questions: because the *how* questions are actually the interesting ones.[6] It's the surface that matters.

JDP: Surfaces are not superficial.

---

5   Leo Spitzer, "Milieu and Ambiance: An Essay in Historical Semantics," *Philosophy and Phenomenological Research* 3/1 (1942): pp. 1–42.

6   Michel Foucault, *The Order of Things: An Archaeology of the Human Sciences* (New York: Vintage Books, 1970).

PART TWO: On Religion, Media, and Practice

JS: What is the topic of *religion* supposed to do for German media theory? Despite all their other differences, media archaeology, actor-network theory, and the study of *Kulturtechniken* seem to converge at the point where the *reality* of actors and their milieux require specification. Actors must be observable in some way, whether in the case of a human body performing a dance, a credit card reader at a supermarket checkout, the stream of information passing in and out of a digital cloud data warehouse, or a culinary technique that is passed on from one generation of humans to the next through their collective labor in kitchens. Analysts must have the confidence to know in each case where to look for the agents and how to trace the consequences of their actions. Perhaps we can say that the biggest difference between proponents of practice theory, such as Couldry, and advocates of competing models for media research is a disagreement about what are the most important actors to observe. Couldry clearly prefers that the focus be kept on *anthropoi*, whereas in other currents of media studies, attention is directed at devices, platforms, infrastructures, and other types of nonhuman actors. But as soon as media analysts introduce religious phenomena into the mix —whatever we might mean by the term *religious* here—confusion and ambiguity abound. Where are the actors? Maybe others can *believe in* the reality of invisible actors, but are we prepared, as media researchers, to accept the alterity, the reality, and the ontological certainty of religious things? The easiest default is to say, "Well, people have their beliefs and their affective states of body and mind, and these are what motivate their commitment to religious principles and shape their conduct in the service of some defined religious purpose." But such an approach ultimately reduces action, practice, and performance in the religious field to the symbolic register. Suppose I am an Amish who shuns clothing designed with zippers. The assumption is that my practice of zipper-avoidance can sufficiently be explained by referencing my prior beliefs about zippers, as one among a range of *modern* technologies and instrumental techniques of which practicing Amish choose not to partake. It is an explanation that conveniently treats Amish references to a seductive Devil or a punishing God as nothing more than elements of their discursive apparatus.

JDP: In other words, one tolerates ontologically dubious entities because one is a functionalist and gives them no more footing than a psychological one.

JS: Yes. But what would be the alternative? Contemporary religious studies has grown increasingly sensitive to the fact that, throughout its history, the very enterprise of studying religion *scientifically* or *objectively* rests upon a particular mode of symbolic violence, whereby the *beliefs of others* are rendered amenable to study by reducing religious conduct, action, and experience to the symbolic level. Is this the same problem that faces religion and media from the perspective of media studies?

JDP: I am reminded here of a story about Niels Bohr. Apparently, someone goes to Bohr's house and sees that he's got a horseshoe hung over the door. And they say: "You don't believe that nonsense, that it's going to give you good luck?" And Bohr replies, "Of course I don't believe it. But I hear it works even if you don't believe it." Many years ago, Gerald Bruns wrote a nice piece on James' trapeze artistry around the topic of religion.[7] James is willing to be a psychologist at some point and to say that religious entities are experiences, and in as much as they are experiences, they are real, we need to take them seriously, since as phenomenological psychologists nothing human is alien for us. So, he doesn't have to commit as to the validity of these experiences whether they are true or false, they just *are*. James opens the door to forms of ontological weirdness, and even is willing to speculate, as in *Pragmatism,* where he says: "I firmly disbelieve, myself, that our human experience is the highest form of experience extant in the universe."[8] The recognition that intelligence doesn't need to take form or take shape in mortal bodies is not unique to pragmatism, certainly. This is something that anthropologists always en-counter when they study religions—that religions have these wild beings that don't behave according to science or other rules but seem to have some kind of efficacy. Should we be pragmatists and say, well, they're working and therefore we'll let them be real. We'll define as real whatever makes a difference, which is James' out. But at some point, the question of ontological validity is always going to keep coming back to haunt you, and James is deep enough to know that. I don't know if this craving for referential presence is unique to the monotheistic tradition. It may be. I mean: You can say, "I believe in God because believing in God does good things for me and for my family and for my com-munity, because it gives me a moral code and a vision of the universe." James calls this *metaphysical comfort*. And he doesn't dismiss it. He's willing to be tough-minded and tender-hearted, recognizing that humans need metaphysical comfort because the world is dark. People die. It's a scary universe and we need to figure out how to live in it. But at some point, if God is nothing more than a therapeutic concoction, then God is no longer a therapeutic concoction.

JS: Precisely. This is the whole problem with arguments about deprivation or some sort of compensatory mechanism. Ultimately, all that analysts are doing is to denude, to render completely innocuous, the alterity of mysterious, transcendent, *religious* phenomena. And then—again—it becomes a kind of Durkheimian exercise whereby the only responsible things left to talk about are the functions that religious phenomena serve culturally, socially, or cognitively for the individuals who engage with them. Because we, the analysts, are supposed to know from the outset they are not really there!

---

[7] Gerald Bruns, "Loose Talk about Religion from William James," *Critical Inquiry* 11/2 (1984): pp. 299–316.

[8] William James, *Pragmatism: A New Name for Some Old Ways of Thinking* (New York: Longmans, Green & Co, 1907).

JDP: How do we know they're not there? Isn't that the ultimate in hubris? That's another Jamesian point.

JS: When you want to study an actor-network system, the maxim always is: Follow the network! Well, why not follow it through a network of prayer and into where the angels go? Why can't we follow the network there? Is it any more or less problematic to want to trace the path of an angel than, say, the influence of a symbol or the spread of information, or other mediated things the existence and movements of which can only be inferred indirectly? Because many of the things that populate the networks that media scholars study are actually invisible anyways.

JDP: Oliver Wendell Holmes, a rival and friend of James, was a kind of stoic, atheist, soldier type who criticized James for wanting to turn down the lights. He thought his friend wanted to shroud certain parts of human experience from the searchlight of inquiry. On the other hand, you know, I think that James is actually shining a flashlight into areas that are *verboten* for secular people. Secular science does not allow you to ask about where the angels dwell, or where the aura is. Faith or belief becomes a psychological condition of interiority, which is a horrible environment for faith to thrive in. If faith is a question of your psychological conviction, then it needs fertilizer because otherwise it is too barren a field to cultivate.

JS: I am reminded here of your recent article, "Recording Beyond the Grave: Joseph Smith's Celestial Bookkeeping," in which you comment on Smith's doctrine that one does not need to bear experiential witness to the baptismal act in order to affirm its authenticity; the record itself will count just as much.[9] In a sense, this question of who is a legitimate witness to a spectacular act of miracle, or to the holy presence of God's terrifying judgment, presents a biting commentary on the very logic of substitution that underpins media research in all its forms—not least, but not only in the domain of *religion and media*. For as media scholars, our attention is being called to the middle place, where we will find the low-hanging fruit that allows us to do our work. It is in the middle of things where we can let a record substitute for a witness. We need only study the record, trusting that it adequately stands in for an absent witness because the latter is unavailable (and perhaps impossibly inaccessible) to us. Without that substitution, we cannot do our work. Likewise, at least as far as the study of religion and media is concerned, perhaps we do not need to find out where God comes from, or whether we were here before God or vice versa. We don't need to go that far in order to have something to say.

JDP: That's the question. Because for so many, *media studies* sounds reductive. To my mother, the term *media* sounds grubby and base and mundane and ordinary and sort of

---

9 John Durham Peters, "Recording Beyond the Grave: Joseph Smith's Celestial Bookkeeping," *Critical Inquiry* 42/4 (2016a): pp. 842–864.

the realm of corruption. Not the realm of the transcendental. And, with Smith, there is something really dry and dusty and bureaucratic about his vision of the redemption of the dead. The dead are saved, of all things, in part by accounting! We don't know what the dead are doing, and we don't need to wait for the black box of the future to know of their assent or rejection of the deed the living do for them vicariously. The way that the transcendental nestles with the mundane in Smith's theology I think is also a very media studies kind of question. I love the quote from Emerson that the invariable mark of genius is to discover the miraculous in the common: a sense of awe or wonder in the fact that we even exist, that we breathe, that we're alive.

JS: I suppose, again, the challenge is how does one make use of this kind of an observation or a starting point without lapsing into the kind of psychological reductionism that turns religious practice into religious *meaning*. Nineteenth- and early twentieth-century theorists of magic, from Tylor to Freud to Lévy-Bruhl, among others, had the hubris to attribute belief in *transcendent causality* to the workings of cognitive dissonance. So-called primitive people, such as practitioners of magic or Biblical literalists, do not possess the detailed scientific understanding of the way the natural world works. They therefore misconstrue the natural causes of, for example, a lightning striking and attribute the event to a supernatural agency. And from that point onward, the *supernatural* expands globally into a compensatory mechanism for everything else beyond our ken or control. Because as you have already pointed out, the universe is a scary place. Life is difficult, precarious, dangerous, and scarcity is everywhere, and so people compensate by constructing *religious explanations* of how the cosmos operates. Miracle, magic, and mystery are the inevitable surplus elements of experience that invite us to create these castles in our mind.

JDP: You just alluded to Dostoevsky's *The Grand Inquisitor*: miracle, magic, and mystery. I'm with Dostoevsky on this: that religion at its best is not in the business of giving answers and closure and resolution. It's helping you to figure out how to manage the open-endedness. Consider here Tanya Luhrmann's study of evangelicals: these are not people who are finding fixed answers.[10] They're finding ways to manage the impossibility of knowing whether there is a God or not. I think that's what religion is: an openness to the question and a toolkit of strategies for dealing with it.

JS: That sort of openness is unnerving for social scientists, who have been trained to debunk and expose that which is hidden. Our methods of critical inquiry belong to an anti-clerical tradition of exposure. If I can show that a given religious performance is merely the product of artifice, that there is a human hand invisibly at work behind religious experience, then I have stripped away its magical power; I have somehow freed both myself and others from the power of its grip. As Bruno Latour, among others, has

---

[10]   Tanya Luhrmann, *When God Talks Back: Understanding the American Evangelical Relationship with God* (New York: Vintage Books, 2012).

argued in recent years, this impulse to debunk is part of a very old story, linked to the history of monotheistic iconoclasm going all the way back to Abraham the idol-smasher.[11] Abraham's acts of destruction, at least in Latour's reading, paradoxically proclaimed that idols must be destroyed because they are both too weak and too strong. Idols are dangerous because they poison people's minds with the *bad idea* of polytheism (although later iconoclasts eventually substitute the many gods for all sorts of other *bad ideas*, including the very idea of religion itself!). But at the same time, the idols are weak, because the things to which they refer have no purchase on the real world. There do not exist many gods, only the one true God. From this perspective, the modern sciences, including the social sciences, are driven by this ever-replenishing impulse to the monotheistic act of iconoclastic destruction. And it is a problem that never goes away because how can one actually remove idols from the world? Does not every act of idol destruction result in the creation of new idols?

JDP: I think the nervousness about granting a kind of ontological space for figments or artifice owes to the other side of monotheism, this blazing, transcendental light of inquiry. There is, after all, a lot of nonsense in the world. Uncovering or unmasking is the classic Enlightenment gesture. Bless it! Sometimes it can be really useful to get to the bottom of things; you need hard investigation. And the appeal to facts is a really key moment. The question is how to avoid letting that rationality take over the entire house. In a court of law, this kind of circumscribed positivism can be really useful. In juridical inquiries it is important to know the facts in terms of assignation of guilt, responsibility, and liability. I think it's important that we figure out what the Nazis did, what happens when police kill people. There are places where empirical, raw fact is crucial, however ultimately shaky that quest might be. I think the anxiety is that the idols are going to take over the house, too: that we'll live in this world of figments.

JS: Does this beg the question: what makes us think that removing the mask is actually liberating? And what do we think is behind the mask anyway?

JDP: What's the famous line? In the French Revolution they tore the masks off of faces, but because that wasn't enough, then they tore off the faces.

JS: To cite Latour yet again, he expresses his fear that: "A Last Judgment has been passed: all our ways to produce representation of any sort have been found wanting. Generations of iconoclasts smashing each other's faces and works. A fabulous large-scale experiment in nihilism. A maniacal joy in self-destruction. A hilarious sacrilege. A sort of deleterious aniconic inferno."[12]

---

[11]   Bruno Latour and Peter Weibel, eds., *Iconoclash: Beyond the Image Wars in Science, Religion and Art* (Cambridge MA: MIT Press, 2002).

[12]   Latour and Weibel, *Iconoclash*, p. 21.

JDP: But of course, fire is useful sometimes. Fire can be terribly destructive. I think reason is like fire. I'm with Horkheimer and Adorno on this. You need a Bunsen burner. You need a torch light. You can do very powerful things with reason. But it can also incinerate the world. Just like fantasy is wonderful, but you don't want to live in fantasyland all the time either. This brings us back to James again. He says we're pinned in between the material world and the idea world. And he does not see a kind of one-to-one mapping. He sees science as a kind of loose foray. I think the best metaphor is actually by a kind of latter-day pragmatist, Willard van Orman Quine, in his *Two Dogmas of Empiricism*, where he says that our knowledge of the world is "a man-made fabric which impinges on experience only along the edges"[13]. Our knowledge has all this fantastic embroidery that might not have anything to do with the world, but it's still a beautiful tapestry, a "web of sentences" as he says. And when you actually look at what we know, it's crumbly. Some evolutionary psychologists who study how human cognition works see us as fabricating all kinds of realities that we think are substantial and solid, because it's evolutionarily useful for us to do so. But our perception is missing the vastness about this world that we live in. So, it's a kind of premature benediction of our blinkered senses to say that we just want *the facts and nothing but the facts*, because the facts and nothing but the facts are evolutionarily limited in the sense that they are dependent on our limited sense organs.

JS: Haven't you just run an end-run around your argument here? If we can reduce the issues of our bafflement with the universe and the limitations of our understanding to a problem of evolutionary cognition, then we can say that an enchanted universe is evolutionarily advantageous for humans, perhaps for the reason that it helps us remain alert to potential dangers. We humans benefit from an active imagination that makes us wonder what is lurking behind the next bush because doing so expresses a survival instinct: to protect ourselves from not walking into bushes and getting eaten by lions. From there, that imagination "desperately outdoes what is required," to quote from James Dickey's great poem, *The Heaven of Animals*.

JDP: So, you're saying that I've just succumbed to the functionalist trap, again?

JS: Well, how does one guard against it? Let's put it that way.

JDP: I don't know. I read a very interesting article a while back about placebos. Apparently, in medical research it used to be that a placebo effect was the ultimate dismissal that a particular therapy doesn't work. But, instead someone realized, wait—if someone feels better if they think that they're getting a drug, why don't we actually use that effect therapeutically? And so, there's a limited, growing embrace of placebos as powerful healing and therapeutic agents.

---

[13] Willard Van Orman Quine, "Two Dogmas of Empiricism," *The Philosophical Review* 60 (1951): pp. 20–43.

JS: It's a wonderful counterexample and it brings us back to Niels Bohr and his horseshoe. The success of the placebo rests on my understanding—should we say, my belief?—that I am getting better, and that in turn has real effects on my neuro-chemistry and my physiology. My brain and body are altered, in a very real sense.

JDP: Well, I don't want to reduce the anthropocentric question about being in the middle to the kind of conundrum: if a tree falls in the forest and we're not there, is there really a sound? But on the other hand, what would a world be like without humans? Richard Wilbur's poem "Advice to a Prophet" ponders this question wonderfully. Would there be an absolute without the sort of brain-mind nexus that we've figured out how to do? And I think the easiest way to think about this—it's not all easy actually—it's the puzzle of mortality and the puzzle of selfhood. Why are you you and why am I me? Why does the world seem so brightly centered around me to me and why does it seem so brightly centered around you to you? This is just an incredibly puzzling and odd fact. And this world, which seems so vibrant and alive, is no longer going to exist for me when I die. Or it may exist for me in some other form, but we know there will be some huge kind of transformation. So, it does seem to kind of point to an intuitive truth about idealism. That the ego constitutes the universe. Because if I'm not alive then all this vibrancy is no longer here. But of course, it still will be here (unless my death is simultaneous with the instant extinction of the whole human species—cheery thought!) For a Freudian, the self is a figment produced as a by-product of physiological systems, a kind of survival mechanism. We're drives or we're genes and we're musculature and we're tissue and we're membranes and we're mostly water. I mean, we are profoundly non-human. The starting point should be that the human is something which is not human. Should we cast out the illusion of selfhood that makes us blind to all the nonhuman processes? But that illusion—that miracle of mind—is still something real and undeniable. The existence of mind is itself connected to the question of figments. How does brain produce mind? That is undoubtedly one of the great twenty-first century questions.

JS: Of course, the brain/mind argument has been going on for a long time in many ways. But it's interesting to think about how such debates work out in the context of media studies because, once again, we're left with a sort of chasm: Where do we think our analyses go? I am thinking here of your assessment in *The Marvelous Clouds*, that the contemporary return to *materiality* is rather tiresome because so much of what we actually need to study is immateriality, "our greatest achievement"[14]. For me, that leads to the question: Which immaterialities do we think are accessible to us and which ones do we feel are *no-go zones* because we're afraid that, by talking about them, we will be indulging in some kind of metaphysical speculation that rubs against the grain of our scholarly responsibility?

JDP: You have described a variant of Wittgenstein's problem. Wittgenstein seems to have treasured metaphysics. He wasn't in favor of abolishing metaphysics; he just didn't think we could talk about it. Which immaterialities are accessible? In that passage in my book, I'm talking about things like points. Is a point something material or not? Euclid has this great definition that a point is *that which has no part*. But obviously, a point matters. The world turns on the Archimedean point. If you can move a decimal point in your bank account, you're going to get really rich or really poor very fast. Christian theologians were worried about introducing a diabolical entity into numbers (such as zero) because here you have non-being with the power to take over and determine all the rest of everything. The zero, of course, is not a number but rather an operator. It brings things into being with its negation. It is part of that study of non-existing entities that run the world, and thus of interest to theology, the so-called *science of non-existing entities* as Deleuze quipped. You know, if we believe in becoming and generation, and genuine novelty, then theology ought to be something of great interest to us.

JS: So, would that be, for you, the best way to describe the task of media studies: the study of non-existing entities that run the world?

JDP: Sure, why not? I touch on this at the end of chapter 7 in *The Marvelous Clouds*. Should the wild, woolly bestiary of immateriality be admitted to media studies? And does theology as a study of non-existing entities have a place? If we take zero as a medium or a decimal point as a medium or language as a medium, we see they clearly have material force but it's very hard to pin them down ontologically. Mathematics largely exists in chalk and in paper: in inscriptions, in operative writing, the media of mathematics. It's not just imaginary entities. It's always material as well. Latour has a review essay about Reviel Netz's work on ancient Greek mathematics in which the former goes ape with delight because the latter demonstrates that ancient Greek mathematics depends upon material practices of diagramming and letter exchanges.[15] Thus, Netz completely undermines the Platonic idea that there are forms out there in the universe. That some *nous* has to be thinking all the time to keep them in being. Ancient mathematics is the material exchange of slate and various diagrammatic objects. One way we can ground immaterial or non-existing entities is in the media practices of inscription and erasure.

JS: This recommendation also brings us back to the question of practice. Your earlier invocation of William James seems particularly apt here, in that Jamesian pragmatism invites the inquirer to suspend nominalist questions and focus instead on process. And the focus on process will allow us to escape from these problems of specification. We don't have to figure out whether it's *A* or *not-A*. We just have to look at the how: What's happening? What's going on here? Perhaps this is what a practice turn for media studies promises? Is this a call ultimately for students of media to be better pragmatists?

---

[15]   Bruno Latour, "The Netz-Works of Greek Deductions – A Review of Reviel Netz's *The Shaping of Deductions in Greek Mathematics*," *Social Studies of Science* 38/3 (2008): pp. 441–459.

JDP: If that's what the *practice turn* means, sign me up. Pragmatism has a kind of behaviorist side. You can read behaviorism as highly reductionist, but you can also read it as a kind of phenomenological respect for things as they are. We're not going to have recourse to mentalistic entities, including our own. We're going to look at how people behave. So, it's a kind of ethnographic imperative. My teacher Hal Miller taught me that behaviorism can be a beautiful philosophy of letting things be as they are, *zu den Sachen selbst*.

JS: What about fantasy? It's about the balance of, you know, we don't want everything to be hypothetical. Because then we lose our bearing in the world. Maybe this is what pragmatism also offers: a sorting out, there has to be a sorting mechanism that allows us to—

JDP: Yes, it is a sorting mechanism. But to what degree is it also a wavering? This is the worry that I have about James and about myself. Am I just trying to enable certain kinds of religious experiences because it's a matter of commitment or is it because there's a genuine truth there? I can see the problem: that genuine truth implies something external to human experience. Why should we buy the positivist line that genuine truth has to be outside of us, which is also a kind of radical Protestant line—that God is outside of you, he's something radically other. Ugh, we are back to an old cursed dualism!

JS: The anthropologist Birgit Meyer has recently written about another rough contemporary of James: Robert Marett, an under-studied anthropologist who developed a robust account of the idea of *awe*.[16] In his attempt to negotiate competing terminology such as *holy*, *numinous*, or *sacred*, Marett proposed the term *awe* in a way that is congenial to the pragmatist enterprise. In Meyer's reading of Marett, *awe*

> calls for detailed attention to the micro-practices of religious fabrication and hence to the production of a surplus, whose emergence needs neither to be attributed to a transcendental force *sui generis* nor to be deconstructed as mere illusion. Instead, it focuses on what I regard as human beings' quite remarkable capacity to engage in co-producing particular awesome effects that they do not reduce to their own actions per se, but experience as marvelous.[17]

Awe is thus something that opens us up to the transcendent, the extraordinary, and so on, but at the same time it is that which roots us in the materiality of bodies, economies, and politics: questions about who experiences awe, in what ways is it experienced, to whose benefit, and at whose expense. Studying the latter does not dissolve the blinding alterity of the former. At least, that's the reading I am keen to pursue.

JDP: One of Peirce's maxims is: *Do not block the road to inquiry*. Openness, that ought to be what we're about. There are more things in heaven and earth, Horatio, than are dreamt

---

16   Birgit Meyer, "How to Capture the 'Wow': R.R. Marett's Notion of Awe and the Study of Religion," *Journal of the Royal Anthropological Institute* 22/1 (2016): pp. 7–26.

17   Ibid., p. 15.

of in your philosophy, right? That's the starting point of any kind of inquiry. Why should we as a starting point say, this is what the universe is? Because the universe keeps getting weirder and weirder and stranger all the time. At the macro level as well as at the quantum level. The observable universe is around 94 billion light years—I was going to say "in diameter" but you can't even talk about diameter because it's not this big sphere but is expanding from any point of view. The Hubble flow, the measure of the average speed of cosmic expansion, is 72 kilometers per second. This morphing is just unfathomable for us. And the observable universe may itself be unimaginably minute compared to the whole shebang. So, in some ways, on Earth we're in this little humid greenhouse, this cosmically anomalous hot house of very bizarre perception where things stay in place. And we flatter ourselves that we're durable and that we know what the world is, what the universe is. The bees and the flies are laughing at us. Or the whales or the bats, with their ability to hear spectra we cannot. They're laughing at us.

JS: You make a similar point in the lecture you gave in 2016 at Concordia University on the American neuroscientist John Lilly's dolphin research, which he conducted in the 1950s and 60s.[18] Lilly's fantasy, as you described it, was that he could somehow gain access to the enormous universe of communications that are intrinsic to dolphins but inaudible to us: that somehow, for Lilly, the only way that alterity can be encountered is to try to tame it by making dolphins learn English and then to audio-tape their "speech," as it were. By slowing the tape down, because otherwise there would be no alterity to encounter. It sounds like the only imaginable way for Lilly to engage with alterity was to find a technical or imaginative means to rein it in. And of course, maybe that's all any humans are ever doing anyways. As Hegel says, you know, you can't—

JDP: You can't jump over your shadow.

JS: Well, at one point does Hegel not say something like this: "to draw a line of a limit is already to see on the other side of it"? In other words, there is no way to encounter the infinite because we've already contained it somehow. How, for instance, can one imagine an expanding universe unless we can visualize its shape, such as in the form of a sphere? So, we can picture in our minds a balloon that fills with air, and that image allows us to say "oh yes, I can picture an expanding universe," but what does it actually mean to contemplate such a terrifyingly paradoxical thought? An expanding universe that expands into what? What could possibly lie beyond the infinite cosmos?

JDP: I think a genuinely religious attitude is one of openness to surprises. This is also exactly the same as a genuinely scientific attitude. And I think that media studies can sober

---

18   John Durham Peters, "John Lilly, Dolphin Voices, and the Tap. Medium," *Public lecture delivered at the Media History Research Centre* (Concordia University, Montréal, Canada. 22 September, 2016b).

us up because it shows us the way that our efforts to encounter the universe or encounter otherness are always mediated by pragmatic tools. I think that's something we should celebrate; it is not a reduction. I don't think Smith's obsession with bookkeeping was a reduction of the divine but was a means of access to it. And my critique of Lilly is that he doesn't realize how dependent he is upon his strategic reductions. Tape and acoustic media (and LSD) were his media to dolphin otherness! Pragmatism gives its blessing to intellectual short cuts. It's the neo-Kantian idea that we can deal with the sensory manifold only through categories.

ULRIKE BERGERMANN

Introduction: Connecting and Dividing Media Theories: Gender, Post-Colonial, and Other Agencies

Media studies as an academic discipline in German speaking countries' institutions has, from its very beginnings, striven to shape not only its subject, the media, but also its working modes. Neither the *Languages and Literatures* departments (and their mainly hermeneutic approaches to, for example, film) nor the social/empirical approaches within *communication studies* seemed to provide substantial background for the analyses of historical and contemporary media cultures and their entanglements with the histories of technology. *Society and the media* or mere user-based perspectives seemed too predictable; while drawing new connections to deconstruction, psychoanalysis, technology and philosophy, as in the work of Friedrich Kittler, opened up new perspectives. To refer to humans or to people, for many scholars, provided all-too-easy explanations. But how, then, questions of power should be addressed remained an open question; the reception of the *Actor Network Theory*, now, can be read as one way of including the *agency* of people within other agencies and analyses of mediated environments. The historiography of media studies, still, reflects an ongoing debate on defining the discipline by way of choosing its roots. What can a turn to *practices* add to this debate?

Practices—comparable to the term *transmission* in actor network theory—connect things and beings, humans and others, apparatuses or objects, in a ritualistic mode: collectively and individually, intentionally or unconsciously, and they are necessarily materialistic, embodied, situated, as well as governed by historically and culturally contingent, immaterial principles, as practice theory argues.[1] At first sight, it looks like an inclusive

---

[1] John Postill, for example, starts his sketch of the history of practice theory from social theory only to turn to media immediately (Nick Couldry's 2004 "Theorising Media as Practice"), calling it a "field-of-practice approach to media." J. Postill, "Introduction: Theorising Media and Practice," in *Theorising Media and Practice*, ed. Birgit Bräuchler and John Postill (Oxford and New York: Berghahn, 2010), pp. 1–32, here p. 3. See also: Theodore R. Schatzki et al. eds., *The Practice Turn in Contemporary Theory* (London and New York: Routledge, 2001). The connection to media and mediality in science and technology studies and practice theory is obvious, see also Léna Soler, Sjoerd Zwart, Michael Lynch and Vincent Israel-Jost, eds., *Science after the Practice Turn in the Philosophy, History, and Social Studies of Science* (New York and London: Routledge, 2014). A volume about praxeology in historiography takes off with a sailor's notebook and the question of how to come back

gesture: Practices address *all* of the elements involved in a given (that is, chosen) situation. Media are single constituencies of practices—the unfolding of a practice can fruitfully be described as a mediation; historically we can have no knowledge of a medium without a respective practice, etc. This section's hypothesis is that the non/disciplines of gender and post-colonial studies, for various reasons, have dealt with the same methodological questions for some time—and that they share many epistemological issues (as well as, obviously, objects) with media studies. Performativity, for example, is a crucial concept in describing the emergence of relatively or at least temporarily fixed identities (according to gender, race, class and their stagings; rituals, institutions and practices, repetitions, power structures).[2] Not everybody and everything involved in a practice has the same agency; questions of power need to be addressed, too.

Connecting/dividing are central figures in media studies' history of thought, be it through McLuhan's love of global connectivity, systems theory's drawing of distinctions, or the deconstructive search for gaps. These theories correspond in one way or another to the mediated practices of connecting and dividing, to political claims for participation, and to new communities. They resonate with senses of belonging and desire, negotiating hegemonies, exclusions, subaltern people and their im/possible agencies, with networks of power, forces of attractions and affects, in moving constellations rather than those of *on/off*. Our history of knowledge is entangled with histories of colonialism and therefore with divisions between speakers and non-speakers, what is sayable and what is not, in redistributions of the visible and the sensible. Taking into account networks and subjects

---

to historical practices via media, considering writing and documenting as practices in themselves; see Lucas Haasis and Constantin Rieske, eds., *Historische Praxeologie. Dimensionen vergangenen Handelns* (Paderborn: Schönigh, 2015). Sociologist Hilmar Schäfer wrote a concise monograph. on the development of practice theory in Bourdieu, Foucault, Butler and Latour, focusing on the body, materiality, affect, or temporality. See Hilmar Schäfer, *Die Instabilität der Praxis. Reproduktion und Transformationen des Sozialen in der Praxistheorie* (Weilerswist: Velbrück, 2013). Hilmar Schäfer, ed., *Praxistheorie. Ein soziologisches Forschungsprogramm* (Bielefeld: transcript, 2016), includes contributions by authors like Schatzki, but also interdisciplinary perspectives, including cultural or media related issues, for example Sophia Prinz on the "Practice Theory of Seeing," or Elizabeth Shove and Mika Pantzar on digital photography and floorball. Sociologist has published volumes on practice theory, cultural analysis, "doing subjects," and concepts of creativity, for example Andreas Reckwitz, *Kreativität und soziale Praxis. Studien zur Sozial- und Gesellschaftstheorie* (Bielefeld: transcript, 2016). Science and technology studies' entanglements with both media and practice theories, and sometimes with gender studies, can be traced prominently through Susan Leigh Star, *Grenzobjekte und Medienforschung*, ed. Sebastian Gießmann and Nadine Taha (Bielefeld: transcript, 2017).

2   See also Candace West and Don H. Zimmerman, "Doing Gender," *Gender and Society*, 1/2 (1987): pp. 125–151; Judith Butler, *Gender Trouble* (New York and London: Routledge, 1990); Hazel Rose Markus and Paula M. L. Moya, eds., *Doing Race: 21 Essays for the 21st Century* (New York: Norton, 2010). For a discussion of postcolonial theory's reception within German media studies see Ulrike Bergermann (under review), "No such Kraftwerk. Germany's Post-Colonial Media Studies," *Grey Room*, special issue, #NGMT17. New German Media Theory. An Update, ed. Moritz Hiller (Cambridge MA: MIT Press, 2018).

that have not been recognized in the creation of an academic heritage, we ask what a *practical turn* might have in store for media theory.

Within German academia, cultural, gender or post-colonial studies, have for a long time been regarded as specialized discourses, as the sole realms of social practices and their subjects. Considering the constitutive role of certain *Others* which shape our basic concepts of representation, authenticity, translation, and other media concepts—relying on divisions like *feminized nature vs. pure reason, the spirit of Europe vs. uncivilized natives,* or *underprivileged masses of media users* and their *killer applications*, we now consider the agencies and practices of those that were said to be non-agents. If modernity implies the division of science and the social, we need to take a look at how media come up in networks that have always been connecting both. *Practical* might be the name for this move within media studies, transforming the very idea of what is particular/subjective/marginal and what is general/universal/normal. *Doing media*, then, comprises diasporas, post-colonies, gendered and racialized subjectivities as places of knowledge production. "Situated knowledge"[3] applies to *the knowledge of media* as well, while technologies elicit new temporal conceptualizations of precedence and antecedence, including both humans and non-humans.

Is there a practice turn in media theory? Or is there the desire to combine several strands of theoretical thinking under a new old umbrella term? If what we consider media are the processes of people and things within contexts and settings, rather than apparatuses, or extensions of users and their intentions; if what happens *within* transmissions, *Kultur-techniken*, mediations, or processing is the most productive way to refer to our mediated culture and the production of knowledge, subjectivities etc., then we may use *practice theory* as a point of reference.

Should we speak of *media-related practices* or *media as practices*? Do we have to choose one definition, one approach within the discipline called media studies, or could we decide to understand and practice media studies exactly as a discipline that does not have to choose? That might not be as easy as suspected, as both approaches imply quite a bunch of different methodologies and assumptions, which might be even contradictory.

Traditionally, practices have been the object or the horizon of studies within areas like anthropology, sociology, ethnography and similar; then, albeit under different names, within science and technology studies (workbench studies etc.) and others. While the aforementioned lack a distinctive notion of media, they connect media studies with the whole field where distinctions cannot be clearly drawn, when bodies, rituals, technologies etc. are concerned. While the concept of *transmission* from actor network theory offered methodologies and even new object descriptions that were fruitful for media studies, actor network theory scholars were so busy distancing themselves from sociology (as can be traced through the history of Latour's and Law's institute and writings), that questions of

---

3   Donna Haraway, "Situated Knowledges: The Science Question in Feminism and the Privilege of Partial Perspective," in *Feminist Studies*, Vol. 14, No. 3. (Autumn, 1988): pp. 575–599.

power and politics were, sometimes explicitly, excluded from the researched networks—as within as the mainstream of Media studies' reception.

I would like to suggest a re-reading of Pierre Bourdieu's *Outline of a Theory of Practice* here. This book, maybe the one that has been quoted most within theories of practice, outlines a working method for how to proceed in order to build up a theory from practice, which traditional methodologies neglect, and considers the traps of objectivity as well as immersion. Bourdieu developed his *Theory of Practice* not as part of philosophical considerations, but as an entangled part of a thick description of Kabyle society. Forced to work as part of the military in the French colony of Algeria, Bourdieu charts the displaced and battered nomad society of the Kabyles through many years and hundreds of pages, and he scrutinizes within that description an analysis of the ethnography of Algerian peoples and others, reflecting and criticizing the modes of investigation. Here is not the time to discuss his suggestions and proceedings, but an opportunity to hint how the history of colonialism has more than once been a trigger for practical theories more than once. Thus, Bourdieu is not only relevant for media theory for his work about and with photography and television, or for concepts like "distinction," *habitus* and masculinity.[4]

Practice media theory is not a program of future studies, not the outcome of a new *turn*, but an effect of reconsidering what has been part of media studies all along. In which ways did the respective processes inform media theory, foster new notions or follow imaginative concepts, or put the whole question of practice vs. theory into new perspectives? Media studies already comprises several of these operations, considering how to *do media*, most prominently in fields like media diasporas, gender, and post-colonial studies. Obviously, media connect and divide on transnational and global scales, and it is through those operations and translations, in new media practices, that spaces of subjectivities, communities, technical networks etc. emerge. Did diasporic mobile networks fundamentally erode container models of (nation) space, as digital commons in migrants' hands indicate?[5] Will *immutable mobiles* become more and more mobile, and practices become ever more important than hardware? To look at practices, though, does not mean to forget the materialities of communication; it is not a mere virtualization, but a shift of focus.[6]

---

[4]   Pierre Bourdieu, *Esquisse d'une Théorie de la Pratique, précédé de trois études d'ethnologie kabyle,* (Geneva: Droz, 1972). German translation: *Entwurf einer Theorie der Praxis, auf der ethnologischen Grundlage der kabylischen Gesellschaft* (Frankfurt am Main: Suhrkamp, 1976). English translation: *Outline of a Theory of Practice* (Cambridge and New York: Cambridge University Press, 1977). Pierre Bourdieu, *La Distinction. Critique sociale du jugement* (Paris: Éditions du minuit, 1979). English translation: *Distinction: A Social Critique of the Judgement of Taste* (London: Routledge and Kegan Paul, 1979). German translation: *Die feinen Unterschiede. Kritik der gesellschaftlichen Urteilskraft* (Frankfurt am Main: Suhrkamp, 1982).

[5]   See for example Vassilis Tsianos et al., *Mobile Commons, Migrant Digitalities and the Right to the City* (London: Palgrave Macmillan, 2015); Brigitta Kuster, *Grenze filmen. Eine kulturwissenschaftliche Analyse an den Grenzen Europas* (Bielefeld: transcript, 2017).

[6]   While Theodore R. Schatzki saw a dichotomy between discourses relying on structure or systems on one side, and practices, materiality and the body on the other, he himself proposed a concept of

The Post-Colony as Matrix of Media(ted) Concepts

Colonialism and its persistence in post-colonial times is entangled with the history of the European enlightenment. The idea of a connective cosmopolitanism, concepts of freedom and autonomy, ethics of humanism on the one hand, and the practices of exploitation of nonwhite people on the other, belong to the legacy of our media-related concepts of *aisthesis*, of vision and truth, of authenticity, the real etc. Post-colonial studies mold *connect/ divide*[7] in their own prominent formulae, such as *double consciousness, hybridity, third space*, or the *Black Atlantic*.[8] Considering Latour's hypothesis that "we never have been modern," we ask: Have media studies never been modern? Which deferrals within media theory respond to post-colonial practices of division?

Performative Subjects. Doing Gender, Doing Race, Doing Media

One might argue that it is precisely in the subjects of gender studies and of the post/colony where the reference points between media studies and those practically inclined theories come together. Discussions about the significance of anthropology or media anthropology including, for example, Erhard Schüttpelz's reading of Mauss' *Körpertechniken*

"order," of "arrangements" of people, artifacts and things. See Theodore R. Schatzki, "Introduction: practice theory," in Theodore R. Schatzki, Karin Knorr Cetina and Eike von Savigny, eds., *The Practice Turn in Contemporary Theory* (London and New York: Routledge, 2001), pp. 1–14, here pp. 6–7. Schatzki does not consider the elements of analyses *symmetrical* or *equal* per se (p. 11); not every tool can be ascribed agency just because it is ascribed to humans, etc. See also Schatzki, "Practice mind-ed orders," in *The Practice Turn in Contemporary Theory*, pp. 42–55. After the turn to transmissions and processings, Hartmut Winkler warns us, we should not neglect the things, storages, and materials. See Hartmut Winkler, *Prozessieren. Die dritte, vernachlässigte Medienfunktion* (Paderborn: Fink, 2015), p. 25.

[7] *Connect* and *divide*, in the first place, are verbs, they denote operations or deeds, they focus on what is done (*agencies* and *practices* might denote the more cultural, or the possibility of the human intentional, side of the process).

[8] W.E.B. Du Bois, *The Souls of Black Folk* (1903); German translation *Die Seelen der Schwarzen* (Freiburg: Orange Press, 2008). See especially discussions of "the veil" on pp. 34, 129, 216–221. Frantz Fanon, *Les damnés de la terre* (1961); German translation *Die Verdammten dieser Erde* (Frankfurt am Main: Suhrkamp, 1966); Frantz Fanon, *Peau noire, masques blancs* (1952); German translation *Weiße Haut, schwarze Masken* (Frankfurt am Main: Suhrkamp, 1980); Homi K. Bhabha, "Von Mimikry und Menschen. Die Ambivalenz des kolonialen Diskurses," in Homi H. Bhabha, ed., *Die Verortung der Kultur* (Tübingen: Stauffenberg Verlag, 2000), pp. 125–136; Homi K. Bhabha, ed., "Interrogating identity. Frantz Fanon and the question of post-colonial identity," in *The Location of Culture* (London; New York: Routledge, 1994), p. 40–65, translated in: Elisabeth Bronfen, Benjamin Marius and Therese Steffen, eds., *Hybride Kulturen. Beiträge zur anglo-amerikanischen Multikulturalismusdebatte* (Tübingen: Stauffenburg Verlag, 1997), pp. 97–122, 123–148; Paul Gilroy, *The Black Atlantic. Modernity and Double Consciousness* (Harvard: Verso Books, 1993); Paul Gilroy, "Der Black Atlantic," in *Der Black Atlantic*, ed. Tina Camp and Paul Gilroy (Berlin: Haus der Kulturen der Welt, 2004), pp. 12–31.

are gendered from the start (if we want to speak of such thing as a starting point here)[9]; Bourdieu unfolded his praxeology in colonial Algeria (with a strong attentiveness for gender in the Kabylic politics of kinship); many of the early influential case studies from actor network theory deal with colonial situations (Law's vessel and maps in Portuguese expansion; Latour's first studies in the Ivory Coast or the Brazilian jungle).[10]

Gender studies, Black studies etc. conceptualized political subjectivities and performativities as well as their materiality in concepts of *Doing Gender* or *Doing Race*. These took white male culture's, politics and science's non-represented, not-mediated, non-agents into theoretical account. Gender performativity fueled critical thought about practices subverting the *structure vs. action*-dichotomy, ideas of precedence and subsequence, highlighting the generative power of rituals, and put forth concepts of media performativity. These practices allow for research questions such as: Did racial discrimination trigger the theorization of visuality, imaging, and technological questions of picturing in a different manner? Does *intersectionality*—as a model for the entanglements of agencies that before were regarded as either connected or divided—correspond with mediated network models? Will Queer Theory have something to offer to non-identical, transversal media concepts?

Practices of *doing gender* are highly mediated—one could even argue that performativity mediates anything involved, and so it comes as no surprise, that *media* in the narrow sense of the word have been taken under consideration when analyzing modes of subjectivities and subjectivations. It is not only the media material, their content and representational politics, that have been scrutinized, but also the practices of consumption, production and circulation, exemplary in their contributions to the respective gender identities and communities. What about digital media, then, if we think about their contested materialities und their often blurred agencies? Peter Rehberg points out the affinities of practice theory and gender studies, quoting from Bourdieu and Couldry about practice theory's overcoming the division between structure and agency in connection with Butler's concept of performativity, arguing that *doing gender* has been at the core of Gender

---

[9]   See for an example, Mauss' account of his analyses when lying in a NYC hospital—Hollywood's globalization and genderings led to a standardized *feminine* walking even in French hospitals. See also Erhard Schüttpelz, "Körpertechniken," in *ZMK, 1/2010, Kulturtechnik*, ed. Lorenz Engell and Bernhard Siegert (2010): pp. 101–120; Erhard Schüttpelz, "Skill, Deixis, Medien. Das technische Können im Labor," in *Mediale Anthropologie*, ed. Christiane Voss and Lorenz Engell (Paderborn: Wilhelm Fink Verlag, 2015), pp. 153–181.

[10] John Law, "Technik und heterogenes Engineering: Der Fall der portugiesischen Expansion [1987]," in *ANThology. Ein einführendes Handbuch zur Akteur-Netzwerk-Theorie*, ed. Andréa Belliger and David J. Krieger (Bielefeld: transcript, 2006), p. 213–236; Bruno Latour, ed., "Circulating Reference. Sampling the Soil in the Amazon Forest," in *Pandora's Hope, An Essay on the Reality of Science Studies* (Cambridge, Mass.: Harvard University Press, 1999); Bruno Latour, ed., "Zirkulierende Referenz. Bodenstichproben aus dem Urwald am Amazonas," in *Die Hoffnung der Pandora. Untersuchungen zur Wirklichkeit der Wissenschaft* (Frankfurt a. M.: Suhrkamp Verlag, 2002), pp. 36–95 [French 1993, first English translation 1995]; see Ulrike Bergermann, "Kettenagenturen. Latours Fotografien, Brasilien 1991," *Fotografisches Handeln*, ed. Ilka Becker et al. (Kromsdorf; Weimar: Jonas Verlag, 2016), pp. 160–181.

Studies from the start. The question of sexuality, however, complicates these theoretical affinities, Rehberg argues, because the desiring body exceeds representations, conscious acts, identities. Do digital media account for something like queer subjectivations and queer communities, asks Rehberg—is there such a thing as a queer subject self/produced in online media practices, e.g. in dating and pornography, through the aesthetics of apps and websites, and their tropes of *the stranger* and *impersonal intimacy*? The very characteristics of gay online sex, its consumeristic and egocentric traits, shows that this asocial community does construct the *homo economicus* as a mediatized and sexualized being at once—and at the same time that this neoliberal subjectivity is subjected to modes of commodification and of resistance to neoliberal agendas, moving in counterpublics beyond consumer capitalism. Rehberg's text explores how media practices enable alternative forms of subjectivity and sociality, where the sexual and the medial are as intimate as anonymous, because "their transformative force, their order-changing activity, lies precisely in the fact that as a practice they move beyond structures of meaning". In this way, Queer Theory, in the end, questions media as sites of meaning: "Hence, what deserves the name 'practice' would be the endless negotiation between those media activities that are familiar and recognizable to us and those we indulge in, precisely because they are not."

Andrea Seier takes up the recent discussions of *New Materialism*, which aim at thinking materiality anew in the light of scientific as well as philosophical concepts. Key author Karen Barad speaks of a "queer performativity of nature," and the works Donna Haraway or Bruno Latour and others addressed materialist/ontological questions in perspectives that did not only stir up concepts within media studies, but are read anew in the light of practice theory.

Barad looks at quantum physics and conceptualizes matter as a kind of doing, a practice of quantums. New Materialism revised the *modern* division of "natureculture" (Latour, Haraway), as well as Gender Studies's concepts of body and agency. Practice theory shares the interest in focusing not so much the subjects and objects but modes of transmission and of doing. So, both meet halfway, but also fall apart again. "For praxeological thinking it seems to be difficult to deal with forms of agencies or incapacities which cannot be observed," Seier writes—the latter would be one of the expertises of Media Studies, theorizing the unseen, the not yet seen, the virtual, the unpicturability of difference.

Like Rehberg, Seier comes back to Butler's *Gender Trouble* and its performative turn rejecting the duality of objective and subjective makings of embodied identities. But she highlights the difference to Bourdieu's separation of the social and the linguistic, as well as Schatzki's critique of a missing dimension of practices in Butler, because of a confusion of discourse and language as well as of subjectivity and individuality. Do *implicit knowledges* imply *implicit politics*? The *agents,* taken seriously by Cultural Studies, in ANT claim to keep a *neutral* position - so that negotiations in the production of truths, of the documentary in media, of critique and resistance, would be addressed differently. Thus, Seier's contribution undertakes a critical re-reading of several theoretical strands and their intersections, bringing them together through a media analysis.

YouTube-videos documenting the transitionings of transgender people enact a current form of "transmaterial gender performativity," and in such depict the limits of new materialist and praxeological approaches. Seier reads this *genderhacking* as a "matter of doses," that is: the practice of taking the substance of testosterone, the alteration of the subject, and the respective modes of producing subjectivity through a series of YouTube videos. These *self-mediations* illustrate the pharmaceutical and biotechnological makings of a body as well as a post-human gender design, a "becoming with technology". The technologies are media and materials, and the private is uncovered as the biopolitical. Barad's understanding of an "ontological queerness of space-time-matterings," the applicability of which comes under critical investigation. Concluding with philosopher and activist Paul Preciado's book on researching and taking testosterone, Seier regards her performative writing as another platform, just like YouTube, enabling the "materializations of political imaginations," and as practice-theories in themselves, using the transgressive capacities of their respective media, the excess in writing, the openness of images.

Canadian media scholars Sourayan Mookerjea and Anne Winkler undertake the effort to decolonize the *practice turn* in media theory, which has remained largely Eurocentric and a-historical. In doing so, they analyze some of the foundational writings of the discipline by McLuhan and Innis, which at the same time have been referred to in order to elucidate the ways in which practice and media theories have always already been connected. Media studies are situated within the *non-Hydra*, that is: the *Herculean* sciences, and could participate in capitalist surveillance practices, or they could illuminate intersectional media politics. Mookerjea/Winkler's analysis starts with the historical invention of new practices of being, belonging and resisting as depicted in Linebaugh and Rediker's book *The many Headed Hydra*. The colonialist practices of conquering, but first of all the practices of resistance in subaltern counter-environments provide the ground for their intermedia research, regarding practices are mediated by power-violence relations. To figure out, in what way is our media world is "a matter of accumulated violence," they refer to their notion of *intermediation*, and then discuss the respective theories and practices in the media used by First Nation activists in Edmonton within a campaign against settler-colonialist memorial politics.

They remind us that Innis was a historian of economic institutions for the British Empire in the Americas, of colonialism and slavery's infrastructures, establishing his communication theory in the time, when colonialism formally ended. Innis' concept of "bias of communication" seeked to depoliticize the term, as did McLuhans *environments*; both use concepts of the senses, of *the eye* or of sound (the bushmen's drum) for media historiographies full of clichés about non-Western immediacy and Western progress, ignoring geopolitical contexts, whereas subaltern counter-environments move within a media ecology of non-teleological time concepts. Both Innis' urban infrastructures and McLuhan's "global village" imply imageries of a city without the rural, without hinterland, margins and the suburban. More aptly, the authors argue, would it be to speak of "assemblages of communication," when it comes to urbanization in Canada, their settler-biopolitical, colonial strategies and the mediated counter/environments. More than half of

Canada's urban populations are indigenous people, who continue to be dispossessed and situated in *wilderness* as metaphorically as literally, and claim their right to the city. The example of the 2001 campaign against the privatization of their spaces in favor of the oil industry and green gentrification in Edmonton encomprises two sites with murals, a public monument, and interventions as an ensemble of media practices contesting the dominant communication channels. Referring to former burial sites and their human remains from colonial war times, the activists "retrieve a decolonizing mass communication system"; coming from a dozen indigenous groups, they do not speak with one voice as opposing Rossdale company, but created a memorial and very contemporary site within a set of murals pointing to the history of the place, Aboriginal genocide, and future demands. In such modes of "critical past-mindedness," the city intermediates practices of belonging.

Karin Harrasser discusses adaptation, inequailty and "interested practices" in the musical practices of Jesuit missionaries in Latin America. For a century, indigenous people of Bolivia were christianized and "reduced," that is: forcibly resettled by Jesuit missionaries.[11] This policy was promoted, documented and driven by music, that is: a hybrid music culture, where European baroque church music took up local practices of music, not only their instruments and performance modes, but also musical forms, genres, melodies, instruments, plays in processions, and related imagery. The notational sheets of the music, the descriptions of the performances, the cultural practices e.g. of the Chiquito and Moxo peoples make up for a "mission culture" which remained a contested issue until today, between questions of indigenous authenticity, tourism, and official politics of re-indigenization.

The missionaries themselves told the tale of Christianization in terms of seduction and adaptation, like the harp player seducing the beasts into "pleasant traps," following the narrative of European media aesthetics' superiority. Harrasser, on the other hand, wants to question this narrative in looking at the forms of "practicing, rehearsing, and performing music as techniques of governing bodies and souls," where the European music and dance practices had to be adapted, too.

Of course, mission in general and the mission's music made use of colonial biopolitics, of policing of the soul; they combined rational planning, bodily force, and pastoral governance of the soul (keeping a schedule, writing, copying, disciplining of bodies for controlled uses of voice and limbs). Guillermo Wilde depicted the hegemonic musical mechanism reinforcing regimes of time, space, and corporeality, forming communities through sonic experiences, putting on stage colonialist ideas of orders of universal harmony. But, nevertheless, coloniality as saturated with mutual and asymmetric interests and of operations with a never fully projectable outcome, we might see something that

---

[11]   The background for the study of a Bolivian archive of musical scores from the eighteenth and nineteenth centuries in Concepción is the history of violence and genocidal colonialism and the so-called *encomienda* system, rewarding conquerors with tribute and/or labor of the conquered people; there were up to 160,000 people forced into mission settlements called *reducciones* in today's Bolivia, Argentina, Paraguay, and Brazil, until 1767.

escapes the narrative of Western superiority. Making the holy mission was sometimes dangerous and precarious, because, following Hennion and Stengers, music is a "risky practice of attachment and invention". In the end, the musical activities in this "ecology of practices" (Stengers) seem to be adaptable and experimental, at least contaminable and unpredictable. Harrasser proposes to consider the transformation "as bidirectional, a mutual usage that is shaped in 'interested' practices". *Interested* is a notion used by Stengers to indicate the aspects of responsibility and intentions in the use of material. Local practices were undone and reshaped, with more or less violence involved, but also the musical practices of the missionaries were changed (taking up everyday music, spiritual elements, the upcoming of affects—for example, Athanaisus Kirchner's widely read music theory referred to non-European music to argue for the universality of the affect of *spiritum*, 1650). Harrasser evaluates the musical practices of appropriating native elements as risky, because colonial Mission culture would always remain fragile and contested. But she goes further and argues that the mere concept of *hybridity* does not take into account the impact of violence on the elements involved—there is no neutral ground for exchange in this network. In the end, she concludes, "it is the use, the need to enact a practice in a *specific* political, cultural and personal situation that renders music a dangerous method."

In contemplating practice theory, Rey Chow refers to elements of Actor Network Theory, to Foucault's technologies of the self and practices of self-examination, or to Althusser on practices of belief—but rather, Chow is interested in *why* there is an interest in practice theory. "If most theories are, inevitably, always already informed by some notion of practice, why has practice become of such interest in our time?," she asks, "have we come to think of practice as so important that we now have a name such as practice theory? What unresolved philosophical, aesthetic, and political issues are signaled by the contemporary investment in practice theory? For what other concepts—or problems, or tensions—is the word 'practice' a stand-in, a veil, a screen?" One possible answer, Chow concludes, could be related to a sense of failure facing the problems of democracy today, where horizontal political architectures give way to hierarchical ones; practices make especially sense when looking for arrangements and processes, that are rather extended than bottom-up. Chow prefers not to use the term *practice* but to look at different practices, at doing knowledge, social performances, gender performances, or doing citizenship, and refers to very specific cultural traditions with their gendered and racialized forms. She goes on to consider networks and agents, transmissions and assemblages, and in what way the question of power comes in.

In the end, Chow questions the idea of the situatedness of the researcher because of its reifying tendencies—while still reminding us of the agency of writing within the academic assemblages.

Peter Rehberg

Grunts and Monsters: Gay Men's Online Media Practices

"[P]hilosophy today is worth less if not undertaken as a quest
to reunite knowledge with practice, thought with ways of life."[1]

Introduction

Historically, queer media practices entail the production of fanzines, independent film-making, or the organization of film festivals. These subcultural activities seem uncon-tested in their social function and their communal and political value of creating queer counterpublics, as historian Martin Meeker reminds us: "[...] the consolidation of gay and lesbian communities depended on the ways people could connect to knowledge about homosexuality."[2] The media practices of the past 15 years that I will focus on in this paper, however—using apps and websites for gay men to chat or hook up—appear much more ambiguous in this regard.[3] Do they enable *queer* forms of subjectivity, do they provide a sense of community? The widespread suspicion about these new forms of interaction concerns both genre and medium. Within the history of visual media, tech-nological advancement has often been closely tied to the genre of pornography, a liaison that triggers moral panic about the representation of sexualized bodies as well as about technology. But the paradigmatic shift that the digitalization of our culture has brought about has been acknowledged by scholars from cultural studies and the social sciences also in less moralizing ways, by thinking about the ubiquity of pornographic images in the twenty-first century and the aesthetic and political possibilities that have come with it as *porn 2.0* or *post-pornography*—to name only two perspectives here.[4]

Talking about gay men's use of online media allows me to situate the discussion about practice theory not just within media studies but also within queer theory. While scholars such as McGlotten and Volkersdorff have used ethnographic methods to get a picture

---

[1] Tom Roach, *Friendship as a Way of Life: Foucault, Aids, and the Politics of Shared Estrangement* (Albany: State University of New York Press, 2012), p. 11.

[2] Meeker, as quoted in Shaka McGlotten, *Virtual Intimacies: Media, Affect, and Queer Sociality* (Albany: State University of New York Press, 2013), p. 5.

[3] See Ken Hillis, *Online a lot of the Time: Ritual, Fetish, Sign* (Durham NC and London: Duke University Press, 2009), pp. 33, 56.

[4] See Tim Stüttgen, ed., *Post/Porn/Politics* (Berlin: b_books, 2010); Susanna Paasonen, *Carnal Resonance: Affect and Online Pornography* (Cambridge MA and London: MIT Press, 2011).

of the new sexual cultures emerging around mobile digital forms of gay representation and communication, and thus already followed a path suggested by the turn to practice, namely to give empirical research a central place within cultural analysis and to emphasize the social function of media, my approach here is a different one. While my ideas are not unrelated to their findings, I am less interested in adding new data or descriptive narratives to this discussion. My project is closer to Tom Roach's attempt to understand these apps and websites based on their aesthetics.[5] I will do this by focusing on some of the familiar tropes from queer theory, such as *the stranger* and *impersonal intimacy* and I will look at these in the context of new media cultures. This is how I hope to delineate a notion of practice that helps us capture the new potentials of these articulations, as opposed to dismissing them as corrupted and impoverished forms of sociality from the start, as is often the case.

My approach—to use strategies familiar from literary studies for reading online sexual cultures—might seem at odds with some of the assumptions of the practice turn, which came into being precisely as a moving away from models of textuality and aesthetics. However, I will show with my discussion how not only sociological but also aesthetic models are helpful when taking into account the practical dimension of media cultures. Moreover, by contextualizing practice also within queer theory, this article is also a reminder that, in order to count as a relevant approach, a turn to practice must entail a turn to politics, as has always been the case in some of the most important works for both practice and queer theory, such as those of Foucault or Butler. Following queer theorists Bersani, Warner, and Roach, I will show how a turn to aesthetics enables us to do precisely that.

To sketch out this project my article is divided into three sections. In the first part, I will present my understanding of practice in relation to some of the methodological and disciplinary questions at stake at the intersection of practice theory, media studies, and gender and sexualities studies. In the second part, I discuss a selected variety of positions of queer theory that allow us to rethink the social from the perspective of the sexual, in order to gain a more nuanced understanding of practice for my particular object of study. In the last section, I will look at my example—the media practice of using gay apps and websites to hook up—and approach it with the terms developed in this article.

Practice Theory and Media Studies

Inherent in the term "practice theory" is a paradox: Is practice still practice, we might ask tautologically, once it has been theorized? Does the otherness of practice—as that which must be more than merely an application of theory—disappear when it is captured conceptually? On the other hand, there is the question of whether a notion of practice that is not also addressed theoretically remains forever locked up as the unattainable other of

---

5   See Tom Roach, "Becoming Fungible: Queer Intimacies in Social Media," *Qui Parle: Critical Humanities and Social Sciences* 23/2 (2015): pp. 55–87.

theory, thus solidifying a restrictive juxtaposition between theory and practice that the project of practice theory precisely aims to overcome.

These difficult questions have provoked a series of different answers within the various strains of practice theory, many of them going back to Bourdieu's notion of habitus.[6] What characterizes a practice based on habitus in this line of thinking is its routine and not quite conscious character. Practices are customary activities, and while, as Postill, following Bourdieu, argues, they are pursued against the backdrop of a doxa that limits their range and meaning,[7] they are also improvised and cannot fully be accounted for by given structures of meaning.[8] The precarious status of practice does not only bring to the fore, however, the difficulties of its conceptualization. At the same time, it promises to provide a more flexible toolkit that seems to be especially useful for the analysis of more recent cultural and social phenomena, which cannot be grasped by more established and contained methods. It is from this perspective that, over the last fifteen years, practice theory has been embraced by media studies.[9] This turn to practice theory is a response to the limitations of some of the most powerful approaches within media studies, such as a sender-response model, an encoding/decoding-model, or a technological determinism. In short, what is newly assessed here through practice theory is what previously used to be addressed under the rubric of "media effects,"[10] a question especially prominent in political, pedagogical, and popular discourse—as the case of online pornography demonstrates in an exemplary fashion.

Moreover, and more importantly in the context of my article, the turn to practice theory must also be seen as a response to the challenges that the emergence and continual transformation of digital media and the cultures created around them have represented over the past twenty years. In this scenario of open-ended practices of media production, circulation, and consumption, the question of "what do people do" in relation to media might be both more easily attainable and more productive than identifying the underlying forces of the seemingly volatile media settings of the twenty-first century.[11] As practice theory contends,[12] generally speaking, neither economy nor the text—and I will come

---

[6] See Pierre Bourdieu, *Outline of a Theory of Practice* (Cambridge: Cambridge University Press, 1977), p. 83.

[7] See John Postill, "Introduction: Theorising Media and Practice," in *Theorising Media and Practice*, ed. Birgit Bräuchler and John Postill (New York and Oxford: Berghahn Books, 2010), p. 8.

[8] See Mark A. Peterson, "'But It Is My Habit to Read the Times': Metaculture and Practice in the Reading of Indian Newspapers," in Bräuchler and Postill, eds., *Theorising Media and Practice*, pp. 127–146.

[9] See Bräuchler and Postill, eds., *Theorising Media and Practice*.

[10] Nick Couldry, "Theorising Media as Practice," in Bräuchler and Postill, eds., *Theorising Media and Practice*, pp. 35–54, here pp. 37, 41.

[11] Compare Ken Hillis, who, for example, reads media practices as new forms of rituals. Hillis, *Online a lot of the Time*, pp. 2–5.

[12] See Couldry, "Theorising Media as Practice," p. 35.

back to discussing their status—would be able to constitute a comprehensive framework for contemporary media studies.[13]

As convincing as it seems to me to loosen and reconsider our theoretical apparatus when faced with the shifts occurring in contemporary media cultures,[14] and testing the promise of the practice turn to do without that apparatus, it should also be noted that some of the assumed methodological limitations of media studies have less to do with lacking the instruments to take into account the dimension of practice. Some of the shortcomings are also the effects of misreadings, for example the failure to acknowledge adequately the notion of textuality as it has been addressed and developed within poststructuralist theory.[15] For, if anything, poststructuralism can be understood as a reaction to the rigidity of a structural approach, that is, it shares one of the impulses that characterizes the turn to practice theory.[16] Therefore, I would suggest, the turn to practice should not so much be understood as a moving away from text as Couldry has it,[17] but rather as the broadening of a discussion already prepared by poststructuralist models of textuality that acknowledge practice—in distinction to structures or values—as a constitutive force of the production of meaning.

I mention this critique of media studies methodology here as a reminder that sociology does not have to be the only discipline to turn to when extending our analysis of media by taking into account the question of practice, like Couldry and others following Bourdieu suggest. An approach that would ground practice theory too securely within sociology and its often structuralist heritage might unwillingly be still subjected, without necessarily acknowledging it, to the paradox of practice theory —that practice ceases to be practice once it has been theorized—and thus risks missing the epistemological challenge that

---

[13]   One way to look at the turn to practice is to understand it not so much as an alternative to but primarily as a postponement of interpretation. Practice theory prioritizes description over hermeneutic deciphering, it challenges our well-rehearsed models of criticism, or what Couldry calls "functionalist ideas" and what Sedgwick names "paranoid readings." See Couldry, "Theorising Media as Practice," pp. 43–45, and Eve Kosofsky Sedgwick, "Paranoid Reading and Reparative Reading, or, You're So Paranoid, You Probably Think This Essay Is About You," in Eve Kosofsky Sedgwick, *Touching Feeling: Affect, Pedagogy, Performativity* (Durham NC and London: Duke University Press, 2003), pp. 123–151.

[14]   In her study of online pornography, Paasonen for instance demonstrated how a psychoanalytical language is not enough to capture the movements taking place in new media settings. See Paasonen, *Carnal Resonance*, Loc 2274, 2288, 2296 of 3979. She suggests the terms "resonance" and "grab" instead, for describing the workings of, in this case, online pornography. See Passonen, *Carnal Resonance*, Loc 3225 of 3979.

[15]   See Mark Hobart, "What Do We Mean by 'Media Practices'?," in Bräuchler and Postill, eds., *Theorising Media and Practice*, p. 63.

[16]   Roland Barthes' notion of the text, for example, already entails a pragmatic dimension, as does Derrida's. See Guido Ipsen, "Communication, Cognition and Usage: Epistemological Considerations of Media Practices and Processes," in Bräuchler and Postill, eds., *Theorising Media and Practice*, p. 184.

[17]   See Couldry, "Theorising Media as Practice," p. 37.

practice constitutes once again. What is at stake here, then, is a thinking about sociality beyond frameworks of totality as, for instance, in Marx or Durkheim. While Couldry does call for a non-unified notion of the social order,[18] a sociality without a signified, the question is, how to prevent sociology itself from becoming the new "functionalist idea" that governs our newly developing knowledge about practices. For the context of my article this means that even if we acknowledge the necessity to understand practices in their social function, sociology might not be the only discipline that deserves attention here in order to make sense of the interrelatedness between media and the social as it occurs through practices. What is at stake with new media practices such as using dating apps and websites is also a reimagining of social relations.

One way of methodologically doing more justice to practice and the paradoxes that emerge when we theorize it, would be to treat it as an object of study that always requires competing theoretical approaches. Thus, practice theory should be understood less as a coherent set of questions, methods, and tools, but rather as a space opened up by the competition of existing theories.[19] As the negative of theory, practice makes theory necessary, we might say; an awareness of practice, however, necessarily must also lead to a failure of theory. This problem can only be responded to by engaging in more than one theoretical approach. Through debate and speculation, the turn to practice thus brings to the fore the practical dimension of theory itself. By exposing and continually negotiating the paradox inherent in practice theory, such an approach might not solve the problems inherent in understanding practice, but it has the advantage of not hiding them either, when translating them into an open-ended conversation about practice and the possibilities of its understanding.

While we need to locate practice at the intersection of different theoretical models in order to acknowledge its very practicity, we must also be aware that practice becomes intelligible only by being identified and named as such,[20] however preliminary and unsteady such designation might be. I find that Hobart's attempt at such a definition best negotiates these competing demands. He names three decisive aspects of understanding practice: "context," "deliberately open," and "order-changing activity." Hobart writes:

> I prefer to think of practices as those recognized, complex forms of social activity and articulation through which agents set out to maintain or change themselves, others and the world about them under varying conditions. Such a working account is deliberately open.[21]

While the aspects of "context" and "deliberately open" reflect the methodological problems sketched out so far, how these circumstances relate to an "order-changing activity" remains more difficult to theorize. This political significance of practice has been emphasized within the theoretical frameworks that prove to be decisive for my object of

---

[18] Ibid., p. 45.
[19] See Hobart, "What Do We Mean by 'Media Practices'?," pp. 56, 60.
[20] Ibid., p. 62.
[21] Ibid., p. 63.

study here, gay men's dating apps and websites, namely gender and queer theory—a field in which the turn to practice has been widely acknowledged.

Gender Studies and Practice Theory

The turn to practice has entered the field of gender and sexuality studies most prominently through the work of Judith Butler. The "dialectical relationship between a structured context and the habituated dispositions people have for acting in those contexts" that we can find in Bourdieu,[22] and the attempt to "overcome the old theoretical division between structure and agency" as characteristic of practice theory,[23] are at the core of Butler's thinking of gender performativity.[24] Many authors participating in the debate on practice theory are indebted to Butler's notions of performance and performativity. While practice has been one of the—if not *the*—key concern of gender studies for quite some time (for example in *doing gender*),[25] its relation to sexuality studies, which is the focus of my investigation here, is more difficult to assess. To be sure, sexuality as a historically constructed social identity, for instance as homo- or heterosexuality, is already part of Butler's analysis of performativity. After all, Foucault's *History of Sexuality*, a narrative that analyzes sexuality as the outcome of disciplinary formations of power, made Butler's project of de-essentializing gender and desire possible in the first place. However, as I will show in my discussion of gay online chat rooms and hook-up apps, interactive digital media create an occasion for displaying sexuality and creating libidinal and affective attachments and connections that exceed the paradigm of representation and its historical or psychoanalytic legacy so powerfully analyzed by Foucault and Butler and a first generation of queer scholars following them. Therewith, it might also shed some light on the question of practice as *order-changing activity*.

If the notion of performativity—here in line with the most influential thinkers of practice theory—acknowledges the tension between script und creation, for the culture of porn 2.0, the assumption and influence of a scripted sexual behavior is less clear. The economy of norms and desires familiar to us from a history of visual culture appears to be less fixed in the digital age. Subsequently, I do not want to follow the most obvious

---

[22]   Peterson, "'But It Is My Habit to Read the Times,'" p. 141.

[23]   Couldry, "Theorising Media as Practice," p. 41.

[24]   Gender performance is characterized by the quotation and enactment of symbolic structures that provide cultural intelligibility. While these reiterations of cultural meaning are coerced and legible as an expression of power hierarchies, due to the temporal structure of their embodiment their successful articulation is never guaranteed. To the extent that they are dependent on practice, they offer the possibility of productive misquotations, which bring about new cultural forms and, in Butler's eyes, will extend the realm of social, political, and juridical recognition. See Judith Butler, *Gender Trouble: Feminism and the Subversion of Identity* (New York and London: Routledge, 1990).

[25]   Already prior to Butler's *Gender Trouble*, the practice dimension of gender was acknowledged. See especially Candace West and Don H. Zimmerman, "Doing Gender," *Gender & Society* 1 (1987): pp. 125–151.

path for a dialogue between practice theory and queer studies, but instead want to suggest that performativity is not necessarily the best concept to work with if we want to grasp what is going on in front of the computer screen. In this paper, I want to rely less on the well-rehearsed models to analyze scenes in relation to media through performative practices. Rather, I am interested in the notion of practice as far as it exceeds the logic of performativity.

In a way that means I want to make a much simpler claim (which will turn out to be also more challenging) which connects those two intellectual projects—practice theory and queer theory in the context of media cultures. For practice theory, according to Postill, acknowledges "the centrality of the human body."[26] It is here that I want to locate the affinity between practice theory, sexuality studies, and media studies.[27]

The sexual and affective body, as I understand it, always exceeds the notion of performativity and its underlying logic of representation. Practice, in my understanding, works here not so much as a negotiation of historically generated, intelligible subject positions but constitutes a more radical break with scripted norms. Consequently, I want to use the term practice here to account for activities that cannot be subsumed by models of representation. Practice theory, then, explores sexual activities in media contexts that create a social relatedness while taking place beyond representation. A sexual body involved in practices is a body we have not fully understood yet, a body we do not really know. It is from this vantage point—what Foucault thought of as the unknowability of pleasure in distinction to the hermeneutics of desire—that the encounter between sexuality studies and practice theory proves to be productive.

The Potential of the Sexual

In their readings of sexual subcultures, queer theorists such as Leo Bersani and Teresa de Lauretis[28] have emphasized a moment of the sexual which is always in excess of its manifestations in fantasies and biopolitical deployments as sexuality.[29] Or, as Tom Roach puts it: "the erotic in its perpetual movement always exceeds sexual identity and

---

[26] Postill, "Introduction: Theorising Media and Practice," p. 9.

[27] This centrality of the human body can also be assumed for media studies: "Media rituals 're-create the illusion of bodily presence, the most basic of all ritual gestures'." Marvin and Ingle quoted in Hillis, *Online a lot of the Time*, p. 12. Hillis names this phenomenon the "sign/body." Hillis, pp. 5, 12. Paasonen makes a similar point in her study of online pornography: "in porn, bodies move and move the bodies of those watching." Paasonen, *Carnal Resonance*, Loc 80 of 3979.

[28] See Leo Bersani, *The Freudian Body: Psychoanalysis and Art* (New York: Columbia University Press, 1986); Leo Bersani and Adam Phillips, *Intimacies* (Chicago: University of Chicago Press, 2008); Teresa De Lauretis, *Freud's Drive: Psychoanalysis, Literature, and Film* (Basingstoke: Palgrave Macmillan, 2010).

[29] What these authors share is an ontological understanding of sexuality as drive theory, based on Laplanche's reading of Freud.

practice."[30] With these queer readings of psychoanalytic theory, a sexual and affective surplus beyond historically given deployments of sexuality is assumed. Another way of putting this is to say that sexuality as practice repeatedly leads to a crisis. If the sexual is not securely captured by historically and discursively anchored practices of sexuality that guarantee its biopolitical status, in its dismantling, sexuality can unleash the sexual as biopotenza in distinction to the governance of biopotere.[31] Could this be a way to locate practice as an "order-changing activity," by asking how the force of biopotenza could be made politically productive as a bodily and affective excess that not only shatters recognizable forms of sociality, but also inaugurates new ones? Conceiving of a public sex culture as an achievement of cultural and political value is not necessarily a widespread view, neither in Europe nor the US;[32] and now certainly less so than during the 1970s: the decade between the sexual revolution, the women's liberation, and the gay and lesbian liberation movements on the one hand, and the emergence of HIV and Aids in the West on the other. Since the 1970s, gay scholars,[33] however, have also continually reminded us of the specific achievements of gay men's public sex culture, in which participation takes place through embodiment and practice. Such readings emphasize the utopian dimension of the gay sex world, which has also been valued as gay men's contribution to rethinking the social and the political, as Michael Warner states it:

"Contrary to the myth, what one relishes in loving strangers is not mere anonymity, nor meaningless release. It is the pleasure of belonging to a sexual world, in which one's sexuality finds an answering resonance not just in one another, but in a world of others."[34]

Beyond the notion of the couple, it is the seemingly apparent *asociality* that invites us here to imagine new, unknown, and more radical forms of community. This perspective does not only do justice to the specificity of anonymous sex between men, but claims to lead to an important rethinking of the political. Before we decipher the ostensibly blunt media practices of using hook-up sites and apps along these lines of thinking, and identify them—somewhat counter-intuitively—as potential sites for alternative forms of subjectivity and sociality, we need to look at the tropes that structure this particular social sphere, which simultaneously promises intimacy and anonymity.

Strangers

Michael Warner's reading of gay men's sex culture introduces a character that plays a leading role in developing alternative ideas of a gay community. Warner reminds us that publics as well as counter publics are always constituted not just through identifiable

---

[30] Roach, *Friendship as a Way of Life*, p. 133.

[31] Ibid., p. 122.

[32] See Michael Warner, *The Trouble with Normal: Sex, Politics, and the Ethics of Queer Life* (Cambridge MA: Harvard University Press, 1999), p. 171.

[33] See Guy Hocquenghem, *Homosexual Desire* (Durham NC and London: Duke University Press, 1993).

[34] Warner, *The Trouble with Normal*, p. 179.

subjects, but also through the presence of the stranger.[35] This proves to be particularly significant for gay men's sexual subculture, a culture "in which intimate relations and the sexual body can in fact be understood as projects for transformation among strangers."[36] In this case, strangely, intimacy does not lead to a sublation of strangeness. In sexual encounters between men, a superficial reification of the stranger's exchangeable body coexists with the experience of intimacy; for it is a form of intimacy that is not anchored in the subject's biography, as a revelation of an interior individuality, which thus would create a special bond between two subjects who know themselves and each other well and experience their bodily encounter as a confirmation of their interior lives. Paradoxically, it is precisely this submission under a well-rehearsed conventional sexual code that gives access to a form of intimacy, an intimacy that is not necessarily that of the subject; for the subject of psychology is not present in these encounters. It is this lack of a demand for recognition or love that reserves some space for the stranger.[37] For Warner, it is politically crucial that the strangeness of the stranger survives in this environment, for it promises to become an exit route from disciplinary regimes of identity that would perpetuate the violence always inherent in the social.

Impersonal Intimacies

This shift in the notion of subjectivity is the condition for a different form of practice. Following Foucault, Roach refers to this movement as the distinction between subjection and subjectivation.[38] Forms of subjection are normative implementations of biopolitical regimes, a manifestation of force within institutional formations or classificatory psychological systems, for instance. Either through discipline or control they suture the subject to established forms of power. A critique of and a freedom from biopolitical regimes cannot rely on a notion of practice that emerged out of this very subjection. It is from here, then, that the emphasis on the absence of individuality, subjectivity, and identity appears politically important and paves the way for an alternative form of practice. "Anonymity and nonidentity thus offer the opportunity for desubjection and subjectivation—in other words, the undoing of socially, historically determined selves and the creation of new ones."[39]

---

[35] See Michael Warner, "Publics and Counterpublics," *Public Culture* 14, no. 1 (2002): p. 55.

[36] Ibid., p. 88.

[37] Moreover, the idea of the stranger is radicalized in the idea of a non-identitarian self. "Becoming a stranger in your own sexuality is about leaving behind the functional structures ascribed to the body and sexuality." Frida Beckman, *Between Desire and Pleasure: A Deleuzian Theory of Sexuality* (Edinburgh: Edinburgh University Press, 2013), p. 118. The stranger does not simply inhabit the place of the other but is already constitutive of the self which, for the authors of the "anti-social turn," leads to a model of sameness that always implies estrangement. See Roach, *Friendship as a Way of Life*, p. 36.

[38] See Roach, *Friendship as a Way of Life*, p. 27.

[39] Ibid., p. 34.

One of the occasions outside of the gay world where one can enjoy the superficial-ity of such practices that would not lead to subjection but to desubjection, would be the chatter at cocktail parties described by Georg Simmel, as Bersani reminds us.[40] Chatter in this setting is not about content or message but should be seen as a social activity of rhythmically connecting subjects independently of psychological depth. Analogously, the practice of cruising for sex represents a form of bodily chatter, or in Foucault's words: "one can meet people who are to you what one is to them: nothing else but bodies with which combinations, fabrications of pleasure will be possible."[41] With this tradition, participating in a gay public sex culture can turn into a practice for escaping one's social and psychological determinations, subjection is replaced by desubjection, normative practices that suture the subject to symbolic and social structures are substituted by movements whose symbolic or social meaning is not determined yet. For Foucault, this implies an overcoming of the category of sexuality as identity and opens up the space for multiple forms of non-identitarian connections beyond fantasy. In public sex, the self is not invested in knowing his or her sexuality, but in using it in order to create new rela-tions. These practices can inaugurate new ways of subjectivity and relatedness beyond the destructiveness of relations based on knowledge and property.[42] They are social activities that simultaneously articulate a critique of the social.

What Foucault, Bersani, Warner, and Roach suggest here is not a model of sociality that would give voice and room for expression to those oppressed in the mainstream public sphere. This is not a program that asks to be represented. Rather, we should think of it as a form of training, an exercise, or what Foucault in his reading of Greek antiquity also called *ascesis*; ascesis not understood as a repression of the drives, but as a physical and spiritual exercise that consists of exposing oneself to the unknown in order to transform the self in the encounter with other selves. A social practice beyond traditional forms of practice, or what queer theorists following Foucault have also named *friendship*: "Friend-ship, as I understand it [...], bespeaks the anarchical contingency of all relationality. In its very nature it is anti-institutional, indeed, it cannot congeal into an epistemological object known as society."[43]

Can Porn 2.0 Bring Us Together?

While queer theory offers us readings of gay men's sex culture in which possibilities of new and undetermined practices continually emerge, it has been questioned whether this understanding of subcultural experiences is applicable to new media cultures. Their forms of subjectivity and sociality are often primarily analyzed in relation to the harm-

---

[40]   See Leo Bersani, "Sociabilty and Cruising," in *Is the Rectum a Grave? And Other Essays* (Chicago: University of Chicago Press, 2010), pp. 45–62.

[41]   Foucault quoted in Roach, *Friendship as a Way of Life*, pp. 34–35.

[42]   Ibid., pp. 130, 132.

[43]   Ibid., p. 13.

ful effects of capitalism. In this regard, the bad reputation of gay online hooking up and dating is as notorious as the popularity of sites such as *Gayromeo* and *Manhunt,* or apps like *Grindr, Scruff,* and *Growlr.*[44] How would they present subjectivities, how would they bring people together? Can they be deciphered with the models of queer selves and socialities introduced by Warner, Bersani, and Roach? To ask these questions seems somewhat counter-intuitive. There is enough evidence to see online media practices as nothing but an expression, extension, and intensification of an alienating and commodified sex culture, as Tom Roach also spells it out for us:

> Everything you may have heard about online dating and hooking up is true: It is steeped in a consumerist logic. [...] It instrumentalizes intimacy and mechanizes the wily ways of desire. [...] It exacerbates the same barbaric impulses—hyper-individualism, cutthroat competition, solipsism, self-aggrandizement—so integral to and rewarded in the marketplace. Indeed, it is difficult to argue that social media at large do little else *but* construct and fortify what Michel Foucault designates *homo economicus*—that calculating spawn of neoliberalism who perceives himself and others foremost as human capital.[45]

Consumption, enterprise, brand creation, self-optimization, efficiency, aggressive speculation, the maximization of individualized pleasure—these are the key terms that characterize the *homo economicus* not just in his professional but also in his sexual endeavors. Submitting to values such as fitness and flexibility appears as typical of neoliberalism which, in our historical present, economically conditions the existence of the subject and the social.[46] Through repeated practices—in a restricted sense of Bourdieu's habitus—a culture of neosexualities implements a hegemonic power structure.[47]

In this perspective, hook-up sites and apps become the breeding ground for neoliberal subjectivity, communication, and relational forms dominated by demands of avail-

---

[44] My reading looks at practices based on visual and linguistic signs and in this regard, we might not find a substantial difference between apps and websites, even though the temporality of the communication with mobile devices seems to be a different one: smart phones or tablets suggest a stronger presence of the user and a faster pace of the online exchange. Another difference can be observed with respect to the identity of these sites and apps. The market of hook-up apps is structured by more specific offers for gay men, according to the compartmentalization of the gay world following body types, age, and fetish.

[45] Roach, "Becoming Fungible," p. 55.

[46] Following Joyce McGougall, Volkmar Sigusch named the commodification of sexual styles known since the nineteenth century as "perversions" as "neosexualities." According to Sigusch, the proliferation and diversification of sexual styles over the past twenty-five years cannot unanimously be read as an act of political emancipation. For they appear as individualized differentiations within a deregulated market controlled by economic forces. See Volkmar Sigusch, *Neosexualitäten: Über den kulturellen Wandel von Liebe und Perversion* (Frankfurt and New York: Campus, 2005).

[47] See Roach, "Becoming Fungible," p. 56; Paasonen, *Carnal Resonance,* Loc 2999 of 3979; José Esteban Muñoz, *Disidentifications: Queers of Color and the Performance of Politics* (Minneapolis: University of Minnesota Press, 1999).

ability and control: a culture of self-sex with no account of otherness. Through them, sexual subjects turn into business people, using the available opportunities for physical self-promotion. Compatibility of preferences can be checked through online lists and the visual display of bodies allows us to make consumer choices driven by an egotistic sexual interest,[48] thus partaking in what Jodi Dean calls "communicative capitalism."[49] If we take these descriptions as apt for the culture of hook-up sites and apps, browsing for sex online appears as a pornifying discipline within a commodified sexual utopia—a rather harmful habit.

Common sense also has it that these occasions to connect with men who want to have sex with men represent an impoverished version of real life encounters. "Virtual intimacies were failures before the fact. If you had to get online to get it, it couldn't be the real thing."[50] In a way this widespread perception is justified by the fact that the relation between digital and non-digital worlds is far from clear here. Are these sites and apps an all-too-efficient way of bringing people together, or do they, quite to the contrary, already exhaust themselves in the exchange of pictures accompanied by sex chat that rarely leads to any action beyond the computer screen? The transition from fantasy to reality, and even their very distinction, remains precarious. Are they perhaps nothing but a *media* practice?[51] While online media practices of self-pornification and sex chat clearly reinforce neosexual paradigms of sexual efficiency, they also present these very practices as continually being in crisis. These activities might be cut off from the real person, and it is unclear whether they will ever lead to a real encounter. But this inevitable moment of crisis also deserves critical attention. "Crisis" here, I want to suggest, should not only be understood as a form of alienation that must be fought at all costs. Our discussion of practice might help us to move beyond such a restricted reading. For it is through this crisis of the neosexual practice that another form of practice becomes possible. The moment of crisis should be taken as a point of departure to think about the ways in which the impersonal intimacies that Foucault, Bersani, and others saw at stake in back room cruising and at S/M sex parties might reoccur in online settings. This would allow us to speak of media practices not only as re-implementing neosexual imperatives of optimizing bodies and pleasures but also as facilitating alternative forms of sociality.

---

[48]   See Volker Woltersdorff, "Paradoxes of Precarious Sexualities: Sexual Subcultures under Neo-Liberalism," *Cultural Studies* 25/2 (2011): p. 169.

[49]   Jodi Dean, "The Net and Multiple Realities," in *The Cultural Studies Reader*, ed. Simon During (New York: Routledge, 2007), pp. 520–537.

[50]   McGlotten, *Virtual Intimacies*, p. 2.

[51]   Given the uncertainty about the social and psychological function and workings of those sites and apps, the difference between hook-up sites and sites that dedicate themselves to cam-sex and produce a user who is not looking for more than visual stimulation gets blurred, as for instance the gay dating site *Manhunt* gives away when it incorporates a video chat function, which appears to be an end in itself, into their set of services.

Virtual Communities

If we bring the questions from the "anti-social turn" within queer theory to our discussion of online hook-up sites and apps, what would allow us to assert that the virtual space is an extension of the back room and, therefore, provides not only a commodified sexscape, but perhaps also the conditions for similar practices of impersonal intimacy in which the stranger is also a friend? Online encounters share many of the features central to readings of pre-digital gay public sex. They are organized around the visual and not around language;[52] they involve the anonymity implied in friendship as estrangement;[53] they can lead to a dissolution of the subject;[54] cruising practices equal browsing practices and "the antirelational ethical principles constituted in the former practices can be found and fostered in the latter."[55] The question remains, how different material conditions, that is, the specific media conditions of online encounters and the practices bound to them, in distinction to the cruising in backrooms, shape and reimage those issues at stake.

It is the presentation through the picture galleries, the performance in front of the webcam and through the chat that become the dominant features of these platforms. In order to understand their social potential, we must understand the aesthetics of these practices. My thoughts here are inspired by a recent discussion of gay online hook-up sites and apps by Tom Roach that also reaches back to his earlier work on friendship. I want to highlight some moments of Roach's reading of visual self-representation and linguistic communication as media practices. While they are embedded within a culture of neosexualities and communicative capitalism, they also announce more interesting forms of being and being together. Through aesthetic media practices they introduce "new mediations of subjectivity,"[56] and can become potentially liberatory.[57] Ken Hillis calls this the "idea of living in art in the here and now of virtual space."[58]

The Monster

Like in *sexting*—the exchange of pornographic selfies on mobile devices—the aspect of self-presentation online that is central to both its production and consumption is the image. Aesthetically, it either adheres to a documentary style of amateur porn or follows well-established pornographic conventions. At least since Debord we know that the picture

---

52 See Warner, *Publics and Counterpublics*, p. 51.
53 See Roach, *Friendship as a Way of Life*, p. 4.
54 See Zabet Patterson, "Going On-line: Consuming Pornography in the Digital Era," *Porn Studies*, ed. Linda Williams (Durham NC and London: Duke University Press, 2004), p. 105; Paasonen, *Carnal Resonance*, Loc 2149 of 3979.
55 Roach, "Becoming Fungible," p. 56.
56 Patterson, "Going On-line," p. 116.
57 See Hillis, *Online a lot of the Time*, p. 33.
58 Ibid., p. 45.

itself can turn into a commodity.[59] Because it is image-based, the culture of hook-up sites and apps first and foremost lends itself to commodification. But does that mean that the function of pornographic images there is exhausted by their value as commodities?[60]

In his reading, Roach does not seek refuge in alternative aesthetics as, for instance, some voices within the post-porn movement do when they claim that new media technologies also offer different visual and body practices and politics.[61] With Sigusch, Roach shares a soberness, to say the least, about the reality of online cruising. But for him, it is precisely the hyper-evidence of the brutal mechanisms of online dating along the lines of racism, ageism, and sexism that deserves attention. The lack of niceness, here, creates the neosexual subject as what he calls a "monster." But the monster is not an uncontested position. Precisely as monster the sexual subject's position is continually in crisis: "This monster . . . is humiliated in the process: the aggressive ego is tempered by the law of equivalence in a (meat) market of substitutable goods."[62] Within a neosexual culture of competition, the adherence to normative bodily aesthetics cannot unambiguously be secured as a narcissistically rewarding strategy but leads to a general form of exchange-ability that involves a humiliation of the ego. In keeping with the queer tradition, Roach states: "it is the very fungibility as superficial types, not unique interiorities, that I find intriguing."[63] What is intriguing here is that a depersonalized visual grammar of online presentation does not provide the means of representation with which a subject could express itself, but what it offers instead is the willful submission under a normative aesthetic code. While one cannot overlook the brutal mechanisms of exclusion coming with this scenario, it also encourages the subject to be substituted by the canonical pictures of a pornified masculinity. The very practice that was supposed to guarantee the sovereignty of the neosexual subject in fact leads to its disappearance. But which kind of practice emerges after this collapse of the neosexual sovereignty?

Grunts

Roach detects fissures in the construction of contemporary neosexualities, not only in visual representations, but also in the linguistic contributions on dating sites and apps. Grunts, jumbles of porn dialogue, hip-hop-slang, bro-speak, and texting shorthand constitute the discursive conventions of online chat.[64] They seem to cater to stereotypical forms of male fantasies, just like the pictures by which they are often accompanied. These incomplete sentences and their lack of eloquence cannot exactly be celebrated for their communicative value. Measured against a notion of communicative intersubjectivity, where "the

---

[59] See Guy Debord, *The Society of the Spectacle* (New York: Zone Books, 1995); Hillis, *Online a lot of the Time*, p. 17.

[60] See Hillis, *Online a lot of the Time*, p. 33.

[61] See Stüttgen, *Post/Porn/Politics*; Paasonen, *Carnal Resonance*.

[62] Roach, "Becoming Fungible," p. 59.

[63] Ibid., p. 69.

[64] See ibid., p. 58.

actors tend to be conceptualized as free and rational agents,"[65] to regard this culture of post-communication as politically meaningful must first appear as a bad joke. But as in visual online forms, there is the question of who is actually represented through these poetics of dumbness that we also find in experimental queer literature.[66]

To answer the question of who is the subject of this sex stutter seems again difficult. Roach compares this situation with the literary device of free indirect discourse in Flaubert.[67] Free indirect discourse complicates the accountability of a literary text for it continually blurs the distinction between author, narrator, and the characters. By turning into a voice that is difficult to detect, it becomes a textual practice that exceeds the regime of representation. In the case of online sex jargon, however, it is not linguistic sophistication that leads to a clever undetectability; the maneuverings of neoliberal rationality, here, are not "outsmarted" through literary or aesthetic techniques but rather "outdumbed." Subjectivity disappears in the midst of the non-distinct stupidity of the practice of pornographic chatter. In its very dumbness, this impoverished communication presents an anti-subjective and anti-social dimension of a language; "what initially, and rightfully, may appear as forums of senseless blather and crass self-interest might also be an active creation of an antirelational discourse."[68] Precisely because of their lack of subtlety, these almost parodically conventional expressions can be read as a form of resistance to neoliberal principles which always rely on the accountability of the subject and the social.[69] Precisely because of its emptiness, porn talk can reside in a place beyond communicative capitalism. It can lead to a "codeless communication,"[70] to a language without value, we might say, which is not yet captured by capital.

Counter Public and Practice

Social theory has shaped our understanding of the public as an exchange of opinions based on rationality. This axiom of our democratic cultures has been questioned in the context of the practice turn: "The conditions of rational calculation are practically never given in

---

[65] Dean, *The Net and Multiple Realities*, p. 522.

[66] For example by Dennis Cooper. See Peter Rehberg, "Pornografie und Bildkritik in Texten des 20. Jahrhunderts," *Handbuch Literatur & Visuelle Kultur*, ed. Claudia Benthien and Brigitte Weingart (Berlin: De Gruyter, 2014).

[67] See Roach, "Becoming Fungible," pp. 68, 76.

[68] Ibid., p. 58.

[69] McGlotten pursues the same question somewhat differently: "Virtual intimacies as immanent and expanding possibilities, might appear to mirror the logic of normative and nationalist structures of power [...] that promise endless freedom and choice. But insofar as they congeal failed, carnal, ambivalent, and over- or hypermediated forms of intimate encounter (public sex, online hookups, predation, and so on), they also reflect the most irredeemable of queer intimacies, intimacies unlikely to be trumpeted as desirable freedoms. In this way, virtual intimacies also resist incorporation into the unreflective, deeply cynical, and/or phantasmatic celebrations of freedom that support homonational and neoliberal ideologies." McGlotten, *Virtual Intimacies*, p. 10.

[70] Hillis, *Online a lot of the Time*, p. 26.

practice: time is limited, information is restricted, etc."[71] Practice theory functions here as an intervention against an idealist vision of the public sphere in the tradition of the Enlightenment. A similar critique was articulated in the study of counterpublics, in which the limits of the notion of the public were not concealed but celebrated. With them, the constitution of the public itself is at stake:

> Counterpublics tend to be those in which this ideology of reading does not have the same privilege. It might be that embodied sociability is too important to them; they might not be organized by the hierarchy of faculties that elevates rational-critical reflection as the self-image of humanity; they might depend more heavily on performance spaces than on print; it might be that they cannot so easily suppress from consciousness their own creative-expressive function.[72]

If we read Warner's theorizing of counterpublics from the perspective of practice theory, we could say that practice becomes the site for queer articulations of social relations that might not always be recognizable as political contributions. Warner writes: "A queer public might be one that throws fits, mourns, 'reads'. To take such attributions of public agency seriously, however, we would need to inhabit a culture with a different language ideology, a different social imaginary. It is difficult to say what such a world would be like."[73]

I want to suggest that a world of virtual intimacies as understood here with the help of Tom Roach's analysis of websites and apps for gay men, a world that Bersani, following Foucault, fleshed out for the pre-digital era, constitutes such a different social imaginary. Now, media practices such as chatting and hooking-up online provide the ambiguous site where neoliberal practices of self-affirmation, and the calculating social and sexual cynicism that comes with it, collapse with the opportunity for a virtual intimacy whose impersonal character leads to the fact that the stranger is also a friend.

If it wants to be a strong concept, practice must have political implications, I argued. To assess the political value of the virtual world of stranger-friends is difficult, for their transformative force, their order-changing activity, lies precisely in the fact that as a practice they move beyond structures of meaning. In that way, they are attached to a sense of futurity. But to translate the transformative experience of impersonal intimacy into recognizable forms of sociality is also a risky business, for this involves some sort of betrayal, as Warner explains about counterpublic strategies: "For many counterpublics, to do so is to cede the original hope of transforming, not just policy, but the space of public life itself."[74] One possibility that remains, is to inscribe non-representational politics into representational politics, as Tom Roach does in his speculations about friendship: "[W]e must nonetheless seek out those social and political forms that best accommodate or ap-

---

[71] Pierre Bourdieu, *In Other Words* (Cambridge: Polity, 1990).
[72] Warner, *Publics and Counterpublics*, p. 89.
[73] Ibid.
[74] Ibid., p. 89.

proximate the antisocial nature of friendship. Only in these forms might we break away from the inherently inequitable and vicious hierarchies of identitarian difference."[75]

A subculture, then, would have to fight for political forms that also make room for this moment of self-transformation beyond representation, identity, and familiar sociality, to cherish its radical otherness as a continual reminder of the preliminariness, inadequacy, and violence of existing social forms.[76] Hence, what deserves the name *practice* would be the endless negotiation between those media activities that are familiar and recognizable to us and those we indulge in, precisely because they are not.

---

[75] Roach, *Friendship as a Way of Life*, p. 118.

[76] As Roach says about Foucault's notion of friendship: "what seems on the surface friendship's greatest weakness is in fact its greatest strength: Its very unrepresentability points toward a politics beyond representation." Roach, *Friendship as a Way of Life*, p. 149. It would be this very impossibility of representing friendship which would guarantee that our thinking about sociality cannot come to a halt.

Andrea Seier

New Materialism Meets Practice Turn.
A Reading of Transgender Knowledge

A third wave of feminist epistemologies and gender studies has been discussed under the names of *new materialism* and *relational ontologies* since the second half of the 1990s[1], rearticulating body concepts as well as concepts of agency, intentionality, vitality, and purposiveness. Scholars like Diana Coole, Samantha Frost, Jane Bennett and Karen Barad consider these concepts as distributed, non/human, and open, where materialities of varying degrees of durability and vitality interfere.

Notions of gender performativity are revised within new materialism. They are reconsidered as the latest version of the modern divide, which tends to subordinate materiality to culture and meaning, as well as bodies and practices to discourses instead of addressing what has been called *natureculture* by Donna Haraway[2] or *modes of existence* by Bruno Latour.[3]

It seems that gender studies is currently much more concerned with a new materialist and ontological rather than a practice turn. But what at first sight seems to be antagonistic, turns out to share common grounds.[4] The emphasis on the material aspects of practices is one of them. Considerations of the implicit and even unforeseen logics of social practices are another. Both praxeological and new materialist approaches refer to Bruno Latour's idea that the social includes not only humans but also artefacts and distributed agencies. And both do not ask so much for the relation between subjects and objects, but for hybrid practices in which connectivities between them (and even between themselves) emerge.

Also, on a methodological level, one can find similar requests. New materialist and especially praxeological thinking prefers empirical studies to critical or conceptual ones,

---

[1] Iris van der Tuin, "'Jumping generations': On second- and third-wave feminist epistemology," *Australian Feminist Studies* 24/59 (2009): pp. 17–31.

[2] Donna Haraway, *Primate Visions. Gender, Race and Nature in the World of Modern Science* (New York: Routledge, 1990).

[3] Bruno Latour, *An Inquiry into Modes of Existence: An Anthropology of the Moderns* (Cambridge MA: Harvard University Press, 2013).

[4] What is more, gender studies is engaged in combining new materialism and praxeology. See for example Susanne Völker, "Prekäre Leben (be-)schreiben: Klassifikationen, Affekte, Interferenzen," in *Geschlechter Interferenzen, Wissensformen. Subjektivierungsweisen. Materialisierungen*. ed. Corinna Bath et. al. (Berlin: Lit, 2013), pp. 209–253.

seeking ontological reasons (new materialism) or preparing empirically-based reports of contingent agencies (praxeology); whereas sociopolitical concepts (like desire or power) and historical contextualizations (like post-Fordism, capitalism, etc.) are misleadingly taken as abstract and immaterial.[5]

In this essay, I am going to discuss the way in which (at least some parts of) gender studies currently reintroduces the notion of *doing gender* within a relational and posthumanist ontology, and in doing so also refers to praxeological thinking.[6] With regard to Karen Barad's work on what she calls a "queer performativity of nature,"[7] I will reflect upon the way current approaches rework the notion of performativity and the political implications this revised version has. The question at stake here is: What happens to the notion of performative social practices within new materialism? How is performativity implied in Barad's proposal to "meet the universe halfway"?[8] Are performative practices still considered as connected to discourse? What happens to the notion of *situated knowledge,*[9] if queerness is no longer discussed as a strategic intervention into concepts of gender identities, but as an epistem-ontological fact (Barad) or at least a widespread incident, which has to be affirmed rather than invented or contested? Is there a roll-back going on regarding the findings of poststructuralism and cultural studies, as Alexander Galloway, Jord/ana Rosenberg and others have argued?[10] Or should materialist and praxeological turns be seen as an update of poststructuralism?

As I will argue, new materialism and praxeological thinking rearticulate poststructuralist terms in a way that has serious consequences in a political sense: What has been discussed as discursive interventions connected to negativity in the work of Michel Foucault, Judith Butler and Gilles Deleuze and Félix Guattari—mainly the term *practices* and the notion of *relationality*—is currently transformed into scientific truth claims. Within

---

[5]   The preference for empirical studies is not true for all approaches within new materialism, but the scepticism towards terms like power, subject, knowledge or capitalism seems to be widely spread. See also Alexander R. Galloway, "A Questionnaire on Materialisms," *October* 155 (2016), http://non.copyriot.com/a-questionnaire-on-materialisms/ (last accessed 29.8.2016). Galloway writes: "Consider climate change. Today's materialist seeks explanations in carbon molecules and oil pipelines, not in, say, the intangibles of greed, desire, or power."

[6]   For a critical discussion of the ontological turn from a queer studies perspective see Jord/ana Rosenberg, "The molecularization of sexuality. On some primitivisms of the present," *Theory & Event* 17/2 (2014), http://muse.jhu.edu/article/546470 (accessed 29.08.2016). S/he calls the ontological turn a "theoretical primitivism."

[7]   Karen Barad, "Nature's Queer Performativity," in *Kvinder, Køn og fordkning (Woman, Gender and Research). Feminist Materialism*, ed., Hilda Rømer Christensen (Odense: Koordinationen for Kønsforskning, 2012), pp. 25–53.

[8]   Karen Barad, *Meeting the Universe Halfway. Quantum Physics and the Entanglement of Matter and Meaning* (Durham NC: Duke University Press, 2007).

[9]   Donna Haraway, "Situated Knowledges: The Science Question in Feminism and the Privilege of Partial Perspective," *Feminist Studies* 14/3 (1988): pp. 575–599.

[10] Alexander R. Galloway, "Queer Atonality," 21 October 2014, http://cultureandcommunication.org/galloway/queer-atonality (accessed 29.08.2016).

poststructuralism, *relationality* was not discussed as a bunch of characteristics of certain entities which could be affirmed, but as an epistemological and strategic concept to help consider entities in an alternative way to the history of thought. This also holds true for the term *practices*.[11]

Whereas both praxeological and ontological turns highlight the contingency of the social in a very convincing manner, they also tend to neglect (material) dimensions of the social. For praxeological thinking it seems to be difficult to deal with forms of agencies or incapacities which cannot be observed. And the ontological turn tends to privilege questions of being to social positionings. If the relationality of *modes of existing* is linked to an ontological uncertainty (as it is the case in Barad's work) and the request to *follow the actors* fortifies a way of thinking which opposes epistemology and praxeology instead of reconsidering their intersection (as it can be encountered in Latour's work), the specific and also material entanglements between social practices and their cultural framings get out of reach. Analyzing YouTube videos by a transgender community, where mostly young people are documenting their gender transitions via hormonal treatments, I will explore a current form of transmaterial gender performativity and highlight the limits of new materialist and praxeological approaches in regard to the historical adjustments of biopolitics, power relations, and media cultures.

Praxeology–Performativity

First of all I would like to point out the fact that some of the current discussions on the relations between epistemology, subjectivity and social practices which come up in new materialism, new ontologies, and new praxeologies, reenact debates on poststructuralism from the 1990s. It is well known that Judith Butler developed her concept of gender performativity in a critical discussion of a praxeological approach, namely of Bourdieu's distinction of *habitus* and *field*. Examining the performative construction of the body, Butler rejected not only the dualities between objective and subjective dimensions of body constructions, but also the dualities of linguistic and social aspects she reveals in Bourdieu's work.

---

[11] See for example Foucault's notion of discourse and relational power, developed in Michel Foucault, *The History of Sexuality: The Will to Knowledge* (London: Penguin, 1998). In *Archaeology of Knowledge* Foucault points to his notion of negativity and "systematic erasure of all given unities" as a specific form of methodology in regard to discourse and statement: "In fact, the systematic erasure of all given unities enables us first of all to restore to the statement the specificity of its occurrence, and to show that discontinuity is one of those great accidents that create cracks not only in the geology of history, but also in the simple fact of the statement; it emerges in its historical irruption; what we try to examine is the incision that it makes, that irreducible—and very often tiny—emergence." Michel Foucault, *The Archaeology of Knowledge and the Discourse of Language* (New York: Pantheon Books, 1972), p. 28.

[C]an the social and linguistic dimensions of the performative speech be strictly separated, if the body becomes the site of their convergence and productivity? In other words, once the body is established as a site for the working through of performative force, i.e., as the site where performative commands are received, inscribed, carried out, or resisted, can the social and linguistic dimensions that Bourdieu insists on keeping theoretically separate be separated at all in practice?[12]

Although Judith Butler in her understanding of performativity highlights the importance of embodiments *as* forms of practicing, authors of the praxeological school of thought like Theodore Schatzki suggested an *undertheorization of practices* in Butler's work. Schatzki claims:

Butler says almost nothing about practices and how they constitute individuals via bodies. Although this lacuna has now been addressed in *Bodies*, her focus there on discourse, "naming," and language confirms a suspicion about *Gender Trouble*, namely, that Butler works with an overly linguistic notion of practice. In *Bodies*, practices are signifying practices, more specifically, practices of signifying through language; and these in turn are chains of declaring and naming acts that reiteratively cite and rework norms and conventions (and do so only as part of these chains, thus as part of practices). Nowhere is the role of nonverbal doings thematized. Perhaps this neglect is simply the flip side of a spotlight on language.[13]

One could argue that the different perspectives of Schatzki and Butler do not get in trouble with each other as long as they are not considered as competing truths. But the confusion of language and discourse[14] and also of subjectivity and individuality[15], which has shaped theoretical debates of the 1990s, is a profound one. And Schatzki's critique of

---

[12]   Judith Butler, "Performativity's Social Magic," in *The Social and Political Body*, ed., Theodore R. Schatzki and Wolfgang Natter (New York: The Guilford Press, 1996), pp. 29–47, here p. 31.

[13]   Theodore R. Schatzki, "Practiced Bodies: Subjects, Genders, and Minds," in Schatzki and Natter, eds., *The Social and Political Body*, pp. 49–77, here p. 64. (emphasis in original)

[14]   By using the term *discourse*, Foucault explored the different forms of relationships between words and things through history, from the Renaissance to modernity. In this sense language and speech are parts of discourse besides other parts like objects and subjects. According to Foucault discourse is not reducible to language but must rather be understood as a formative social practice that constitutes its objects and also subject positions which make statements possible. In his book *Archeology of Knowledge* Foucault writes: "Of course, discourses are composed of signs; but what they do is more than use these signs to designate things. It is this more that renders them irreducible to language and to speech. It is this 'more' that we must reveal and describe." Michel Foucault, *The Archeology of Knowledge* (London and New York: Routledge, 2002), p. 49. Michel Foucault, *The Archaeology of Knowledge and the Discourse of Language* (New York: Pantheon Books, 1972), p. 48–49.

[15]   The term *subject* refers to possible and impossible subject positions that according to Althusser and Foucault are considered as an intersection between self-formation and formation through others. Processes of subjectivation are in this sense acts of decentering and precede a given individual. Butler's work on gender performativity combines Althusser's notion of interpellation with Foucault's notion of subjectivation and points to the fact that the act of interpellation can be misleading because it needs to be decoded by the individual.

Butler's work is based on this confusion. It is engaged with truth production, discussing flip sides (language/practices), where passages should be the topic to discuss.

Interestingly enough, these pretended flip sides currently reappear, although in a newly arranged manner. While offering different alternatives, praxeology and new materialism share a certain scepticism against an approach which addresses subjectivity instead of individuality and practices which imply discursive and also non-discursive practices.[16] Practices, within the practice turn, are understood as bodily activities, in which the body is not considered as an instrument used by a human agent. It is rather constituted through embodied practices including skills, learning and knowledge.[17] In this view, knowledge is only gained through bodily activities which include thinking processes. The notion of appropriation is strictly related to these bodily activities, whereas other forms of dealing with knowledge and cultural norms—maybe those which cannot be observed like indecisiveness, hesitation, quarreling, or disbelief—are more or less excluded.

Praxeology focuses on so-called *implicit knowledge*, which time and again facilitates the confusion between a semiotic understanding of language and the concepts of performativity and discourse according to Foucault and Butler. This is mainly the case because the idea of an implicit or tacit knowledge[18] highlights dispositions of ability, perception, agency, and decision making, which all refer to individuals or groups rather than to the cultural conditions of subjectivation. What praxeology and new materialism share is that they tend to displace the consideration of probabilities of doings and sayings through an observation of their stabilities and destabilization within hybrid networks. They also both refer to the methodological recommendation from actor network theory to "follow the actors,"[19] which means to situate the question of stability and destabilization within the nuanced changes within the actor's trajectories rather than dealing with the cultural framings of these trajectories. Actor network theory's proposal *to follow the actors* acknowledges the claim from cultural studies that actors have their own philosophies which should be taken seriously. In Latour, the actors' knowledge is not a minor knowledge in comparison to scientific knowledge, thus it should not or even cannot be analyzed as relating to a *deeper truth*. In Latour's view, it primarily has to be described and reported.

---

[16] For a résumé of current debates in German-speaking countries, see Hilmar Schäfer, ed., *Praxistheorie. Ein soziologisches Forschungsprogramm* (Bielefeld: transcript, 2016).

[17] Theodore R. Schatzki et al., eds., *The Practice Turn in Contemporary Theory* (London: Routledge, 2001).

[18] Michael Polanyi, *Personal Knowledge. Towards a Post-Critical Philosophy* (Chicago: University of Chicago Press, 1958).

[19] Regarding the performative dimension of agency, this notion tends to reestablish older binaries between structure and agency, base and superstructure, which poststructuralist approaches reflected intensively. Latour writes: "Using a slogan from actor network theory, you have 'to follow the actors themselves', that is try to catch up with their often wild innovations in order to learn from them what the collective existence has become in their hands, which methods they have elaborated to make it fit together, which accounts could best define the new associations that they have been forced to establish." Bruno Latour, *Reassembling the Social. An Introduction to Actor-Network-Theory* (Oxford: Oxford University Press, 2005), p. 12.

Whereas the cultural studies' approach is interested in the question of how it is possible to escape from hegemonic ideologies and interpellations, Latour's advice to follow the actors promises to avoid questions of ideology. What goes along with this is an understanding of practices which differs from Butler's and Foucault's in a very profound way. A praxeological understanding of practices refers to practices in the sense of truth claims rather than of controversial negotiations of truth production. And, as a second aspect, it separates practices from power relations. Both aspects let an understanding of practices emerge that cannot be linked to Foucault's or Butler's work, although time and again they are referred to as trend setters or even initiators of the praxeological turn.[20]

When Turns Meet: New Materialism Meets Practice Turn

Also, within new materialism, social practices are of particular importance, although they are explored with a slightly different focus: practices are not only social and performative practices. As embodied practices they are also distributed material practices. In combining quantum physics and queer studies, Karen Barad conceptualizes matter *as* a doing, or, to be more precise, as a queer *onto-epistemological* quantum practice.[21] As a physicist working on what she calls "agential realism,"[22] she insists on thinking of matter as an active agent in its ongoing materialization, as generated and generating, produced and producing. The notion of appropriation of cultural knowledge is at stake here: If bodies are conceptualized as parts of the world, instead of entities dealing with the world, appropriation is itself questioned and transformed into a notion of ongoing interferences. It is the impossibility and failure of appropriation that is stressed in this view rather than its success.

Accordingly, the political agenda of gender studies changes: While earlier works on gender performativity highlighted the violating biopolitical power of gender norms, new materialist thinkers like Karen Barad propose relational ontologies, which address the

---

[20] See also Frieder Vogelmann, "Zur Archäologie der Praktiken. Eine Komplikation praxeologischer Foucault-Deutungen. *XXII. Deutscher Kongress für Philosophie, München, 11.-15. September 2011*, https://epub.ub.uni-muenchen.de/12428/ (accessed 12.10.2016). For a critical discussion of Latour's work from a postcolonial perspective see Ulrike Bergermann, "Kettenagenturen. Latours Fotografien, Brasilien 1991," in *Fotografisches Handeln*, ed. Ilka Becker (Weimar and Kromsdorf: Jonas, 2016), pp. 160–181.

[21] Karen Barad, *Meeting the Universe Halfway*, p. 185. Barad writes: "We don't obtain knowledge by standing outside the world; we know ontology is a reverberation of a metaphysics that assumes an inherent difference between human and nonhuman, subject and object, mind and body, matter and discourse. Onto-epistem-ology—the study of practices of knowing in being—is probably a better way to think about the kind of understandings that we need to come to terms with how specific intra-actions matter. Or, for that matter, what we need is something like an *ethico-onto-epistem-ology*—an appreciation of the intertwining of ethics, knowing, and being—since each intra-action matters, since the possibilities for what the world may become call out in the pause that precedes each breath before a moment comes into being and the world is remade again, because the becoming of the world is a deeply ethical matter."

[22] Ibid., pp. 132–133.

ethical implications of an anthropocentric way of doing politics and science. Questions of ethics, accountability, and political critique are raised in a way that is much more connected to the explicitly non-Marxist actor network theory than it is to earlier forms of materialist thinking. As Alexander Galloway notes:

> Not too long ago, being a materialist meant something rather specific, despite the capacious complexity of the term; it meant one was a Marxist. These days materialism generally means non-Marxism, or some variant thereof. What happened? As it was formulated in France in the eighteenth century and then more broadly across Europe in the nineteenth century, materialism was concerned chiefly with what Marx called the "sensuous activity" of society and politics, an undertaking guided by strict adherence to the modern if not nihilist mantras of secularity and critique. Today's new materialism means something different. Methodologically speaking, the new materialism is dog-whistle politics for three things: empiricism, pragmatism, and realism.[23]

The notion of a performative agency of matter and bodies is contrary to both Marxism and social constructivism, where matter counts as passive and immutable, a static entity waiting to be completed by an external force like culture or history, as Karen Barad claims.[24] Her concept of a posthuman performativity is supposed to overcome the juxtaposition between passive matter and active cultural forces.

New Performativities: Ontologizing Queerness

Butler's *Gender Trouble* (1990) suggested replacing sex-/gender-relations with a concept of gender as a cultural norm and pointed out that this norm tends to naturalize a heterosexual matrix. Karen Barad picks up and reworks this idea. She advises feminist thinkers to deal with the fact that their concepts of performativity not only challenge traditional divisions of knowledge production (sciences/humanities), but, in an unintended way, also assist them. Feminist notions of performativity were, as Barad points out, usually concerned with the human body and excluded other forms of non-human agency and entities. As an alternative to this exclusion, Barad suggests to combine queer and science studies, quantum physics and gender studies and to overcome the distinction of labor they produce. She discusses scientific knowledge production as an agential cut[25] through the world, which seems to separate (although unsuccessfully) the social from the scientific sphere, but cannot succeed in drawing these boundaries sharply.

---

[23] Galloway, "A Questionnaire on Materialisms." Galloway's conclusion, at this point, is perhaps a bit too generalized. At least, it does not apply for Donna Haraway in the same way as it does for Karen Barad's work. See also Astrid Deuber-Mankowsky, "Diffraktion statt Reflexion. Zu Donna Haraways Konzept des Situierten Wissens," *Zeitschrift für Medienwissenschaft* 4/1 (2011): pp. 83–92.

[24] Karen Barad, "Posthumanist Performativity: Toward an Understanding of How Matter Comes to Matter," *Signs* 28/3 (2003): pp. 801–831, here p. 821.

[25] The term *agential cut* implies a specific understanding of agency that is not reduced to human bodies. It points to the fact that practices of discursive classifications have to be understood as enactments. They do not *happen* by themselves, they have to be performed in order to take place.

In her article on nature's queer performativity,[26] Barad discusses the blurring boundaries between scientific and social forms of knowledge in regard to blizzards, animals, and atoms.[27] She claims that all these phenomena hold forms of queer in-between-existence, not only in the sense that they depend on practices of knowledge production, but also in the sense that, as phenomena of intra-active natureculture, they can also question our knowledge of causality, agency, and communication.[28] For feminist thinking, such an approach, promoting an ontological queerness of atoms, blizzards, and electrons, is a challenge. In a highly challenging twist for gender and queer studies, Barad suggests understanding culture as something that (not only humans but also) nature does. What is targeted here is a revised idea of an ontology that is separated from concepts of hierarchy, exclusion, and totalization, and that tries to come to terms with forms of being, appearing, and existing that traditional models of metaphysics have excluded. [29]

But what could be the use of defining matter as *ontologically queer* and ontology itself as *queer deviation*?[30]

It seems that, although concerned with their ongoing deconstruction of boundaries, relational or queer ontologies are unable to address their own partiality. Surely aiming

---

26 Karen Barad, "Nature's Queer Performativity," pp. 25–53.

27 In Barad's sense queerness should not be thought of as reduced to humans, gender identities or culture. Rather, she suggests to complicate the relations between nature and culture as well as forms of causality with the term queer. More generally speaking she describes the constitution of time and space as queer, in the sense that 'queer' it is no longer an opposite figure to ontology, but in its very center: "Queer is not a fixed determinate term; it does not have a stable referential context, which is not say that it means anything anyone wants it to be. [...]What if queerness were understood to reside not in the breach of nature/culture, per se, but in the very nature of spacetimemattering?" Karen Barad, "Nature's Queer Performativity," p. 29.

28 Blizzards are discussed here through different discursive layers, ranging from physics to literature and diaries from colleagues. Within these layers blizzards emerge as forms of nonlocal communication processes between heaven and earth. As phenomena they can neither be separated from knowledge nor are they immaterial fiction. Moreover, they subvert models of stable agency, of sending and receiving, of activity and passivity, as Barad points out. Processes of sending and of receiving are interrupted and transformed in a way scientists are still trying to find out.

29 As Galloway notes: "Ontology reproduces the very structure of queer alterity, given how ontology tends to be transcendental, abstracting, totalizing, and tied historically to concepts of hierarchy and morality, etc. 'Ontology,' Frantz Fanon wrote in *Black Skin, White Masks*, 'does not permit us to understand the being of the black man.' And thus, by homology, ontology does not permit us to understand the being of the queer." This response seems absolutely valid and yet at the same time somewhat limiting. Absolutely valid—in the sense that metaphysics has often been used as a weapon against the poor, women, people of color, or anyone on the losing end of moral or metaphysical models of alterity. But also limiting—in the sense that ignoring such questions will not magically cause them to disappear; any theoretical undertaking, when pursued long enough, must come to terms with questions of being, appearing, and existing." Galloway, "Queer Atonality."

30 Donna Haraway, "Situated Knowledges," p. 581.

at a deconstruction of fundamentalist cuts between entities, they let deconstruction itself get fundamental.[31]

While the practice turn dissociates itself from intellectualism and textuality, it promotes a rigorous scientification, locating truth within practices in opposition to concepts and theories. An understanding of theory *as* practice—in the sense of an enabling of positioning—is now turned upside down and transformed into a scientific methodology itself. In other words: A practice of theorizing as problematization linked to negativity—like a "systematic erasure of all given unities" (Foucault)—is not considered as an alternative approach to science. Rather it becomes itself a scientific truth claim.

Everything is a Matter of Doses: Genderhacking on YouTube

When the social is understood as an ongoing association of hybrid collectivities, the consideration of self-mediation practices is obvious. [32] YouTube channels and social media platforms as well as practices of self-monitoring in areas like medical health care, sports, and fitness are discussed in this context. From a posthuman and techno-optimist perspective, Rosi Braidotti has argued that current technologies are *queering* the human body in many—not only sexual or intimate—ways. Electric toothbrushes, cybersex, touchscreens, and cosmetic surgery are everyday technologies with the potential, according to Braidotti, to subvert gendered subjects in the sense that they open straight subject positions towards a becoming of an undifferentiated other, of a *becoming with technology*. Braidotti calls these technologies "queering devices." [33] While it seems to be rather difficult to share this

---

[31]   Such a notion of uncertainty, which is considered as a universalized assumption, situated in neither history nor politics nor cultural contexts, can also be found in Bruno Latour's work. In his introduction to actor network theory, Latour claims: "The world is not a solid continent of facts sprinkled by a few lakes of uncertainties, but a vast ocean of uncertainties speckled by a few islands of calibrated and stabilized forms." Bruno Latour, *Reassembling the Social*, p. 12.

[32]   Self-mediation as a term is used by Sarah Kember and Joanna Zylinska to refer to performative accounts of selfhood, accounts "in which the self does not precede or remain independent from processes of mediation but is rather called into being in and through those processes." Sarah Kember and Joanna Zylinska, "Sustainability, Self-Preservation and Self-Mediation," in *Life after New Media. Mediation as a Vital Process*, ed. Sarah Kember and Joanna Zylinska (Cambridge MA: MIT Press, 2012), pp. 129–152, here p.132.

[33]   Rosi Braidotti, "Meta(l)flesh," in *The Future of Flesh: A Cultural Survey of the Body*, ed. Zoe Detsi-Diamanti et al. (New York: Palgrave Macmillan, 2009), pp. 242–261. Like Barad, Braidotti uses the term *queer* in a new way, which is not necessarily linked to gender relations but to the boundaries between human and non-human entities. Addressing this perspective, the feminist journal *Feministische Studien* has called a volume *The Queerness of Things not Queer* (2, 2012). What is basically registered under this title is a self-reflective discussion within queer studies, triggered by queer of color critique, queer disability studies, crip theory and affect studies. *Things* do not only imply objects here but also normalized knowledge formations, relations, practices which seem to be *excluded* from queerness at first sight. In these approaches a new form of queer reading is emerging in the sense that queer studies asks gender studies to broaden its critical impact, to release its fixation on the critique

optimism,[34] posthuman entanglements can at least be described as forms of distributed embodiments,[35] which oscillate between location and dislocation and shape current modes of existing in lots of different ways.[36]

Regarding the embodiments of gender differences, a section of videos on YouTube is revealing. In these videos, mostly young people (from about 15–40 years old), who identify as *transgender*, *non-binary* or *gender-fluid*, share their experiences with a sort of posthuman gender design. But who is queering whom, or what, one could ask with Braidotti and Barad? How do the videos relate to an ontological queerness of spacetimemattering? Do the videos matter at all in relation to this approach? And how far could one address the forms of distributed embodiment with a praxeological approach?

The videos, shot in private rooms or work places, focus on gender transitions, mainly body and voice transformations, documented weekly or monthly. The protagonists link their gender transitions to rather different *materials* like hormonal treatments, surgeries, gender trainings, but compared to autobiographical documentaries from the 1990s, the hormonal treatments have pretty much come to the foreground of self-narration. As hormonal treatments are on their way to normalization or at least becoming more widely spread, they are also suitable for media representations as they produce a slow and gradual passage which can be observed in all its intermediate stations.[37] Most of the videos are composed in a similar way. They start with or without a trailer, providing names, nicknames and timelines (*seven weeks on testo, 2 months on T* etc).[38] In many cases the video begins with a greeting (like in *Hi Youtube* or *Hi Internet*) and a comment on the seriality of video production itself (like in excuses that there has not been a video for a long time,

---

of binary concepts bound to the heterosexual matrix, and to address also other forms of domination and governmentality. Within these fields there are lots of different approaches and not all of them follow a Deleuzian feminism like Braidotti does. See the work of Jasbir Puar on homonationalism as another example of combining Deleuze with affect and postcolonial studies. Jasbir K. Puar, *Terrorist Assemblages. Homonationalism in Queer Times* (Durham NC: Duke University Press, 2007).

[34] Braidotti claims: "[…] technology today lies in a sexually undecided position, an in-between state such as transsexuality; it is a queering device. […] [T]he embodied agent is unhinged from its classical frame of sexual difference, floating into a sort of undifferentiated process of becoming-other." Rosi Braidotti, "Meta(l)flesh," p. 249.

[35] Maud Radstake, *Visions of Illness: an Endography of Real-time Medical Imaging* (Delft: Eburon, 2007).

[36] In a critical discussion and finally in opposition to Braidotti, Simon Strick has pointed to the straightening devices of the iPhone. See Simon Strick, "The Straight Screen. Begradigungsarbeiten am iPhone," *Feministische Studien* 31/2 (2013): pp. 228–244.

[37] Hormonal treatments also create timelines and technical terms like "hormoniverary". See for example the videos of Ashley G., a male to female trans person: https://www.youtube.com/watch?v=xQOniMh_T5c (accessed 06.05.2020).

[38] See for example the videos of a British trans guy who calls himself Finn, *the Infinncible*, who is working very hard to document his experiences and runs his own YouTube channel. He also uses other channels, utilizing the legal limits of each device. Like others he now and then points to the fact that his video production started in 2014 as a practice of documenting his transition, but holds its own momentum: https://www.youtube.com/user/FinnTheInfinncible.

or a note that the video is just in time, following the regular frequency like a week or a month).[39] What follows are detailed reports of body changes, the enthusiasms they produce as well as the challenges of dealing with them in everyday life. Although or just because the boundaries between nature and culture and other respective binarisms are eroding, they are still echoed and reflected in the video diaries. Similar to the way in which the contraceptive pill has shaped heterosexual romances since the 1950s, they reveal that dating experiences and desire are closely linked to pharmaceutical and biotechnological treatments of the gendered body. Moreover, pharmaceutical and biotechnological treatments are themselves gender technologies which give everyday practices a certain shape and direction.

Aesthetically the videos use the imagery and *technologies of confession* that are widely spread on YouTube. They use the format for self-narration, but also to provide information, encouragement and support for the community. The directors and main actors place themselves in front of their computer and its camera, alone or with their partners. Their rooms are partly seen in the background, cats and dogs come and go. Whereas techniques of self-narration and their restrictions are surely important, what comes to the fore is the transition of bodies, voices and gestures, which are shown, described and evaluated. Features and narration patterns of the genre of "makeover television"[40] are installed, enhanced with detailed personal experiences, oscillating between appropriation and ongoing alteration. Usually, growing hair is staged in close ups, changing shapes of muscles are shown and described in detail. Gender transition is technically feasible, although in everyday life it is not a cakewalk. And when voices drop, time and again the actors discuss if this is an effect of a bad cold or of testosterone. Timelines as well as recaps and compilations from several years of transition support the intrinsic interconnection between evaluation and affects, for actors as well as for viewers. The correlation between growing or losing hair, shifting voices and changing moods is conceptualized in a very intense way.

The atmosphere these videos conjure switches between a spirit of departure from people who acquire and reclaim the means of gender production, the melancholy of its constitutive futility, and the sweeping and sometimes deflating impressions of the leftovers the so-called everyday practices are made of. In other words: *the private is biopolitical.* And practices, including media practices, are criss-crossed with and shaped by power-knowledge.

Do-It-Yourself or Who is Directing Everyday Life?

While some of these videos and their directors are dealing with transitions supposed to have a male or female gender identity as a *result*, there are others in which the ambitions and destinations of the transition are rather unclear. Moreover, destinations and ambitions

---

39 The desire and also the impertinence of sharing the process of transition as a form of labor are addressed in these moments.

40 Dana Heller, ed., *Makeover Television. Realities Remodelled* (London and New York: I.B. Tauris, 2007).

often change during the transition, partly because of the everyday experiences with a new gendered body, revealing the governing dimension of gender differences in everyday life.[41] Practices of embodiments turn to those everyday laboratories the YouTube videos are part of. They reflect and in the long run modify the components of what Barad calls the transmateriality of gender, and what Helen Hester in a more historical sense has called the "pharmaceutically-mediated nature of contemporary sexual embodiments."[42] The difference between sex and gender implodes in favor of an understanding of gender as a transmaterial interference in which hormones and video cameras, personal documents and dating practices are implied. What molecules effectuate in bodies and minds still needs to be mediated. It is performed and also observed by others. And it is translated in language. The restrictiveness and impossibility of this *translation* is addressed in almost every video. "I don't know how to express it …," "it's so hard to put it in words …" are sentences repeated over and over again. It is the entangled and also dispossessed body which is reflected in these moments.[43] Language and naming as well as medical and pharmaceutical treatments are both forms of dispossession and tools to deal with these dispossessions. They hold promises, and they account for experiences of alienation. And, maybe even more importantly, alienation can be promising, as the videos highlight. A huge amount of the videos struggle with a logic of cause (a shot of testosterone) and effect (feeling pain, feeling more clear, more active, self-confident etc.). But how would a methodology which is strictly *following the actors* deal with this? What kind of understanding of *the actors* would this imply? Would testosterone be implied as an *actor*?

Surely the directors of the videos are experts in gender theory. And many things that they address are usually beyond perception, at least outside of the transgender community. What they explore are not only the conditions of embodiments of gender knowledge, but also the ways common practices of hormonal treatments and medical sex change actually rebuild gender norms in a pharma-technological and mediated way.[44]

But what is striking is that the gender knowledge which the videos provide is gained through everyday practices already deeply invaded by pharmaceutical and psychological discourses as well as biochemical transformations of feelings and affects. This leads to the assumption that the juxtaposition of theory and practice, embodiment and knowledge, doing and saying seems to be implausible.

---

[41]   Young females taking testosterone are talking about the fact that they are addressed in a different way and also feel more self-reliant on testosterone. In sum, positive and negative experiences with hormonal treatments and social interactions are discussed and often lead to a critical reflection on the transition process.

[42]   Helen Hester, "Synthetic Genders and the limits of Micropolitics," *displace ... ment* 6 (2015), https://repository.uwl.ac.uk/id/eprint/2732/1/synthetic-genders-and-limits-micropolitics (accessed 06.05.2020).

[43]   Judith Butler and Athena Athanasiou, *Dispossession: The Performative in the Political* (London: Polity, 2013).

[44]   See also Paul B. Preciado, *Testo Junkie. Sex, Drugs, and Biopolitics in the Pharmacopornographic Era* (New York: Feminist Press, 2013).

Tacit knowledge of gender norms becomes manifest in the videos, and though dealing with them, their renewed embodiment is an ongoing challenge, a mission, and also a sort of cliffhanger. Tricks and tactics (like passing), skills, and empowerments (for surgery or using hormones) play as important a role in the videos as forms of insecurity, regretting, precariousness, and anxieties. All of these *body situations* are traced back to biochemical substances in one way or the other as well as to practices of mediation like the videos themselves or exercises of gender performance in everyday life. Again and again the protagonists comment on their own performances in previous videos, discussing possible reasons for moods, feelings etc. In a literary sense they get a picture of themselves which they review, verify, and reassess. And it is hard to tell whether these video diaries explore an inventive and self-determined approach to gendered self-facilitation by hormones, one that holds the potential to counteract neoliberal market economics, or if they are situated at the very center of these logics, because they discuss appropriations of gender norms as a question of choice. Surely this cannot be discussed as an either-or question, because the videos show a huge amount of different forms of dealing with gender transitions, which range from self-optimization to self-care, from self-protection in a binary gendered world to those examples which attack binary gender rules and regulations. And of course—as new materialism, affect studies, and the praxeological turn would argue—there are many more aspects to discuss within these practices of gender transition than those of shifting power relations. But at least in my view, the aspects which make the videos specifically interesting are not linked to a consideration of an ontological queerness which the videos display and are part of. What seems to be more important is how they point to the shifting relations between biopolitics, desire, and gendered bodies. Within this view, gender knowledge is neither linked to a fundamental queerness nor to practices of embodiments which are somehow detached from discourse. Neither practices nor entangled materialities should be considered here as what Donna Haraway has called "the real game in town,"[45] compared to historically and geopolitically situated discourses. They are surely both essential elements within negotiations of gender relations, but at the same connected and even enabled through biotechnologies and biopolitics.

Conclusion: The Medium is a Chemical Message

As far as the YouTube videos are concerned, praxeological and new materialist approaches would either deduce gender as a social order from those practices (practice turn) or read these videos as an indicator for the more general precariousness of the gendered subject (new materialism). From Latour's perspective, the analysis would address individual embodiments on a micro-level in a very detailed way. From Barad's perspective one could argue that the bodies presented in these videos are not only situated in the world, but constituted "along with the world" as ongoing interferences.[46] In a certain way, the

45   Haraway, "Situated Knowledges," p. 577.
46   Barad, *Meeting the Universe Halfway*, p. 160.

videos affirm logics of a distributed embodiment rather than conceptions of a whole body. And they do emphasize dislocation and alteration, although they also highlight the need for location and self-disclosure.

The videos surely acknowledge the relationality and hybridity, the contingencies and also the temporality of the social. But without any references to history and biopolitics, these insights seem rather pointless. Instead of verifying the contingencies of the social beyond truth politics, it would be reasonable—if following Karen Barad and Bruno Latour at all—to combine their approaches with the reflection of the biomolecular reinvention of the gendered body after the Second World War. Paul B. Preciado elaborates in his/her book *Testo Junkie*:

> After World War II, the somatopolitical context of the production of subjectivity seems dominated by a series of new technologies of the body (which include biotechnology, surgery, endocrinology, and so forth) and representation (photography, cinema, television, cybernetics, videogames, and so forth) that infiltrate and penetrate daily life like never before. These are biomolecular, digital, and broadband data transmission technologies. The invention of the notion of gender in the 1950s as a clinical technique of sexual reassignment, and the commercialization of the Pill as a contraceptive technique, characterized the shift from discipline to pharmacopornographic control. This is the age of soft, feather-weight, viscous, gelatinous technologies that can be injected, inhaled—'incorporated.' The testosterone that I use belongs to these new gelatinous biopolitical technologies.[47]

Like Barad and Latour, Preciado insists on the entanglement of micro and macro levels and on an anti-essentialist, relational approach. But the notion of relationality is linked here not only to the history of (gender) knowledge but also to its historical adjustments. It is concerned with the ways in which hormonal treatments like the contraceptive pill and other forms of biotechnologies were involved in rebuilding gendered bodies and sexual subjects in the 1950s. In these days new consumer cultures and new media like television and video supported not only the prevalence of pornography. They also coincided with pharmaceutical proceedings, and the overlapping of these two developments – new media technologies and new pharmaceutical proceedings – produced new forms of sexual subjectivities and desires according to the requirements of a post-Fordist order of the social. Post-Fordism should not only, like Preciado emphasizes, be linked to immaterial labor, cognitive or communicative regimes—as is very often the case—but should also be analyzed as an increased biopolitical productivity of desire and an ongoing circuit of desire-frustration-desire-frustration.[48]

---

47 Paul B. Preciado, "Testo Junkie. Sex, Drugs, and Biopolitics. Excerpt," April 2013, *e-flux journal* 44, http://www.e-flux.com/journal/44/60141/testo-junkie-sex-drugs-and-biopolitics/ (accessed: 15.10.2016).
48 See also Lara Rossana Rodriguez, "Transgressive Truth Telling. *Testo Junkie: Sex, Drugs, and Biopolitics in the Pharmacopornographic Era* by Paul B. Preciado," *Transgender Studies Quarterly* 1/3 (2014): pp. 449–454.

Using a very powerful image, Preciado discusses and compares the contraceptive pill as a form of power with the apparatuses of the panopticon, and argues that power since World War II is getting miniaturized, infiltrating, soft, more or less noticeable, liquid. Almost invisible, it ritualizes bodily practices every day. And as "the body swallows power,"[49] as Preciado claims, to refuse the prescriptive, prepackaged, regimented genders is what s/he suggests.

Describing his/her own non-prescribed use of testosterone gel as drug use, as erotic act, and also as a *molecular revolution*, Preciado writes:

> As a body—and this is the only important thing about being a subject-body, a techno-living system—I'm the platform that makes possible the materialization of political imagination. I am my own guinea pig for an experiment on the effects of intentionally increasing the level of testosterone in the body of a bio-female. Instantly, the testosterone turns me into something radically different than a cis-female. Even when the changes generated by this molecule are socially imperceptible. The lab rat is becoming human. The human being is becoming a rodent. And, as for me: neither testo-girl nor techno-boy. I am just a port of insertion for $C19H28O2$. I'm both the terminal of one of the apparatuses of neoliberal governmentality and the vanishing point through which escapes the will to control of the system. I'm the molecule and the State, and I'm the laboratory rat and the scientific subject that conducts the research; I'm the residue of a biochemical process. I am the future common artificial ancestor for the elaboration of new species in the perpetually random process of mutation and genetic drift. I am T.
>
> I do not want the female gender that has been assigned to me at birth. Neither do I want the male gender that transsexual medicine can furnish and that the State will award me if I behave in the right way. I don't want any of it. I am a copyleft biopolitical agent that considers sex hormones free and open biocodes, whose use shouldn't be regulated by the State commandeered by pharmaceutical companies.[50]

What Preciado highlights in his/her performative writing, also holds true for the bodies in the transgender videos: They are platforms that enable the materializations of political imaginations. These imaginations need to be embodied in order to *exist*, to be in and part of the world, and they also change during this embodiment. Preciado's writings as well as the YouTube videos demonstrate that the tools for manipulating one's own body are ready at hand, and they invite us to think about possible interventions (beyond diets and sports).

Preciado describes his/her own *intoxication procedure* as a theory of the self,[51] and, one could argue, it surely is a practice-theory of the self, and a self (-made) theory at the same time. The *body-essay Testo Junkie* refers to the bodily activities and affects of the author and is still considered as fiction. It uses the transgressive dimension of language,

---

[49] Paul B. Preciado, *Testo Junkie*, p. 15.

[50] Paul B. Preciado, "Testo Junkie. Sex, Drugs, and Biopolitics. Excerpt."

[51] At the beginning of the book Preciado writes: "This book is not a memoir. This book is a testosterone-based, voluntary intoxication protocol, which concerns the bodies and affects of BP. A body-essay fiction, actually. If things must be pushed to the extreme, this is a somato-political fiction, a theory of the self, or self-theory." Paul B. Preciado, *Testo Junkie*, p. 11.

without mixing up language and discourse, or subject and individual: "I'm not interested in my emotions in so much as their being mine, belonging only, uniquely to me. I'm not interested in their individual aspects, only in how they are traversed by what isn't mine."[52]

To study our entanglement with what Preciado calls the *pharmacopornographic regime*, queer ontologies are neither disturbing nor helpful. And the focus on performative practices is surely necessary, but only useful if not opposed to theories and biopolitics which help to shape them. The popularity of queer ontologies and the practice turn should be further discussed as a symptom of these biopolitical shapings of bodies (and universities). While focusing on actors, agencies and transmaterialities as truth claims, they are—one way or the other—dealing with truth politics and current forms of bodies' dispossessions. So be aware of scientific turns suggesting to get *closer to the world* while dismissing transversal perspectives. The drawings of inside-outside boundaries of knowledge are still "theorized as power moves, not moves towards truth."[53]

---

[52]   Ibid., p. 12.
[53]   Haraway, "Situated Knowledges," p. 577.

Sourayan Mookerjea and Anne Winkler

Decolonizing Media Studies: Settler-Colonialism and Subaltern Counter-Environments

Introduction

Given the media saturation of every nook and cranny of contemporary social life, media theory is poised to serve as the privileged critical idiom of our era. This chapter contributes to the elaboration of such a radicalized critical project by offering an account of intermedia research which seeks to decolonize the *practice turn* in media theory. Prominent accounts of the practice turn[1] seek to break through the current impasses of audience research, and the stalemate between readings of media texts and case studies of the political economy of culture industries, by bringing media studies into more intense dialogue with the social sciences. But the so-called *practice turn* in the social sciences remains largely Eurocentric, in some cases ahistorical, and generally not well equipped to address the contradictions of our contemporary deepening of convergent ecological and social crises, nor to deal with their politics.[2] Intermedia research, drawing upon the traditions of Canadian communication theory, Marxist cultural studies, and global decolonization theory, intervenes on just these issues.

We theorize both media and practice here with reference to settler-colonial capitalist urbanization as a historical formation of communication practices, and examine contestations over the ways the settler-colonial city of Edmonton, Canada remembers its history and so intermediates practices of belonging through its place identity. One of these contestations of place identity and common history involves the successful efforts of a coalition of First Nations and Metis community activists to reclaim a historically significant place in Edmonton, the site of indigenous and fur trade graveyards, from the dual oblivion of energy development and green gentrification. The second site we examine here is the

---

[1]   Nick Couldry, *Listening Beyond the Echoes: Media, Ethics, and Agency in an Uncertain World* (London: Paradigm Publishers, 2006); Birgit Bräuchler and John Postill, eds., *Theorising Media and Practice* (New York and Oxford: Berghahn, 2010).

[2]   Theodore R. Schatzki, *Social Practices: A Wittgensteinian Approach to Human Activity and the Social* (Cambridge: Cambridge University Press, 1996); Andreas Reckwitz, "Toward a Theory of Social Practices, Developments in Culturalist Theorizing," *European Journal of Social Theory* 5/2 (2002): pp. 243–263; Emil Visnovsky, "The 'Practice Turn' in the Contemporary Socio-Human Sciences," *Human Affairs* 19 (2009): pp. 378–396.

modification of two large multi-paneled murals on parallel walls of Edmonton's Grandin/ Government Centre Light Rail Transit (LRT) Station, which were unveiled on March 21, 2014, just ahead of the final public hearing of the Truth and Reconciliation Commission of Canada (TRC). The commission examined the cultural genocide of indigenous peoples through an official policy of assimilation implemented by residential schools.

These interventions into the circulation of signs, through which wealth and power normally police rights to the city, open an era of indigenous urban activism that coincides with a demographic shift wherein the majority of indigenous people in Canada now live in urban centers; with escalating racist-sexist violence directed at indigenous women; with escalating police racism directed at indigenous men and women; with an economic boom, depending on tar sands development, resulting in both rapid, uncontrolled urban development and inflation in Edmonton, and its recent bust. The Truth and Reconciliation process[3], a focal point of this urban activism, has also involved an efflorescence of cultural political art and media seeking to radically restructure all channels of communication between new immigrant Canadians and indigenous peoples through what we call a political poetics of Treaties.[4]

We begin, however, with a discussion of an intermedia theory of the commons as this has developed in relation to research carried out at the Intermedia Research Studio at the Department of Sociology, University of Alberta, in recent years.[5] The first section

---

[3]   The Truth and Reconciliation Commission of Canada was struck in 2009 to hold public hearings and listen to the experiences of survivors of the residential school system that was used by the Canadian state for over one hundred and fifty years as a tool for the assimilation of indigenous peoples. Over one hundred and fifty thousand children were taken from their families to board at these schools to devastating effect; many died, suffered physical and sexual abuse or were worked to ill health. While the program's official mandate was assimilation, in actual practice residential schools were one more tactic of the colonial capitalist state's social engineering of racial apartheid and its results recognized by Chief Justice Beverly McLachlin of the Supreme Court of Canada as cultural genocide. The last residential school in Canada closed in the 1990s. The TRC process was mandated by the Indian Residential Schools Settlement Agreement, the result of a class action suit launched by survivors against the Government of Canada. From the time the Commission began its work, the questions of truth and reconciliation with respect to this history of cultural genocide have transversed the field of politics in Canada such that all political positions come to be evaluated in relation to the memory politics of decolonization mobilized around this enduring intermedia ritual.

[4]   Sourayan Mookerjea, "Petrocultures in Passive Revolution, or, the Autonomous Domain of Subaltern Geo-Politics" in *Petrocultures: Oil, Energy, Culture*, ed. Sheena Wilson, Adam Carlson and Imre Szeman (Montreal: McGill Queens University Press, 2017).

[5]   Sourayan Mookerjea, "Montage and Spatial Ethnography: Crystalline Narration and Cultural Studies of Globalization," *Symploke* 9/1-2 (2001): pp. 114–131; Sourayan Mookerjea, "Allegorical Stereotypes: Calendar's Filmic Concept of Global Flows," *Space and Culture* 5/2 (2002): pp. 103–121; Sourayan Mookerjea, "Native Informant as Impossible Perspective: Information, Subalternist Deconstruction and Ethnographies of Globalization," in *Canadian Review of Sociology and Anthropology* 40/2 (2003): pp. 125–151; Sourayan Mookerjea, "Autonomy and Video Mediation: Dalitbahujan Women's Utopian Knowledge Production," in *Indigenous Knowledge and Learning*

of the chapter takes up the question of theorizing media and social practices and sets out the stakes for decolonizing the practice turn in media studies. The subsequent section addresses the question of intermediation in relation to a practice theory of the commons that we assemble through an encounter between Canadian communication theory and cultural studies. The final two sections of the chapter then return to the specific (but for media studies, non-canonical) intermedia practices of "right to the city"[6] urban practices of living in common.

Resituating Social Practices

The practice turn promises to elude the impasses of media studies without abandoning the strengths of formal analyses, ideology critique, or the critique of political economy, by proposing to study media practices in their full range, including practices of production, distribution, appropriation, resistance, reconstruction etc. The practice turn's call for a closer engagement with the social sciences' problematic of social practices, for decentering media practices in relation to a broad field of social practices, for purging media studies of its *embarrassing functionalism* are all indeed paths intermedia research also takes. In this regard, intermedia research also proposes the principle of (re)turning to practices but goes farther than what has been called *the practice turn* in the social sciences, by including in this principle its corollary that all practices are mediated. Intermedia research endeavors not to fall prey to the empiricist delusion of an immediacy of practice for two reasons.

As Couldry observes, media practices stand out insofar as they represent or model other social practices out of which they themselves are then produced, such that media practices "have consequences" that bear upon non-media practices.[7] For intermedia research the freeze frame of cause and effect must be released into narrative dialectical motion as soon as it has been registered. The concept of *social practice* itself projects but another reification and so intermedia research proposes a very different kind of social science than the dominant colonialist patriarchal one. In the critical social sciences at least, the problematic of practices has been increasingly reworked to include their mediation not only by meaning, structure, and contingency but also by power, history, and environments.[8]

---

in Asia/Pacific and Africa, ed. D. Kapoor and E. Shizha (New York: Palgrave Macmillan, 2010); Sourayan Mookerjea, "Cosmopolitanism's Other Utopia: The Humanities, Cultural Studies and the Time Bias of Communication," *Contours: The Journal of the Institute for Humanities* Spring/ Summer (2011): pp. 32–41, *http://www.sfu.ca/humanities-institute/?p=581* (accessed 23.09.2013); Sourayan Mookerjea, "Notes on time bias poem no. 3/In memoriam: device for falling into the rift between history and memory," *TranscUlturAl: A Journal of Translation and Cultural Studies* 8/1 (2016), https://ejournals.library.ualberta.ca/index.php/TC (accessed 15.05.2016).

6   Henri Lefebvre, *Writings on Cities* (Cambridge: Blackwell, 1996).

7   Couldry, *Listening Beyond the Echoes*, p. 41.

8   Arjun Appadurai, *Modernity at Large* (Chicago: University of Chicago Press, 1996); Akhil Gupta and James Ferguson, *Culture Power and Place* (Durham NC: Duke University Press, 1997); Sherry B. Ortner, *Anthropology and Social Theory: Culture, Power and the Acting Subject* (Durham NC:

Building on such developments, we take our point of departure, however, from the critique of reification at the heart of Dorothy Smith's[9] critical institutional ethnography and from the critique of northern theory developed by Raewyn Connell.[10]

Both Smith and Connell turn to practice but for them there is no practice in its elemental immediacy that serves as the foundation of any old ontology or the model of a new practical logic. Rather, for Smith, practices of everyday life are always underway and connected to the politics of social reproduction, practices inseparable from the social division of labor and power struggles involving patriarchal, heteronormative, and racialized systems of oppression. Smith's critical ethnography studies the institutional, indeed usually *textual*, processes by which this realm of the political struggles of everyday life becomes reified into normalized, ranked, routinized, controlled, and depoliticized practices of what she calls patriarchal capitalist relations of rule. Smith thus endeavors to show how practices of everyday life, in their concrete specificity, are nevertheless mediated by abstract power relations.

Raewyn Connell adds another dimension to such critiques of a depoliticizing immediacy. Referring specifically to the practice theory building of Bourdieu and Giddens, among others, Connell reminds us that we are never for a split second outside of history and able to start theorizing clean from some godly or Cartesian ideal starting point. Connell recounts the emergence of the social sciences through the historical project of colonialism and is primarily concerned with its attendant intellectual division of labor whereby the colonies serve as field sites for the resource extraction of data and the metropole headquarters for the value-added practice of theorizing finished thoughts for export. Of course, these colonial vectors of academic knowledge production still operate today as everyone outside the triangular trade between the US, the UK, and Great Power Europe will readily affirm. But Connell reminds us that the colonial project was all about re-assembling the social in the colonies and this involved not only the violence of conquest, war, enslavement, and witch-burning but the epistemic violence of presuming to clear the ground of all extant knowledges and their practices to start with a clean slate. "Terra nullius, the colonizer's dream, is a sinister presupposition for social science," Connell writes, and it "is invoked every time we try to theorize the formation of social institutions and systems from scratch, in a blank space. Whenever we see the words *building block* in a treatise of social theory, we should be asking who used to occupy the land."[11] Every treatise of social theory[12] that

---

Duke University Press, 2006); Marshall Sahlins, *Culture in Practice: Selected Essays* (New York: Zone Books, 2000).

[9]   Dorothy E. Smith, *The Conceptual Practices of Power* (Toronto: University of Toronto Press, 1990), pp. 67–69; Dorothy E. Smith, *Texts, Facts and Femininity: Exploring the Relations of Ruling* (London: Routledge, 1990), pp. 71–74.

[10]   Raewyn Connell, *Southern Theory: The Global Dynamics of Knowledge in Social Science* (Cambridge: Polity Press, 2007).

[11]   Ibid., p. 47.

[12]   For example Schatski, *Social Practices*; Raimo Tuomela, *The Philosophy of Social Practices: A Collective Acceptance View* (Cambridge: Cambridge University Press, 2002).

forgets the colonial history of the present and the world history of ongoing decolonization struggles, or proposes to found social theory as a social ontology of practice built
out of elementary building blocks—whether of utility calculations or norms or habitus
or the pragmatics of meaning or *we attitudes* or chains of speech acts—only repeats this
patriarchal epistemic violence of world conquest. Once we frame the abstraction *practice*
out from the teeming heterogeneous welter of specific things people actually have been
doing around the world, it matters little whether we pronounce upon it the depoliticizing
invocations of language games or of binary oppositions or of an embodied, reflexive,
performative *causa-sui*, etc. The concept cannot be electrified into life from dead, blank
space without theory rising to the concrete singularity of this or that specific historical
and political situation. As with Smith, Connell also insists that the abstraction *practice* is
useful for theorizing—not because it pulls the rabbit of *agency* out of the hat of *structural
constraint*—but only insofar as we find the *histories of repoliticization* this reification
both holds and conceals.

   Connell's re-situation of the history of the social sciences in relation to colonial history
is therefore usefully supplemented by Peter Linebaugh and Marcus Rediker's account of
the violent creation of the new worlds of trans-Atlantic capitalism in their magnum opus
The Many-Headed Hydra.[13] These British historians retrace the connections between the
European enclosures, colonization, and plantation slavery forged through the new media
ecologies of the Atlantic merchant and naval fleets. Their history emphasizes the rebel-
lions, revolts, mutinies, desertions, movements of slaves, indigenous people, maroons,
sailors, pirates, witches, soldiers, and subaltern women servants and preachers against
the making of Atlantic capitalism from the sixteenth century to its stabilization in the
eighteenth century. Drawing upon the rhetoric of proprietors over this three century-long
cycle of conquest, revolt, and repression, they describe this world historical struggle as a
herculean war of property against the many-headed Hydra of resistance. The significance
of Linebaugh and Rediker's account for our discussion here is the light it sheds on our
understanding of the social sciences. As the warships of proprietors built a new world
economy and a new imperialist Westphalian inter-state system, so were a series of colonial
sciences invented to govern and manage this new set of problems, crises, and resistances
that would come to be called (and in the nineteenth century theorized as) *society*. For
example, William Petty's first treatise on "political arithmetic," a forerunner of political
economy, was written in order to help consolidate Cromwell's re-conquest of Ireland. In
opposition to this intersecting system of oppressions being assembled at a world scale,
agricultural people, hunters and gatherers, pastoralists, forest dwellers who were flung
together into new political and productive relations on the decks and holds of ships, on
plantations, colonies, in the forests of this new world-scale distribution of events and
processes, did in fact invent new practices of being, belonging and resisting. We call such
chronotopes of collective resistance to the accumulated violence of "society" *subaltern*

---

[13]   Peter Linebaugh and Marcus Rediker, *The Many-Headed Hydra: Sailors, Slaves, Commoners, and
       the Hidden History of the Revolutionary Atlantic* (Boston MA: Beacon Press, 2000).

counter-environments. We will return to this concept of *subaltern counter-environments* below, but for now we can note that what feminists such as Dorothy Smith and Raewyn Connell, among others, theorize as the everyday practical sphere of social reproduction mediating all social production, is comprised of just such survival practices of subaltern counter-environments.

Only for such a herculean science set to the task of civilizing hydrapolitics is society, and social practice, identical with itself in an immediacy that represses the accumulated violence of capitalist society through a rhetoric of law and peace. For intermedia research, however, practices are mediated by power-violence relations, which, in turn, are mediated by insurgent and creative practices of everyday life. We insist on the conjunction of violence with power for several reasons. Whereas Foucault dismisses the question of violence because power is not always violent, feminist and anti-racist scholarship draw attention to the link between power and violence in compelling ways, and have forged concepts of institutional and symbolic violence to do so. Moreover, Fanon's[14] argument that colonialism is violence suggests to us that Anibel Quijano's[15] theorization of our contemporary, global colonial matrix of power is also a matter of accumulated violence. Indeed, such accumulated violence allows us to understand why and how different power machines of oppression intersect. Even the case of the power relation of exploitation, of the allegedly pure economic, nonviolent and *free* coercion of market mechanisms, involves the violence of cost externalization to bodies and their ecologies. But then the key implication of theorizing social practices in terms of their intermediation with power and accumulated violence for the practice turn in media studies needs to be underscored. Intermedia research takes care not to be co-opted by herculean science and become a mere service provider of surveillance over practices in their creative flux and heterogeneity. Intermedia research questions come from sources very different than the interests of capitalist property; they are rather drawn from the theory and praxis of social justice movements and their contradictions but necessarily remain autonomous from them. In this regard, they remain in fidelity to cultural studies' inaugural insight that everyday political struggle over-determines social practices so that the only kind of media studies worth doing is one that can illuminate the conjunctural terrain of intersectional cultural politics.

Intermedia Theory

We now turn to outlining the theoretical concept of *intermediation.* The lens through which we refract several theoretical arguments regarding media, practices, the social and the commons is the work of the Canadian political economist and communication theorist Harold Innis and his student, Marshall McLuhan. We have found it helpful to bend some of their ideas to the purposes of decolonizing media theory.

---

[14]   Frantz Fanon, *The Wretched of the Earth*, trans. R. Philcox (New York: Grove Press, 1961).

[15]   Anibel Quijano, "Coloniality of Power, Eurocentrism and Latin America," *Nepantla: Views from the South* 1/3 (2000): pp. 534–580.

As a historian of economic institutions crucial to the establishment of British Empire in the Americas, Innis was keenly alive to the importance of the problems of communication for the working of markets and other institutions for capital accumulation; in the Atlantic cod fisheries, the fur trade, the Atlantic triangular trade, the opening of the Canadian West via railroad construction, the wheat boom and immigration, all of which are key episodes of Canadian settler-colonial nation-building.

Innis develops his communication theory just as the British Empire is replaced by the leadership of Pax Americana and the globalization of the system of nation-states through decolonization and the Cold War. The large sweep of this history is a crucial context for understanding Innis' *bias of communication* thesis, its constellation of concepts—"monopoly of knowledge"; "margin of empire"; "strategy of culture"—and his denunciation of our "obsession with present-mindedness," which he theorizes as the "space bias" of modernity.[16] In this diagnosis of some kind of hegemony of space characterizing the modern, Innis keeps the illustrious company of theorists such as Lukács, Heidegger, Debord and Lefebvre, among others.[17] But it is the way Innis formulates the issues that is important to us here, not the least of which is his mobilization of the concept of bias itself.

His critical target is the claims of the new discipline of neoclassical economics (a herculean science *par excellence*) to constitute a *value-free* science. But rather than evoking the typical issues of perspective, opinion, and prejudice that are standard fare in discussions of media, Innis appropriates the term *bias* from electrical engineers and more specifically from the circuitry of telegraphic signaling, where a direct current is used to establish a reference point enabling an alternating current to amplify a signal. Innis' metaphor figures "the mediation of mediation," so to speak; the mediation of communication by its social, historical, and material immanence, just as "cutting on the bias" in tailoring creates a special property of the cloth cut. Bias, in Innis' hands, is then a characteristic of sensuous and material practice rather than belief or opinion. Innis' historical research investigates media with regard to whether their institutional mobilization turns up the bias of communication for strategies of projecting imperial power across space or over time. In developing this historical analytic, Innis posits as his normative ideal a bias set to balance the contingencies of space and time. Empires able to balance the communicative imperatives of space and time endure, Innis suggests, quite unlike the British Empire, then in free fall. Innis' historical studies are only prolegomena for his central concern— capitalist modernity and its cutting edge, the British Empire.[18] The communicative space bias of the modern, then, has to do with a system of communication not only making world scale markets possible, but also mediating this space of accumulation with modes of

[16]   Harold Innis, *The Bias of Communication* (Toronto: University of Toronto Press, 1951), p. 87.

[17]   Georg Lukács, *History and Class Consciousness*, trans. R. Livingstone (Cambridge MA: MIT Press, 1972); Martin Heidegger, *Being and Time*, trans. J. Stambaugh (New York: Harper & Row, 1962); Guy Debord, *The Society of the Spectacle*, trans. Fredy Perlman (Detroit: Black and Red, 1977); Henri Lefebvre, *The Production of Space* (Oxford: Blackwell, 1991).

[18]   Harold Innis, *Changing Concepts of Time* (Lanham MD: Rowman & Littlefield Publishers, 2004), p. 120.

political power—competitive and warring absolutist empires and then nation-states—on which the accumulation of capital depends but which accumulation then also fuels. Innis links modernity's space bias to the dominance of one mode of communication, which he describes as "industrialized communication based on the eye."[19] We would today call it information or, after Guy Debord, spectacle.

Indeed, one of the enduring contributions of Innis' communication theory is the way his "practice turn" enables us to conceptualize information historically and socially. In this regard, a key virtue of Innis' historical approach to theorizing information—in relation to the history of writing systems but also to the emergence of prose, various genres of reports, the news, ads, indices, prices, statistics, soundbites, capta, and so on—is to pose the problem of information in terms of what we today call media ecology.

This dialectical, media-ecological aspect of Innis' work was deeply important to McLuhan, as it is for our mobilization of the concept of intermedia now. Building on Innis' theorization of Canada's postwar passage between the British Empire and American imperialism and his recognition of the key global role that the quintessential American invention—the transnational corporation—would play, McLuhan's version of the story tells of the "world environment" projected by the American superpower and, in turn, theorizes Canadian society in terms of its cultural borderlines as the hidden ground of a counter-environment, an idea to which we will return below.[20]

As is well known, McLuhan's field theory of media environments takes the argument to its logical conclusion, by including all technology under the rubric of media since all technology communicates and extends the human senses; all technologies mediate by changing patterns and scales of perception. McLuhan ultimately develops his insight that "the message of a media is another media"[21] into his tetradic hermeneutic of "retrieval, reversal, obsolescence and extension"[22] which, we suggest, sow the seeds of a new intermedia dialectic.

To see how, we need to return for a moment to Innis' bias of communication thesis and note that space bias and time bias are not binary either/ors for Innis. Indeed, the concept of bias, as we have seen, belongs to the world of analog communication. Within the structural dominance of modern space bias, then, the time bias of communication offers the possibility of what Innis calls a "strategy of culture" that, he argues, might be able to offset the space bias of industrialized communication based on the eye from its inside. As a "strategy of culture," Innis' plea for time directs us to the ethico-political core of the problematic of communicative practice. "Culture is concerned," he writes, "with the capacity of the individual to appraise problems in terms of space and time and with

19 Innis, *The Bias of Communication*, pp. 79–81.
20 Marshall McLuhan, "Canada as Counter-Environment," in *Canadian Cultural Studies: A Reader*, ed. Sourayan Mookerjea et al. (Durham NC: Duke University Press, 2009).
21 Marshall McLuhan, *Understanding Media: The Extensions of Man* (New York: Signet Books, 1964), p. 24.
22 Marshall McLuhan, *Laws of Media: The New Science*, ed. Eric McLuhan (Toronto: University of Toronto Press, 1988), p. 116.

enabling him [sic] to take the proper steps at the right time."[23] Innis' cultural politics is still one that is committed to a humanist mobilization of high culture against the cultural imperialism of American mass culture. But even here there is a twist, insofar as Innis also finds in oral tradition, where popular culture re-enters the discussion, another possibility of a strategy of culture against present-mindedness.[24] The temporal possibilities of an oral tradition, its ritualized everyday echoing durations, and its rhizomatic institutions of memory are, for Innis, the subalternized bias of time immanent to the space bias of industrialized communication based on the eye. In this way, the theory of communicative bias then opens the door to some kind of dialectical interrogation and cultural political intervention in our media ecology.

McLuhan's version of this Innisian dialectic probes the possibilities of resonating intervals of televisual acoustic space against the hegemony of Gutenberg's linearity. But most readings of McLuhan ignore the geopolitical context that we have seen to be decisive for both Innis and McLuhan.[25] Consequently, they also ignore a parallel branch in McLuhan's media theory, which explores what he calls the cultural borderlines that makes Canada different from both the US and Europe. McLuhan here proposes the concept of a counter-environment in relation to the US-led world information environment. As a counter-environment, aspects of Canadian history and society serve as the United States' hidden ground, McLuhan argues, enabling the workings of this world environment to become visible in new and critical ways.[26] We cannot pursue McLuhan's explorations of counter-environments and cultural borderlines further here but will appropriate this concept of counter-environment for our purposes of naming the non-identity of *society* as discussed above. For us, subaltern counter-environments refer to the time-biased sacrificial ground of everyday social reproduction (often enough rendered theoretically invisible) upon which history's victors stage their figures of events.[27] Moreover, we propose to appropriate the first branch of McLuhan's media theory as well and suggest that his signature thesis, "the message of a media is another media," taken to its logical conclusion, enables us to pull out an intermedia theory of the commons from Marx's version of the concept of *mode of production*, through his theorization of labor as "a process in which both man [sic] and nature participate."[28]

---

23   Innis, *The Bias of Communication,* p. 85.

24   Ibid., p. 76.

25   Joshua Meyrowitz, *No Sense of Place: The Impact of Electronic Media on Social Behaviour* (Oxford: Oxford University Press, 1985); Joshua Meyrowitz, "Morphing McLuhan: Medium Theory for a New Millennium," *Proceedings of the Media Ecology Association* 2, (2001): pp. 8–22; Shaun Moores, *Media/Theory: Thinking About Media and Communications* (New York: Routledge, 2005), pp. 44–45.

26   McLuhan, "Canada as Counter-Environment," pp. 71–86.

27   Sourayan Mookerjea, "Epilogue: Through the Utopian Forest of Time," *Canadian Journal of Sociology/Cahiers Canadiens de sociologie* 38/2 (2013): pp. 233–254.

28   Karl Marx, *Capital* 1, trans. Ben Fowkes (London: Penguin Books, 1967), p. 177.

In the introduction to the *Grundrisse*,[29] Marx sets these concepts of labor and production, society and nature in motion as a vicious circle of chickens and eggs, of a double mediation, which short-circuits attempts to read these concepts either purely ontologically or with historico-positive immediacy. For Marx, "all production is appropriation of nature on the part of an individual within and through a specific form of society."[30] All human collective forms of life are mediated by relations with nature, but all human relations with nature are mediated by "social" relationships which are, in turn, but specific kinds of nature. Different modes of social reproduction organize these intermediations differently. "Production in general is an abstraction," writes Marx[31] regarding his materialism of "sensuous praxes."[32] The redundancy built into the terms *inter-mediation* then turns out to be rather serendipitous in evoking this double mediation characterizing the conditions of possibility of every kind of commons, which are all media technologies in McLuhan's sense.

Urban Intermedia

Before turning to the intermedia practices, one further implication of this theoretical framework needs to be set in place. As Henri Lefebvre and David Harvey argue, the history of capitalism is almost essentially the spatial history of modern urbanization.[33] Contemporary social geographers argue that this process is planetary in scale such that the reach of urban infrastructure, pollution, transportation, and communication has indeed created if not quite a *global village* then at least what McLuhan described as a new world environment, though a toxic one. The challenge now is one of grasping not just the persistence of the rural with the (sub)urban[34] but rather the resonating intervals between urbanization and its resource hinterlands of mountains, forests, oceans, deserts; its agricultural and other modes of eco-social reproduction on which urban practices continue to depend. Our conception of urban architecture as intermedia includes such subaltern counter-environments as the city's resonating intervals with its manifold socio-ecosystemic borderlines. Practices of urban development are precisely mediations of shifts in scale from the singular human body to fossil fuel speed, insofar as both accumulated colonial violence and urban form are immanent constraints upon embodied practice. Moreover, media scholars and social geographers have increasingly understood urban practices in terms of their spectacular media cultures of consumption, financialization, and branding as well as their infrastructures of surveillance and repulsion.[35] Intermedia theory helps us grasp how the building

---

[29] Karl Marx, *Grundrisse: Outlines of Political Economy*, trans. M. Nicolaus (London: Penguin, 1973).

[30] Ibid., p. 87.

[31] Ibid., p. 85.

[32] Karl Marx, *The German Ideology*, trans. S. Ryazanskaya (Moscow: Progress Publishers, 1964).

[33] Lefebvre, *The Production of Space*; David Harvey, *Rebel Cities: From the Right to the City to the Urban Revolution* (London: Verso, 2012).

[34] Monika Krause, "The Ruralization of the World," *Public Culture* 25/2 (2013): pp. 233–248.

[35] SARAI, *Sensor, Census, Censor: A Report* (New Delhi: Sarai Media Lab, 2007).

of so-called smart cities as a *pris(on)m* of sensors with their fountains of data streams continue the herculean projects of nation-building and settler-colonialism. In this regard, they continue the historical process of enclosure of the commons in which the space bias of *industrialized communication based on the eye* has played a decisive role. Urbanization in Canada, we argue, needs to be understood as an intermediated process based on the articulation of various settler-biopolitical and colonial-governmental strategies with diverse assemblages of communication. If the city as a livable place depends upon the urban commons created by the everyday spatial practices of its inhabitants,[36] then media practices, we argue, need to be theorized in terms of subaltern counter-environments.

Indigenous people residing in cities constitute the fastest growing segment of Canadian society. In 2006, 56% of these Canadian indigenous people, consisting of Inuit, Métis and First Nations, lived in urban areas (Indigenous and Northern Affairs Canada). Striking about this group of people is their marginalization within Canadian society, which is evident in terms of socio-economic indicators such as income, employment, housing quality, education, and poverty rates.[37] The practices of intermediation that we discuss below assert a decolonizing *right to the city* which re-places indigenous peoples in the urban commons since settler-colonialism has dispossessed them through enclosure and apartheid, subalternizing them in *wilderness* discursively and reserving them in industrialized nature politically.

Decolonizing Media Politics and the Right to the City

In 2001, a coalition of indigenous and Métis community activists intervened in an ongoing conflict between a power utility being prepared for privatization and residential property owners in a well-connected and gentrified neighborhood called the Rossdale Flats on the banks of the North Saskatchewan River, as it winds through central Edmonton. This intervention began when activists put up crosses marking a field beside an electrical power plant as a sacred graveyard and, after five years of public protests, consultations, traditional ceremonies, public hearings, newspaper and online debates, culminated with the City of Edmonton unveiling a public monument commemorating the site. Reading this intervention as an ensemble of media practices enables us to grasp how this practice contests the dominant channels of communication between Canada and indigenous peoples and so further refine our intermedia theory as well.

In 2001, the then part-publicly owned electrical power utility, EPCOR, announced the expansion of its power plant in Rossdale. This expansion was opposed by a hastily formed Rossdale residents' association greenishly named Concerned Citizens for the Edmonton River Valley (CONcerve). Such projects for producing urban space embody what urban

---

36 Lefebvre, *The Production of Space*; Harvey, *Rebel Cities*, p. 68.
37 Evelyn Peters, ed., *Urban Aboriginal Policy Making in Canadian Municipalities* (Montreal: McGill-Queen's University Press, 2011), p. 7.

geographers call "urban growth machines."[38] They typically articulate public relations strategies with legal and administrative procedures. Urban growth machines reconfigure urban imaginaries to sell their vision of the urban commons to publics and authorities. Indeed, both campaigns used a standard mix of public relations strategies, economic forecasting, and administrative processes to pursue their agendas. As we shall see, this conflict exemplifies a contradiction immanent in the reproduction of urban commons. EPCOR's expansion plan appealed to a dominant narrative of technological nationalism.[39] Technological development is a synecdoche for nation-building framed as progress and urbanization in this imaginary, which also threw in a few weak claims about greener buildings to solicit support for the expansion.

This strategy was opposed by an elitist "deer park" environmentalism.[40] Thus CON-cerve threw its considerable private resources behind another plan to conserve and develop an existing chain of public parks throughout the Edmonton River Valley as a valuable commons critical to Edmonton's environmental viability, to act as the city's lungs just like Central Park, it was argued, does for New York.[41]

Intervening in the middle of this classic battle between progress and conservatism, the activists' reclamation of a patch of the Rossdale Flats with grave markers communicates an indigenous *treaty right to the city* politics. The immediate effect of this alleged discovery of a burial site was to stop EPCOR's development plans, make CONcerve pull back and require the city administration to become more centrally involved in the conflict. But the ensuing public relations campaign mounted by the indigenous-Métis coalition, to push the City into building a monument to commemorate the site, *extended* a different channel for the circulation of signs through which Edmonton's urban imaginary is sustained.

As a resource dependent, settler-colonial city, unable to exert effective *world class* agency in the global economy to which it is connected, Edmonton's urban imaginary is marked by a characteristic disavowal of place and history involving desperate imitation of capitals of culture and cultures of capital elsewhere. Emblematic of this disavowal are, on the one hand, the obligatory, imitative but stunted corporate skyline, signaling a civic commitment to worldly progress, industry, technological instrumentality, and on the other, the new Art Gallery of Alberta, which is supposed to somehow evoke the North Saskatchewan River and the Aurora Borealis simultaneously and still look like a new art gallery in any capital of culture—signaling now a civic commitment to transcendence, leisure, refinement, and consumption, if not a toe-hold in the brave new world of creative economies. Perhaps the most egregious symptom of this disavowal, however, is Edmonton's

---

38   Neil Brenner, *Spaces of Neoliberalism: Urban Restructuring in North America and Western Europe* (Oxford: Wiley-Blackwell, 2003).

39   Maurice Charland, "Technological Nationalism," *Canadian Cultural Studies: A Reader*, ed. Sourayan Mookerjea et al. (Durham, N.C.: Duke University Press, 2009).

40   Mike Sadava, "River valley serving only the affluent, Reimer says," *The Edmonton Journal* 1, (25.04.1991): B1.

41   Scott McKeen, "What's better: an old power plant or a new theme park? Councillors' vision will be on display in Rossdale debate," *Edmonton Journal* 24 (2003): B1.

Fig. 14: Anne Winkler, Rossdale Burial Site Crosses, 2015. Edmonton, Alberta.

displacement of its own origins in the fur trade era trading post called Fort Edmonton that had over the years occupied various sites along the river flats. When a museum and theme park was built for the national centennial in 1967 to tell the story of Edmonton's history, the replica fort theme park was moved several turns up the river for the convenience of a new prestigious suburban neighborhood. Debates about civic identity in Edmonton have almost always been contained within the alternatives of an urban austerity and discipline, supposedly reflecting the instrumentality and efficiency of loyal workers who supply services for the oil patch up north, and blue chip trophies of elite distinction such as the West Edmonton Mall, which could boast being at one time the world's largest mall before being dwarfed by developments in Dubai and Beijing. The crosses that appeared mysteriously overnight in Rossdale and the intermedia campaign for commemoration then confronted Edmonton's phantasmatic identity of spatial transcendence (as *Western civilization*) with the ghostly historicity of a specific, settler-colonial, place (see Figure 14).

For the graveyard in Rossdale Flats was not a new discovery. There exists an oral tradition of the river crossings at the flats being the sacred site for cemeteries for thousands of years. According to indigenous oral tradition, the Flats were a *pehonan*, a gathering place, where pow wows, the sacred Goose and Sun Dances were performed, and where the Wolf Track migration route crossed the Saskatchewan River. This indigenous place-making of the river ford is why the fur trade was drawn to the area and why various fur trading posts, including Fort Edmonton itself, were ultimately built on these flats. After colonial enclosure, Treaty payments were made at annual ceremonies held at the flats. Along with ancient cemeteries here, several graveyards connected to these trade forts contain the remains of Cree, Blackfoot, Métis, Sarcee, Dene, and French fur traders, as well as of employees of the Hudson's Bay Company. An official oral history of the Flats commissioned as a result of indigenous community activism also records accounts of construction workers unearthing human remains while building the residential neighborhood of Rossdale in the 1960s. In the course of urban development in the post-enclosure settler-colonial period, from 1907 to the present, these burial sites keep being forgotten and buried and then periodically rediscovered.[42]

Indeed, this reclamation of the Flats turns up the time bias of the PR conflict over urban development and in doing so produces instead a common public memory of a different history of the commons and its enclosure in which the fur trade and the Treaties figure centrally. Brought into relation with this subaltern counter-environment, both progressive and conservative projections of the urban commons are turned inside out by this indigenization of urban identity. The publicly funded power plant expansion was meant to make EPCOR's assets more attractive for its eventual privatization.[43] Park conservation development in the river valley is also more about raising property values through the capture of monopoly rent through proximity to the park than it is about creating a more egalitarian city not requiring the heavy policing of Indigenous Peoples in public spaces. By placing the historical contingencies of the fur trade and colonial enclosure in this intermedia counter-environment, this media practice makes the contradictions in both hegemonic versions of the commons apparent, through their reversal. Far from presenting opposing political visions of the future of Edmonton, both progressive and conservative projects in fact have always relied upon each other to create the "not in my backyard" fetishism of industrial and capitalist development, in which there are no losers or victims because they have been racialized into invisibility. From the first crosses reclaiming a part of Rossdale Flats to the public commemoration ceremony at the unveiling of the monument, the assertion of indigenous urban identity intermediates the possibility of belonging in common, by displacing the dominant myths of nation-building and rendering obsolete at least a certain style of civic branding, and by retrieving histories of racialization and enclosure.

Similar intermedia effects of obsolescence and retrieval can be discerned in the second practice we consider here, the modification of the murals at the Grandin/Government Centre LRT station and its supplementation by a new series of panels. These murals reject unequivocally settler-colonial history by inserting indigenous culture and bodies into pub-

---

[42] Jacqueline Pelletier et al., *Rossdale Flats Aboriginal Oral Histories Project: Report of Findings*, ed. Edmonton Aboriginal Urban Affairs Committee (City of Edmonton: Edmonton, 2004); Heather Zwicker, "Dead Indians, Power Conglomerates and the Upper Middle Class: Commemorating Colonial Conflict in Edmonton's Rossdale," presentation, *Canadian Association of Cultural Studies Second Annual Conference*, McMaster University, Hamilton, Ontario, February 2004.

[43] Cameron Wall, "Legality of EPCOR Privatization Challenged in Court," *Metro News*, September 11 (2009).

lic consciousness and memory while also reconfiguring historiography. Importantly, they place indigenous peoples into the city, for *the urban* and *the indigenous* continue to signify as an oxymoron in the ideology of *Western modernity*; in Peters and Andersen's words, "throughout the twentieth century, urban locales have been understood in the academy and more broadly as places where Indigenous culture goes to die."[44] Blomley describes the colonization of North America and its urbanization as a process that necessitated *active place making*, which involved forgetting aspects of the past and reconstructing others, both culminating in the incompatibility of city and indigeneity.[45] According to Blomley, settler-colonial urbanization requires that "native people must be conceptually *removed* from urban space. If located anywhere, native people are frequently imagined in the past or in nature. In either case, they are placed outside the city." In this way, nation-building and urbanization go hand in hand: "This place is to be made into a white place through physical settlement and occupation."[46]

The composite artwork that today defines the Grandin/Government Centre LRT Station and provocatively places Canada's indigenous peoples in the context of the contemporary city began to take shape when, in 1989, the *Francophonie Jeunesse de l'Alberta* commissioned the first mural to honor Father Vital-Justin Grandin (1829–1902), who founded new missions and churches throughout what is now Alberta and whose work led to the construction of new hospitals and schools. The francophone artist Sylvie Nadeau originally painted three panels, which remain on display. The right side depicts a contemporary scene of the surrounding Grandin neighborhood, featuring two Catholic churches, Grandin School, and a multigenerational group in the middle. The center panel includes tepees pitched in front of the trading post Fort Edmonton, a steam locomotive, and several small indigenous figures whose gazes do not meet that of the viewer. The left panel features the most prominent figures in the entire series: Father Grandin and a Grey Nun holding a Métis child (see Figure 15).

In the distance behind them rises an institutional structure that may denote a residential school, in front of which another Grey Nun stands among a group of Aboriginals, some of whom are wrapped in Hudson's Bay Company blankets. The latter image in particular has been the source of much controversy, for it can be interpreted as a celebration of cultural assimilation. In fact, the TRC's final report describes government policy, including the mandatory attendance at residential schools by indigenous children, more forcefully as "cultural genocide."[47] Although Nadeau has stated that the building does not portray a residential school, it must be pointed out that Grandin did work to expand the residential

---

44 Evelyn Peters and Chris Andersen, eds., *Indigenous in the City: Contemporary Identities and Cultural Innovation* (Vancouver: University of British Columbia Press, 2013), p. 1.

45 Nicholas K. Blomley, *Unsettling the City: Urban Land and the Politics of Property* (New York: Routledge, 2004), p. 114.

46 Ibid.

47 *Honouring the Truth: Reconciling for the Future.* Summary of the Final Report of the Truth and Reconciliation Commission of Canada. (Truth and Reconciliation Commission of Canada, 2015), p. 1.

Fig. 15: Sylvie Nadeau, Bishop Vital-Justin Grandin Mural, 1989. Grandin LRT Station, Edmonton, Alberta. Photograph by Anne Winkler.

school system. These actions were motivated by his conviction "that attempts to *civilize* and evangelize native adults would have negligible results and that it would be preferable to concentrate on weaning children from their traditional lifestyle."[48]

In juxtaposition with Nadeau's representational painting, Métis artist Aaron Paquette's counter-mural, entitled "Stations of Reconciliation (A Conversation)," on the opposing east wall is composed of stylized indigenous imagery in bold colors that symbolically encapsulate 10,000 years of indigenous history in Edmonton. The White Buffalo, a sacred animal, is flanked on both sides by a wolf, bear, and raven (see Figure 16).

The Thunderbird stretches across the entire mural. The authorized meaning of these figures includes peace, renewal, hope, protection, healing, and destruction. Of the ravens, Paquette writes: "They are a bridge between worlds, warning of death, but also in many legends are the bringers of light. They wake up the world."[49] Two end panels on either side of the work depict medicine drums embellished with the only two human figures on this wall. Similar pieces, but painted by Nadeau and featuring an indigenous girl and boy, now also frame her original mural. Together, the four medicine drums tie together the murals

---

[48] Ramsay Cook and Jean Hamelin, *Dictionary of Canadian Biography: Volume XIII 1901–1910* (Toronto: University of Toronto Press, 1994), p. 401.

[49] Aaron Paquette, "The Stations of Reconciliation (A Conversation) – Artist Statement," *http://www. aaronpaquette.net/?p=4778* (accessed 01.11.2014).

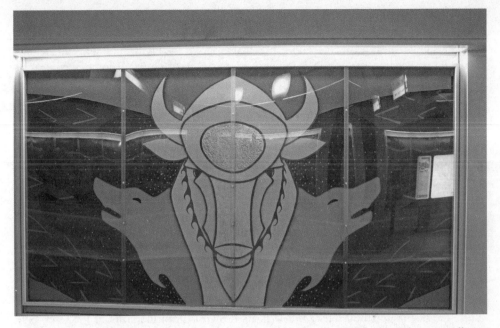

Fig. 16: Aaron Paquette, The Stations of Reconciliation, 2014. Grandin LRT Station, Edmonton, Alberta. Photograph by Anne Winkler.

on the opposing walls. Yet this linking does not mask the murals' profound differences, which run much deeper than their representational styles. In their juxtaposition, they render visible opposing historiographies and differing claims of place, belonging, and ownership, which culminate in an unequivocal assertion of Indigenous Peoples rights to the city.

We argue that these renovations of the LRT murals, achievements of the militancy underlying the Truth and Reconciliation process and the cultural politics of asserting a Treaty right to the city, are to be grasped as an ensemble of intermedia practices that intervene in Edmonton's transit commission's public address system. Such a transit communication system is but one component of a settler-colonial urban governmental apparatus of enclosure, though it is one with its own singular effects. The industrially functional, visually austere, and kinesthetically "prickly" design of most of Edmonton's LRT stations combines commands about public safety, hygiene, morality, security, and police in order to massify, accelerate, and circulate bodies between production and consumption. In doing so, this aesthetic design endeavors to depoliticize the mass transit body it makes possible. In relation to this flow, the mural modifications, we argue, re-politicize this mass transit body, however transitorily, by extending it into a counter-environmental common place that asserts in its own singular way *a Treaty right to the city*. In relation to settler-colonial fears and anxieties regarding the indigenous body's intrusion into interdicted spaces, spaces that solicit and support the gaze of settler-colonial surveillance, the murals assert a decolonizing distribution of the visible.

Not only does this intervention retrieve a decolonizing mass communication system invented by Diego Rivera and the Mexican Revolution but, like the Rossdale memorial, Paquette's indigenization of Nadeau's triptych of progress and civilization turns up the time bias of this space through its public remembering of racialization and colonial enclosure. Indeed, Grandin Station is the LRT stop for the Province of Alberta Legislature, which was built on the last site of Fort Edmonton not far from the Flats. The mural modification thus also claims place through time as it works at decolonizing the LRT station, a neighborhood, an entire city, and even a nation. For Paquette, what is at stake is the rediscovery of "true" history. He writes: "Inside the Thunderbirds are carried the reminders of the true history of this place. The land on which the City of Edmonton has been built has been inhabited for over 10,000 years. Our history is longer than Canada, than Rome, than Christianity and the Pyramids. And it has continued unbroken to today."[50]

One of the most important practice effects of this intervention, then, lies in what the mural modification renders obsolete. As Jennifer Esposito points out, "we must continually critique and examine representations of racialized bodies, especially those bodies already marginalized within the system of racial hierarchies."[51] The decision not to decommission the preexisting mural allows for a pointed interrogation of the ideology of cultural assimilation and the paternalistic iconography of racialized bodies dispossessed of agency. While the display of the Métis child with its brown skin in the arms of the Grey Nun may have provoked discomfort in the past, the addition of the Paquette painting affirms that it got history wrong and incomplete. Moreover, the mural's location in the physical and symbolic center of Alberta's capital city indicates that the colonial genre of Nadeau's 1989 mural will no longer go unchallenged. In fact, it signals a shift in the dominant urban imaginary of settler-colonial technological nationalism, or at least its possibility.

Nevertheless, at the very limit of its intermedia practice effects of retrieval, obsolescence and extension, this work of public art also stands on the brink of undoing, contradicting, and thus *reversing* its own potential to intervene in the colonial urban imaginary. For example, the mural obscures the great diversity of indigenous groups in Edmonton and Alberta, which include the Métis, Beaver Nation (Dene Zaa), Blackfoot Nation (Siksika, Piikani and Kainai), Chipewyan Nation (Dene Suline), Cree Nation, Sioux Nation (Dakota), Ojibwe Nation (Anishinaabe), Sarcee Nation (Tsuu T'ina), Slavey Nation (Dene Tha'), Stoney Nation (Nakoda/Assiniboine); each with different traditions, languages, and cultural symbols. This diversity brings with it great challenges when it comes to formulating a united and powerful voice in decolonizing projects, which was particularly visible in the consultation process leading up to the building of the memorial at Rossdale power plant. Indeed, cultural-political representations of intersectional differences among indigenous

---

[50] Paquette, "The Stations of Reconciliation," 2014.

[51] Jennifer Esposito, "Negotiating the gaze and learning the hidden curriculum: A critical race analysis of the embodiment of female students of color at a predominantly White institution," *Journal for Critical Education Policy Studies* 9/2 (2011): p. 95, http://www.jceps.com/wp-content/uploads/PDFs/09-2-09.pdf (accessed 01.06.2017).

people is now crucial for the development of critical past-mindedness, especially if the challenges posed by the eruption of class inequality among indigenous people are to be addressed. Equally as problematic as rendering the complex simple are the medium and the site of the work, which sanitize and order the messy. As it stands, in their seemingly permanent form, the murals provide the mistaken sense that the work of decolonizing the city has been completed or at least is in full swing. It signals closure when this intervention should be read as only a beginning. Unless ways are found to continue to activate the initial militancy of the intervention, the still provocative murals are in danger of turning into merely depoliticized decoration unable to provoke critical past-mindedness.

In this chapter, we have sought to decolonize the practice turn in media studies by arguing for an intermedia theory that reconstructs the concept of media practice in terms of the production of urban space and its intermediation by a politics of the commons. In doing so, we have implicitly argued against approaches that claim to apprehend social practices with an immediacy that transcends the politics of social reproduction. Our discussion of the two examples of intermedia practice has rather attempted to demonstrate that practices are better grasped in their articulation through social processes of de-politicization and re-politicization and, therefore, in relation to the *longue durée* of subaltern resistances to colonial enclosure, if the practice turn is to make any significant contribution to the critical social scientific understanding of our times.

Karin Harrasser

Sweet Trap, Dangerous Method. Musical Practice in the Jesuit Reductions of Chiquitos and Moxos in the Eighteenth Century[1]

When I became interested in the musical practices of Jesuit missionaries in Latin America, my first research trip brought me to Concepción, a small town in the Bolivian *llanos* (the eastern lowlands). It hosts an archive of musical scores from the eighteenth and nineteenth centuries containing approximately 3,100 folios of scores, predominantly European Baroque music. The scores were archived and made accessible during the last twenty years. Before that, people from local villages had kept them privately, sometimes over centuries. Some scores had been copied time and again after the expulsion of the Jesuits from South America (1767), and sources from the nineteenth century testify that they were still in use around 1840. The former mission complex of Concepción also hosts a small museum that documents the history of the town. Between 1690 and 1767, various indigenous groups (were) converted to Christianity and were resettled into towns, now known as *reducciones*. The resulting hybrid "mission culture," [2] and especially its musical aspect, has become a contested issue in Bolivia's cultural politics at the beginning of the twenty-first century. "Mission culture" is an important economic factor, as the opulently renovated mission churches and a biennial festival of Baroque music attract visitors from all over the world. At the same time, the claim that "mission culture" is the proper cultural expression of the Chiquitos is controversial not only with regard to Evo Morales' politics of re-indigenization.

Instruments from the eighteenth century are on display at the museum as well as wooden figures of Jesus Christ, San Miguel, and Jesuit saints that were and are still carried about as part of processions. Also, we find a woodcut of unknown date showing

---

[1]   Meanwhile this article has been published in German: "Riskante Praktiken der Bekehrung. Die musikalische Kolonisierung der Sinne," in *Sensibilität der Gegenwart. Wahrnehmung, Ethik und politische Sensibilisierung im Kontext westlicher Gewaltgeschichte*, ed. Burkhard Liebsch (Hamburg: Meiner, 2018), p. 61–81. (= Sonderheft 17 der Zeitschrift für Ästhetik und Allgemeine Kulturwissenschaft).

[2]   The term "mission culture" is used for a wide range of practices that resulted from cultural activities by several Catholic orders in the Amazon region. It is specifically employed to describe the historical epoch of the Jesuits' activities in Paraguay, Argentina, Brazil, and Bolivia. See David Block, *Mission Culture on the Upper Amazon. Native Traditions, Jesuit Enterprise, & Secular Policy in Moxos, 1660-1880* (Lincoln NE and London: University of Nebraska Press, 1997).

Fig. 17: Display in the museum at Concepción, Bolivia, © Karin Harrasser 2014.

Martin Schmid, SJ (the acronym for the members of the Societas Iesu or Jesuit Order): the designer of the local churches (called *templos*) and the person who was responsible for the introduction and cultivation of the European musical tradition in Chiquitos in the eighteenth century. In one of the exhibition rooms, documentary images are shown: Images of the town before the renovation in the 1990s, a *traditional music ensemble* (legend) with violins. On its left, another image is placed, same size, same framing, also black and white. And it looked quite familiar to me. It depicts a man, sitting on a big stone, playing the oboe. From behind and from the sides, two natives, adorned with loincloths, painted, bow and arrow in their hands, are listening and watching with great interest. And yes indeed: It is a frame showing the famous scene from Roland Joffé's movie *The Mission* (1986,) where Jeremy Irons lures the natives out of the woods by playing the oboe.

The more I studied the *reducciones,* the more it became apparent that this fragment from a feature film rendered *documentary* (a black and white image adjacent to images of *real* music making) resonates with Jesuit propaganda about their mission settlements from the seventeenth century: From the beginning, the *padres* were eager to communicate their "success." The myth of their peaceful and productive strategy of seduction and adaptation (as opposed to the cruelty of the *encomienda* system and the illegal but nonetheless practiced man-hunt) was disseminated with great coherence. We find it in travel reports, in published letters, and subsequently as part of the collections of *relatos* (reports) that were published from 1640 onwards. The collections were so popular that they were translated into several languages (French, English, German).[3] The biblical figure associated with the

---

[3]   The German edition translates some of the original sources and parts of the French "Lettres Edifiantes": Joseph Stöcklein, ed., *Der Neue Welt-Bott. Mit allerhand nachrichten deren Missionarii Soc. Iesu. Allerhand so Lehr- als Geist-Reiche Brief, Schrifften und Reis-Beschreibungen, welche von denen Missionariis der Gesellschafft Jesu, aus beyden Indien und anderen über meer gelegenen*

Jesuits' *conquista spiritual* (this was the title of a 1639 book by the missionary Antonio Ruiz de Montoya[4]), was David, who used the *kinnor* (a harp) to heal Saul from a demon. Another frequent reference is Orpheus' ability to tame the beasts with music. It is stunning that even critics of the Jesuits' all-encompassing government perpetuated this myth. The narrative is reproduced over and over again. In René Fülöp-Miller's widely read book from the twentieth century, for example, we can find the following:

> When the first Jesuits explored the virgin forests of Paraguay along the river banks, any kind of missionary work seemed well-nigh impossible, for the Indians persisted in timidly fleeing from them. But the fathers noticed that, when they sang religious melodies in their canoes, the natives peeped out of the bushes here and there to listen to them, and gave signs of extraordinary pleasure. This discovery supplied the missionaries with a method of enticing the Indians from their forest haunts. They took musical instruments on their voyages, and played and sang to the best of their ability. "The Indians fell into the pleasant trap," writes Chateaubriand in his *Spirit of Christianity*. "[…] Bows and arrows fell unheeded from the hands of the savages, and their souls received the first impressions of a higher kind of existence and of the primitive delights of humanity."[5]

Even if commentators were critical concerning the Jesuits' *powers*, this narrative remains an affirmation of the alleged superiority of European media, aesthetics, and modes of government.[6] In what follows I shall therefore offer a perspective on musical practice that questions this narrative and its prerequisites from different angles: I will frame practicing, rehearsing, and performing music as techniques of governing bodies and souls that surpass concepts of seduction, manipulation etc. The reductions should rather be understood as experimental sites to explore ways of governing that were, to some extent, coherent with theo-political concepts of the Early Modern era but also transformed them: Music was not simply utilized, but had to be adapted, and thereby conversely reshaped theo-political concepts of European origin. Music and dance practices were not imposed monodirectionally and fully intentionally. It seems rather that their dominant role in spiritual and community life during the time of the Jesuits stems from a specific understanding of music that had been in place before the *padres*. But how did the Jesuits make use of the numerous music and dance practices (and of the religious concepts) they encountered? To what extent did they become part of the indigenous world? And in what way had musical

---

ländern, seit An. 1642 bis auf das Jahr 1726. […] (Augspurg and Grätz: Philips, Martins and Joh. Veith seel. Erben Buchhandlung, 1726).

4   Antonio Ruiz de Montoya, *Conquista Espiritual hecha por los religiosos de la Compañía de Jesús en las provincias del Paraguay, Paraná, Uruguay y Tape* (1639) (Bilbao: Imprenta del Corazón de Jesús, 1892).

5   René Fülöp-Miller, *The Power and Secret of the Jesuits* (New York: G. Braziller, 1956), pp. 356–357.

6   For a critique of the myth of Western superiority in media technology that focuses on writing, see Erhard Schüttpelz, *Die Moderne im Spiegel des Primitiven. Weltliteratur und Ethnologie (1870-1960)* (Munich: Wilhelm Fink, 2005); Erhard Schüttpelz, "Die medientechnische Überlegenheit des Westens. Zur Geschichte und Geographie der immutable mobiles Bruno Latours," in *Mediengeographie. Theorie, Analyse, Diskussion*, ed. Jörg Döring and Tristan Thielmann (Bielefeld: transcript, 2009).

practice to be re-invented, sometimes against the guidelines of the Catholic Church? I will discuss episodes from different sources that hint at the precarious nature of music, dance, and theatrical performance as techniques for governing bodies and souls. The very feature that makes music a powerful tool of conversion and government renders it a dangerous method: The affects addressed and invoked by and in music cannot be firmly linked to certain *contents of faith* easily. With Antoine Hennion and Isabelle Stengers, I will frame music as a risky practice of attachment and invention. Music and dance have often played important roles in indigenous resistance and in uprisings, especially in millenialist movements, but also in individual reactions towards the Jesuits' regime. I will discuss some examples of a reverse-engineering of theological concepts and of music and dance.

In general, I want to stress the complex dynamics of the reworking of the senses, bodies, and souls in the process of conversion and education. The Jesuit activities were adaptable and experimental, one could even say: opportunistic. Mission (the monodirectional propagation of a message) and transmission (an error-prone and multidirectional mode of transference) are interrelated and produce puzzling effects.

Biopolitics and Government

The settlements in Chiquitos and Moxos were founded and managed by the *Compañía de Jesús* from about 1691 until its expulsion in 1767. The *reducciones* were spread out in a vast region that is now on Bolivian, Argentinian, Paraguayan, and Brazilian territory. The settlements had from 500 up to 10,000 indigenous inhabitants, and at its peak an estimate of over 160,000 people lived in mission settlements. In Chiquitos, in Moxos, but also in the Guaraní missions, the whole community was involved in both religious and profane musical activity. Music was part of efforts to remove indigenous groups from their nomadic mode of existence to a *civilized* life style.

Certainly, the process of resettlement of the indigenous groups was not as peaceful as depicted in some of the *relatos*. Even Jesuit sources speak of massive physical violence. One of many examples are the reports of the Bavarian *padre* Julian Knogler, who is quite open about the violence involved in the founding of the *reducción* Santa Ana de Chiquitos. He calls the very process "Geistliche Jagd" ("spiritual hunt") and describes in detail how the *padres* employed 50–60 converts to search and hunt down a group.[7]

The initial act was collective baptizing. Subsequently, the neophytes underwent conversion to a monotheist, universalist religion. This included acquiring practices of prayer, listening to biblical stories, and instruction in central theological concepts. Indoctrination took place in native languages. This is one of the reasons why the *padres* were also the first ones to write grammar books of the respective languages. The standard narrative of the founding of a *reducción* goes as follows:

---

[7]   Franz Josef Merkl, ed., *Ein Jesuit aus Bayerisch-Schwaben bei den Chiquitos in Bolivien: Die Aufzeichnungen des Julian Knogler SJ 1717-1772 aus Gansheim* (Donau-Ries and Augsburg: Wissner, 1999).

This multitude of nations began to be brought under the rules of society [the *Societas Iesu*, KH] around the middle of the last [seventeenth, KH] century, by means of presents, persuasion and promises. Through the constancy of the missionaries in their endeavors and exertions, and at the cost of the lives of some of them, these wild beasts were tamed. They managed to make men out of them in order to make them Christians. In the process of reduction ample and regular towns were built [...] magnificent temples were erected with beautiful ornaments, in which on festive days one can hear an excellent music of voices and instrument: organs, harps, harpsichords, violins, string basses [*violones*], flutes, shawms, etc.[8]

The report, however accurate it may be, stresses certain motifs that also reoccur in many other sources: Firstly, the Jesuits' ability to construct an orderly and productive community that expresses itself in musical performance of great excellence. A prominently mentioned feature is the fact that in the settlement, *a multitude of nations* was under one rule; another topos is the Jesuits' strategy of evangelization with *presents, persuasions and promises* as opposed to forced conversion and physical coercion. The concept of the *reducción* was not of Jesuit origin though. It was the result of an ongoing conflict between the Spanish Crown and the *conquistadores*. Since the early sixteenth century, laws had been implemented to protect the indigenous communities from the most excessive forms of exploitation by the settlers. At the same time, these laws aimed at regulating and controlling them. In the sixth volume of the *Leyes de Indias* from 1681, it is stated that the "Indios" should be treated as persons who could not be sold and enslaved, deserved protection from slave hunters and from the *encomienderos*, plantation owners who mistreated them as cheap, or often free labor. Yet at the same time, a number of other regulations were also decreed. The *reducciones* were said to have proven to be "los medios mas convenientes, para que los Indios sean instruidos en la Santa Fé Catolica, y Ley Evangelica, y olvidando los errores de sus antiguos ritos, y ceremonias vivan en concierto, y policia, [...] resolvieron, que los Indios fuessen reducidos á Pueblos, y no viviessen divididos, y sepearados por las Sierras, y Montes [...]."[9]

The act of *reducing*, in the sense of *concentrating*, the indigenous people is a means to collectivize a population dispersed in mountains and plains, to give them *Santa Fé Catolica, policía* and *concierto*, so to speak: religion, governance, and community. Their *reduction* should *make them forget* their idolatrous rites and ceremonies. To achieve this, the settlements were built and governed following a standardized pattern that rendered the territory *urban*.[10] The first activity the law envisaged was the construction of a church with a door and a lock (due to the Indios' alleged lack of a sense for private property).

---

[8] Cosme and Bartolomé Bueno, quoted in Leonardo J. Waisman, "Urban Music in the Wilderness. Ideology and Power in the Jesuit Reducciones, 1609-1747," in *Music and Urban Society in Colonial Latin America*, ed. Geoffrey Baker and Tess Knighton (Cambridge: Cambridge University Press, 2011), p. 210, footnote 5.

[9] Julian de Paredes, *Recopilacion de Leyes de los reynos de Las Indias* (Madrid: Iulian de Paredes, 1681), 6/III.

[10] Compare Geoffrey Baker and Tess Knighton, *Music and Urban Society in Colonial Latin America*, especially Baker's introductory essay.

Spatial discipline was considered a key factor.[11] The rural settlements were designed in the typical checkerboard pattern around the Plaza Mayor, which was lined with the buildings of civil and ecclesiastical government. Temporal discipline was considered another key: Together with the church, a sun-dial and a clock tower were erected in order to battle the assumed careless attitude attributed to the natives. Equally important were legal discipline, respect for authority and social hierarchy as well as reading and writing skills as prerequisites for *buen policía*. The local chiefs (*caciques*) and noble families (*la familia*) were thus given functions and they played a certain role in enforcing local regulations, for example in matters of jurisdiction. As the *reducciones* were considered projects to increase the *cultural state* of the indigenous people, the betterment of material comfort and of the religious cult were part of the project. Remarkable efforts were made for the latter: Churches were decorated abundantly, instruments were imported and shipped to remote places, and soon workshops were set up to produce both sophisticated art work as well as trumpets, violins, and even organs.[12]

Considering that colonial biopolitics of monodirectional exertion of power; of extinction and extraction of bare life was the dominant model of political economy, the *reducciones* appear as early examples of a governmental mode. The *padres* (not all of them Jesuits) developed a strategy of politics of welfare, caring for people's lives instead of threatening to take it. I therefore suggest that the *reducciones* should be considered as early experiments for a genuinely modern way of *policing* that combined rational planning and pastoral governance of the soul.[13] It is worth reframing such a Foucauldian perspective with a broader colonial one as it shows that the colonies were testing grounds both for the feudal, sovereign model (with its threat to take life) and the governmental model. The atrocities of the sovereign model were brought to its excessive limits while, at the same time, *softer* models of governance were introduced.[14]

Instead of a "Sweet Trap": A Political Anthropology of Mission Sound

Music was omnipresent in the missions: Starting with mass in the morning, continuing with music that accompanied daily work until common singing and music-making in the evening. Both children and adults were systematically taught to sing and to play an instrument. The ecclesiastical festivities must have been impressive events. The scores archived in Concepción contain spiritual and worldly music: passions, lamentations,

---

[11] Guillermo Furlong, *Antonio Sepp S. J. y su gobierno temporal (1732)*, Escritores Coloniales Rioplatenses (Buenos Aires: Theoria, 1962).

[12] Waisman, "Urban Music in the Wilderness. Ideology and Power in the Jesuit Reducciones, 1609-1747," p. 210–211.

[13] Michel Foucault, *Security, Territory, Population: Lectures at the Collège De France, 1977-1978* (New York: Picador, 2004).

[14] The Jesuits were not against slavery in general. They *used* African slaves in their plantations as well. See Karin Harrasser and Gudrun Rath, "Arbeit und die Grenzen des Lebens. Zur Kolonialität und Modernität von Plantage und Jesuitischer Reduktion," *Historische Anthropologie* 24/2 (2016): pp. 216–239.

and songs of praise in Latin and in the indigenous languages. Over time, the repertoire increased impressively: Antiphons, litanies, motets, vespers, polyphonic masses; but also: sonatas, minuets, concertos and dances that—very likely—were performed on occasions of communal life rather than at religious festivities. Italian Baroque can be identified as a major inspiration. It was Domenico Zipoli, a former court composer and a member of the *Compañía de Jesús* since 1716, living in the La Plata region, who initially provided the *padres* with new compositions. But the *padres* wrote music themselves as well, and they asked their European colleagues to send scores. The already mentioned Martin Schmid composed quite a number of pieces.

Music was employed as a pedagogical tool on several levels. It was a means to teach and enact the gospel and the legends of the saints. The most impressive example from the Chiquitos archive is a one-hour oratory on the life of Ignacio de Loyola by Domenico Zipoli and Martin Schmid. Its music was clearly meant to address the listeners affectively. The musical style is late Italian Baroque, already meant to depict psychological processes, for example the temptation of Ignacio by the devil or the confession of friendship with Francisco Xavier. The arias are musically spectacular and are arranged as duets of seduction and dedication.

Music was also a means to incorporate a certain *ethos*. Anton Sepp and Martin Schmid give a good account of all the aspects involved[15]: Keeping a schedule, learning to deal with written texts, patient copying of scores, and of course the disciplining of bodies for a controlled use of the voice and of the extremities that followed an idea of modesty and spiritedness. Also, music was used as the silver bullet to create an experience of the new religion and a way of living in the new order in harmony. I also have the impression that music was used as a community-forming tool that went beyond spoken language because the Chiquitos missions always consisted of up to ten different groups speaking different languages, the so-called *parcilidades*.

Guillermo Wilde[16] has studied the music in the Guaraní missions and has developed the key elements of a "political anthropology of mission sound." For Wilde, the "sonic experience" in the missions served "as a hegemonic mechanism that reinforced regimes of temporality and corporality."[17] He refers to Antonio Manuel Hespanha, who analyzed European political treatises of the era. The superposition of an understanding of politics as a correct exercise of life and politics as an instrument at the service of the common good are central features. The concept of *affectio* was a central operator in this superposi-

---

15 Martin Schmid, *Pater Martin Schmid SJ, 1694-1772. Seine Briefe und sein Wirken*, Beiträge zur Zuger Geschichte 8 (Zug: Kalt-Zehnder, 1988); Anton Sepp and Anton Böhm, *Reissbeschreibung wie dieselben aus Hispanien in Paraquarien kommen. Und kurtzer Bericht der denckwürdigsten Sachen selbiger Landschafft, Völckern und Arbeitung der sich alldort befindenten P P Missionariuorum. [...].* (Nuremburg: Joh. Hoffmanns, 1696); Antonio Sepp, *Continuación de las labores apostólicas*, Colección América (Buenos Aires: Editorial Universitaria de Buenos Aires, 1973).

16 Guillermo Wilde, "Toward a Political Anthropology of Mission Sound. Paraguay in the 17th and 18th Centuries," *Music & Politics* 1/2 (2007), http://dx.doi.org/10.3998/mp.9460447.0001.204

17 Ibid.

tion. According to the paradigm (formalized, among others, by Saint Thomas), relations between the things that comprised the order would be maintained by love or some similar affect. Like nature, the social consisted of an organic network of sympathies. Thus "subordination" did not represent a lesser dignity but rather a specific place in the universal order, which allotted obligations and rights to each position. Angels and other supernatural beings, animals, inanimate objects, corporations, children, and the deceased, or even God Himself—all had protected rights and duties. Music and ritual were central to both *visualizing* and *enacting* this order; in more recent terms: the harmony of the social order was constituted in a performative manner. Not only actions such as genuflection (repeatedly mentioned as a proof of faith), the kissing of hands or face, the sexual relations within a family, were bound up in the nature of things; it was musical performance that both guaranteed and substantiated the truth of the very order. Although heterogeneous, the things of creation in this political doctrine should work together toward a common end, creating a universal polyphony. Hespanha notes that the perfection of creation was seen as residing in the heterogeneity of things as they "wove themselves together, sharing an objective as if a polyphonic texture encompassed the universe."[18] The idea of universal harmony was as a consequence invoked through the image of a choir of many voices or an orchestra that represented diversity and the unity of the world at once.

In the South American missions, we find more than faint echoes of this concept. European observers perceived the settlements of the New World as exemplary realizations of the ideal republic: The Jesuit José Manuel Peramás referred to the missions of the Guaraní of Paraguay in terms explicitly drawn from Plato's Republic.[19]

Although negative, evidence for the political character of the concept of musical harmony can be found in the description of indigenous music and society. In a report on the "Life and Death of *padre* Cypriani Baraza," printed in *Der Neue Welt-Bott*, the Moxos were said to live like wild beasts, without any discipline of time and space (they eat when- and wherever they feel like it). They were reported to be drinking and dancing in furor, accompanied by "instruments out of tune" ("auf den ungestimmten Hall gewisser Instrumente") in order to worship their idols.[20]

Risky Practices

Up to this point musical practices in the *reducciones* have been interpreted within the framework of governmental politics according to Michel Foucault: The various modes of practicing music in the mission present music as political technique. Musical practice connects the individual body with the collective body. It is a recursive practice in the

---

[18] Ibid.

[19] José Manuel Peramás, *La república de Platón y los guaranies* (1791) (Buenos Aires: Emecé Editores, 1946).

[20] Joseph Stöcklein, "Bericht von dem Leben und Tod Vener. Patris Cypriani Baraza, aus der Gesellschaft JESU, deren Moscheen in America erster Apostels und Blut-Zeugens Christi […]," in *Welt-Bott*, Part V, 1704-1711, Letter Nr. 112: pp. 62–71, here p. 63.

sense that it represents what is operatively performed.[21] The orchestra and the choir are symbols of the new order while, at the same time, enacting it. Some of the components of this symbolic apparatus can furthermore be conceptualized as techniques of the body and of the self: By learning to play the instruments, to control the pitch of the voice in a new way, to read the scores, to stand in line, to form a choreography, the christened individuals literally *become* Christians. This perspective is certainly important to understand the cultural violence at work in colonial situations. Still, in the rest of this essay I will develop a different perspective that is meant to complement and complicate what has been said: I will follow a praxeological trajectory which stresses the fact that "to practice" is more than an exact reproducing of an already established routine. Practice always encompasses moments of variation or even of invention. Antoine Hennion has developed a concept of musical practice as a never fully projectable mediation. I will take this as a starting point. Musical practice (including the alleged mere "reproduction" of scores) is conceptualized by Hennion as "the emergence of previously unknown beings and objects."[22] In his (pragmatist) take, even the most mimetic reproduction of a musical piece brings about new subjectivities and things. Additionally, I will take into account Isabelle Stengers' "ecology of practices."[23] She brings in an important caveat for my case: the fact that practices need to be considered within power relations, that invention is never free from traces of violence. She insists that in colonial/modern situations of learning and knowing, somebody usually plays the god-trick and declares him- or herself free from subjective interests. Although the missionaries were not scientists in the full sense, they delegated their interests and desires: to their mission. It was not *them* who *wanted* something; they considered themselves tools (or media) of some higher interest. If we consider the milieu of conversion/coloniality as saturated with mutual and asymmetric interests and of operations with a never fully projectable outcome, we might see something that escapes the narrative of Western superiority.

What kinds of music and dance did the Jesuits encounter? They got to know a multitude of groups, languages, and cultural practices. Therefore, we have to be cautious with generalizations. A number of cultural and religious practices were, however, shared in different places in Moxos and Chiquitos. Music, dance, and the consumption of *chicha* (maize beer) were widespread features in rituals that were supervised and performed by holy persons. The Jesuits labeled them *magicians* or *priests*. Fernández gives a detailed account of such

---

[21] Thomas Macho, "Zeit und Zahl. Kalender und Zeitrechnung als Kulturtechniken," in *Bild-Schrift-Zahl*, ed. Sybille Krämer and Horst Bredekamp (Munich: Fink, 2003); Bernhard Siegert, "Kulturtechnik," in *Einführung in die Kulturwissenschaft*, ed. Harun Maye and Leander Scholz (Munich: Fink, 2011), pp. 172–192.

[22] Antoine Hennion, "The Work to be Made: The Art of Touching," in *Reset Modernity!*, ed. Bruno Latour and Christophe Leclerq (Cambridge MA and London: MIT Press, 2016), pp. 208–214, here p. 209.

[23] For a reading of *ecologies of practice* in the framework of media ecology and the coloniality/modernity debate, see Karin Harrasser and Katrin Solhdju, "Wirksamkeit verpflichtet. Herausforderungen einer Ökologie der Praktiken," *Zeitschrift für Medienwissenschaft* 14 (2016): pp. 72–86.

a person's tasks and practices for the Maniacas, who were later *reduced* to one of the Chiquitos missions. One becomes a *mapono* by bodily and spiritual techniques: fasting, consuming inebriant substances, making spiritual encounters with animals, and having illuminating episodes of illness. Fernández speaks of "exercises and ecstasy" ("Übungen und Verzückungen"[24]), a vocabulary common for a Jesuit disciple who had gone through the Ignatian exercises. The *mapono* (often, but not necessarily, a man) is described to be the intermediary to the deities. S/he employs gestures familiar to the European observer: the sprinkling of fluids (*Weyh-Wasser*). The Maniacas celebrated elaborate *masses* for what Fernández calls a *diabolic trinity*. For this purpose, the *temple* was bisected with a curtain of branches and foliage. Behind that curtain, the trinity of *Omequeturiqui* (father), *Urasana* (son) and *Uropo* (spirit) manifested itself while the village was singing, dancing and drinking. Only the *mapono* was allowed to enter the sanctuary. S/he delivered the requests of the villagers but also flew with the gods. Fernández reports that sometimes the whole building would rise and come down with a big crash. The *mapono* travels into the lap of a deity Fernández is not quite sure how to describe: It is either a devil, or the mother of *Urasana* and wife of *Omequeturiqui*.[25] Taken together, the scenario is not so different from practices of Jesuit Catholicism that embraced the worship of Mother Mary and built on an ecstatic encounter with Jesus as a result of elaborate exercises of body and mind. Conversely, in the eyes of the *Maniacas* the Jesuit *padres* must have resembled their own priests (abstinence, prayer, meditation, a life beyond the communal and sexual arrangements of a group). Consequently, the *padres* were often feared because they were considered powerful magicians. Nicholas Griffiths therefore considers the religious practices of the Jesuits "Christian magic" and he calls them "Christian shamans."[26] And indeed: The reports are full of miracles that not only demonstrate the power of faith to the European reader but give a hint to what extent the missionaries adapted indigenous practices. With regard to music and dance, they employed a double strategy: They allowed traditional music and dance to be part of the liturgy and of the abundant culture of (worldly) celebration *and* they engaged heavily in the teaching and performance of European music. Bach and d'Orbigny, who reported on Chiquitos in the 1840s, 70 years after the Jesuits' expulsion, are impressed by the quality and variety of the performed music: They recount celebrations spanning many days in which all villagers take part in all sorts of music, theatre, and dance performances. The performers seemingly changed easily from Italian orchestral music to traditional dance and back.[27]

---

[24] Juan Patricio Fernández, *Erbauliche und Angenehme Geschichten derer Chiquitos, und anderer von den Patribus der Gesellschaft Jesu in Paraquaria Neu-Bekehrter Völcker; [...]*. (Vienna: Paul Straub, 1729), p. 305.

[25] Ibid., pp. 293–303.

[26] Nicholas Griffiths, *Sacred Dialogues. Christianity and Native Religions in the Colonial Americas 1492-1700* (Great Britain: Lulu Enterprises, 2006), pp. 185, 208.

[27] For example Alcide Dessalines d'Orbigny, *Fragment d'un voyage au centre de l'Amérique Méridionale* (Paris: P. Bertrand, 1845), p. 54ff.; Moritz Bach, *Die Jesuiten und ihre Mission Chiquitos in Südamerika. Eine historisch-ethnographische Schilderung* (Leipzig: Ritter, 1843), p. 47ff.

Another frequently reported amalgamation of European sounds and sounds from the woods, of Catholic ritual and local modes of worship, were the Corpus Christi processions in Chiquitos:

> The plaza, a big square space, was adorned by the Indians with arches built from tree branches, from which hung a few fruits. Amidst this green foliage, there fluttered, restrained by light ribbons, a multitude of birds of different species, diverse colours and various shapes: wild ducks and geese, parrots and numerous beautiful species, toucans with disproportionate beaks, longer than the rest of their bodies. Add to this the "maximos," similar to peacocks, and the ostriches with their erect neck and long legs. To the bases of the arches were tied wild beasts from the forests, such as anteaters, wild boars, different kinds of deer, foxes, armadillos, hares and other species. All these animals, in the manner of a (religious) service and of a silent homage, extolled the strength and majesty of the God who was to walk by [...].[28]

The mix of natural and artificial sound was carefully staged: the animals were captured specifically for the event (and released afterwards). The abundant use of local flower and feather patterns was incorporated from native modes of worship. Attachment to local deities was quasi *reframed* within the Catholic system without being totally abandoned. Spatial and temporal arts were deliberately employed to bridge a situation of intimate co-existence with forest and land with life in a delimited settlement, with its geometric architecture, its time structured not by eternal rhythms but by the clock.

As Martin Zillinger notes, "media history of the Christian mission soon encounters conditions that are not exhausted in the question of standardizations and formattings that mobilize ideas, practices, and specific formats (Latour's 'immutable mobiles'). [...] Rather, the missionary societies always had to mobilize various resources in order to actualize the universalistic horizon of conversion in situ."[29] This is quite obvious in Chiquitos. I want to take the argument a step further: What if we consider the transformation as bidirectional, a mutual usage that is shaped in *interested* practices? Stengers uses the term *interested* to indicate that practices are bound up with efficacies that in turn afford responsibility, even more so if we take into account that *intention* (for example to proselytize) never transmits directly, but rather via all sorts of mediators and against resistances. In a more or less destructive way, local practices have been reshaped, but also the missionaries and their way of *doing faith* have changed. Kristin Dutcher Mann argues that it was the mission experience that profoundly altered the Jesuits' understanding of the relationship between music and spirituality. Both Ignatius and the Catholic doctrine after the Council of Trent were skeptical about the use of elaborate, polyphonic music in church. Discussions about liturgy and music were framed by the concern of an *abuse of the Mass* as a spectacle. The

---

28 José Manuel Peramás, *De vita et moribus tredim vivorum paraguaicorum,* partial facsimile in Schmid, *Pater Martin Schmid SJ, 1694-1772. Seine Briefe und sein Wirken,* p. 237, English p. 236, trans. Leonardo Waisman.

29 Martin Zillinger, "Christian Modernizations. Circulating Media Practices of the Mission Along the Nile," *L'Année du Maghreb* 11 (2014): pp. 17–39, here p. 18.

use of secular instruments and of the musical style of the court was under suspicion of inspiring covetousness, irreverence, and superstition.[30] Ignatius wrestled with the place of music in the order and came to the conclusion that too much music should be avoided: "If it were to follow my taste and inclination, I would put choir and singing in the Society; but I do not do it because God our Lord has given me to understand that it is not his will—nor does he wish to be served by us in choir, but in other matters of his service."[31] It was never an official dogma, but in general it was believed that strong affects caused by music were a threat to real spirituality.[32] All evidence from Chiquitos and Moxos point to the opposite: The archives are not only full of elaborate church music of a fashionable style at the time but also of worldly music of all sorts (dances, sonatas, etc.).

What happened in music theory? Athanasius Kircher, whose *Musurgia Universalis* (1650) was available in any Jesuit library, also in the *colegios* of New Spain, went as far as to consider certain intervals to be universal in their ability to produce the affect of *spiritum*. It is striking that he uses evidence from non-European music to underline his argument: "This is why all people use the *genus diatonicum* in their song; the Turkish priests in their *alla, alla* move *per tonos & ditonos;* the Chinese, when they are praying to their idol *Canfutium,* they sing *Chuypò, chuypò,* from the 8th to the 4th and back from the 4th to the 8th. The same is true for the *toupinamba* in the New World."[33]

This is close to heresy: If *the spiritual* is universally invoked by certain intervals, how could one distinguish the Christian God from *idols* such as *Canfutium*? There is no space here for an in-depth discussion of the problem, but it was indeed one of the major problems for the missionaries to distinguish *proper* faith from *masked* faith and to demonstrate of Christian faith that it really *meant* something else.

It was not only in theoretical terms that the colonial experience was a transformational force. I want to argue that it reshaped the self-concept of the missionaries. This becomes evident in the letters of Martin Schmid, SJ. Before coming to Chiquitos from Switzerland, he was not a professional musician (or an architect), but as a missionary he taught himself and the new Christians to play all sorts of instruments: the trumpet, the cittern, flutes, violins, the organ. He became a professional instrument maker and a composer (and architect). It is the mission, he states in a letter to a brother, which was able to awaken these abilities, "so that we know more here than what we know, and we

---

[30]   Kristin Dutcher Mann, *The Power of Song: Music and Dance in the Mission Communities of Northern New Spain, 1590-1810* (Stanford CA: Stanford University Press, 2010), p. 51.

[31]   Quoted in ibid., p. 59.

[32]   Ibid., p. 61.

[33]   "Daher gebrauchen alle Völcker in ihren Gesängern das *genus diatonicum*; die Türckischen Priester in ihrem *alla, alla*, gehen *per tonos & ditonos*; die Chinenser wann sie ihren Abgott *Canfutium* anbeten singen sie *Chuypò, chuypò,* von der 8. in die 4. von der 4. wider in die 8. Also auch die *toupinamba* in der Neuen Welt." Athanasius Kircher, *Musurgia Universalis. Reprint der deutschen Teilübersetzung von Andreas Hirsch, Schwäbisch Hall 1662* (Basel, London, New York and Prague: Bärenreiter, 2006), p. 151.

Fig. 18: Athansius Kircher, *Musurgia Universalis*, example for "spiritual" music from the New World, p. 151.

are more able here than we are able."[34] And he continues: He is a missionary not *even though* he sings, dances and plays instruments, but *because* he does so. He anticipates that his brother might not like the idea of a dancing priest. He therefore asks his reader to consider that even the feet of those who herald the gospel should be set splendidly.[35] Also, he would do nothing but follow David's example who danced around the Ark of the Covenant with much grace. Although he uses figures of the Old Testament in order to convince his fellow brother, it is evident that it was the everyday practice that inspired the new self-conception of Martin Schmid as a "dancing and singing priest." Furthermore, the practice of spreading the gospel in aesthetic rather than in conceptual ways enabled him to discover new skills and unknown aesthetic options.

Appropriation/Inversion

Can we take the perspective of interested practices one final step further to investigate inversions of the Jesuit practices? The sources available are highly biased in these cases. Counter-appropriations are framed as heretic or diabolic, as a relapse into the state of superstition. Their genres are didactic miracles and visions ("Gesichte"). A case that is only loosely connected to musical performance might be of interest, as it demonstrates the difficulty of discriminating between Catholic and indigenous contents of faith and shows how deeply unsettling the practices to stimulate affects employed by the Jesuits were. It is the story of a *miraculum* centering around the practice of flagellation. Flagellation was a frequent practice with multiple meanings in the *reducciones*. The whip was used

---

34 "ut sciamus hic plus quam sciamus, possmus plus quam possimus." Letter to P. Joseph Schumacher, SJ, San Rafael Chiquitos, 10th October, 1744, Schmid, p. 84.

35 "speciosos esse debere etiam pedes evangelizantium," Schmid, p. 85.

to discipline the neophytes. It was worn and shown as a symbol of power by the *padres* while overseeing work or worship. Ritualistic flagellation was, furthermore, a central element in liturgy, especially (but not exclusively) during Holy Week. In the fasting period, the parish assembled once or twice a week in church for sessions of flagellation that were orchestrated with music and sometimes culminated with the appearance of the devil in person: A masked man would enter the church and would howl, produce a lot of noise, and chase the flagellants.[36] Also, as part of the staging of the Passion of Christ, it was considered a great honor to be part of the group of 3–4 people who would enact the physical suffering of Christ.

If we take these multiple meanings and instances as a background, the following epi-sode, concerning the conversion of a "magician" recounted by Fernández, is puzzling. The "magician," an "intimate of the devil," had recently come to San José and wanted to live in a Christian way, but he is constantly in danger of falling back, of becoming "a wild animal" again. He is tempted by the devil: Lust and thoughts about his former religion make him fall into a feverish condition in which he envisions a crowd of devils ("eine Schaar Teuffel").[37] They flee the church and condemn the faithful who are currently in church using the whip on each other. The devils try to persuade the man to return to the woods and to take up his old religion again by pointing out that a religion that makes people flagellate each other cannot be something good. They threaten to flog him the same way as can be seen in the church ("wir werden dich mit eben solchen Schlägen abbleuen").[38] The genre does not allow for anything else but a compunctious conversion in the end, but nonetheless the episode shows how prone the bodily techniques introduced by the Jesuits were to appropriations of all sorts.

For the Guaraní, Antonio Ruiz de Montoya reports cases of counter-appropriation of the musical and theatrical practices of the Jesuits. He reports an uprising led by the *caci-que* Miguel Artiguaye. The exodus of 300 people from a *reducción* starts with an ecstatic speech by Artiguaye, in which he accuses the *padres* of having stolen their freedom. The *sacerdotes* have not sent them the promised god but the devil. With "furor diabolico" Ar-tiguaye ends his speech with the following words: "We can no longer suffer the freedom of those who wish to reduce us to their bad way (of living) on our own ground."[39] The subsequent exodus is performed with great theatricality: Everybody assembles on the plaza, adorned with beautiful feathers, with bows and arrows, arks are erected, and the whole village leaves "with much grandeur and the sound of tambourines and flutes."[40]

---

[36] Bach, *Die Jesuiten und ihre Mission Chiquitos in Südamerika. Eine historisch-ethnographische Schilderung,* pp. 59–60.

[37] Fernández, *Erbauliche und Angenehme Geschichten derer Chiquitos, und anderer von den Patribus der Gesellschaft Jesu in Paraquaria Neu-Bekehrter Völcker; [...].* p. 135.

[38] Ibid., p. 136.

[39] "Ya no se puede sufrir la libertad de estos que en nuestras mismas tierras quieren reducirnos á su mal modo." Antonio Ruiz de Montoya, *Conquista Espiritual hecha por los religiosos de la Compañía de Jesús en las provincias del Paraguay, Paraná, Uruguay y Tape,* p. 58.

[40] Ibid., p. 59.

Although the *padres* feared for their lives, they were obviously impressed by the spectacle that literally inverts the Corpus Christi processions.

Montoya, who was active in Paraguay in the seventeenth century, observed an exodus led by a charismatic leader. Alfred Métraux studied what he called millenialist movements with an "indigenous messiah" for a later period.[41] Such movements were frequent throughout the eighteenth and nineteenth century, also in Chiquitos and Moxos.[42] Métraux is convinced that the basic pattern of the charismatic leaders—a redeemer who leads the suppressed into a "land without evil" (by means of excessive dance, by the way)—was widespread in cultures of the Amazon before the Europeans arrived. It is hard to judge based on the written sources: The Catholic figures, narratives, and practices (of punishment and redemption) were in some places syncretically mixed with indigenous ones, in other cases they were openly rejected. Some of the messiahs claimed that they would lead people back to their former way of existence, some claimed to incorporate Jesus Christ and bring them to paradise. In any case, the encounter with the Christian missionaries forged tools of resistance, practices that emerged out of a dense web of routines, skills, affects, attachments, and symbolic practices. Practices of conversion and cultural transformation included images (both Christian and indigenous) and written texts (books, scores), but their staging and bodily enactment are the clue to understanding how the reworking of both Catholic and indigenous culture was shaped into what is, probably too neutrally and one-dimensionally, called *Mission Culture*. Rather, we should speak of a dangerous method and of risky practices that produced an often contradictory *assemblage*; an *assemblage* that might have *worked* quite well in some places for a certain amount of time, but that remained contested and fragile throughout.

Concluding Remarks

Although we can observe certain moments of hybridization and syncretism, especially if we consider the long-time effects of the Jesuit enterprise in the region, I hesitate to be content with the explanatory value of the terms. I have the feeling that the notion of syncretism tends to brush over processes of imposition and of physical and symbolic violence. If everything is connected in a cosmic dance of symbols, things, and agencies, then violence, suffering, and inequalities tend not to matter enough. There is no neutral ground on which two (or more) cultures can meet under Spanish rule in the seventeenth and eighteenth century. This is why I stressed biopolitics and the political nature of music in the first part of this text. As a counterbalance to the danger of affirming European superiority even through its critique (as a unidirectional dispositive), I tried to carve out moments of deflection and inversion of affective techniques. It is the use, the need to enact a

---

[41]   Alfred Métraux, *Kult und Magie der Indianer Südamerikas. Magier und Missionare am Amazonas*, trans. Isotta Meyer (Gifkendorf: Merlin Verlag, 2001), pp. 11–37.

[42]   Gary Van Valen, *Indigenous Agency in the Amazon: The Mojos in Liberal and Rubber-Boom Bolivia, 1842-1932* (Tucson: University of Arizona Press, 2013).

Fig. 19: Minuet in A-major, R 82, f 44 V, Archivo Musical de Chiquitos.

practice in a *specific* political, cultural and personal situation that renders music a dangerous method.

Much needs to be done to arrive at a theoretical model that can de-colonialize our perspective on constellations like these. One major obstacle is the nature of the archive we are forced to work with: We can try to carve out stories about resistance and appropriations, to untie reports of indigenous practices from their condemnation, to uncover the interestedness of everybody involved. We can follow the vector of practices in Hennion's sense: The emergence of new subjects and objects, the necessary establishment of new relations with every enactment. But still: these documents, like all documents, are corrupted transmitters. This is especially true for the scores now neatly conserved in the archive. Not only because they have materially faded, but because all the words, gestures, signs, and bodies that are missing in this story, all the local resources and living bodies that were mobilized in the name of God and the new order are missing in the scores as well, almost at least. Media studies of coloniality are, perhaps, studies of missing transmitters in the first place.

Probably we can start by honoring the dead who have not left letters and reports. I therefore dedicate this text to Pablo, whose name is written after the double bar of a little minuet I practiced while I wrote this (see figure 20). The piece is quite hard to play for an inexperienced musician like me. And I do not know who Pablo was. Did he write the piece? Did he copy it? Was it written/copied for him in order to be performed in public?

For what public did he play it and who danced to the music? Who were the dancers and what did they wear? Did they dance a fashionable minuet or a dance from the old days? Did they enjoy dancing or was it a duty imposed on them to please *padre* Martin Schmid? Or did he perhaps dance himself, putting his feet splendidly in order to please the Lord? I cannot answer any of these questions. They might remain unanswered but they can be ghostly guides to our colonial past and present.

Practice is a Screen. Minor Assemblages of Gender, Race, and Global Media

INTERVIEW WITH REY CHOW, BY ULRIKE BERGERMANN

UB: What is practice theory (if there is such a thing)?

RC: Practice can mean so many different things. In the English language, one thinks immediately of artistic practices (singing, playing a musical instrument, doing calligraphy, rehearsing for a dance performance), sports practices, legal practices, clinical practices, and so forth. In these ordinary examples, the connotations of practice have to do with techniques (which require long periods of training to reach excellence, if not perfection), on the one hand, and with a vocation or profession based on specialized skills, on the other. One also thinks of practice in other senses: routines guided by rules (like driving on the right or left side of the road), customs (like eating turkey for Thanksgiving dinner; exchanging presents at Christmas), and rituals (like the last rites ceremony in Hinduism by which a dead person is sent off to their ancestors). These social, cultural, and religious practices connote communally shared ways of doing things that are repeated over time, often passed down generations. Within the academy, the word practice is usually invoked with institutional nuances. In the study of Anglo-American literature, for instance, there is *practical criticism*, a type of critical engagement centered on the specifics of an isolatable literary text or collection of literary texts. There, the point is not exactly practice as a duration of training time or as a vocational enterprise; rather, it is a method of studying literature—a manner of appreciating a literary text, you might say—that sets itself apart from philosophical discussions of ideas. A kind of criticism that is practical—that is, concrete rather than abstract—is thought to be appropriate and correct for literature. I bring up *practical criticism* in this context because I think it may have something to tell us about the current interest in practice theory.

So, what might be considered practice theory (today)? I tend to think that the answer is wide open at one level because no theorist would say that his/her ideas do not somehow involve an explicit or implicit notion of practice. At the same time, it seems that *practice of a certain kind* is really what we are talking about, no? Would this be practice involving the physical body and involving many rather than few people? *Embodied* and *widely shared*—two criteria to keep in mind.

Among well-known contemporary theorists, Bruno Latour comes readily to mind at this juncture. His attempt to underscore the collective nature of scientific and social scientific explorations in such ways that not only humans but animals, plants, soil, and mechanical objects collaborate in a relay of efforts in research experimentations and findings, is a good instance of theoretical thinking based on a refreshing notion of practice. (Actor Network Theory fits the criteria of being embodied and widely shared). A few decades ago, Michel Foucault, as we know, wrote about the techniques of the self as part of a larger study of practices of self-examination and self-mastery in Greco-Roman antiquity. Unlike Latour's, Foucault's emphasis is not exactly the networking of players and their actions but rather the micro-applications, involving both body and mind, specific to the ancients' (as opposed to Christianity's) instructions regarding the care of the self. Foucault's work is exemplary in its understanding of human society as constituted by practices—a word he usually invoked in the plural. I want to mention another important figure: Louis Althusser. In his famous discussion of ideology, you recall, Althusser discusses the relation between practice and belief by drawing on Blaise Pascal's rather blasphemous suggestion: you kneel and say your prayers, then you believe. By going through the motions, literally, we can find God. If we think of kneeling and praying as practices, what Althusser has given us is nothing short of a practice theory—that is, a theory for which practice precedes everything else, including belief. Slavoj Žižek, who is fond of citing Althusser's reference to Pascal, terms this kind of *materiality*—based in physical moves but expressing itself as something lofty and spiritual—*the sublime object of ideology*. Rather than only the church, Žižek also associates this sublime object with the functioning of the totalitarian state.

If most theories are, inevitably, always already informed by some notion of practice, why has practice become of such interest in our time? To this extent, I think it is insufficient to determine *what* practice theory is, whether it exists as a body of work which authors can be identified with and so forth. Far more crucial, it seems to me, is another set of questions: how—by what processes, controversies, and antagonisms—have we come to think of practice as so important that we now have a name such as practice theory? What unresolved philosophical, aesthetic, and political issues are signaled by the contemporary investment in practice theory? For what other concepts—or problems, or tensions—is the word *practice* a stand-in, a veil, a screen?

In some ways, our interest in practice may be symptomatic of our collective sense of failure at arriving at any genuine sense of democracy around the globe today. Through practice, we are perhaps holding on to the possibility of *dignifying—of giving due recognition to*—all classes, people, things, and actions that used to be marginal or off-limit to thought proper. An invigorating, egalitarian realignment of society, practice is the sign by which everyone, everything, and every act may become more or less equal or at least comparable. In this vein, practice has in fact assumed the *conceptual* status of an arbiter of value, a conceptual status that was once occupied by more elite descriptors (such as genius, giftedness, talent, wealth, superiority, etc.). With the spotlight on practice, value itself has shifted from the more traditional bases in transcendent (and hierarchical) meanings to horizontal arrangements, accompanied by preferred criteria such as immanence, singularity, and experience.

As in the case of the old-fashioned *practical criticism*, then, the turn to practice, together with the invention of practice theory, carries with it a politics and an ethics of our time, perhaps even a code of good and bad in tune with the new age.

Practice/Media/Theory

UB: Proclaiming a *turn to practice theory*, at the same time, may be a self-fulfilling prophecy: you name it and do it, and it is there. This interpellation of an academic community can be motivated, as you suggest, by a diffuse sense of political exigencies (following the idea that academic thinking and the real political world were not very close). Media studies in Germany is following different threads here, either highlighting practice analyses within a possible history of the discipline, or elaborating ethical perspectives within media-related work, or picking up some of the vocabulary and stripping it of its political contexts for a formal use. What would be the possibilities of doing media studies relating to *practice*? Neither a definition of *practice* nor *medium*, but rather a look at the performative epistemological power of the notions is a good point of departure, as you said. So, my next question would be: how to conceptualize that *media*—taken as sets of practices, subjects, (technical and living) things—connect and divide, and always involve ethics? Can you offer an outline of such a reference frame for media and practice?

RC: Because the concept of practice is so broad—in this sense it is not unlike the concept of media itself—it would perhaps be more productive to specify different practices and the ways they connect or divide, carry ethical implications, and evolve historically. I am less certain of there being any overarching frame of reference that would explain all examples of (media) practices.

There already exist many possibilities of doing media studies through practice at different levels. For instance, at Duke University, where I teach, some colleagues actively engaged with media theory and media philosophy also maintain multi-year *labs* to pursue collaborative research (with colleagues and students) on particular themes. I believe these labs are, pedagogically speaking, not unlike seminars or workshops where we experiment with ideas in a collective fashion, though of course the labs are typically equipped with technological means of testing, communicating, and measuring ideas through controlled uses of computer networks. Labs allow for a quantifying approach to media studies. To that extent, one type of practice in media studies is that of having quantifiable metrics, involving algorithms, for instance.

On the other hand, practice may also be defined in terms of social purpose or communal utility. Some studies of the visual arts, like film, video, or documentary, may be explicitly tied to social causes, such as ending poverty, bringing attention to the precarious lives of migrants, or charting the historical transformations of a particular ethnic neighborhood. In such cases, the media involved are understood both as means of capture and narration *and* as ways of intervening in the social scenarios presented, with the view to raising audiences' consciousness and/or soliciting their participation. Putting media studies at the service of social causes in this manner is one of the obvious practical connections we can make across communities inside and outside the university. But it is equally important to remember that there is often a gap between academic studies and social causes—and that such a gap is not necessarily a bad thing: it reminds us of media studies' autonomy; the fact that there are aspects of media studies that cannot simply be instrumentalized for utility purposes (like serving the public).

What you call the performative epistemological aspect of practice is most evident, it seems, when the intimate aspects of oneself, such as one's inscription into the conventional sexualization of human bodies (male/female), can no longer be assumed as natural but must, on some occasions, be deconstructed and reassembled, as in the case of transgender people. Here the body itself serves both as a medium and a site of practice. As you may have heard, in the state of North Carolina, the State Legislature passed in spring 2016 what is called HB2 (House Bill 2), which, among other things, stipulates that people must use public bathrooms that correspond to their sex at birth. This travesty of a law is clearly not enforceable—unless the state requires people to produce their birth certificates whenever they go to the bathroom, or installs what one of my colleagues aptly calls *genitals inspectors* in public spaces—but its passing was really staged as a hostile confrontation, the point being to shame people who have chosen to undergo biomedical procedures of gender reassignment. While it has been prevalent to focus attention on the personal dimensions of these transgendered practices, in which the individual body is de facto both a lab and a social cause, it is crucial not to lose sight of the state's strategies—in this case, of deploying the law—for surveillance, control, and propaganda. The state, too, is actively involved in such media practices of gender reassignment, by performing epistemological as well as ideological and managerial functions in these communications with the ordinary citizen.

Mediated Bodies, Ethnicized/Racialized Bodies

UB: As you say, the body is a medium and a site of practice, and it is as well a name for a spatio-temporal unity of agencies, a mediatized thing insofar as we can only conceive of it in mediated ways; and insofar as it is through this that the world is programmed, pictured, made; and insofar as no performative would be possible without its materiality—there is just no way you could describe a body as not mediated, and as not always already part of a set of practices. Does that hold true for ethnicized/racialized bodies in the same way?

RC: The (post)colonial situation offers an excellent instance of how bodies can be ethnicized or racialized. I think the *how* is crucial here, because it is not as though ethnicity or race is a type of stable content, something well understood in advance, that we can simply locate in some bodies while other bodies are free of such content. Instead, to ethnicize or racialize really involves establishing a certain boundary, drawing an invisible line, between us and those who are not like us (and who therefore must be eliminated or made to disappear from *our* space). So how are bodies ethnicized or racialized in some colonial/postcolonial situations? You must have heard of the controversial historical case of *suttee* (widow burning or women's acts of self-sacrifice on their husbands' death in some parts of India), footbinding in premodern China, and clitoridectomy in some parts of Africa. These longstanding cultural practices were each mediated by local kinship custom, class hierarchy, and economic considerations, as well as by local ideological debates and rationalizations. Each practice also incited resistances, revolts, and conflicts among its local practitioners. During the recent colonial era, however, as Europeans, including missionaries, educators, and travelers, arrived in these places and learned about such practices, they were typically scandalized by what, from their civilized perspectives, appeared to be savage cruelty and inhumaneness, and many of them mobilized efforts to eradicate these practices. In response, local groups, often led by patriarchs and nationalists, would defend the practices in terms of native or national tradition, with which foreigners, they argued, had no business interfering. This, then, was the type of fraught scenario that Gayatri Chakravorty Spivak once described as "white men saving brown women from brown men."

My point is that these female bodies *become* ethnicized or racialized only in the process of this struggle between colonialist rescue and nationalist defense—that they *become* brown, yellow, or black women, with specific characteristics differently amplified in each case, as colonialist and nationalist forces each use them to stake out their self-serving interests. On the one side, the female bodies were mediated by the rhetorics of science, enlightenment, and Christian benevolence: *We, the most advanced citizens of the world, must save these poor brown, yellow, and black women from their own people!* On the other side, the same bodies were mediated by conservative ideologies of traditionalism: *These women's bodies bear the signs of our culture, our nation, our history! We must be the ones to determine the pros and cons of these practices, not the bloody foreigners!* Even today, we continue to hear echoes of this type of confrontation every time a country such as China, Iran, or Iraq complains about Western powers meddling in their *internal* affairs. Indeed, if we take something like *freedom of speech* not as an indestructible universal ideal, as it is thought to be by some, but rather as a kind of body (or more precisely a type of embodied practice), then the typical outcry we hear in Western reports against how this body/embodied practice is abused in places like China and some Islamic countries is very much a replica of the way female bodies were ethnicized and racialized during those earlier, colonial encounters.

And in a situation such as that of contemporary Germany where, within a very short period of time in 2015–16, there has been an unprecedentedly large influx of immigrants from war-torn Syria and other countries in the Middle East and Africa, immigrants who arrive with very different cultural, religious, and gender practices from those of the Germans, I suspect that we are going to witness increasingly problematic attempts to ethnicize and racialize—bodies and embodied practices, including embodied practices of speech—through the tensions and conflicts between different groups competing for economic resources and social recognition. This will be painful, given the history of the Holocaust, which was, of course, an earlier instance of precisely such an effective program of ethnicizing and racializing bodies and embodied practices by the state in the form of an *us* versus a *them*. This artificial but real boundary became the rationale for genocide. There have long been studies of the practices specific to the Nazi regime, including studies of Hitler himself as a media phenomenon—indeed, as an artist. They are worth revisiting for purposes of charting the relations between media, practice, and ethnicization/racialization of bodies.

Networks and Agents in Practice

UB: A new way of charting these relations could be a reference frame sketching the body and the media as provided by network theory—would you agree? Mediating bodies, as you say, is one discursive practice, its performative power constitutive of realities; and the bodies themselves are not only mediated but also exist as media and mediating agents at the same time.

I guess we can make the most of media studies here by enlarging the notion of network theories: A *network* comprises *media* in a narrow sense—the apparatuses, the technologies—as well as the users, the institutions, and immaterial *things*, the cultural history of the respective imaginary (for example the belief in the documentary status of special transferences). Actor network theory, here, focuses on the *transmissions*, the work between these nodes, that make up a (media) network. Media, then, are the temporal entities of what is connected through transmissions. To say that media connect and divide is not to say that their contents are inclusive or hostile, but to consider media in terms of what is being done, the ongoing result of *doing media*. The problem with actor network theory is that it has hardly been able to take power structures into account. We might easily think that whatever constitutes a network is free to join the conversation; and the limited choice of network elements is not usually seen within political or economic contexts—as actor network theorists would argue, any larger-scale question is already inherently present within the smaller frame. A racialized or gendered body, a certain movie camera, a history of documentary practices, and a landscape, for example, would make for a singular analysis and incorporate larger structures as well. A medium, then, is not a tool, not a neutral thing as opposed to ideology, but is as material as it is political as soon as it is in practice.

It might sound strange to look at fascist race politics as a media network, but only as long as you associate media analysis with *the other of politics*. Otherwise, I would not know how to look at Hitler but as an agent. To include the question of responsibility (which is not simply *distributed within a network*) is a necessary step for actor media theory.

Do these theoretical considerations make sense for you, or would you rather take off from specific materials and topics?

RC: I am in general agreement with you that one issue with actor network theory remains the unavoidable question of power (what you call responsibility). In suggesting that different kinds of agents be embraced under actor network theory, Latour, I believe, is asking us to recognize the agency of non-human as well as human players in the way our world works. He is excellent in helping us understand how, for instance, a scientific or anthropological expedition may involve not only the human specialists themselves but also various types of mechanical equipment, natural elements (down to the soil and the worms in it), institutional offices, transportation means, communication technologies, etc. I don't think that actor network theory has been conceptualized to skirt the issue of power; if anything, thinking in terms of a network of actors (or actants) renders the notion of power highly complex. Latour's theorization is Foucauldian in that regard, because power, as Foucault writes, is not a thing that you can possess or pin down but rather a social and discursive relation—between different parties, between different classes, between different groups of actors. And, as Foucault also argues, power is not only a negative, prohibitive exercise of force (in the form of *No!*); it is, more importantly, a positive, enabling exercise, the force of *Yes!* This notion of power—as what makes things possible, what generates rather than forbids, what proliferates rather than restricts—remains entirely germane to our thinking about media's power to connect and divide.

I like your emphasis on media's capacity for transmission. Thinking about media in these terms allows us not to lose sight of the element of temporality, as you say, and not to lose sight of the processual aspects of media practices, which are always in-between temporalities, criss-crossed by multiple temporalities, rather than beginning and finishing once and for all.

By substituting the term *network* with *media*, and by coining the phrase *actor media theory*, (instead of actor network theory), do you mean to have *media* take on all the potentiality carried by the notion of *network and* do something more at the same time? And what would that something more be? Would it be the capacity for dealing with power, temporality, and the specificities of an embodied practice or situation? I guess I am not sure why the term *network* cannot handle all that.

I recall how, when I read through some of the papers for the DFG symposium, I was struck by how open and yet unsatisfying the concept of *media* remains, simply because media and its cognates—from *medium* and *mediality* to *intermedia* and *intermediate* (used as a verb), to *mediation* and *remediation*—are used to talk about so many different things across identities, cultures, and time periods. I felt, and continue to feel, that it behooves us to clarify the epistemological, theoretical, and practical status of the term media. Is *media* interchangeable with terms such as *agency*, *matter*, and *art*, or does it refer to tools, gadgets, and devices used in contemporary everyday life such as smartphones, websites, and apps? Does the term *media* encompass not only objects of an instrumental nature but also art making, political activism (such as protests and acts of memorialization), social relations (involving bodies, encounters, intimacies, and communities), and colonial administrative work (including musical teaching and training, and their documentation)?

My hesitation to replace *network* with *media* also has to do with the fact that, even as we speak, some theorists are already using the term *media* in a sense that brings it close to *network*. In the more classic sense, *media* tends to mean either a carrier (as in a medium) or something that mediates, that comes between (as in the English noun *intermediary*). In these classic usages, *media* is aligned with more traditional disciplines such as philosophy (for example Nietzsche, Hegel), sociology (for example Niklas Luhmann), technologies of communication (Marshall McLuhan, Friedrich Kittler, and their followers), the arts (for example Theodor Adorno), the everyday (for example Sigmund Freud, Walter Benjamin), and the nonhuman world (for example Vilém Flusser). In the meantime, some scholars have begun shifting the word toward a newer, more fluid kind of nuance, so that *media* now means something like *assemblages* in the sense we have learned from Deleuze and Guattari. It seems to me that *assemblages* are comparable to *networks*.

Assemblages and Politics

To take up, at this point, your vivid scene of "a racialized or gendered body, a certain movie camera, a history of documentary practices, and a landscape": We can think of each of these components of the scene as a minor assemblage with its own micro-history, but we also need to ask how they all work *together* as a singular group (though not a totality). And it is this process of working together that must be analyzed in terms of the politics of power, of multiple actors and their interactivity with one another, correct? The absence of any one of these components would alter the nature of the analysis—for example a movie camera, a history of documentary practices, and a landscape, without a racialized or gendered body; or a racialized or gendered body, a movie camera, and a landscape, without the history of documentary practices, and so on. So, the notion of *connect* that was a theme of our DFG symposium is very much about the *possibilities* as much as the forms of togetherness, the forms of collaborative coexistence, and their multiplication. As some of the workshop papers showed, however, media practices are typically marked by ambiguities. If they serve as connectors, they also easily turn into impediments and divides. If they help to manage and govern, they are also the occasion for deception, exploitation, abuse, or violence. If they generate communities, they seem as readily to confront us with the bodies, voices, gestures, and life stories that have been excluded, that are, for one reason or another, missing.

With such ambiguities come the ethical conundrums that some of the panelists sought to address: How do media practices organize, facilitate, and/or challenge the shifting but ever-present boundaries between the inside and the outside, as for instance the inside and outside of capitalist markets, of colonial enclosures, of gender inequities, or of sexual intimacies? And what happens when the very media practices—call them networks or assemblages if you like—available for academic study (such as the sociological, anthropological, historical, scientific, and other disciplinary accounts mentioned in the different papers) have themselves erased the plurality of voices and agencies that form the original settings, the original settings these accounts are supposedly documenting and transmitting as *historical knowledge* or *historical evidence*?

UB: Yes, speaking of networks certainly would not help, if this was simply meant as another mode of enlarging the frame of reference. I understand it as the opportunity to conceptualize not a bigger, but a different setting, which might include practices (so, I would not exchange *media* with *agency*). Reconsidering *media* as assemblages, then again, things might work as Turing proposed: Do not ask if the computer can think, but ask how to rethink *thinking*.

At the same time, it is important to be reminded that academic work might fall short of taking practices into account, no matter what (*networked*) frame of reference it uses. This might be the point where the situatedness of the researcher comes in, in all its contingency, responsibility, and accountability for the choice of frames—whether these frames are called media, media assemblages, actor networks, or whatever suits the analytical purpose, as long as it makes sense, produces some knowledge, as in *doing gender*. And, finally, would this kind of impersonal identity have a special relation to her object of study, a kind of performative making of her object, or an active part of the assemblage?

RC: By *impersonal identity*, do you have in mind factors that are not specific to a particular individual but that may bear relevance to the work at hand in a collective manner, what you call *situatedness* in all its contingency, responsibility, etc.? I guess my response is that, yes, such situatedness should have a special, active relation to the researcher's object of study. The important thing, however, is not to turn such situatedness into a prescriptive condition. Some forms of work may defy expectations of the performative role as played by their particular situatedness, so to speak, and surprise us. There has to be room for that. An Asian American author, for instance, should not be expected to produce work that always reflects her historical condition of being classified as Asian American; a woman artist, for instance, should not be expected to produce artworks that necessarily speak to the experience of being a woman. A German-Turkish documentarist should not have to produce work that can be identified as *essentially* German-Turkish. Otherwise, *situatedness* can easily turn into a form of reification (of class, race, gender, location, cultural origin, or ancestry) despite its political astuteness.

To me, this is a major problem with many well-intentioned, politically progressive attempts to represent non-Western cultures and peoples around the world: such attempts often end up reproducing or reinforcing stereotypes. Consider the example of modern and contemporary Chinese art: it is frequently sold to Euro-American audiences as art produced in a repressive political regime, in which freedom of expression is heavily censored. What is being sold, in other words, is not only the art itself but the idea (and ideology) that the purchaser in the West is a morally virtuous *savior* of these poor folks who are victimized by their own government. Among Chinese artists and filmmakers, the joke is that if you want your work to win recognition in the West, you should produce it in such a way that it will be banned by the Chinese government; such banning has proven, time and again, to be the royal road to the hearts and minds—and wallets—of Western viewers! The phenomenal success of a multimedia artist like Ai Weiwei illustrates my point. To that extent, *situatedness* can be tricky because it easily involves preconceived ideas, which may have already placed or situated people in stereotyped ways before their work has had the chance of being seriously considered. Ironically, even a repressive state apparatus, such as the People's Republic of China, must be recognized as a player—an actant or actor—in this international network or assemblage. In many ways, the PRC's often rigid and punitive practices are *enabling* Chinese art productions to thrive in the neoliberal global market, where connoisseurs' narcissistic investments in their own moral superiority make censored artworks an irresistible attraction. Much like the European rescuers of native female bodies in the colonial era (as mentioned above), and much like the cosmopolitan guardians of free speech in today's global media circuits, these art connoisseurs, too, are an active part of the performative assemblages generated around these exotic, because censored, art objects.

UB: So that the promises of *practices* for media studies, in the form of potentially larger, more inclusive communities (with gendered, racialized, and other kinds of situated agents), come with their own traps. Practice theory needs to keep the concept of *practices* as suspended—and as open—as the objects, media, and subjects they serve to connect and/or divide.

RC: Yes, very much so!

ERHARD SCHÜTTPELZ

Introduction:
Media Theory Before and After the Practice Turn

Dedicated to the Memory of John J. McGraw (1974–2016)
Anthropologist and participant at our conference

Classical Media Theory

When media theory finally broke through the shell of communication theory at the end of the 1950s, Marshall McLuhan defined the agenda for decades to come in his opening sentences of the *Report on Project in Understanding New Media*:

> Our media have always constituted the parameters and the framework for the objectives of our Western World. But the assumptions and parameters projected by the structures of the media on and through our sensibilities have long constituted the over-all patterns of private and group associations in the West. The same structuring of the forms of human association by various media is also true of the non-Western world as of the lives of preliterate and archaic man. The difference is that in the West our media technologies from script to print, and from Gutenberg to Marconi, have been highly specialised.[1]

Media theory, as we can tell from these classic sentences, was looking for structure: the constitution of different *forms of human association* and *sensibilities* by the structures of media. And media theory was based on a structure of its own: There is an *invariant*, namely the invariant potential of human interaction that manifests itself in oral cultures, and in its pure form is not as *highly specialized* as in postliterate cultures, or rather, not specialized at all. There is an *independent variable*, namely the historical sequence of media innovations, happening *in the West* and diffused from the West. And there are *dependent variables*, the *forms of human association* and the *parameters and the framework for the objectives* of our and other worlds. The aesthetic and perceptive *sensibilities* have a special role in this functional equation, because it is *on and through* them that the structures of media are projected. Thus, in McLuhan's version of media theory, they are both part of the dependent variables and *the medium of media*, as one could say. In the corpus of media theory derived from this framework, media practices could only be secondary to

---

[1]   Marshall McLuhan, *Report on Project in Understanding New Media* (Washington DC: National Association of Educational Broadcasters, 1960), p. 1.

media. Media theory was based on the assumptions that social practices were contingent upon the *forms of human association* structured by different media, and that epistemic practices were contingent upon *the parameters and the framework for the objectives of our Western World* being constituted by media in the first place. And even apart from social and epistemic practices, in this version of media theory, media are *primary* in a very general sense—at least McLuhan gives no clues how they derive from non-media or act as dependent variables in other theoretical contexts.

McLuhan's three sentences summarize the position of a highly successful strand of media theory that could be called *classical media theory*. The invariant, the independent variable and the dependent variables remained in place, and so did the primacy of media. Classical media theory turned out to follow an East-bound and mostly North Atlantic trajectory in the Cold War: from Edmund Carpenter and Marshall McLuhan in Canada (starting in 1954) to Jean Baudrillard and Paul Virilio in France (converting to media theory after May 1968), and finally to Vilém Flusser (in the 1970s), and Friedrich Kittler (in the 1980s). In Germany, classical media theory had a lasting impact on media studies and media history, especially in the guise of Kittler's *media archeology*; not so much because it was the dominant theory (which it never was), but because the international success of German media theory seemed to be focused on this local brand of classical media theory—to the detriment of the internal diversity of German media theory, which diversity has largely been ignored internationally since the 1990s. In the U.S., the center of media innovations and pacemaker for their global diffusion, classical media theory was bound to remain a controversial and surprisingly exotic position—which made its adoption all the more challenging or even romantic.

Three major accomplishments of classical media theory, in Germany and elsewhere, may be named as follows:
- stressing the *materiality of communications*, in other terms:
- looking for the *infrastructural realities* of information and communication technologies, and localizing the medium in their material and immaterial infrastructures;
- and last but not least—acknowledging *the Medium as the Message*, the medium as the main message that can neither be corrected nor effaced by more messages, because it is already effected by practicing the conditions of its techno-legal constitution.

Thus, early on, media theory and classical media theory achieved a level of theoretical complication that overturned the reductions of functionalism. And even if McLuhan's formula for one reason or other seems slightly obsolete today, we would certainly wish to keep the three accomplishments of early media theory and their challenges: the materiality of communication, the infrastructural focus of media theory, and the medium as message.

Classical Media Theory in the Digital Age

Classical media theory may not be dead, but after more than fifty years, it has begun to smell funny. There is more than one reason for this change: theory has moved on, but media have changed as well. To characterize the stakes of media theory today, we have to reflect both changes. On the one hand, digital networked media came as a surprise for media theory, though both networks and computers had been objects of theoretical curiosity from the start, and in spite of the fact that McLuhan's media theory had its own impact on the world of computing, for example with Alan Kay and his concept (inspired by a reading of McLuhan's work) of both the computer and its user turned into reciprocal media.[2]

Classical media theory could inspire the digital world, but once computing encompassed all former media, classical media theory was at a loss what to say in structural terms. It seems that the asymmetries of classical media theory were not made for the new circumstances. Digital media have become *primary* indeed, and *more primary* than all former media. But with a vengeance, or even an irreducible paradox: The success and the versatility and volatility of computing technologies have made the causal or historical *impact* of media, of digital media, and even of something called *digital media technology* highly problematic. As a consequence, the whole idea of distinguishing media as *independent variables* from practices or messages or *forms of human association* as *dependent variables* seems to lead into contradictions, at least in three respects: concerning the processes of digital innovation; the problems of focusing *the medium* and *the computer*; and the fundamental blurring of the technical and social.

First: Do media form *social practices*, or are they determined by their social or rather socio-technical modeling? If apps for instance are designed for their messages, or even for their social patterns and practices, does the message now configure the medium? Come to think of it, it will be hard to deny that digital media are time and again reconfigured to suit new tasks and already existing practices, though of course any software will give rise to new tasks and thus escape its functionalist definitions. But it has become very difficult if not downright impossible to make media practices secondary to media now, because on a practical and material level, all we have are different bundles of operational chains across several networked hardware and software artefacts. Choosing a medium—making a phone-call, looking for a reference, making up one's mind to watch a video with friends, posting, mailing...—is choosing a practice first, an interactional sequence for operational chains assembling different semi-automatic media genres for preliminary services. Old media and new media alike have turned into *media genres* run by combinations of software packages, by bundles of operational chains and their algorithms.

Second: There are lots of digital media, but where exactly are *the media* of platforms, apps, or data mining? When computing pervades everything, even the computer disappears as an identifiable entity. Cars, washing machines, security locks are special-purpose computing devices, and so are mobiles or e-books—and some of them are called *computers*, some of them are called *media*, some of the displays are computer interfaces, other interfaces conceal that fact, and the differences are quite arbitrary, to say the least. Right after growing up *before the computer* we suddenly woke up to live *after the computer*, and

---

[2]   Alan Kay, "User Interface: A Personal View," in *Multimedia: From Wagner to Virtual Reality*, ed. Randall Packer and Ken Jordan (1989) (New York: Norton, 2002), http://www.vpri.org/pdf/hc_user_interface.pdf (accessed 05.04.2018).

there was no Turing machine to guide us either—because digital networked computing devices never were Turing machines, and because the Turing myth has been thoroughly debunked.[3] Thus, neither will *the medium* define *the computer* nor vice versa, it seems.

Third: In defining the media of computing, or, indeed, in defining what digital media are, paradoxically, we refer more and more to sociotechnical categories, and these categories turn out to be quite arbitrarily *socially defined* categories. For instance, if we define or reconfigure what a computer is or what it is not; or what *digital TV* is, or why to call it *TV* at all. Neither the computer nor the TV set nor the TV genre are defined by technology nor by the past of TV or of computing, but by convenience and institutional design. And this difficulty nowadays applies basically to all old media turned digital, and to all digitally-born media, software and data flows.

To summarize: Classical media theory was ill-prepared for the digital world, and the asymmetrical structure of classical media theory seems to be ill-suited for digital networked devices. Of course we have to concede that classical media theory suspected that much, and predicted a future where *the media* would no more be the media of the past, or not be media at all—anymore, nevermore. But even these earlier predictions of a digital *media convergence* or of a digital *end of media* turned out to be inadequate. At least for the time being, media have not gone away and the terminal equipment of end-users has not converged. Worse than that, it has become completely arbitrary which digital artefacts or digital interfaces are called *media* or not; digital networked interfaces with interactive communication facilities being so ubiquitous that calling them *media* has become both a scientific necessity (to understand the everyday world of work, pleasure and infrastructure) and a statement without theoretical clues (once all technological artefacts participate in digital networks and the one network that is called an *internet*).

The Challenge of Symmetry in Media Theory

Classical media theory is not dead, but it smells funny. Media have changed, and theory has moved on. Concerning theory, we can take a short cut by comparing classical media theory to a line of research on modern technology that was developed slightly later, from the 1970s, as science and technology studies. Science and technology studies and media theory never really converged or even intersected until after their formative periods; with one telling exception that will be used as the exception that proves the rules of both fields.

Classical media theory was based on McLuhan's structural assumptions, that is, on a set of strong *asymmetries*: media innovations vs. a timeless invariant, independent vs. dependent variables, West vs. Rest. These asymmetries were to prove their point in media history, which in Canadian, French and German versions remained a success story of

---

3   Maarten Bullynck et al., "Why Did Computer Science Make a Hero out of Turing?," *Communications of the ACM* 58/3 (2015): pp. 37–39.

technological innovations, of *media impact*, and of *the rise of the West*. In comparison with the theoretical development of science and technology studies and related fields, these asymmetries were the strengths of media theory when it seemed strong, and they appear as weaknesses in alternative historiographical strategies, and in more sophisticated theory-building. In *We Have Never Been Modern*, Bruno Latour summarizes three methodological accomplishments of science and technology studies (and actor network theory), expressly named as three *principles of symmetry*:

1. David Bloor's *principle of symmetry*, the heuristic maxim to describe and explain *successful and failing* developments in the same terms and by the same factors (a principle unfailingly ignored in popular histories of science, technology and media).
2. A heuristic principle of symmetry for the contributions of *human and nonhuman* agencies (which is ignored in a purely sociological explanation of technological decisions, or in purely technological explanations of social processes, which both remain asymmetric but challenge each other's asymmetries in zig-zag fashion,
3. A principle of symmetry between *modern and non-modern* collectives, running counter to the assumptions of the singularity of modern collectives.[4]

A quick glance at McLuhan's statement (see above) or a more thorough look at the corpus of classical media theory reveals that classical media theory has never bothered to revise any of those asymmetries:

1. Classical media theory was written as a *technological success story*, the technological innovations being due to cognitive advances, and the failures due to cognitive failures or social resistance.
2. Media innovations constituted the basis for new *group associations*; thus (and in distinction to many other theory developments) the *nonhuman agency* of media was characterized as stronger than any human agency.
3. Concerning *the West and the Rest*, the theory and historiography of classical media theory was unabashedly Eurocentric: "the difference is that in the West our media technologies ... have been highly specialised," as McLuhan wrote in the beginning, and as Kittler confirmed to the end.[5]

This striking contrast between the symmetries of science and technology studies and the asymmetries of classical media theory may explain why the latter may appear old-fashioned or even exotic to historians of technology, media technology included. But the shortcomings of classical media theory may appear curable: its cognitive and social failures may be acknowledged, and, if classical media theory was bound to an unbroken

---

4   Bruno Latour, *We Have Never Been Modern* (Cambridge MA: Harvard University Press, 1993).
5   Friedrich Kittler, "Geschichte der Kommunikationsmedien," in *Raum und Verfahren*, ed. Jörg Huber and Alois Martin Müller (Basel and Frankfurt am Main: Stroemfeld/Roter Stern, 1993), pp. 169–188.

chain of accumulating innovations from the West, innovations from the non-West may be included. The asymmetry of nonhuman over human agency may appear as a virtue of classical media theory; after all, this asymmetry (of *technological determinism*) was the rule in popular histories of technology (and thus a vice), but unusual in sociological representations of material culture and material innovation (and thus a virtue, or at least a virtual virtue). It might even seem that the asymmetry of non-human agency is what is missing in *social constructions of technology* and makes them able to become symmetrical by complementing one type of asymmetry with its counterpart.

But the three principles of symmetry are not easily attained, and the asymmetries of classical media theory are not easily cured. Bruno Latour's seminal article "Drawing Things Together" is a case in point, because Latour takes up one of the lasting challenges of classical media theory, the debate about the "Great Divide" between oral and literate societies, and proposes a different and much smaller divide based on the symmetry of human and non-human agency, on the heuristic symmetry of success and failure, and on striving at a possible symmetry of *West and Rest*. Latour's description of Western innovative writing techniques looks deceptively similar to its sources in classical media theory and its cognates; but its preconditions and consequences are dissimilar and set it apart from the reasoning of classical media theory. "Drawing Things Together" takes a practice-theoretical approach to the problem of the so-called "Great Divide," though this fact may easily be overlooked in a reading informed by the premises of classical media theory. Whereas McLuhan and his followers take it for granted that "the assumptions and parameters projected by the structures of the media ... have long constituted the over-all patterns of private and group associations," Latour's theory of *immutable mobiles* aims at a *binocular* of social practice and technological innovation, or—to make it more sym-metrical—of technological practice and what he calls an "agonistic situation." He writes:

> My contention is that writing and imaging cannot by themselves explain the changes in our scientific societies, except in so far as they help to make this agonistic situation more favorable. Thus it is not all the anthropology of writing, nor all the history of visualization that interests us in this context. Rather, we should concentrate on those aspects that help in the mustering, the presentation, the increase, the effective alignment or ensuring the fidelity of new allies. We need, in other words, to look at the way in which someone convinces someone else to take up a statement, to pass it along, to make it more of a fact, and to recognize the first author's ownership and originality. This is what I call "holding the focus steady" on visualization and cognition. If we remain at the level of the visual aspects only, we fall back into a series of weak clichés or are led into all sorts of fascinating problems of scholarship far away from our problem; but on the other hand, if we concentrate on the agonistic situation alone, the principle of any victory, any solidity in science and technology escapes us forever. We have to hold the two pieces together so that we turn it into a real binocular.[6]

---

[6]   Bruno Latour, "Visualisation and Cognition: Thinking with Eyes and Hands," *Knowledge and Society: Studies in the Sociology of Culture Past and Present* 6 (1986): pp. 1–40.

Latour thus rejects both the premises of classical media theory and of the social construction of technology school and other sociological schools: neither is technology shaped only to the demands or interests of social organizations or institutions (in this case, administrative and colonialist institutions and scientific organizations and networks), nor are media shaped according to a series of purely technological innovations (because their success and their shape depend on the *effective alignment* with social organizations that adopt and transform them). Only a *binocular* of social and technical factors, of human and nonhuman agency, and of the contingent history of success and failure, can explain—or describe—why media have turned out to be what they are.

After the Practice Turn: Media History and Media Theory

Thus, Latour's theory of *immutable mobiles* may be read as a paradigmatic case study for a media theory that strives to turn the asymmetries of classical media theory into the symmetries of science and technology studies (or of actor network theory). Obviously, this theory and its historiography leaves classical media theory behind, but in which direction? If we take seriously Latour's insistence on a binocular between the *agonistic situation* and the techniques of visualization employed—being part, resource and object of an agonistic situation—it is definitely a matter of practical concern to decide about the socio-technical arrangement and the conjunction between human and nonhuman agencies, between Western and non-Western innovations, and between success and failure. There are no *a priori* considerations that could shift the balance once and for all in favor of the social situation or the technical resources, or of Western or non-Western, successful or failing media innovation. Latour's *binocular* of agonistic situations and visualization techniques explains the success and failure of specific media through the success and failure of their practices of innovation, distribution and use. The inverse position—to explain media practices via the affordances of existing media—now seems not only clumsy, but runs counter to what we know about the instability of current and of historical media, and the material and personal efforts that were and are necessary to stabilize and standardize media and scientific instruments in the past and present. The consequences of this historiographical revision can be summarized in three respects:

1. Classical media theory was often indistinguishable from a *philosophy of history* or an evolutionist scheme of stages and steps taken by a privileged part of humanity for the rest of humanity to join via the diffusion of innovations. Because diffusion and colonization were indeed part of modern media history and early modern history, it is all the more necessary to decolonize the narratives and assumptions of media theory. And one of the ways of decolonizing media history and media theory consists in the acknowledgment that European media history (and European settler-colonial history) after Gutenberg was based on *philosophies of history* or even religious and secular *salvation histories* put into practice. Classical media theory, from this perspective, was no explanation of the indigenous *philosophies of history* documented between Gutenberg and Marconi and in

computerization movements and their propaganda, but had the weakness of falling prey to variations of the genre.[7] The focus on the contingencies of media practices promises to resolve this conundrum, and maybe even the fascination of classical media theory *philosophies of history*. After all, arguing through a *philosophy of history* or *salvation history* was a long-standing habit of media histories told by missionaries, engineers, politicians, marketing people and administrators alike, deeply ingrained into their contempt of, for example, illiterate populations abroad and at home. But if the belief in and the spreading of this assumed *philosophy of history* is and was a practical matter, it has to be studied in its practical circumstances and consequences, and in most cases history will tell that a philosophy of history, and a media philosophy of history will fail to live up to its own promises and aspirations. For example, printing after Gutenberg was lauded for its ability to print scale-free quantities of identical copies, but it was only in the nineteenth century when these promises made sense—there was no media practice between 1450 and 1750 that could live up to this utopian wish, and there was no progress of skills or equipment that could fulfill these promises.[8] The *printing press as an agent of change* was definitely linked to its promises of salvation history and philosophies of history, but the history of these changes developed in contingent ways that ran counter to the official doctrines, propaganda or marketing strategies.

Thus, spelling out the promises and campaigns of *philosophies of history* reveals a whole set of modern media practices and enables a more precise history (and especially prehistory) of classical media theory, which relativizes the evolutionist frameworks that were both used and frustrated in colonialist, imperialist and Eurocentric history. There is no media evolution to explain the history of mankind, but evolutionism certainly was a factor in modern ideas of diffusion, distribution and innovation. The new historiographical position could be summarized as follows:

2. It is not *one* development or evolution which explains the history of media and media innovations. On the contrary, it is *the unique history of human societies and their manifold media practices* that explains the transformations of media and their development, including the asymmetries of power built into media or sustained by media practices and other social practices, and including discourses of *one development*. And if media technologies are partly built in an incremental fashion, or by accumulating and combining existing devices, the history of this accumulation is not self-explaining, but needs the full story of accumulating devices and non-accumulative skills, and of accumulation and loss; for example of empires breaking down and their scribal, linguistic and artisanal skills being lost or radically transformed.

In this respect, the core argument remains the same: It is not the history of accumulations that explains the history of media innovations, but the unique history of incremental

---

[7]   Adrian Johns, "Gutenberg and the Samurai: Or, the Information Revolution is History," *Anthropological Quarterly* 85/3 (2012): pp. 859–883.

[8]   D. F. McKenzie, "Printers of the Mind: Some Notes on Bibliographical Theories and Printing-House Practices," *Studies in Bibliography* 22 (1969): pp. 1–75.

or non-incremental media practices that explains the sequences and asymmetries of accumulation.

3. This history is non-evolutionist, non-Eurocentric, and it bypasses all dogmas of classical media theory, including the assumption of *media primacy*. Media may have been primary in many respects concerning practices developed *after the fact* of existing artefacts and communication channels, but they are neither primary to media practices, nor necessarily primary to non-media practices.[9] Media infrastructures may be built upon and in conjunction with non-media infrastructures; and they may even have been the *dependent variable* in configurations of necessarily pre-existing *independent variables*. Before writing, there was the neolithic revolution followed by urbanization; before modern media, there was the Industrial Revolution followed by a *control crisis* that gave rise to new management methods and the *Visible Hand* of new administrative hierarchies; before the computer, the world had become computable in many, if not most respects.[10] Again, it is not a scheme of stages or steps that explains this sequence, but the unique history of specific towns and regions that explains the appearance of *steps* and their indigenous representations in the mission statements of local and translocal *philosophies of history*, classical media theory included.

What is true about the history of media, is also true of the historical present. The contributions to this section on media theory and the practice turn show how media theory copes with the new situation of post-classical theorizing and post-classical media. The challenge of symmetrical media theory is here to stay, and it will take some time to cope with its complications. After all, debugging Classical Media Theory will be twice as hard as writing it in the first place, because Classical Media Theory more often than not was written as cleverly as possible.

---

9   Erhard Schüttpelz, "Media Revolutions and other Revolutions," *Zeitschrift für Medienwissenschaft* 17 (2017): pp. 147–161, https://www.zfmedienwissenschaft.de/online/media-revolutions-and-other-revolutions (accessed 12.08.18).

10 James R. Beniger, *The Control Revolution: Technological and Economic Origins of the Information Society* (Cambridge MA: Harvard University Press, 1977); Alfred D. Chandler Jr., *The Visible Hand: The Managerial Revolution in American Business* (Cambridge MA: Harvard University Press, 1977).

Dawid Kasprowicz

New Labor, Old Questions: Practices of Collaboration with Robots

Runaround[1]

In his short story *Runaround*, published in 1942, Russian-American novelist Isaac Asimov tells the story of an adventurous collaboration. A robot named Speedy has been sent to the planet Mercury with his two human partners Gregory Powell and Mike Donovan. While the men have to repair a mining factory, Speedy is sent off to excavate an amount of selenium from a hazardous crater. The selenium is required for the functioning of photocell banks that keep solar radiation away from Donovan and Powell. However, Speedy does not return, and without the selenium the photocell banks cease to function. Without them, Powell and Donovan are in danger of burning to death from the intensity of the sun's radiation. Finally, both make their way outside in protective suits to search for Speedy. When they find him, Speedy is walking around in circles while mumbling verses from the Victorian composer duo Gilbert and Sullivan. Programmed with the three laws of robotics, Speedy must obey the commands of human beings, but at the same time, he has to protect his own continued existence.[2] Since he fears entering the crater, these two rules are in contradiction and Speedy is stuck, unable to make a decision.

Asimov's short story entails several anxieties that tend to reemerge in contemporary discussions about the co-presence or cooperation of humans and robots. Dysfunctional robots such as Speedy, out of control or even dangerous to their human partners, are not solely the content of science-fiction plots. The growth of scientific fields like social robotics in the last fifteen years, the upcoming introduction of health and care robots, and new mobile robots for industrial labor have provoked new definitions of the status of robots and, in general, of the social status of computational, non-organic agents.[3] On the

---

[1]   I thank Thomas Turnbull and Carsten Ochs for comments, critique and corrections on a previous draft of this article.

[2]   The third law is that a robot may not injure a human being. To obey a human being may not conflict with this third law. Finally, the protection of the robot's existence may not conflict with both rules. The famous three laws of robotics have been taken up several times, especially in debates about robot ethics. See Roger Clarke, "Asimov's Laws of Robotics: Implications for Information Technology," in *Machine Ethics*, ed. Michael and Susan L. Anderson (Cambridge: Cambridge University Press), pp. 254–284.

other hand, the robot can also be portrayed as the next step in a capitalist-driven techno-industrial revolution.[4]

But I will leave these larger questions aside and instead focus on a concept that first flourished within the Artificial Intelligence (AI) community during the 1990s, but which retains importance for contemporary developments in embodied robotics. The concept I wish to focus on is that of collaboration: to work together to achieve a common goal. I will argue that in understanding human-robot collaboration, one has to go beyond the communication structures and techniques of information processing and also look at collaboration as a social practice between humans and machines. By practice I mean, on the one hand, the cooperation of materials for the robots' hardware, computer programs and simulations, and on the other the non-discursive practices of human postures, gestures, and certain *body knowledges*.[5] These aspects will be discussed with reference to the epistemology of specific AI models. I will begin this discussion with a description of the decisive change in AI models that occurred at the beginning of the 1990s. Within this historical development, an epistemological shift from the computation of intelligent agents towards the modelling of social performance will be important, since it conjures up the notion of negotiating agents, that is, agents who have to weigh their intentions against their collaborators, in response to both machines and humans. The description of this important development within AI will be followed by an analysis of a research project on human-robot collaboration. In this research project, engineers discussed the various functionalities of an autonomous robot that can be trained to carry a heavy plate with a human collaborator. In these discussions, the notions of negotiation and delegation form constitutive parts which show how human-robot collaboration is not only a formal processual language of actions, but also initiates a discourse around the *ordering* of other social practices.[6] These can vary from new gestures between man and robot to completely new factory designs due to the mobility of the human's partner.

In the final part I will take up these new constellations of human and robot in order to offer a possible relationship between media theory and practice theory. My argument is that these collaborations pose new problems to old questions of trust, responsibility, and control in labor practices. They do not manifest in single practices of human or artificial agency but in the materializations that occur after both agents have done *their* work. Departing from this destabilization of social roles and anthropological categories, media will be described—in the context of human-robot interactions—as the materialization of negotiated relationships (which challenge both the status of social practices as well as of single social actors). This conception of media neither emphasizes communication

---

4   In Germany, the term "Industry 4.0" was coined in 2011 by the Ministry of Education and Research to describe the advent of a widespread digitalization of industrial processes, including machine-to-machine communications in smart factories.

5   Lucy Suchman, "Subject Objects," *Feminist Theory*, 12/2 (2011): pp. 119–145, here p. 121.

6   Nick Couldry, "Theorising Media as Practice," in *Theorising Media and Practice*, ed. Birgit Bräuchler and John Postill (New York and Oxford: Berghahn Books, 2010), p. 49.

processes nor ontological arguments relating to the concepts of the hybrid or the cyborg. Rather, materialized negotiations of relationship resettle the effects of media on the threshold between the formalizations of social practices, such as negotiation and delegation, and their implicit depths.

This encounter between media and practice theory could therefore help us to look deeper into the reconstruction of collaborative practices, since it involves both the historical-epistemological dimension of AI models as well as the situatedness of the programming and training of a robotic system.

Collaborative Systems—Practices of Negotiation

Production environments in general, and the factory in particular, have long been a field of operation for robots. Think only of large assembly lines stacked with robotic arms, a situation in which one does not necessarily think of practices of collaboration. Made for repetitive tasks like welding doors on automobiles, the first robot for industrial purposes, built in 1961, was equipped with a control system based on binary digits, a memory system, and a digital servo-mechanical controller.[7] The beginning of industrial robotics from the early ages of digital computers has led to several utopian ideas about societies delegating all industrial work to machines while leaving humankind free to pursue less onerous tasks.[8] In the early 1960s United States, this confidence in technological innovations led to the development of ideas about the simulation of human thinking through a computer program. Five years after the foundation of AI as a research discipline at a conference in Dartmouth, New Hampshire in 1956, and the emancipation from early cybernetics and operations research, the proclaimed goal was to program a machine that could think like humans and even solve ever more complex problems.[9]

However, in the late 1970s and the 1980s, *good old-fashioned* AI fell into a crisis when it became obvious that it seemed impossible to simulate a human cognitive system through the processing of programmed representations. Instead of encoding sequences of actions in symbolic orders, an alternative approach was developed by researchers such as Rodney Brooks and Tom Ziemke. They stressed the aspect of a dynamic and emergent learning behavior. This shift in the conception of robots, from programmed to primarily embodied

---

[7] The company Unimat designed their first robot for the assembly lines of General Electrics and later also for General Motors. See Robert Staff, "The Rise and Fall of Unimation Inc. – Story of Robotics Innovation & Triumph that Changed the World," *Robot Magazine*, December 2, 2010, http://www.botmag.com/the-rise-and-fall-of-unimation-inc-story-of-robotics-innovation-triumph-that-changed-the-world/ (accessed 10.04.2015).

[8] A representative example is Marshall McLuhan's idea of "paid learning" of employees who could learn humanistic subjects while robots would do their work. Marshall McLuhan, *Understanding Media* (Cambridge MA and London: MIT Press, 1964), p. 70.

[9] See Allen Newell and Herbert A. Simon, "Computer Simulation of Human Thinking," *Science* 134 (1961): pp. 2011–2017 and Marvin Minsky, "Steps Towards Artificial Intelligence," *Proceedings of the IRE* 49/1 (1961): pp. 8–30.

agents, changed the semantic orientation from a "top-down" to a physically "bottom-up approach."[10] This epistemological shift is the point where both media and practice theory enter the discussion of human-robot collaboration. There are two reasons for this:

Firstly, in order to talk about robots, you have to build them. Intelligent, computer generated systems are not enough. Secondly, once built, the robots should emerge within an open, non-predetermined environment. In this coupling of system and environment, one could raise the question of whether one observes an action, a practice, or just an emergent aspect of running algorithms. However, in the early 1990s, the protagonists of embodied mind theory, Francisco Varela, Evan Thompson and Eleanor Rosch, described the cognitive activity of embodied systems as "context dependent know-how":

> Indeed, if we wish to recover common sense, then we must invert the representationalist attitude by treating context-dependent know-how not as a residual artifact that can be progressively eliminated by the discovery of more sophisticated rules but as, in fact, the very essence of *creative* cognition.[11]

The concept of a *creative cognition* refers to another key concept of this turn in robotics: situatedness. Both determine the prima facie principle of knowledge about the world through practice in the world, from basic interactions to complex practices like collaborations. What does this mean for the AI community? At the beginning of the 1990s, several AI disciplines, such as cognitive science or machine learning, changed their priorities, moving from information processing in individual intelligent machines to the social agencies of machines when interacting with other machines or when humans interact with machines. The background of this switch in AI not only marks a reaction to the increased attention gained by researchers from the field of embodied robotics. With regard to AI's big question about the function of the human mind, alternative models were developed in the 1980s which answered the question of connectionism in language-based cognitivism. In the view of the connectionists, the world outside should not be represented in symbolic sequences, nor linearly processed through a man-made program. Instead, it should emerge through the activation of neural networks similar to our nervous system. In this model, input and output units are analogous to sensory and motor neurons, but the important part between these neurons are the so-called *hidden units*. Hidden units have stronger and weaker connections—known as weights—which can be trained so that for each new input unit the net adapts its weight and the output units increasingly resemble the desired output units, for example the expected movement of a robotic arm.[12] In these

---

[10]   See Rodney A. Brooks, "New Approaches to Robotics," *Science* 253 (1991): pp. 1227–1232 and Tom Ziemke, "The Construction of 'Reality' in the Robot: Constructivist Perspectives on Situated AI and Adaptive Robots," *Foundations of Science* 6/1 (2001): pp. 163–233.

[11]   Francesco J. Varela et al., eds., *The Embodied Mind. Cognitive Science and Human Experience* (Cambridge MA: MIT Press, 1995), p. 148.

[12]   James Garson, "Connectionism," 19 February 2015, *Stanford Encyclopedia of Philosophy*, http://plato.stanford.edu/entries/connectionism/ (accessed 20.02.2016)

models, the weights of several connections between the different units should not be fully determined by the input of the operator outside of the system. But what does this mean for a practice of collaboration?

While researchers in embodied robotics saw hidden units as independent operators, built into the bodies of men, animals, and machines to generate a fitness in the world through interaction, AI researchers, working with connectionist models, focused more on modelling cognitive phenomena.[13] However, at the beginning of the 1990s, an increasing number of disciplines like pedagogy, ethnology, psychology, and social psychology were also influenced by connectionist approaches as they created their own models of distributed cognition and de-centralized learning.[14] At the same time, the commercialization of the internet began after the introduction of the World Wide Web by Tim Berners-Lee and the first graphical web browsers, such as *Mosaic* in 1993. The epistemological encounter of computer network structures and socially distributed cognition is an event that was not missed by the AI community. In her Presidential Address in 1994, Barbara Grosz, the head of the American AI Association, declared that the idea of collaborating machine systems could become feasible if AI managed to "look beyond individual intelligent systems to groups of intelligent systems that work together."[15] Soon models of social practices circulated in the community, trying to shape the differences between interaction and cooperation, between the delegation and the adaptation of goals.[16] Italian cognitive science scholar Cristiano Castelfranchi even addresses the problem of social practice as a way to reconcile the two different streams in robotics:

> Emergence and cognition are not incompatible with one another; neither are they two alternative approaches to intelligence and cooperation. On the one hand, cognition has to be conceived as a level of emergence (from sub-symbolic to symbolic; from objective to subjective; from implicit to explicit). On the other side, emergent and unaware functional social phenomena (ex. emergent cooperation, and swarm intelligence) should not be modelled only among sub-cognitive agents

---

[13]   Tom Ziemke and Noel E. Sharkey, "A Stroll Through the Worlds of Robots and Animals: Applying Jakob von Uexküll's Theory of Meaning to Adaptive Robots and Artificial Life," *Semiotica* 134/1 (2001): pp. 701–746, here pp. 705, 711.

[14]   This theoretical movement can only be broached briefly in this context. Relevant works are those of Edwin Hutchins (sociology), Jean Lave (learning as situated practice), or Lauren B. Resnick (social psychology), for example. See Lauren B. Resnick et al., eds., *Perspectives on Socially Shared Cognition* (Washington DC: American Psychological Association Press, 1996): pp. 1–22.

[15]   Her words for the urgency to keep pace with the upcoming internet are no less demanding: "The thing is, even after you get in the club, there's not much help getting what you really need. AI can play a unique and pivotal role in improving the situation, making the Superhighway an *information* superhighway, not just a *gigabit* superhighway." Barbara Grosz, "Collaborative Systems. AAAI-94 Presidential Address," *AI Magazine* 17/2 (1996): pp. 67–85, here p. 68.

[16]   See Michael Luck and Mark d'Inverno, "A formal framework for agency and autonomy," in *Proceedings of the First International Conference on Multi-Agent Systems*, ed. Victor Lesser (Menlo Park CA: AAAI Press, 1995), pp. 254–260 and Grosz, "Collaborative Systems."

[…], but also among intelligent agents. In fact, for a theory of cooperation and society among intelligent agents […] *mind is not enough.*[17]

Without deepening the question of differences between sub-cognitive and intelligent agents, one must first distinguish coordination from collaboration. For Barbara Grosz, cooperation can also imply signing a contract. To pursue one's own goals by committing certain services or goods to each other while in collaboration, all agents have their own intentions which they should subordinate to the common goal of the group.[18] Moreover, the agents must share the same environment and information resources to do that. This implies several complications—especially for the computation of the agents. The group's goal as well as the *personal* goals can both change as well as be in conflict. So, basically, the question becomes, how can you formalize and program the *intentions* of machines and humans in a collaborative setting? The urgency for machines to *negotiate* starts here:

> Each of the collaborating agents has multiple desires not all of which can be satisfied. It will have plans for actions it is carrying out to meet some desires, plans that include various intentions. It must ensure that its intentions don't conflict (a property that distinguishes intentions from desires). In considering whether it will do something, an agent must weigh current intentions with potential intentions. There are significant computational resource constraints. As those who have worked on real-time decision making know, all the while the world is changing—agents can't think forever. They must choose what to think about and whether to stop thinking and start acting. As Voltaire would have it, "the best is the enemy of the good." Collaborating agents need to reconcile competing intentions while respecting time constraints.[19]

Here social and technological practices intertwine, and social imaginations of collaboration become obvious on the level of technological problems. Moreover, technological constraints determine the framework of negotiations between diverse agents. What can be negotiated is part of the calculation but also part of a calculation model. In the context of AI, this is not as trivial as it sounds. It entails a shift in the AI expert themselves, from a computer engineer specialized in programming code to an interdisciplinary scholar, increasingly working in the fields of social psychology, sociology, and anthropology.[20] At the same time, the question of reconciliation of intentions is deeply entangled with the

---

[17] Christiano Castelfranchi, "For a Science of Layered Mechanisms: Beyond Laws, Statistics, and Correlations," 3 June 2014, *Frontiers in Psychology* 5, https://www.frontiersin.org/articles/10.3389/fpsyg.2014.00536/full (accessed 22.07.2017).

[18] Grosz, "Collaborative Systems," p. 80.

[19] Ibid., p. 81.

[20] Ibid., p. 83. This would open up another theoretical background in psychology and cognitive science that has not yet been recapitulated for media studies, especially with regard to the influential use of buzzwords like "smart environments." Approaches like distributed cognition, analytic philosophy of intentions, or groups as information processors in psychology produced a wide range of theories and models around the question of social practices, especially information processing and learning, with different agents in shared environments. See Verlin Hinsz et al., "The Emerging Conceptualization

question of how many things the agent can learn to resolve a certain number of problems in finite states—which relates directly, and this is still an open question, to the task of practically solving problems with or without computers in computational complexity theory.[21] In short, a problem is practically solvable if the computation time only increases like a polynomial function of the problem size and not faster: say, exponentially. Because "the world is changing," as Grosz writes, the agents "weigh current with potential intentions," turning the technologically feasible into social practices of collaboration and driving the once so individualistic mechanism of cognition into the realm of social performance.[22] In such a situation, non-action of an agent is thereby not only noise, it is understood as non-collaborative behavior.

In describing this epistemological shift in AI from individual to collaborative agents, two points must be retained: Ethnomethodologists such as Steve Woolgar and science and technology studies scholars such as Lucy Suchman have criticized cognitive theory practitioners as well as those working in embodied robotics for not having been aware of the social implications and effects of their work in their description of the behavior of agents.[23] While this is true, epistemological shifts like the one here described in AI imply more than new conceptions of cognitive systems. They depend on a new approach toward computerized agents, following the advent of the internet, but primarily the multidisciplinary movement of modelling of collaborative practices through socio-cognitive theories.

But what does it mean for a human to negotiate with a collaborative autonomous agent? Does the concept of practice only fit the collaborative working and the construction of models, or is there also a practice of the robot that should be questioned? To explicate these questions, I will look at an example from robotics research to see how this notion of collaboration and the task of weighing intentions are handled by another important practice: delegation.

---

of Groups as Information Processors," *Psychological Bulletin* 121/1 (1997): pp. 43–64 and Michael Bratmann, "Shared Cooperative Activity," *Philosophical Review* 101 (1992): pp. 327–341.

[21] This is put as the equation P=NP, where NP is the set of all problems that have a solution, algorithmic or not, and P is the set of problems for which there is an algorithmic solution, both within polynomial, that is tolerable, time. See Lance Fortnow, *The Golden Ticket* (Princeton NJ: Princeton University Press, 2013, pp. 4–5.

[22] Steve Woolgar, "Reconstructing Man and Machine: A Note on Sociological Critiques of Cognitivism," in *The Social Construction of Technological Systems. New Directions in the Sociology and History of Technology*, ed. Wiebe E. Bijker et al. (Cambridge MA and London: MIT Press, 1989), p. 306.

[23] Ibid., p. 317; Lucy Suchman, *Human Machine Reconfigurations* (Cambridge: Cambridge University Press, 2007); Lucy Suchman and Randall H. Trigg, "Artificial Intelligence as craftwork," in *Understanding Practice. Perspectives on Activity and Context*, ed. Seth Chaiklin and Jean Lave (Cambridge: Cambridge University Press, 1996), pp. 144–178.

Collaboration as Homotopy—The Practice of Delegation

In a paper from 2009, the engineers Paul Evrard and Abderrahmane Kheddar from the French Center of Scientific Research (CNRS) describe the simulation and construction of a robot which carries a metal plate together with its human partner.[24] What they try to find out is not only if the technical conveyance works but also if the human partner relies on the robot's suggestion as to where it would be logistically useful to deposit the plate. Through on-line calculation of the sensed haptic cues, the robot *recognizes* the intentions of its human partner and has to interpret them as well as try to anticipate the next movement so that it can finally negotiate "its own *programmed* intentions."[25] The aim of the project is to avoid the classical dyad or constellation of a constant follower and leader by developing ergonomically correct body postures for the human worker through smooth recommendations, so-called "internal forces as hypothetical haptic cues for communication."[26] In this case, the robot does not react to cues of a leader or a follower but to transition probabilities. For its programmers, these recommendations are part of a collaborative practice in the socio-dynamic environment of a factory. Evrard and Kheddar called their model "homotopy switching,"[27] after the mathematical principle of homotopy. Homotopy (etymologically, *homo* is same and *topos* is place), means that two different functions describe homotopic equivalent spaces that constantly deform into one another between two points. So, to avoid the two hierarchical extremes of follower and leader, the formalization of another practice is needed: delegation.

Delegation here is not only understood as the challenge of splitting up tasks within the computational architecture, or organizing competences in a hierarchical structure, but as a process of turning the models of collaboration into a work-setting of human and robot, who have to overcome the problems of competing intentions.[28] The human worker has to

---

[24] The robot is human-like not humanoid, which means it has extremities like a human but not a human-like skin.

[25] Evrard and Kheddar discretize haptic movement in four parts: 1. the basic controller with some intended trajectories; 2. a haptic pattern identification as an on-line recalculation of the adjusted trajectory; 3. haptic semantics for the interpretation of the received cues and 4. a haptic pattern communication so that the human partner understands the intents of the robot. Paul Evrard and Abderrahmane Kheddar, "Homotopy Switching Model for Dyad Haptic Interactions in Physical Collaborative Tasks," in *World Haptics – 3rd Joint EuroHaptics conference and Symposium on Haptic Interfaces for Virtual Environment and Teleoperator Systems*, ed. IEEE Technical Committee on Haptics (Salt Lake City: IEEE Digital Library, 2009), p. 45.

[26] Evrard and Kheddar, "Homotopy Switching Model," p. 45.

[27] Ibid.

[28] In this sense, my use of the term delegation emphasizes the idea of encouraging agents, both human and non-human, to do things. Thus, technics and media are not conceived as tools but as materializations of such delegations. See, for a similar definition, Bruno Latour's concept of delegation for actor network theory: "For the word delegation to hold, the ANT theory of action, that is, how someone make another do things, has to be kept in mind. If such a dislocation is missed, delegation becomes another causal relationship and a resurrection of a *Homo faber* fully in command of what he—it's

trust the robot's intentions; he has to withdraw from his own intentions and relate to the robot's haptic cues to carry the metal plate. In this way, the object of negotiation is not only the goal-oriented intention but also the social roles in the practice of labor. Delegation as a part of collaborative practice implies the transference of intentionality into non-living objects, something Freud once described as uncanny when referring to "our primitive fore-bears" and their belief in animism.[29] But whilst for *our primitive forebears* ritual practices should enliven the non-living object, in the case of homotopy switching one has to rely on the learning algorithm of the autonomous agent which calculates optimal switching:

> This role switching should occur in a smooth way, so that i) the human partner has time to react and to negotiate progressively the role sharing and ii) the motion of the robot is not abrupt and jerky. Moreover, a smooth transition between the leader and follower roles, and its timing, is necessary to translate *progressive negotiation* and *hesitation*. When switching abruptly between these states, the only way to translate hesitation is to oscillate from one state to the other while trying to decide what to do. On the contrary, if the switching is smooth, the role redistribution and sharing is progressive. This allows each partner to have knowledge and understanding on what the collaborative partners' intents are.[30]

However, to delegate leadership through the negotiation of role sharing requires time-critical transitions so that the movements will not become *jerky*, or, in general, uncanny. What is at stake here is the materialization of a relationship through negotiated action, and this relationship does not depend on whether one, both, or none of the parties in this collaboration are humans. In this constellation of materialized practice, it is this dissolution of explicit agencies through the practice of delegation that leads to a trade-off between potential and current intentions of a human and an artificial agent, trade-offs where the only interface is the behavior of the metal plate. On the one hand, this collaborative prac-tice seems to be another case of hybridization in a technological scenario, a situation in which more and more robots could become part of our life in a constantly data-gathering environment. On the other hand, these developments in human-robot collaboration open up a wider discussion that directly relates to the question of the post-human in media and practice theory. My key point here is less an emphasis on a transformative process of humankind, than on how these practices of delegation de-center the human agent and ideas of authority, trust, and sovereignty. The worker is not the master of their bodily posture, nor of the workflow, but delegates both to the robot. And in some cases, the human worker is forced to trust the robot, for example, in the case of robotic arms that no longer need a fence to separate the human area of movement from that of the robot. Industrial robotic arms whirl around the employee's head and beside their body. Here, the programmed trajectories concern the employee's movements, the probability of their

---

almost always a 'he'—does with tools." Bruno Latour, *Reassembling the Social. An Introduction to Actor-Network-Theory* (Oxford: Oxford University Press, 2005), p. 70.

[29] Sigmund Freud, *The Uncanny* (London: Penguin Classics, 2003), p.155.

[30] Evrard and Kheddar, "Homotopy Switching Model," p. 46.

next gesture, the hierarchy of postures, as well as the segmentation of the body.[31] The safety of the employee must be assured, but this should not happen at the expense of efficiency. Consequently, engineers create solutions for a hazard-free human-robot collaboration, but some of them argue that the European ISO-Norm 10218, which regulates speed and distances in the encounters of robots with employees, would be too "restrictive and overly undifferentiated, and therefore strongly limit the performance of the robot."[32] This performance, however, requires a collaborative training with the human partner to learn, through torque and visual sensors, what an intended and non-intended movement of the human partner is, what kind of physical forces are at play, and how they can be read as virtual forces for computer simulations that can calculate "exploratory, tactile behavior."[33] It is up to the human partner to learn how to grasp a robot's arm, how to lead it to a desired position, and how to keep his routine, habituated body postures without having the uncanny feeling of sorting stock items while a metal arm flops in his back.

What is at stake here is that the old practice of delegation encompasses not only technical issues but questions of sociability, legal norms, ergonomic standards, and design features. This raises the further question of how these single robotic actions are linked to routine practices in the work process. In doing so, it also shows what kind of operations must be involved in human-robot collaboration, beyond pure programming tasks, to transmit and translate non-technical aspects like intuition, smooth haptics, or trust into machines. These concepts do not exclusively implicate formalized rules. They point to a tacit knowledge, a feeling of how things could be done, not only how they have to be done.

Of course, on the one hand, the homotopic space is a highly hypothetical and context-dependent model.[34] On the other, however, these modellings of collaborations evoke new forms of practices that challenge our self-conceptions of movement, social forms, and gestures in resisting a definite attribution of agency to one or another of the collaborators. I will call these processes, from the transformation of this anthropological knowledge to its retroaction on man-machine interactions, *media as materializations of negotiated relationships*. In this sense, practices of collaboration cannot be explained through a strong conception of media (here, for example, with the dominant role of miniaturized

---

[31] This presupposes the storage of movements which is made possible through movement tracking techniques. They can be either done by trackers attached to bodies in virtual reality environments or with motion capture techniques. Meanwhile, robotic engineers also use physical mock-up bodies which are connected to a virtual body, in which feedback responses are calculated that the physical robot is not yet able to conduct. In all cases, the robot first has to collect the body's data to be able to collaborate with it. See Morana Alač, "Moving Android: On Social Robots and Body-in-Interaction," *Social Studies of Science* 39/4 (2009): p. 493.

[32] Sami Haddadin et al., "Requirements for Safe Robots: Measurements, Analysis and New Insights," *The International Journal of Robotics Research* 28/11–12 (2009): p. 1509.

[33] Sami Haddadin et al., "It Is (Almost) All about Human Safety: A Novel Paradigm for Robot Design, Control and Planning," in *Computer Safety, Reliability and Security*, ed. Friedemann Bitsch et al. (Berlin: Springer Publishing, 2013), p. 209.

[34] Evrard and Kheddar, "Homotopy Switching Model," p. 47.

and connected computers) nor can they sufficiently be grasped as an *anchoring role* that ties together other practices.[35]

Media as Materialized Negotiations of Relationships

In this last part, the example of collaborative practices will be discussed in the context of a possible relationship between media and practice theory. If media studies' aim in investigating robotics is to explain not only the new interactions with robots and how they change our perceptions about man, but also how computer and robotic engineers transform anthropological concepts in their development of models of human-technological encounters, then the issue of how to converge the practices of constructing robots and the epistemology of their models should rightly be examined.

However, with the influence of constructivist theory, ethnological laboratory studies focused on the diverse practices of scientists at work and on their (re-)productions of ontological distinctions with the help of techniques like inscriptions and visualizations.[36] Especially in science and technology studies, developments in feminist theory, stemming from the movements of the 1970s and 1980s, found their way into laboratory studies that investigated the practices of scientists and computer engineers.[37] The deconstruction of binary oppositions, the nucleus of a socio-political agenda in feminist theory, became a point of departure when looking to the scientific practices of constituting and attributing reality to living or non-living, natural or artificial entities and their bodies.

Current science and technology studies scholars of human-machine interaction follow the track just outlined, describing techno-biological couplings and focusing upon the social situatedness of constructions in robotics. As such, they try to frame the multiple socio-dynamic agencies between man and machine, between the scientist and the computer engineer, as well as the objects surrounding them. Morana Alač, for example, has investigated engineers who built a humanoid robot for the purpose of making the robot sensible to its environment. Here, the humanoid robot's conception of its environment is achieved via sensorial extensions, through microphones and video-cameras which transform a data-gathering body into a social one without explicitly referring to knowledge derived from models based on embodiment and cognition in robotics.[38] To achieve this,

---

35   Couldry, "Theorising Media as Practice," p. 48.

36   See Bruno Latour and Steve Woolgar, *Laboratory Life. The Construction of Scientific Facts* (Princeton: Princeton University Press, 1986) and Andrew Pickering, "From Science as Knowledge to Science as Practice," in *Science as Practice and Culture*, ed. Andrew Pickering (Chicago: University of Chicago Press, 1992), pp. 1–26.

37   See Lucy Suchman, *Human Machine Reconfigurations* and Lucy Suchman, "Feminist STS and the Sciences of the Artificial," in *The Handbook of Science and Technology Studies*, ed. Edward J. Hackett et al. (Cambridge MA and London: MIT Press, 2008), pp. 139–164.

38   Morana Alač, "Moving Android," pp. 493–494. For a discussion of the design and maintenance of a social robot which interacts with toddlers through its gestures and its mimics while being programmed online in a room next to the interactions, see Morana Alač, "'Points to and Shakes the

engineers performed the gestural movements several times in front of the robot, breaking down their body movements into component parts. While coordinating their constructed movements for the robot, they turned the material and time-specific practices of their individual bodies into a universal body-language of the robot.[39] Alač describes this with the term "intra-actions":

> The details of gestural intra-actions between human and machine challenge the idea that the human body primarily belongs to a single individual who exchanges information with the external world, as implied by the "distributed body" and the concept of embodiment proposed by contemporary cognitive science and social robotics. Rather, the practitioners' interaction with their colleagues and their engagement with technology show peculiarities of the human body in interaction. Such a body expands and contracts while its dynamic, multiparty configurations change with the context and participation framework.[40]

The concept of intra-actions[41] offers a means to look closely at the re-construction of the human body through negotiations with the robot's body and vice-versa. Like in the homotopic space, the construction of agents and their bodies becomes "bidirectional" as Alač calls it.[42] But although Alač uses her laboratory study to identify an important gap between algorithmic-governed bodies on the one hand and imitated bodies of purely supervised learning on the other, she still makes use of notions like the prosthesis, the cyborg, or hybridization.[43] Counter to this, using my example of collaborative practices, I argue that one cannot fully grasp such phenomena with concepts like these, which have been previously used to mediate, on an ontological level, between the impact of new technological phenomena and their feedback upon on our notions of human, of nature, and, not least, of society. As I have tried to show, collaborative robotics are first embedded into models, in which they mediate social practices like negotiation and delegation as well as concepts like trust, leadership, or sovereignty. That is why an ahistorical approach to the modelling of robot-human interaction risks ignoring the specific tension between the model-designed collaboration and the collaboration as a *bidirectional* but goal-orientated process in labor practice. Alač's critique of the concept of embodiment opens up the importance of intra-actions, but there is a need to highlight the epistemology of robotics articulated in the models. In complex relationships like those involved in industrial labor, models and

---

Robot's Hand.' Intimacy as Situated Interactional Maintenance of Humanoid Technology," *Zeitschrift für Medienwissenschaft* 15/8 (2016): pp. 41–71, http://www.zfmedienwissenschaft.de/online/points-and-shakes-robots-hand (accessed 25.06.2017).

[39]   Alač, "Moving Android," p. 508.

[40]   Ibid., pp. 496–497.

[41]   The concept of intra-action comes from Karen Barad's *agential realism* and the idea of dynamic (re-) configurations of nature and culture through ongoing interrelationships. Barad refers here to the quantum physics of Niels Bohr. See Karen Barad, *Meeting the Universe Halfway* (Durham NC: Duke Press, 2007).

[42]   Alač, "Moving Android," p. 522.

[43]   Ibid., p. 523.

practices refer to each other. For example, the employee who does his routine movements under the arm of a collaborative robot delegates not only a part of the collaborative task to the robot but negotiates his body position toward it. In this case, models of adaptable robots must be simulated on computers and physically tested. One could say that models and tests as well as the living and non-living bodies are in discursive and non-discursive negotiations with one another.

That is why I argue here for a relationship of practice and media theory and speak of media as materialized negotiations of relationships instead of hybridizations or cyborgs, which are somewhat overdetermined terms in both practice and media theory. Negotiation and delegation are not technology-driven forms of communication but social practices that materialize in movements, in body postures, or in new relationships in factory architectures. They do not transform something ontologically as the notion of the hybrid suggests. Rather these practices split up the anthropocentric notions of trust, authorship, or sovereignty between several living and non-living agents. As such, negotiation and delegation lead to the transformations of these anthropocentric notions through socio-technological couplings and through integration within the robots' models rather than through human-driven ideas. It is important to note that, as a result of this coupling and integration, anthropocentric notions like trust are redefined ex ante. In robotics discourse, this reintroduces old questions of industrial labor within a new architecture of factories as embedded systems, so-called "cyberphysical structures."[44] In this structure, human and robot represent one-third of the physical part while the rest is composed of computers processing data through the internet and by sensors embedded in floors and walls.[45] Such cyberphysical factories raise questions ranging from *who is the leader and who is the follower of an action?* to *what amount of trust has to be generated through the semantics of the robots' models* (for example formalizing intuitive gestures) *and the robots' performances* (for example in the case of *smooth haptics*)?

In this paper, my argument has been to show how the fixed roles of agents migrate and transform *in the* working practice, and thereby necessitate a translation of tacit knowledge into programming languages or into so-called autonomous or self-organized systems. In the model of the homotopic space, the question of whether the robot collaborated or not involved a comparing of the joint-torque output visualized on the computer screen with the report of the robots' human partner. Thus, human-robot collaborations demand that engineers reset their understanding of bodily movements and the expectations they place on the resultant labor practices. In doing so, engineers must adjust the border between formalized models of movement and bodily and tacit knowledge. This border is never fixed but is the result of feedback loops in collaborative practices that materialize as negotiated relationships—in the case of a robot carrying a heavy plate, for example.

---

[44] Edward A. Lee and Sanjit A. Seshia, *Introduction to Embedded Sytems. A Cyber-Physical Systems Approach* (Berkeley: LeeSeshia.org, 2011).

[45] Ibid., p. 12.

To take into account how the delegations and negotiations of the employee are entangled with new movements or gestures to communicate safety norms, to share responsibility, or just to perform—as a technique to show understanding in the collaboration—is a
crucial factor in what German media studies scholar Karin Harasser has termed situations
of part-sovereign agencies.[46]

Of course, this definition of media as materialized negotiations of relationships is wide
and it is hard to show any relationships that are not grounded in some kind of materialization. But it is important to pay attention to the multiple levels of socio-technological
encounters of human and robot before restricting this *physical one-third* to the effect of
a computerized, *smart* environment.[47] Hence, studying materialized negotiations forces
one to look out for media of translation processes which exist between the formalization
of social practices and the tacit knowledge of bodily routines.[48] In doing so, the aim is to
question how the formalizations of practices and bodily routines are rearticulated, not as
slave-and-master structures but as recursive models in situations of ambiguous agency.

Models and computer simulations of collaboration are not excluded from the laboratories of robotics, they mediate practices of negotiation and delegation, amongst other
things. Herein, embodiment need not refer to a singular concept of bodies but to a recursive
process of negotiation of social relationships through bodily movements and gestures. This
recursive negotiation raises several questions: What kinds of movement must a robot do
to keep up the relationship with its partner? What does it mean to create models that make
haptic interactions intuitive, in the sense of the robot meeting the expectations of its partner
and avoiding an uncanny encounter? By attending to such questions, it becomes apparent that materialized negotiations of relationships include both the knowledge inherited
by the models as well as their transformations and adaptations through non-discursive
practices. Thus, media and practice theory share a common goal in interrogating the
border between bodily knowledge and the formalization of this knowledge in models

---

[46] Karin Harasser, *Körper 2.0. Über die technische Erweiterbarkeit des Menschen* (Bielefeld: transcript,
      2013), p. 116.

[47] In the last ten to fifteen years, *smart environments* have often indicated, for media theorists at least,
      a situation where machines communicate beyond the perception of humans. Geographer Nigel Thrift
      coined here the term "technological unconscious." See Nigel Thrift, "Remembering the Technologi-
      cal Unconscious by Foregrounding Knowledges of Position," *Environment and Planning D: Society
      and Space* 22/1 (2004): pp. 175–190. Aspects of smart environments such as microtemporality of
      data-traffic, the protocols sent between machines through decentralized networks, are taken up by
      media theorists to diagnose a new technological condition wherein the becoming of psychic, social
      and ecological entities is interrelated. Scholars such as Mark Hansen refer to these phenomena as
      conditions of an environmental twenty-first century media, where "[…] media catalyze a shift in the
      economy of experience itself, prior to, and without any necessary relation with, human affairs." Mark
      B.N. Hansen, *Feed-Forward. On the Future of Twenty-First Century Media* (Chicago: University
      of Chicago Press, 2015), p. 8. Similarly, the German media studies scholar Erich Hörl speaks, in
      relation to the ontogenetic model of the French philosopher Gilbert Simondon, of a "metastable
      relationality." See Erich Hörl, "The Technological Condition," *Parrhesia* 22 (2015): p. 10.

[48] Michael Polanyi, *The Tacit Dimension* (Chicago: University of Chicago Press, 2009).

and computer simulations. In collaborative practices, such as those described here, this dynamic border becomes obvious in the materialization of labor. Such practices change the social order of man as the leader and the machine as follower or tool.

With this approach, the category of intelligence which still dominates robotics discourse becomes secondary. Instead the main focus should be on the practices of robots and the formalizations of the tacit knowledge that are embodied by them. Without falling victim to an industry-driven optimism, one can safely say that collaborators like Speedy will not wait on distant planets but will soon enter into processes of negotiation and delegation with us here on earth.

MARTIN STERN AND DANIEL RODE

A Question of Style!
Body-Camera Usages in Snowboarding:
A Praxeological Approach to the Study of Media[1]

Introduction

The ways in which modern technologies like camcorders and smartphones have become part of our lives have proliferated. YouTube trends and the *selfie* wave in everyday practices, or the production and distribution of video films in action sports like snowboarding are only some examples. Descriptions of these developments as ongoing processes of individualization featuring narcissist self-display miss the point: we are looking at highly social, collective practices that stretch over space and time. Consequently, a narrow empirical focus, for example on the technical device (camcorder, smartphone) or isolated activities, leads to a limited understanding of those practices. To overcome these restrictions, we turn to practice theory as a possible *new way* of researching.

Seventeen years after Schatzki and others promoted a "practice turn in contemporary theory,"[2] the vocabulary of this re-orientation—*practice* and *practices*—as well as its main objectives[3] have found their way into various research contexts and have established practice theory as a research approach.[4] Not surprisingly, media studies has also made attempts to turn to this new program.[5] Focusing on a study in snowboarding, where style becomes the central criterion,[6] we argue that for media studies, practice theory is not *just*

---

[1]   We would like to thank all participants of the beautifully organized symposium for their critical discussion of a preliminary version of this contribution. We are especially indebted to Erhard Schütt-pelz for his feedback and for him pointing out his reading of Marcel Mauss, as well as to Dawid Kasprowicz for his extensive and insightful comments, which have found their way into various passages of this text.

[4]   Thomas Alkemeyer et al., eds., *Praxis denken: Konzepte und Kritik* (Wiesbaden: Springer, 2015); Frank Hillebrandt, *Soziologische Praxistheorien: Eine Einführung* (Wiesbaden: Springer, 2014); Davide Nicolini, *Practice Theory, Work, and Organization: An Introduction* (Oxford: Oxford University Press, 2012); Reckwitz, "Toward a Theory of Social Practices"; Robert Schmidt, *Soziologie der Praktiken: Konzeptionelle Studien und empirische Analyse* (Frankfurt am Main: Suhrkamp, 2012); Joe Rouse, "Practice Theory," in *Philosophy of Anthropology and Sociology*, ed. Stephen Turner and Mark Risjord (Amsterdam: Elsevir, 2006), pp. 499–540; Allan Warde, "Consumption and Theories of Practice," *Journal of Consumer Culture* 5 (2005): pp. 131–153.

a social theory to fall back on, but rather represents a certain style of doing research, the implications of which touch all levels involved.

To characterize this style, we argue that practice theory is best adapted by media studies as a methodology (section two). We then draw on a study in the field of snowboarding (section three) to discuss a praxeological concept of media, which centers on the material and corporeal dimension of the usages that constitute mediality (section four). We conclude by discussing style as a concept for praxeological research that might be fitting for the study of (media) practices well beyond the field of action sports (section five).

Practice Theory

Serving as a starting point for our investigation of a possible relationship between practice theory and media studies, we will give a brief account of our perspective on practice theory, highlighting some of the points recently made in the German-speaking discussion.[7] This results in maintaining that practice theory should be adapted by media studies as a methodology.

Practices: A Performative Approach

In attempting to distance themselves from holistic and individualistic approaches to explaining social life, practice theories[8] make an important claim: "the regularity of behavior, the orderliness of social events and the structuredness of social relations, all those fundamental characteristics of the social, are produced in and through social practices."[9] It is the notion of performativity,[10] of doing culture[11] that is applied to practices as *basic units* of the social, and of these theories.[12] In reference to Wittgenstein, Heidegger, But-

---

[7]   Thomas Alkemeyer et al.,"Kritik der Praxis: Plädoyer für eine subjektivierungstheoretische Erweiterung der Praxistheorien," in *Praxis denken*, ed. Alkemeyer et al. (Wiesbaden: Springer Fachmedien, 2015), pp. 25–50; Reckwitz, "Toward a Theory of Social Practices"; Schmidt, *Soziologie der Praktiken.*

[8]   We use the plural to highlight what many authors have pointed out: Practice theory is not a unified theory, but rather a set of approaches that share several common features. For attempts to systematize these features, see Reckwitz, "Toward a Theory of Social Practices"; Schatzki et al., *The Practice Turn in Contemporary Theory,* pp. 1–5, and also Rouse, "Practice Theory." However, we will also use the singular form, thereby stressing the "family resemblance" of these related approaches. See Ludwig Wittgenstein, *Philosophical Investigations*, 4th edition (Chichester: Wiley-Blackwell, 2009).

[9]   Schmidt, *Soziologie der Praktiken: Konzeptionelle Studien und empirische Analyse*, p. 10. The translation of all German references was done by us. For the sake of better readability, this will not be indicated after every quote.

[10] Jörg Volbers, *Performative Kultur: Eine Einführung* (Wiesbaden: Springer, 2014).

[11] Karl H. Hörning and Julia Reuter, eds., *Doing Culture: Neue Positionen zum Verhältnis von Kultur und sozialer Praxis* (Bielefeld: transcript, 2004).

[12] Reckwitz, "Toward a Theory of Social Practices," p. 245. Schatzki points out that the notion of practice as performance is "central to any analysis of human existence": "the continuous happening at the core

ler, Bourdieu, and others, practice theories maintain that the principles that regulate and govern social life as we observe it do not exist *outside* of social practices, in some kind of structures or the minds of individuals. Rather, these principles are "accomplished"[13] in and through "an open ended, spatially-temporally dispersed nexus of doings and sayings."[14] A process that, in turn, shapes the doings and sayings as this or that practice. From this perspective, sociality is *done* in and through characteristic entanglements of human and nonhuman *Partizipanden*.[15]

Such a performative approach entails a new attention to the contributions of all entities involved in these accomplishments—including media and especially the human body—and for the tacit knowing[16] that these contributions rest on: The body incorporates and communicates certain nonpropositional abilities and, as an acting body, constitutes

---

of human life *qua* stream of activity . . . reminds us that existence is a happening taking the form of ceaseless performing and carrying out." More importantly, he links this to the often-cited concept of practices as "a temporally unfolding and spatially dispersed nexus of doings and sayings" by writing: "Each of the linked doings and sayings constituting a practice is only in being performed. Practice in the sense of do-ing [sic], as a result, actualizes and sustains practices in the sense of nexuses of doings. For this reason, a general analysis of practices qua spatiotemporal entities must embrace an account of practice qua do-ing [sic]." Theodore R. Schatzki, *Social Practices: A Wittgensteinian Approach to Human Activity and the Social* (Cambridge: Cambridge University Press, 1996), pp. 89–90.

[13] Harold Garfinkel, *Studies in Ethnomethodology* (Cambridge: Polity Press, 1967). Ethnomethodology uses the concept of *accomplishment* to analyze ordinary situation *as if* this *being ordinary* must be achieved by the participants via certain methods. See Harvey Sacks, "On Doing 'Being Ordinary'," in *Structures of Social Action: Studies in Conversation Analysis*, ed. J. M. Atkinson and John Heritage (Cambridge: Cambridge University Press, 1984), pp. 413–429. As Breidenstein et al. note, by understanding practices as ongoing accomplishments, the practical knowledge of how to do certain things in a certain social context and of how the social world is implicitly understood can be analyzed. Georg Breidenstein et al., *Ethnografie: Die Praxis der Feldforschung* (Konstanz and Munich: UVK/Lucius, 2013), pp. 28–31. See also Nicolini, *Practice Theory, Work, and Organization*, pp. 134–161.

[14] Theodore R. Schatzki, "A Primer on Practices," in *Practice-Based Education*, ed. Joy Higgs et al. (Rotterdam: Sense Publishers, 2012), pp. 13–26.

[15] Stefan Hirschauer, "Praktiken und ihre Körper. Über materielle Partizpanden des Tuns," in Hörning and Reuter, eds., *Doing Culture*, pp. 73–91. Hirschauer's term "Partizpanden" avoids an a priori subject-object distinction and stresses that people, bodies, things, artifacts, and other living beings all contribute to a practice coming to be performed. The different practice theories take material artifacts into account as carriers (*Träger*) and anchors of practices, consider them to unfold certain affordances in connection to the practical knowledge of the human participants, and—in case of actor network theory—treat them as active participants (actants). The point is to stress that practice is not controlled by a single class of participants (*Teilnehmerschaft*), but unfolds as a however (a)symmetrical distributed performance. In media studies, *media* mainly refers to the technical communication artifacts of certain practices and their *contributions*, which are conceptualized in various ways. For an entertaining overview, see Nele Heinevetter and Nadine Sanchez, *Was mit Medien...: Theorie in 15 Sachgeschichten* (Paderborn: Fink, 2008).

[16] Michael Polanyi, *The Tacit Dimension* (Chicago: University of Chicago Press, 1966).

social practices as bodily performances.[17] Along this line of thought, practice theories also reformulate the concepts of agency and subjectivity: agency does not result from intentional and autonomous subjects that exist prior to practice; participants rather constitute themselves as specific subjects in the respective practices.[18] Thus, taking a practice theory approach to one's research entails employing a perspective that focuses on the performativity of the researched practices,[19] which may be, ontologically, analytically, and methodically speaking, quite a drastic shift from other research approaches.[20] Such an approach, however, includes a number of pitfalls that we will discuss by touching on a point we have, so far, left out: the concepts of practice and practices.

Practice vs. Practices

Up to this point, our explications contain several tensions that require further discussion. On the one hand, there are practices (in German: *Praktiken*) as a basic unit of social analysis, defined as "a nexus of doings and sayings,"[21] "a routinized type of activity which consists of several elements, inter-connected to one another."[22] This nexus becomes analyzable as, for example, "a way of cooking, of consuming [... and] forms so to speak a *block* whose existence [...] depends on the existence and specific interconnectedness of these elements."[23] On the other hand, there is practice (in German: *Praxis*), as a pres-

---

[17] See Pierre Bourdieu, *The Logic of Practice* (Stanford CA: Stanford University Press, 1990); Michael Meuser, "Zwischen 'Leibvergessenheit' und 'Körperboom'. Die Soziologie und der Körper" *Sport und Gesellschaft* 1, (2004): pp. 197–218. Elaborating on the body in practice theory would exceed the space given. However, we want to point out that regarding every practice as what Reckwitz calls a "skillful 'performance' of (human) bodies" ("Toward a Theory of Social Practices," p. 251) entails that we not only have a body and are a body, but, as Annemarie Mol and John Law put it, "we also do (our) bodies." Annemarie Mol and John Law, "Embodied Action, Enacted Bodies: The Example of Hypoglycaemia," *Body & Society* 10, (2004): pp. 43–62, here p. 45. This means that the body gains its socially intelligible existence only as a certain practice-specific body—which may vary from practice to practice. We enact our *body multiple* in practice as particular *Umgangskörper*. See Annemarie Mol, *The Body Multiple: Ontology in Medical Practice* (Durham NC: Duke University Press, 2002); Gunter Gebauer, *Wittgensteins anthropologisches Denken* (Munich: Beck, 2009), pp. 95–101.

[18] See Thomas Alkemeyer et al., eds., *Selbst-Bildungen: Soziale und kulturelle Praktiken der Subjektivierung* (Bielefeld: transcript, 2013); Alkemeyer et al., "Kritik der Praxis"; Andreas Gelhard et al., eds., *Techniken der Subjektivierung* (Munich: Fink, 2013).

[19] And also on the performativity of the researcher's practices. We will come back to that point in the section "Praxeology as Methodology."

[20] For media studies, Nick Couldry thus calls practice theory a "new paradigm" and Mark Hobart agrees that the consequences touch on questions of ontology, epistemology, and politics in rather radical ways. Nick Couldry, "Theorising Media as Practice"; Mark Hobart, "What Do We Mean by 'Media Practices'?" in Bräuchler and Postill, eds., *Theorising Media Practice,* pp. 55–75.

[21] Schatzki, *Social Practices*, p. 89.

[22] Reckwitz, "Toward a Theory of Social Practices," p. 250.

[23] Ibid., p. 250.

ent and, therefore, contingent "stream of activity,"[24] which can only be retrospectively conceived as a performatively structured social situation.[25] Alkemeyer et al. identify two subfamilies in the family of practice theory that differ in their focus either on practice or on practices. The latter analyzes social life as something that is organized in the form of practices as routinized activities. Thereby, from a *theater perspective*, the participants of a practice merely appear as its *carriers* (*Träger*):[26] they carry out the conventionalized activity at a certain point of time and in a certain place.[27] Such a conceptualization runs the risk of neglecting the active and often creative contributions of the subjects.[28] It also disregards the contingency of the situation that the participants are confronted with, instead overstressing the *routinization* and *conventionalization* of activities. At worst such an approach risks simply reversing the dichotomies it seeks to overcome by regarding practices as somehow given entities that structure social life: social practice remains something that is structured—in this case by practices.[29] On the other hand, there are approaches which focus on practice as a present stream of actions that is marked "by insecurity, unpredictability, and contradicting conditions."[30] While being able to focus on the creative practical achievements of the participants by reconstructing their disparate perspectives, these approaches risk falling back to "subjectivist explanations of the constitution, modification, and exceeding of social order."[31] Therefore, Alkemeyer et al. argue that if practice theories want to present *new ways of thinking* to avoid individualism and holism and cater to the complexity of the social life they seek to empirically investigate, they need to systematically confront those two perspectives with each other.[32]

Praxeology as Methodology

What are the benefits, though, of this methodological confrontation of *Praktiken* and *Praxis* perspectives? Firstly, the interplay between *from above* and *from within* perspectives on social situations forms a way of being able to empirically grasp the simultaneity of forming and being formed, constituting and being constituted that a performative approach to practice(s) stresses.[33] Secondly, each of these analytical perspectives appears as something that is methodically constructed.[34] This ties in with the conceptualization of practice

---

24   Schatzki, *Social Practices*, p. 90.
25   See Alkemeyer et al., "Kritik der Praxis," p. 27.
26   Alkemeyer et al., "Kritik der Praxis," p. 28.
27   See Reckwitz, "Toward a Theory of Social Practices," p. 250.
28   Alkemeyer et al., "Kritik der Praxis," p. 28.
29   Thomas Alkemeyer et al., "Anliegen des Bandes," in *Praxis denken: Konzepte und Kritik*, ed. Thomas Alkemeyer, Volker Schürmann and Jörg Volbers (Wiesbanden: Springer, 2015) pp. 8–9.
30   Alkemeyer et al., "Kritik der Praxis," p. 28.
31   Ibid., p. 28.
32   Ibid., pp. 28–29.
33   Ibid., p. 29.
34   Ibid.

theory not as a social theory, but as a methodology.[35] Reducing praxeology to a social theory, Schmidt argues, spoils its empirical-analytical potential and neglects the specific relation between *theory* and *practice* that practice theory promotes.[36] When regarded as a methodology, it becomes apparent that practices are not *something given* that can simply be observed as a certain practice, but that this observational perspective is and has to be methodically constructed. By systematically reflecting on this, practice theory seeks to avoid the *scholastic fallacy* of mistaking the researcher's theoretical categorizations as the "logic of practice."[37] According to Schmidt,[38] practice theory destabilizes the conceptual separation of the spheres of theory and of the empirical by, on the one hand, regarding empirical *data* as something that is always subject to its theory-driven production (*Theoriegeladenheit von Empirie*).[39] On the other hand, even if not explicitly "grounded"[40] in empirical research, theory is regarded as implicitly relying on everyday empiricism (*Empiriegeladenheit von Theorien*).[41] The kind of theory-building that practice theory claims for itself is situated so *close* to the field, that theoretical conceptions are constantly irritated by the practices they analyze, leading to a modification of the theoretical assumptions and a critical assessment of the research practices.[42] A praxeological analysis thus reflects on itself as an analytical practice among other practices[43] and is regarded as "primarily a reflexive *modus operandi* of doing research, that is, a methodology of praxeolization."[44] On the level of research methods, praxeology calls for ethnographic approaches as ways of gaining bodily *apprenticeship* in the field[45] while variating between different forms, levels, and sites of involvement[46] to methodically *manufacture* different perspectives.

Our account of practice theory has taken us—not quite coincidentally—from theoretical reflections on basic concepts of social study, to the task of *manufacturing* and me-

---

[35] Schmidt, *Soziologie der Praktiken*, pp. 28–50.

[36] Ibid., p. 28.

[37] Bourdieu, *The Logic of Practice*; Pierre Bourdieu, *Pascalian Meditations* (Stanford CA: Stanford University Press, 2000).

[38] Schmidt, *Soziologie der Praktiken*, pp. 30–31.

[39] Stefan Hirschauer, "Die Empiriegeladenheit von Theorien und der Erfindungsreichtum der Praxis," in *Theoretische Empirie. Zur Relevanz qualitativer Forschung,* ed. Stefan Hirschauer and Gesa Lindemann (Frankfurt am Main: Suhrkamp, 2008), pp. 165–187, here p. 167.

[40] Barney G. Glaser and Anselm L. Strauss, *The Discovery of Grounded Theory: Strategies for Qualitative Research* (Chicago: Aldine Pub. Co., 1967).

[41] Hirschauer, "Die Empiriegeladenheit," p. 168.

[42] Hillebrandt, *Soziologische Praxistheorien*, pp. 26–30.

[43] Robert Schmidt and Jörg Volbers, "Siting Praxeology. The Methodological Significance of 'Public' in Theories of Social Practices," *Journal for the Theory of Social Behaviour* 41 (2011): pp. 419–440, here p. 432.

[44] Schmidt, *Soziologie der Praktiken*, p. 36.

[45] Loïc Wacquant, "Carnal Connections: On Embodiment, Apprenticeship, and Membership," *Qualitative Sociology* 28 (2005): pp. 445–474.

[46] Erving Goffman, *Behavior in Public Places: Notes on the Social Organization of Gatherings* (New York: Free Press, 1966).

thodically controlling analytical "lenses,"[47] to ethnographic research methods. Following this, practice theory can enter a *relationship* with media studies as one possible *way of worldmaking* among others.[48] In the conceptual framework of practice theory, the social world can be analyzed as a conglomeration of situated, embodied, and knowledge-based performances between humans and (electronic, digital or virtual) artifacts. Those "skilful [sic] performance[s]"[49] include active decision-making and creative or even subversive acting by the participants while from a certain *distance* appearing as ordered and conventionalized practices that bear certain "family resemblances."[50] But how does this world *made* by a praxeological approach relate to the study of media?

Our engagement with this question takes us to the field of snowboarding. We draw on an ethnographic study in this field to serve as an example for a praxeological style of doing research on media.

The Mediality of Snowboarding[51]

Snowboarding belongs to an open family of new sports that do not subscribe to the orientations and values of traditional sports, such as competition within a normative and standardized frame, or sports performances as objectified measurements of abilities. Instead, the focus is on a specific style, which is performed in a constellation of high-tech, play, and risk.[52] The playful use of new technical equipment—here the snowboard—produces new qualities of movement and new body-techniques[53]—such as high jumps that conquer the vertical space or gliding at a high speed—and thereby suspends the habitual movements and orientations of everyday life. In their spectacular performances, the riders take high risks and try to capitalize on the unforeseen, but they only earn recognition and status in the field if this is done in good style. The demonstration of *style-competence* is the central ability to be part of the community.[54] This *community of style* exists as an ever-evolving

47 Nicolini, *Practice Theory, Work, and Organization*, pp. 213–240.

48 Nelson Goodman, *Ways of Worldmaking* (Indianapolis: Hackett Pub. Co., 1978).

49 Reckwitz, "Toward a Theory of Social Practices," p. 251.

50 Wittgenstein, *Philosophical Investigations*, §67.

51 The empirical example is derived from research in a larger project on performativity and is part of an ethnographic study that also included paragliding and climbing practices. The study relied on participant observation in various places and practices, photo-stimulated episodic interviews and media analysis. See Stern, *Stil-Kulturen*. For this paper, the material has been thoroughly re-evaluated.

52 Martin Stern, "Konstellationen von Technik, Spiel und Risiko im Sport," in *Kalkuliertes Risiko: Technik, Spiel und Sport an der Grenze*, ed. Gunter Gebauer et al. (Frankfurt am Main and New York: Campus, 2006), pp. 38–49; Stern, *Stil-Kulturen*.

53 Marcel Mauss, "Techniques of the Body," *Economy and Society* 2 (1973): p. 7088. For a reading of Mauss' theory as a practice theory, see Stephan Moebius, "Entwurf einer Theorie der Praxis aus dem Geist der Gabe. Die Praxistheorie von Marcel Mauss und ihre aktuellen Wirkungen," in *Erleben, Erleiden, Erfahren: Die Konstitution sozialen Sinns jenseits instrumenteller Vernunft*, ed. Kay Junge, Daniel Suber and Gerolde Gerber (Bielefeld: transcript, 2008), pp.171–199.

54 Stern, *Stil-Kulturen*, pp. 151–195.

spatially and temporally dispersed constellation of practices, people, *spots*, technical and virtual artifacts.[55]

Micro Analysis and Style-Building: The Role of Video Technologies

An integral part of the new sport of snowboarding is the production and distribution of photos and videos. While on and off the slopes, the riders constantly shoot each other with photo and video cameras. Afterwards, they edit and analyze these photos/videos by using slow-motion, reverse and fast forward, stills, cutting, enlargement, and screen-shots. Some of this *footage* is then distributed online and circulates amongst the community. The production of images in snowboarding thus relies on practice-specific usages of digital technologies. Firstly, the video cameras are equipped with *fish eye* lenses; secondly, the videographers position themselves in a specific way to film only specific *tricks* from a certain angle. Thirdly, the possibilities of digital media-players are used to analyze specific details of the movements, and fourthly, of the endless possibilities of the editing program, only certain functions are used in a specific way.

The crucial point that reveals itself when focusing on these video practices is that the use of digital media does not simply produce portrayals of the bodily practices. Rather, the ways in which camcorder, computer, and software are employed create new perspectives and possibilities for the riders to picture movements and bear notions of style. The *freeze-effect* of the screen-shot produces a theatricality of stop-motion as part of the style, which stands in a strong tension to the speed and high dynamics of the movement. This work on the microstructure of movements can be discussed as analytic reflexivity of the digital perspective that, firstly, overcomes the restrictions of perception in action and, secondly, shows how the main issue of *style* can be perceived, communicated, or understood through the specifically created pictures and videos. Thus, the use of video technologies forms a constitutive element of the way the practices of the snowboarding community unfold by enabling a microanalytical work on the body and thereby mediating the production and distribution of style.[56]

---

[55]   Ibid.

[56]   With Walter Benjamin we might call this a new *Spielraum*—created by the "optical unconscious" brought to light through the camera—that transforms the whole practice of snowboarding, as we will show in the next section: In their moves, in the spatiotemporal organization of their "sessions" all the way to their distinctive behavior, the riders sub/consciously take the video practices into account. Their performances, similar to film actors' performances, are geared for an audience of experts, in this case *experts of style*—a style that is constituted in the intertwining of media and sports practices. Walter Benjamin, *The Work of Art in the Age of its Technological Reproducibility, and Other Writings on Media* (Cambridge MA: Belknap Press of Harvard University Press, 2008).

Micro Analysis and Style Building: Body Techniques and Forms of Movement

When switching positions and focusing instead on the ways in which the bodily practices of snowboarding are conducted and on how the different moves and tricks are performed, another part of the *working cycle* of style building is revealed. From this perspective, it becomes clear that the theatricality of snowboarding is not restricted to the digital sphere, but is closely related to the performance in the specific *spots*, the spatiotemporal arrangements (fragmentation), as well as the reflexive body as *carrier/producer/performer* of style.

Firstly, the analytic reflexivity of the digital perspective is part of a *working circle* that installs a new reflexivity of the body and brings forth and forms its movements and techniques. The work on the microstructure of movements, as outlined earlier, transforms both notions of style and of body techniques: Snowboarders transform gestures to poses and aim to realize a stop-motion effect in the movement itself. Movement and stop-motion, speed/dynamic and freezing in still-frame (for instance at the highest point of a jump) become constitutive characteristics of this embodied style.

Secondly, the spatiotemporal structuring of these practices caters to this style and the video practices by showing a fragmentation: The ideal framing for this orientation is no longer an extensive ski run but its fragmentation into single spots, that allow an optimized focus (presentation and reception) on the micro-analytical style of the performed movement (like a single jump).

Thirdly, as specifically performed micro-gestures and poses, the style is not restricted to the sphere of sports: brought forth and embodied in this interlaced and mutually dependent process of highly reflexive mobilization and mediatization, the body techniques become a new part of the body knowledge. Overcoming a dichotomous perspective that separates *knowing how* and *knowing that*, body and mind, this knowledge takes the form of a specific style (of talking, of dressing, of gesturing etc.) that affects other fields outside of the sport. In this perspective, the gestures gain a quality of citation that refers to a quite exclusive and distinctive field by transgressing this field and, at the same time, emerging in everyday life.[57]

The practice of snowboarding thus constitutes itself as a community of style spread over space and time. The "nexus of doings and sayings"[58] in which style is produced, refined, and distributed is reciprocally constituted by the technical media and the body. Just as the body techniques and movements induce distinct ways of using camera and software, so these usages allow for a specific work on the body. In our praxeological analysis, style is then revealed not only as a criterion for sports performance, but as a part of practical knowledge (Bourdieu) that connects and divides people, places, technologies, and practices; that facilitates social communization and distinction. Following these insights, the last two sections of our paper propose a praxeological rendering of media/mediation and discuss style as a theoretical concept of relevance well beyond the field of snowboarding.

---

[57] Stern, *Stil-Kulturen*, p. 265.

[58] Schatzki, *Social Practices*, p. 89.

Media and Practice

Our analysis has shown that, in the researched field, style is constituted in the dynamic interrelation of body techniques and digital technologies, and that this style provides the *social glue* holding together the bundle of practices we commonly refer to as snowboarding.[59] In this respect, we referred to the mediality of snowboarding and to style-building as being mediated by body-media usages. Both formulations require further discussion, which starts with a praxeological rendering of the term media.

The body techniques, poses, and micro-gestures that can be observed in the movements and in the behavior of the snowboarders as well as in the images produced by them, form an unwritten[60] and ever-evolving code that all members of the snowboarding community share. As *membership* in these practices cannot be fully grasped with references to concepts of propositional knowledge, we rather pointed to the ability to embody this code in a style that resonates within the community. In that sense, we consider the body to be a medium of these practices, because the ways in which it is used and the ways in which it acts lead to social differentiation and connection.[61] The mediality lies in the symbolic distinction that is achieved by virtue of the body.[62]

This distinction works all the more effectively because the "style competence"[63] becomes part of the snowboarders' "practical sense"/"feel for the game"[64] and thus part of their social persona. However, that does not mean that such a sense is only developed implicitly. As we have shown, in the snowboarding community a great deal of activities and technologies are explicitly geared towards developing and refining the bodily movements, gestures, images, and their style. In particular, this refers to the ways in which digital video technologies are employed. Social distinction qua style is not only accomplished by virtue of the body, but also by the specific usages of those digital technologies. Thus, they become media of the snowboarding practices. In this perspective, the (inter)mediality of snowboarding lies in the specific ways in which body and digital video technologies are used in relation to each other.

---

[59] More precisely, we should say informal freestyle snowboarding. In the perspective presented here, snowboarding cannot be seen as a homogenous field, but as a field of different bundles of style, which include racing, freeriding, or freestyle.

[60] It could be debated whether the various pictures and videos can be regarded as a form of writing.

[61] See Erhard Schüttpelz, "Körpertechniken," *Zeitschrift für Medien- und Kulturforschung* 1 (2010): pp. 1–20.

[62] Ibid., p. 13.

[63] Stern, *Stil-Kulturen*, pp. 167–169.

[64] Bourdieu, *The Logic of Practice*, p. 66.

A Praxeological Concept of Media

This leads us to formulate a praxeological rendering of the term media, which, along the line of conceptualizing praxeology as a methodology, should be considered a heuristically analytical *lens* for empirical research.

We have established practices as performative formations, which exist as emergent, contingent streams of activity while from a certain distance appearing as structured and conventionalized units that are connected over space and time. What the body or subjectivity really is, is decided in the practice-specific accomplishments. Those accomplishments are skillful performances that rely on the embodiment of a practical knowledge in figurations of human participants, artifacts, and symbols. Remaining inside this framework, media cannot be regarded as entities that exist independently of the practices. Rather, a medium is constituted as a medium by its use.[65] Because the body or a video camera are arbitrary in character, the different, characteristic ways of using them have a socially distinctive function.[66] In those usages, the practice-specific mediality of the body and of video technologies is accomplished while, at the same time, the activities constitute themselves as this or that practice.[67]

Such a performative take on media, we hold, can serve as an analytical tool. It does not decide the question of what is considered a medium a priori, but rather provides us with a set of questions to be answered empirically: What is mediated and how is it mediated? How exactly do different entities play together to create symbolic distinction and connections? Asking those questions generates analytical perspectives that allow us to investigate how certain practices unfold over space and time—that is, how they are mediated over space and time—without falling back to structuralist assumptions. Before illustrating this with the help of our example from snowboarding, we map out a methodological framing for this claim by referring to what Schmidt and Volbers call the "publicness of practices."[68]

The Publicness of Practices

According to Schmidt and Volbers, practice theory regards local sites and situations as well as the corresponding transsituative contexts and structurations as public. Publicness, then, describes a "shared space in which situated practices and their contexts are constituted."[69] This space, as a processual, relational space, is constituted by the "linkages

---

[65] See Stefan Münker, "Media in Use: How the Practice Shapes the Mediality of Media," *Distinktion: Scandinavian Journal of Social Theory* 14 (2013): pp. 246–253.

[66] See Schüttpelz, "Körpertechniken," p. 13.

[67] See Daniel Rode, "Praktiken, Subjekte, Medien? Überlegungen zu einer praxeologischen Ausrichtung medienpädagogischer Forschung," *merz (Medien + Erziehung)* 59 (2015): pp. 72–78.

[68] Schmidt and Volbers, "Siting Praxeology," pp. 424–431.

[69] Ibid., p. 424, emphasis in original.

between embodied participants, artifacts, places, and surroundings."[70] Thus, publicness is not confined to a shared presence in the situation, but depends on shared attention, which is given "wherever participants of practices, in their activities, attend to the fact that the artifacts, symbols, and practices given to them are also available to other participants."[71] Shared attention refers to a practical knowledge that manifests itself—and thereby the contexts that are relevant for the practice—in the specific constellations of embodied participants, artefacts, and symbols. The point that Schmidt and Volbers make is that publicness can then be regarded as transcending the actual presence of the participants while certain practices, artifacts, symbols as well as the bodies of the participants function as carriers and producers of such a public space beyond immediate co-presence.[72] Furthermore, the public sphere of practices is *in collective ownership*—it is not controlled by a single person or entity—and is thus marked by "a plurality of perspectives."[73] Shared reference is achieved in a joining of perspectives, while in each perspective, what is public can appear differently depending on the position in the public space as well as the acquired dispositions.[74]

Following this, the interconnectedness of practices and bundles of practices over space and time can be analyzed by the "reconstruction of this context of reference between embodied social participants and artifacts,"[75] that is, by reconstructing how the plural space of shared reference is constituted. We argue that reconstructing the mediality of this public space is one analytical strategy to be considered here. Such a strategy caters to the research interest and topics of media studies but has yet to be integrated into the praxeological research program.[76] It rests on the understanding that the shared attention of the participants and the practical performances are mediated and draws on the performative concept of media we have proposed above to create an analytical focus. Our analysis in the field of snowboarding can be regarded as an illustration of such an approach: When asking what connects and divides the different people, places, artifacts, and activities that might or might not be part of the snowboarding community, and when establishing positions in the field to follow the shared references,[77] the specific

---

[70]   Ibid. For this relational understanding of space, see Martina Löw, *Raumsoziologie* (Berlin: Suhrkamp, 2013).

[71]   Schmidt and Volbers, "Siting Praxeology," p. 424, emphasis in original.

[72]   Ibid., pp. 425–427.

[73]   Ibid., pp. 427–428, emphasis in original.

[74]   Ibid., p. 428.

[75]   Ibid., p. 427.

[76]   Knorr Cetina and Brügger's analysis of the global financial trade market can be considered one example for analyzing a global phenomenon and its dependence on technical communication media as "a technical-material and technically-mediated, public micro-social order." Schmidt and Volbers, p. 428; Karin Knorr Cetina and Urs Brügger, "Global Microstructures: The Virtual Societies of Financial Markets," *American Journal of Sociology* 107 (2002): pp. 905–950.

[77]   When looking *over the shoulder* of different riders, the various efforts to gain an individual style can be observed. When *zooming out*, it can be seen that individual styles can only exist within a group

interplay of the body and of digital video technologies comes into focus. In their specific relation to each other, they reveal themselves as media of style. Not only does this generate a distinct understanding of the process of subjectification of the snowboarders and its extension beyond the sports practices.[78] It also raises the question whether the concept of style derived from this field of study might have a programmatic character that could be useful for researching other (media) practices? This will be our point of discussion in the final section of this paper.

Outlook: The Concept of Style

In this contribution, we have argued for practice theory to be considered a specific style of doing research. We have characterized this style on the levels of social ontology, epistemology, methodology and methods, and have illustrated the implementation of such a research perspective by drawing on a study in the field of snowboarding.

To make observable how people, places, digital technologies, body techniques, gestures, and digital images are connected and divided over space and time to form the phenomenon called freestyle snowboarding, the praxeological perspective offers a notion of publicness as a plural space of shared awareness.[79] This notion leads us to consider the mediation of these practice constellations: a medium connects and divides because it enables symbolic distinction and social differentiation. But from a praxeological point of view, mediality is not decided a priori. Rather, a medium is constituted as a medium by its usages and thus only exists in the form of practice-specific accomplishments (skillful performances) that rely on the embodiment of a practical knowledge in figurations of human participants, artifacts, spatiotemporal arrangements, and symbols. In this regard, a praxeological approach widens the focus to take all potential media into consideration.

We have shown that this understanding of media/mediation—used as a theoretical *visual aid*—brings into focus style as the central concept of the field of snowboarding. Formed in body-media usages, style can be regarded as an embodiment of practical knowledge that constitutes snowboarding as an ever evolving, plural, and decentral community of style and that transgresses into everyday practices as part of a person's distinctive behavior.

For a theoretical concept of style developed from this analysis, we can rely on Ludwig Wittgenstein's considering of style as the image of man and can regard style as a general feature of human social existence that is distinctively formed in (and forms) different "language games":[80] Social practices produce specific *Ausdrucksformen* (forms of expression) —they produce (corporeal, linguistic, pictorial) images—and in the practice-specific usages of these images, meaning is constituted. Style can then be considered to

---

style, that group style and individual style are co-constitutive, and that they rely on different forms of mediation. When shifting away from the sports practices, it becomes obvious that this specific style becomes part of everyday practices beyond the field of the sport.

[78] Stern, *Stil-Kulturen*, pp. 197–267.

[79] Schmidt and Volbers, "Siting Praxeology," pp. 424, 428, 432.

[80] Stern, *Stil-Kulturen*, pp. 198–205.

be embodied social meaning:[81] the constitution of social practices (and their subjects) is always reliant on processes of style making. With Nelson Goodman, this specific embodiment of a certain style can be referred to as a way of worldmaking, which hinges on different practices, techniques, and media: rather than simply portraying a given world, photographic images and their usage, bodily performances, or scientific discourses all constitute their own specific worlds.[82]

Style then forms a central feature of a complex nexus of explicit and implicit knowledge, speech, writing, and digital images, movements, body techniques, and gestures as well as technical infrastructures. The description of how a style is mediated allows for an understanding of how—in a specific bundle of practices—these different parts are interconnected. Thus, especially for highly mediated and spatiotemporally dispersed fields of practices, style might serve as a theoretical concept suited to guide empirical research. As we have shown, such research in the field of snowboarding reveals a world that, following Goodman, is made through specific intersections of body knowledge, body performance, and media performance.[83] For the field of practice theories, this worldmaking constitutes a (scientific community of) style that, according to the various scientific self-descriptions we have referred to, is characterized by a performative approach that reflects on one's own research as practice amidst practices. Simply put: we have shown that researching media via a praxeological approach might very well be considered a question of style.

---

[81] Ibid., p. 203.
[82] Ibid., pp. 205–215.
[83] Goodman, *Ways of Worldmaking*.

CARSTEN OCHS

Privacies in Practice

> "This is the plot of my philosophical tale: that ontology is
> not given in the order of things, but that instead, ontolo-
> gies are brought into being, sustained, or allowed to wither
> away in common, day-to-day, sociomaterial practices."[1]

Introduction[2]

As media connect and divide, they at the same time contribute to practicing the public/
private distinction. For example, doors, as media, may create inside/outside distinctions
which help to generate *private spheres*,[3] while corridors and walls assist in producing
privacies in eighteenth century houses.[4] Yet, in contemporary discourses, what is no-
toriously problematized is rather *informational* instead of *spatial* privacy. And also, in
informational terms we are dealing with media practices that connect (for example hard-/
software for emailing) and divide (for example cryptographic tools to disable third parties from wire-tapping). Having said this, the issue of privacy is not only a topic media
theory is bound to deal with but also a highly contested one for, historically speaking, the
advent of digital media technologies obviously results in comparatively novel practices
of digital networking that, in turn, profoundly challenge the modern way of practicing
the public/private distinction.[5]

---

[1] Annemarie Mol, *The Body Multiple: Ontology in Medical Practice* (Durham NC: Duke University
Press, 2002), p. 6.

[2] This contribution was enabled by a grant of the German Federal Ministry of Education and Research
awarded to the interdisciplinary research project *Privacy Forum* (see https://www.forum-privatheit.
de/forum-privatheit-de/index.php). I am indebted to Jörn Lamla, whose advice and critique is a
constant source of inspiration. I also would like to thank all members of the research project for
valuable feedback. Finally, I thank all participants of the Third Media Studies Symposium of the
German Research Foundation for their thorough peer review. In case of remaining inaccuracies, the
author was not able to integrate peers' outstanding expertise.

[3] Bernhard Siegert, "Türen. Zur Materialität des Symbolischen," *Zeitschrift für Medien- und Kulturforschung* 1/1 (2010): pp. 151–170.

[4] Anthony Giddens, *Die Konstitution der Gesellschaft. Grundzüge einer Theorie der Strukturierung*
(Frankfurt am Main: Campus, 1995).

[5] As they participate in constituting practices (see below), media technologies generally may stabilize
as well as destabilize ways of practicing the public/private distinction. *Novel* technologies thus likely
have repercussions for established practices. Unsurprisingly, then, the proclamation of the "end of

One major political problem in popular discourses on privacy and surveillance as well as in academic debate is that these discourses tend to operate with a bourgeois idea of privacy[6] that seems to be as deep-rooted as it is inadequate to account for contemporary sociotechnical practices. Privacy more often than not is conceived as withdrawal from sociality, thus enabling citizens to cultivate inwardness, morality, and autonomy,[7] whereas in contemporary social formations, actors strive to achieve autonomy by *social networking* rather than *retreat*.[8] Nevertheless, there are privacy problems to be encountered, say, in *Online Social Networks* (OSNs); however, unfortunately, a bourgeois discourse that treats privacy as retreat from the social is doomed to miss these problems right from the outset. It is therefore only consistent that theory discourse on privacy has recently begun to put collective dimensions center stage:[9] "Expecting that people can assert individual control when their lives are so interconnected is farcical [...] we need to let go of our cultural fetishization with the individual as the unit of analysis. We need to develop models that position networks, groups, and communities at the center of our discussion."[10] The aim of this paper is to contribute to such a conception of privacy. In addition to *collectivity*, there are two further conditions a general theory of privacy has to fulfil: *plurality* and *scalability*. Specifying these suggests how the issue is to be approached:

A theory of privacy has to be pluralistic, for in empirical practice the label *private* is applied to a diverse range of phenomena, such as mental processes (privacy of the mind), decisions (decisional privacy), knowledge (informational privacy), the body (private parts), resources (private property), space (spatial privacy), and institutional spheres

---

privacy" frequently coincides with the advent of new media. See Dietmar Kammerer, "Die Enden des Privaten. Geschichten eines Diskurses," in *Medien und Privatheit*, ed. Simon Garnett et al. (Passau: Karl Stutz-Verlag, 2014), pp. 243–258.

[6]   Colin Bennett, "In Defence of Privacy: The Concept and the Regime," *Surveillance & Society* 8/4 (2011): pp. 485–496; Carsten Ochs, "Die Kontrolle ist tot – lang lebe die Kontrolle! Plädoyer für ein nach-bürgerliches Privatheitsverständnis," *Mediale Kontrolle unter Beobachtung* 4/1 (2015), http://www.medialekontrolle.de/wp-content/uploads/2015/11/Ochs-Carsten-2015-04-01.pdf (accessed 04.03.2019).

[7]   Jürgen Habermas, *Strukturwandel der Öffentlichkeit. Untersuchungen zu einer Kategorie der bürgerlichen Öffentlichkeit* (Frankfurt am Main: Suhrkamp, 1990), pp. 113–114; Andreas Reckwitz, *Das hybride Subjekt. Eine Theorie der Subjektkulturen von der bürgerlichen Moderne zur Postmoderne* (Weilerswist: Velbrück, 2006), pp. 92–97; Alan F. Westin, *Privacy and Freedom* (New York: Atheneum, 1967), pp. 31–37.

[8]   Felix Stalder, "Autonomy Beyond Privacy? A Rejoinder to Bennett," *Surveillance & Society* 8/4 (2011): pp. 508–512.

[9]   Paul Dourish and Ken Anderson, "Collective Information Practice: Exploring Privacy and Security as Social and Cultural Phenomena," *Human-Computer Interaction* 21 (2006): pp. 319–342; Helen Nissenbaum, *Privacy in Context. Technology, Policy, and the Integrity of Social Life* (Stanford CA: Stanford University Press, 2010); Beate Roessler and Dorota Mokrosinska, eds., *Social Dimensions of Privacy: Interdisciplinary Perspectives* (Cambridge: Cambridge University Press, 2015).

[10] Danah Boyd, "Networked Privacy," *Surveillance & Society* 10 (2012): p. 350.

(public authorities/private economy, lifeworld etc.).[11] Whereas these dimensions are to be distinguished analytically, they are obviously connected empirically (closing the door, for example, may be at once about spatial and informational privacy), which is why it is impossible to treat them separately.[12]

The labels of *public* and *private* are also applied at very different scales. Habermas, for example, conceptualizes the *private sphere* explicitly as a *societal sector,* that is, he conceives public/private in terms of a macro distinction.[13] In contrast, the bulk of privacy theory and general discourse centers on profoundly individualistic notions of privacy,[14] thus conceiving it as a micro distinction. As both ways of applying the distinction are encountered in empirical practice, neither conception is wrong; still, neither manages to cover the variable scales of privacy either.

Consequently, I will develop here a theory of privacy that sets out from *collectivity*, is able to integrate *plurality*, and allows for *scalability*; it goes without saying that it furthermore is bound to operate with a *sociotechnical understanding* of privacy. The provisos thus established obviously call strongly for an approach grounded in practice theory, for the latter *traditionally* adopts a perspective that centers on collective action;[15] that allows accounting for phenomena on variable scales;[16] and that is most suitable to deal with materiality and plurality, that is, with the multiplicity of materially performed ontologies.[17]

In what follows I will successively unfold my argument, resulting in a revised notion of privacy. For a start, I will strike a rather abstract note and develop a concept that fulfils the conditions formulated above. This is followed by an analysis of the ways current practices of digital networking subvert the public/private distinction. Finally, I will present an ethnographic case that articulates empirically the conceptions developed in this contribution.

---

[11] Edward Shils, "Privacy: Its Constitution and Vicissitudes," *Law and Contemporary Problems* 31/31 (1966): pp. 281–306; Beate Rössler, *Der Wert des Privaten* (Frankfurt am Main: Suhrkamp, 2001).

[12] Carsten Ochs, "Privat(heit) im Netz(werk). Internet Privacy zwischen kollektiver Normierung und individueller Kalkulation," in Garnett et al., eds. *Medien und Privatheit*, pp. 189–208.

[13] Habermas, *Strukturwandel*, p. 89.

[14] Rössler, *Der Wert des Privaten*; Bennett, "In Defence of Privacy."

[15] Etienne Wenger, *Communities of Practice: Learning, Meaning, and Identity* (Cambridge: Cambridge University Press, 1998); Barry Barnes, "Practice as Collective Action," in *The Practice Turn in Contemporary Theory*, ed. Theodore R. Schatzki et al. (London: Routledge, 2001), pp. 25–36; Bruno Latour, *Reassembling the Social: An Introduction to Actor-Network-Theory* (Oxford: Oxford University Press, 2005).

[16] Giddens, *Die Konstitution der Gesellschaft*; Anselm Strauss, "A Social World Perspective," *Studies in Symbolic Interaction* 1 (1978): pp. 119–128; Theodore R. Schatzki, "Materiality and Social Life," *Nature and Culture* 5/2: pp. 123–149.

[17] Mol, *The Body Multiple*.

Sociotechnical Formations: Landscapes of Partaking and Experience

A general theory of privacy must be able to integrate all the relevant ontological aspects: mental, decisional, informational, bodily, resource-related, spatial, institutional. Typically, we are used to drawing the public/private distinction in respect to all these dimensions, and, from a practice theory point of view, this is precisely what privacy is about: *practicing the drawing of the public/private distinction*. Why talk of a distinction here? The crucial point is that any time privacy is raised in practice it is about distinguishing something from something else, and about limiting something vis-à-vis something else.[18] This, in turn, raises the question *what* is limited in each of the dimensions. What we need is a fairly abstract specification so as to be able to cover multi-dimensional heterogeneity. Yet, as we deal with *practices* here, it seems vain to strive for some unambiguous *definition*; instead, our specification is meant to describe privacy practices' "family resemblance."[19] And whereas "[p]ublic and private are the common referents to deep and basic domains of social experience,"[20] *private* usually implies the confinement of the consequences of some action,[21] that is, the interruption of a chain of action. Combining both of these intuitions, we may account for privacy's family resemblance as follows:

The distinction *private* generally refers to the teleological shaping of *experienceability* (*Erfahrbarkeit*): it opens up the *experiential realm* of an actor/group of actors A (positive aspect) by limiting the range of possibilities (negative aspect) of a related actor/group of actors B to *partake* in A's mental content, decisions, knowledge, body, space, resources, or social realm. B strives to constitute itself as an actor by partaking in (that is, taking a part of) some of A's features, and as this affects A's experiential realm, B's partaking may be normatively blocked in favor of the privacy-enjoying entity A. The teleological nature of privacy is evident: the limitation of B's partaking serves the purpose of creat-

---

18 My highlighting of the practice of distinction drawing is not meant to evoke some structuralist idea of binary oppositions forming the ground of sociality, although Bourdieu seems to suggest that public/ private is a kind of basic opposition ordering social life also in non-modern anthropological settings. For example, the everyday life of Kabyle tribes appears to be basically structured by applying the distinction outside of, as well as within the homes of, Kabyle families; thus the distinction features *reentries* in the sense that it is re-applied in social areas that were themselves distinguished before with the aid of it (e.g. privacy in the private home). While I do not claim public/private to be an anthropological universal, I will provide quasi-empirical evidence for the reentry logic of the distinction below. Pierre Bourdieu, *Entwurf einer Theorie der Praxis auf der ethnologischen Grundlage der kabylischen Gesellschaft* (Frankfurt am Main: Suhrkamp, 1979), pp. 39, 56.

19 "…we see a complicated network of similarities overlapping and criss-crossing: sometimes overall similarities, sometimes similarities of detail. (…) I can think of no better expression to characterize these similarities than 'family resemblances'." Ludwig Wittgenstein, *Philosophical Investigations* (Oxford: Basil Blackwell, 1958), pp. 66–67.

20 Joe Bailey, "Some Meanings of 'the Private' in Sociological Thought," *Sociology* 34/3 (2000): p. 384.

21 John Dewey, *Die Öffentlichkeit und ihre Probleme* (Bodenheim: Philo, 1996).

ing, establishing, or maintaining A's experiential realm. Note that *actor* here may refer to various kinds of human/non-human, individual/collective agents.[22]

Having said this, the limitation of partaking may be understood as an abstract, virtual, cultural technique[23] underlying all privacy practices. While the specifications provided indicate how privacy practices draw on this technique, they require further explanation:

Partaking and experience: Taking up the now-widespread non-essentialist idea that actors are constituted by all the other agents constituting an actor's network,[24] we may start from the premise that everyday practices in large part consist of partaking in other minds, bodies, resources etc. *Partaking* here is more or less literally understood as *taking a part*: a mental, spatial, visual etc. feature of some other entities' existence so as to draw on it for one's own constitution. In many if not most cases this happens in a rather unproblematic way, such as when people shake hands, explain something to each other, confess their love to each other, consult each other, share their food, hang out with their friends, when someone dresses up to go out, or makes available some ground for people to pitch their tents on, etc. There are myriad instances of such partaking each and every day. However, in some cases B's partaking in A's features may disturb or even destroy A's *experienceability*, that is, A's possibilities and potentials to have specific experiences. "Experience" here refers to the entirety of *what* is experienced *in what way* and *by whom*; it is not reducible to subjective perception or the like, since it features *objective* traits and constitutes subjectivities in the first place.[25] Experience includes "primary experience" as well as "derived refined objects," that is, second order experience that is made by reflexively referring to primary experience.[26] Consequently, A's experiential realm may be destroyed by B in a range of ways. For example, if B installs a camera in A's apartment to watch the latter getting undressed, they may constitute themselves as a sexual perpetrator: they visually partake in A's bodily features to constitute themselves as a voyeur-actor. The action destroys A's experiential realm, for instance the way A may experience their own body, for it now is impossible for A, say, to develop a specific bodily-experiential sense of self.[27] This goes whether or not A knows about the camera: if they know, they might avoid certain actions. If they don't, still their experiential realm is disturbed, for the latter is no subjective affair.

---

[22] I have to thank Tanja Bogusz for pointing out to me the potential usefulness of the notion of *partaking* (*Teilhabe*).

[23] Carsten Ochs, "Kulturtechnik, Praxis, Programm: Begriffsinventar zur Erforschung der Anthropo-Logik der Digitalisierung," in *Digitalisierung. Theorien und Konzepte für die empirische Forschung*, ed. Gertraud Koch (Konstanz: UVK, 2017), pp. 21–54.

[24] Latour, *Reassembling the Social.*

[25] John Dewey, *Erfahrung und Natur* (Frankfurt am Main: Suhrkamp), pp. 25, 226–227.

[26] Ibid., p. 21.

[27] This suggests that enjoying privacy is in no way tantamount to holding a dominant position, and rightly so. For example, data protection rights aim to make "users" enjoy privacy precisely so as to *attenuate* the power asymmetry between individuals and powerful organizations. Martin Rost, "Zur Soziologie des Datenschutzes," *DuD – Datenschutz und Datensicherheit* 37/2 (2013): pp. 85–91.

It is in this sense that practicing the public/private distinction limits the possibilities to partake in others' minds, decisions, bodies, spaces, resources, information, and societal-institutional spheres.[28] Whatever dimension we focus upon in each case, we may conceive of privacy as limitation of partaking for the sake of opening up *experienceability* in the sense just specified.[29]

The teleological nature of privacy becomes visible when we consider the case of imprisonment. Being in jail limits the potential partaking one can perform but we certainly do not talk about the privacy of the prisoner; quite the contrary, for the limitation of partaking in this case does not occur to enlarge the room to maneuver of the agency in question (the prisoner) at all. Thus, any form of privacy features a limitation of partaking, but not vice versa. To count as privacy, the limitation of partaking must aim at serving the agency concerned,[30] and the limitation must be performed at the outset to serve this teleological purpose. For example, if B enjoys the privilege[31] of first class travel as opposed to A, then we have here a limitation of A's possibilities to partake, with B's room to maneuver being larger. Yet, this does not seem to have anything to do with practicing the public/private distinction, for in the case of the privilege we do *not* have a limitation of A's possibilities to partake *for the sake of* opening up B's experiential realm or space

---

[28] The specification provided also preserves the etymological root of privacy, as the term stems from the Latin *privare*, meaning to deprive: what an actor B is deprived of is the potential to make certain experiences, thus opening up possibilities for an actor A to have in turn particular experiences.

[29] Any exclusive grounding of privacy in the notion of property in an economic materialist fashion amounts to *an essentialism* that I am strictly arguing against, and for two reasons: *first,* modern ideas of property (*Eigentum*) tend to confuse the latter with wealth (*Besitz*), the actual *capital* of capitalism. While *Eigentum* is material resources (premises, land), space (residence) and social sphere (family); at the same time, *Besitz* cuts off all the other modes of experience so as to preserve exclusively the material resources aspect that then may be turned into capital. Hannah Arendt, *Vita Activa oder Vom tätigen Leben* (Munich and Zurich: Piper, 2002), pp. 73–81; Michel Callon, *The Laws of the Markets* (Oxford: Blackwell, 1998). Second, and even more importantly, "it is the very variability of the private/public distinction that is sociologically striking." Bailey, "Some Meanings of 'the Private'," p. 384. Consequently, privacy's *genealogy* cannot be reduced to private property either. This is exemplified by attempts to conceive of information as private property around 1900: as they applied an old notion to a new entity, Warren and Brandeis as well as Simmel had the greatest difficulties coming to terms with the novel situation. Samuel D. Warren and Louis D. Brandeis, "The Right to Privacy," *Harvard Law Review* 4/5 (1890): pp. 193–220; Georg Simmel, "Das Geheimnis und die geheime Gesellschaft," in *Georg Simmel Gesamtausgabe, Band 11: Soziologie: Untersuchungen über die Formen der Vergesellschaftung*, ed. Otthein Rammstedt (Frankfurt am Main: Suhrkamp, 1992), pp. 383–455. A comparative reading of the work of, say, Elias, Arendt, Habermas, Sennett, Goffman, and Foucault further illustrates the multiple historical trajectories of privacy.

[30] Of course, what I am talking about here is clearly restricted to societally normative ideas, that is, as a sociocultural category, privacy is portrayed as being good for those who enjoy it—whether this generally holds true in practice is a whole different question.

[31] I am indebted to Michael Waidner for bringing up the question of privilege.

of potentialities—the privilege B enjoys is only a secondary effect but was not implied as a *telos* at the outset.

Collectivity: Terms such as *privacy* and *private* in the sense established here denote a specific network configuration. Agencies involved in this may be human or non-human, *individual* as well as a *collective*. Being spied upon by some automatic recording device when meeting with friends in the gazebo is a violation of collective privacy, although there is no human spy directly involved. The operation may allow someone to constitute themselves as blackmailer at the expense of those being spied upon—the latter's experiential realm may be disturbed.

In the sense explicated, then, social formations can be considered sociotechnical landscapes structuring the potentials, possibilities, and opportunities to partake in others' features, thereby determining the experiential realms of these others. Therefore, privacy, even in its most bourgeois and isolated form, is never about some isolated individual refraining from *society*; nor is it about some sphere to be distinguished *in toto* from *the public*. Practicing the public/private distinction rather *puts actors into specific relations and shapes the latter; it consequently is social through and through as it sociotechnically mediates the partaking of some in others' features and thus shapes their experiential realms: their room to maneuver. Stabilizing the way the public/private distinction is practiced (with the term "practice" usually indicating precisely the very stableness of behavior*[32]) is thus tantamount to generating more or less stable power differentials.*[33]

This makes the following a pressing question: what are the components providing for such stabilization? My premise is that, in a very broad sense, it is sociocultural rules that structure activities. Due to lack of space I cannot provide a satisfying account of the ramified discussion regarding social rule following, which takes off at the latest with Wittgenstein's considerations put into writing in the *Philosophical Investigations*. Although the latter as well as the discussions they induced are of central relevance for practice theory, all I can do is to state that, from my point of view, in order to be called *practice*, some activity (actions, events, processes) must feature an empirically observable *patterning*. It is in this sense that it must be structured. What provides for structuration,[34] in turn, is

---

[32] Bourdieu, *Entwurf einer Theorie der Praxis*; Giddens, *Die Konstitution der Gesellschaft*.

[33] At this point the ambivalence of privacy shows: whereas Marxists and feminists tend to throw a rather suspicious glance at it, data protectionists praise privacy. The divergence of the perspectives is caused by the fact that privacy may have empowering as well as discriminating effects. And it is crucial that, say, feminists and data protectionists talk about very different practices and actors (patriarchy vs. women; monopolistic enterprises vs. *users*) and different potentialities being foreclosed or opened up—*they talk about different privacies.* I am indebted to Regina Ammicht-Quinn, Jessica Heesen, and Tobias Matzner for pointing out to me the ambivalence of privacy early in the process of working out the scheme at hand.

[34] *Structuration* here is used in the style of Giddens' *duality of structure* theorem, that is, in the sense of rules and expectations that change their status from virtual to actual existence only by being performed. This idea of performative structuration is similar to what Butler calls the performance of "the

implicit expectations[35] and practical understandings,[36] explicit discursive rules, durable inscriptions into documents[37] possibly tied to institutionalized sanctioning apparatuses, and the material scripts that things, hardware and software perform.[38]

It is easy to detect how these specifications relate to the practice of drawing the public/private distinction, since the latter features structuration in any of the forms identified: there are tacit privacy expectations,[39] just as there are explicit discursive rules (*spying among friends, that's going too far!*); there are durable inscriptions explicating rules (*Private Ground—Keep Out!*), just as there are very durable explicit rules inscribed as law (which nevertheless must be interpreted to function, for example the privacy rules specified in the German *Volkszählungsurteil*) and thus tied to sanctioning apparatuses. Last but not least, there are hard- and software scripts, such as doors or Facebook's so-called *privacy settings*, that certainly and profoundly contribute to the way the public/private distinction is performed in practice.

All these human (people) and non-human (media technologies) components and their inscriptions collectively perform, at least potentially, when it comes to practicing the public/private distinction (no performance, no privacy nor publicity), and it is an empirical question *how* those components co-operate in practice (jointly, mutually enforcing, in parallel, independent of each other, interfering, contradictory etc.). As regards current practices, there are certainly contradictions observable,[40] and I will provide a basic analysis of these below. What is required prior to this is a specification of the way *modern* practices of drawing the public/private distinction were generally stabilized.[41] And as far

---

law." Still, I extend the notion of *structure* by including also rules performed by non-human entities. Giddens, *Die Konstitution der Gesellschaft*, pp. 69, 77–81; Judith Butler, *Körper von Gewicht. Die diskursiven Grenzen des Geschlechts* (Berlin: Berlin-Verlag, 1995), p. 37.

[35] Harold Garfinkel, *Studies in Ethnomethodology* (Cambridge: Polity Press, 1984), pp. 35–36.

[36] Theodore R. Schatzki, "Practices and Actions: A Wittgensteinian Critique of Bourdieu and Giddens," *Philosophy of the Social Sciences* 27/3: p. 304.

[37] Michel Callon, "Techno-Economic Networks and Irreversibility," in *A Sociology of Monsters: Essays on Power, Technology and Domination*, ed. John Law (London and New York: Routledge, 1991), pp. 132–164.

[38] Bruno Latour, "Where Are the Missing Masses? The Sociology of a Few Mundane Artifacts," in *Shaping Technology/Building Society. Studies in Sociotechnical Change*, ed. Wiebe E. Bijker and John Law (Cambridge MA: MIT Press, 1992), pp. 225–259.

[39] Garfinkel, *Studies in Ethnomethodology*, p. 75.

[40] Carsten Ochs, "Wettrüsten der Skripte. Widersprüchlichkeiten soziotechnischer Privatheitspraktiken im Internet," in *Im Sog des Internets. Öffentlichkeit und Privatheit im digitalen Zeitalter*, ed. Ulrike Ackermann (Frankfurt am Main: Humanities Online, 2013), pp. 111–129.

[41] Pointing to the stabilization of the distinction means to account for the distinction's permeability, for if the distinction was hermetically sealing off a private from a public realm once and for all, stabilization would not be required. From this it follows that the distinction is firstly never absolute but subject to constant sociomaterial reenactment, and, secondly, that crossing the boundary may reproduce the latter: there was no boundary to be crossed if the latter was not re-performed by the crossing.

as modern *societies* are concerned, the public/private distinction plays the role of a *structural principle*;[42] that is to say, the distinction and the rules that specify how it be applied pervade and thus structure *all modern practices*.[43] This is a fairly strong contention which requires justification; in the next section I will provide one, and in so doing carve out the core of the privacy theory that I put up for debate here.

Social Worlds Practicing Privacies

According to Giddens,[44] public/private as a macro distinction separating public authorities from private economies is one of the central structural principles of modern capitalist societies.[45] However, as I have argued above, in practice the distinction not only occurs on the macro level but features multiple ontologies. To account for these, I next turn to *social world theory*. As Strauss explains, social worlds are scalable social aggregates with fluid boundaries constituted and maintained by collective core activities (that is, practices).[46] In this sense, sociomaterial practices in fact establish social worlds, the boundaries of which are neither rigid nor fixed once and for all, but are constantly defined, contested, and negotiated within and outside social worlds.[47] Social worlds operate at any scale, and they *consist of* activities, sites, technologies, and organizations.[48] To this effect they are

> groups with shared commitments to certain activities, sharing resources of many kinds to achieve their goals, and building shared ideologies about how to go about their business. Social worlds form fundamental building blocks of collective action [...] Society as a whole, then, can be conceptualized as consisting of a mosaic of social worlds.[49]

Here is a visualization of this *mosaic*:

---

42   Giddens, *Die Konstitution der Gesellschaft*, p. 240.

43   Löw presents class and gender as examples of structural principles: no matter what section of society one investigates, class- and gender-related rules are among the defining aspects shaping social relations (albeit not the only ones). Martina Löw, *Raumsoziologie* (Frankfurt am Main: Suhrkamp, 2001), pp. 173–183.

44   Giddens, *Die Konstitution der Gesellschaft*, p. 238.

45   See also Habermas, *Strukturwandel*, p. 83.

46   Strauss, "A Social World Perspective," pp. 121–122.

47   Anselm Strauss, "Social Worlds and Legitimation Processes," *Studies in Symbolic Interaction* 4 (1982): pp. 171–190.

48   Strauss, "A Social World Perspective," p. 122.

49   Adele Clarke, "Social Worlds/Arenas Theory as Organizational Theory," in *Social Organization and Social Process. Essays in Honor of Anselm Strauss*, ed. David R. Maines (New York: de Gruyter, 1991), pp. 119–157.

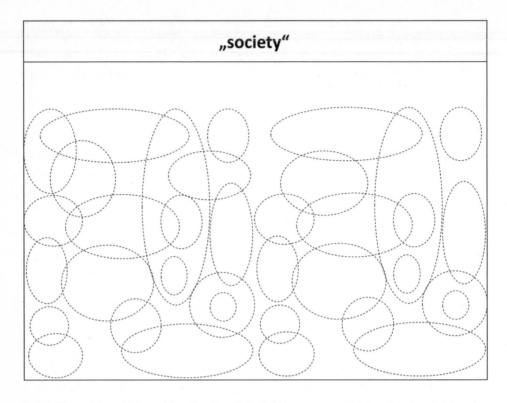

Fig. 20: The *social world theory* idea of society. Dotted circles represent social worlds composing society. Actors may belong to different social worlds at once; social worlds may overlap and contain sub-worlds (for example the social world of winter sport contains the sub world of alpine skiing, of snowboarding, of ski jumping etc.). The box ("society") does not feature clear-cut boundaries either. Giddens, *Die Konstitution der Gesellschaft*, pp. 216–222.

By assigning the public/private distinction the role of a structural principle, I claim that both all the worlds and the societal *whole*[50] are structured by the distinction; this happens in four different ways:

Internal structuration: All social worlds have normative rules that specify how the public/private distinction shall be applied internally in practice. This means that internal practices are partly structured by limiting the partaking in others' minds, bodies, space, resources, information etc. to the use of individual actors or the entire social world (notably without there necessarily being *discursive* concepts of *public* and *private* in use). Some social worlds draw on the distinction as a *Leitdifferenz* (guiding distinction), in the sense that the distinction defines even the core practice of that social world. For example, the

---

50   The societal *whole* obviously has become a rather problematic idea for social theory. I cannot deal with this here, so I simply resort to a *weak* notion of society in the sense of an operational fiction.

core *Cypherpunk* practice of encrypting digital communication is explicitly structured by a hyper-individualistic idea of privacy, whereas post-privacy adherents structure practices by actively un-limiting the partaking of others in one's data. Relevant rules and concepts may be explicit or implicit; for example, whether or not discursively articulated, in the social world of pornography there apply other rules concerning the visual and tactile partaking in others' bodies than in the world of Catholicism.

External structuration: There are countless social worlds that perform their primary activities without needing to render explicit their idea of properly applying the public/private distinction. For example in the social world of Catholicism, actors may structure their activities via clinging to distinctions such as sacred/profane; however, as soon as these social worlds come into contact with other social worlds, practices may be structured by the public/private distinction also from *outside*. If, for example, a priest attempts to dictate to females to wear long skirts, actors of other social worlds—the social world of legal practice, say—may intervene. They might point to the fact that the rules of Catholic doctrine do apply privately, but not in the *whole* of society; thus, priests may not straight-forwardly partake in others' decisions to wear long skirts or not: decision making is limited to the wearers. Also, members of the social world of Catholicism enjoy privacy in this sense: they may decide for themselves whether or not to follow the priest's prescription. The social world's practices are thus partly given shape from outside, and priests have to take the public/private distinction into account *willy-nilly*.[51]

Global declaration: There are social worlds (and practices) that are declared in their entirety as public or private, for example the practices of the state's social worlds are by definition public. This is not to say that whatever a member of the state apparatus does counts as public, but only those practices that belong to their public role. When it comes to politically delicate actions, actors oftentimes strategically capitalize on that. When former German Minister for Economic Affairs and Energy, Sigmar Gabriel, was criticized for attending a discussion with supporters of the so-called *Pegida* movement, for example, he immediately replied that in fact he participated as a *private individual*.[52] Referring to the term *private* here is meant to say that his attendance should not be considered as part of the Minister's public role; it shall go unnoticed by *the public*. Whatever one might think of such an argument, it still illustrates that it is *practices* that are declared public/private, not actors. Besides, when the technique of limiting partaking in others' features

---

[51]   As is apparent, the example chosen is a culture-specific one, originating from (an idealized version of) the historic trajectory of modern practices. This is, however, per se not problematic, for *any* account of the public/private distinction whatsoever necessarily relates to specific cultural settings: there is no practicing the public/private distinction *as such*. Whether modern societies live up to their own self-descriptions is, of course, open to debate, however, to be able to start the debate at all it is required to clarify how these societies historically stabilized their practices of applying the public/private distinction in the first place. We will see below how the traditional practices analyzed here are unsettled by current developments.

[52]   Kurt Kister, "Dreifach daneben," 25 January 2015, *Süddeutsche Zeitung*, http://www.sueddeutsche.de/politik/gabriel-bei-pegida-diskussion-dreifach-daneben-1.2319848 (accessed 10.02.2019).

is applied in the *public realm*, practices cannot be declared private anymore, but only *secret*: for example, partaking in knowledge about the practices of the secret services for non-members is quite limited, but still those practices do not count as private; likewise, although citizens have limited opportunities to partake in certain activities of the state, we would not call these activities private but rather *state secrets*. In contrast, even though economic practices in their entirety are declared private in capitalist societies, they may feature a certain kind of *publicness*. Internet businesses, for example, are private corporations, but they may still breach their *users*' privacy. Here we have a kind of re-entry, insofar as within the field of economic practices, which is itself distinguished with the aid of the public/private distinction, this distinction re-emerges on another scale. Internet businesses oftentimes harness the resulting confusion, when they consider themselves to be bound to rather weak data protection regulations due to their *private* status: they must comply, or so they claim, to *private* law, instead of *public* law. Thus, they claim a specific form of privacy (a historically evolved macro distinction) for themselves while downgrading another: their so-called *users*' privacy.[53]

Operational fiction of totality: Finally, we need also to account for the notion of *the* public. As Habermas was aware that *the* public, in terms of space, issue, and communication, is divided into numerous sub-publics,[54] I would like to argue that the idea of a public totality might be understood as an *operational fiction*; that is, *the* public at least exists in the minimal form of an idea or fiction which actors draw upon in order to orient their actions. From a social world point of view, the fiction of *the* public envisages a situation where society-as-a-whole, that is, all the social worlds constituting the societal mosaic, may partake in some of the features of an actor. Empirically speaking, it is rather improbable that, say, some information is in fact received by the totality of all members of all social worlds. So, what we mean when we say some information ends up *in public on the internet* is that *potentially* everybody may partake in this information. In a similar vein, we can transfer such an understanding from the informational to the spatial realm: for example, *public space as such* is deemed to stand open to everyone's partaking in general.

These conceptions make for the following model:

---

[53] Facebook's Mark Zuckerberg is quoted as follows: "To get people to this point where there's more openness—that's a big challenge.... But I think we'll do it. I just think it will take time. The concept that the world will be better if you share more is something that's pretty foreign to a lot of people and it runs into all these privacy concerns." David Kirkpatrick, *The Facebook effect: and how it is changing our lives* (London: John Murray, 2010), pp. 199–200. Meanwhile, Facebook does not seem to be particularly keen on sharing its algorithms, databases, or revenues (private property).

[54] Jürgen Habermas, *Faktizität und Geltung. Beiträge zur Diskurstheorie des Rechts und des demokratischen Rechtsstaats* (Frankfurt am Main: Suhrkamp, 1992), pp. 451–452.

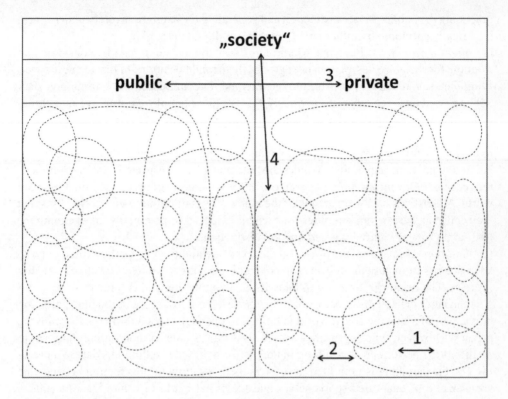

Fig. 21: The social world model of privacy: Dotted circles represent social worlds, numbered arrows visualize the four axes generated by the four forms of practicing the public/private distinction.

Although the rigid idea of private vs. public sphere is dissolved here into manifold practices of drawing the public/private distinction, privacy is still not conceived as the *individual preference* of some isolated, atomistic actor. Instead, we are able to identify four types of practicing the public/private distinction: first, *within* social worlds (1); second, *among* social worlds (2); third, as *macro distinction* dividing society in a binary fashion (3); and fourth, as *operational fiction of totality* (4). The next section will analyze how practices of digital networking put pressure on all of the axes.

Four Types of Digital Pressure on the Public/Private Distinction

Throughout this text I have emphasized on various occasions that my analysis deals with a modern way[55] of practicing privacies. I will now show how all four modern ways of

---

[55] Bruno Latour, *An Inquiry into Modes of Existence. An Anthropology of the Moderns* (Cambridge MA: Harvard University Press, 2013).

practicing the public/private distinction and generating the axes are severely undermined, historically speaking, by rather novel practices of digital networking.

(1) *Internal violations*: Peer groups and circles of friends surely can be considered an example for social worlds. Within peer groups there might be norms of discreetness specifying that, say, if something is told to one member in confidence, this information shall not be passed on to the others.[56] Obviously, this is a fine example of normative rules structuring the way the public/private distinction is practiced within social worlds as regards information: partaking in information is limited for all members except for those party to the confidential conversation, thus opening up a space of potential experiences for the latter: a room to maneuver that includes the potential to have restricted communication. If the receiver of the information passes it on, this is a violation of privacy within the social world. Against this background, one of the major effects of online social networks is that they constantly create opportunities for such violations, thus potentially undermining the traditional way of internally practicing the distinction.

(2) *Violations among social worlds*: Medical confidentiality is an explicit rule bound to keep doctors from passing information concerning a patient's state of health to, say, life insurers. The insurer's partaking in knowledge about the insured is limited, so as to enable the latter to have insurance even if they have a chronic disease or the like; partaking on the part of a specific social world is limited to open up a space for the party enjoying privacy. However, when quantified selves feed fitness data into an online platform to monitor their performance, resulting in the platform provider selling this data to a health insurer, the partaking is unlimited, insofar as there is a flow of information between the social world of quantified sports-selves and the social world of health insurers (this is what Nissenbaum calls a *violation of contextual integrity*[57]). In this sense, digital practices have the potential to unsettle the traditional way of practicing the public/private distinction *among* social worlds.

(3) *Privacy violations among social worlds globally declared as public/private*: Historically speaking, as was stated above, the macro distinction was applied in practice to limit the partaking of public authorities in private social worlds (including private economies). Once the macro distinction was in place, citizens' doings and sayings were *none of the state's business*, their practice was private business, with public authorities not being entitled to partake in informational, tactile, decisional etc. terms. According to the normative idea, the limiting of the public authorities' partaking opened up a space of potential practices for citizens. However, secret services practicing industrial espionage digitally threaten the practicing of public/private as macro distinction. It is therefore rather consistent that when Germany's major IT industry association BITKOM addressed German

---

[56] Carsten Ochs and Martina Löw, "Un/faire Informationspraktiken: Internet Privacy aus sozialwissenschaftlicher Perspektive," in *Internet Privacy. Eine multidisziplinäre Bestandsaufnahme/A Multidisciplinary Analysis*, ed. Johannes Buchmann (Berlin and Heidelberg: Springer, 2012), pp. 15–62.

[57] Nissenbaum, *Privacy in Context,* pp. 129–157.

public authorities to warn against industrial spying, they did so under the *rubric threat to the private sphere*.

(4) *Total privacy breaches in the face of the operational fiction of the public*: A *total* privacy breach is perceived any time we operate with some undifferentiated idea of digital data *ending up on the internet*. Because of their unlimited replicability, persistence, and searchability,[58] such data *never seem to vanish*. This results in a situation in which the entirety of the social worlds making up the mosaic of society potentially have access to, and thus may partake in, this data. This in turn may restrict the room to maneuver of the actors concerned. Empirically speaking, it is rather improbable that all social worlds do access certain data; however, even the potential for this to happen amounts to a privacy breach. The so-called *right to be forgotten* on the internet is an attempt to diminish the probability of privacy breaches of this very type.

Some Practice, Finally: A Case in Point Instead of a Conclusion

Having analyzed the way the public/private distinction is practiced in modern social formations, and the fourfold ways digital networking practices put pressure on entrenched modes of distinguishing public and private that limit partaking in others' minds, bodies, spaces, resources, knowledge, or institutional spheres, I would like to conclude by presenting a case in point that demonstrates how the conceptions developed so far in a kind of thought experiment style do actually materialize in empirical practice. I will therefore finally introduce an ethnographic case derived from a series of interviews conducted in 2016 in Germany. In the course of the interview series, we recorded 14 conversations with male and female representatives of all of the seven internet-usage milieus identified by the SINUS Institute in 2012.[59] We treated our interviewees in the style of Mol[60] as auto-ethnographers of their own everyday practices, and thus avoided the usual mistake of asking interviewees explicitly about their ideas concerning privacy. The latter strategy typically only discloses discursive rhetoric; instead we invited people to indulge in narrations and reconstructed their (privacy) practices from the resulting auto-ethnographic stories.

The case that I will present was selected because it concerns a person who presents herself in relation to *overall society* as somewhat marginalized; revealingly, despite this self-positioning at the societal *periphery*, our research partner nevertheless actualizes the conceptions developed above. The case is constituted by a 46-year-old housewife and mother of one who begins her self-description by talking right from the very beginning of the interview about her sexual practices in the BDSM scene (Bondage & Discipline, Dominance & Submission, Sadism & Masochism). Let us call this person by the pseud-

---

[58] Danah Boyd, "Social Network Sites: Public, Private, or What?" *Knowledge Tree* 13 (2007), http://www.danah.org/papers/KnowledgeTree.pdf (accessed 14.05.20), p. 2–3.

[59] Deutsches Institut für Vertrauen und Sicherheit im Internet, *DIVSI Milieu-Studie zu Vertrauen und Sicherheit im Internet* (Hamburg: DIVSI, 2012).

[60] Mol, *The Body Multiple*, p. 15.

onym of *Laura*. Laura got divorced from the father of her daughter some 15 years ago, and she is now married again. While she acts as a *Domme*, that is, plays the dominant role, her current husband used to practice the submissive part, but he has now *retired* from practicing BDSM altogether. Laura had a hard time after her divorce; she recovered and reinvented herself as a sadist BDSM practitioner, and since then, she indulges most intensely in this practice: she spends the greatest part of her time in this social world; many if not most of her social contacts are involved in BDSM; her daughter and future son-in-law practice BDSM; and her husband used to practice BDSM, too. When starting to chat on the internet each day in the early morning, when exchanging recipes via the internet, when discussing the best cruise agencies, Laura always makes use of her corresponding BDSM platform on the internet. At the same time, internet usage, in her case, largely serves the purpose of organizing her social world of BDSM.

As Laura is not in paid employment, work and leisure are not separated into different social worlds for her, as is the case for her husband, who works for a bank. In this sense, Laura's everyday life is not differentiated into too many social worlds; BDSM constitutes her major *lifeworld* in many respects, and she seems to achieve recognition and status mainly within this world. Laura explicitly distrusts *society*—she distrusts chains of action that stretch beyond her social near-field influence. She presents herself energetically as a conspiracy theorist, when claiming that "the really rich" once a year meet with all the heads of government so as to casually determine the course of the world for the next twelve months. The importance of the social world of BDSM for her social existence is in reverse proportion to the semiotic irrelevance she assigns to *mainstream society*: "I watch as little news as possible. I'm interested in things that I may influence in my own environment."[61]

A superficial glance at Laura's social existence might mistakenly conclude that she does not *need* privacy or *is post-privacy*, since her narrative does not stick to the bourgeois principle of keeping details of one's sex life to oneself. However, not submitting to bourgeois rules is not tantamount to the general absence of structuring. There is indeed internal structuration, normative rules that determine the limitation of partaking and the establishment of experiential realms in the social world of BDSM. For example, as Laura explains, she usually knows the first names of her submissive male partners, and perhaps she might know roughly about the region where they are from; but she would never enquire their full name and address. Even more importantly, she would not tell anybody about whom she practices BDSM with, nor what they do exactly. So, not even within the BDSM world does she release information about the actual sexual practices she performs with specific others (there are exceptions, she says, for instance at parties; yet on those occasions all practitioners performing *publicly* agree to do so). In this sense, there are normative rules structuring the limitation of partaking in others' activities, establishing an experiential realm strictly reserved to practitioners: there is internal structuration of applying the public/private distinction in the social world of BDSM. What is more, Laura's

---

[61]   Quotations are my translations from the German transcript.

answer to people asking her in chat rooms about her techniques and preferences is: "I don't tell this to some totally unknown guy whom I haven't met."

When it comes to information flow from the social world of BDSM to outside social worlds, normative expectations are even stronger. Laura explains that most practitioners in the social world of BDSM use nicknames, that is, pseudonyms to disguise to external worlds their membership in the BDSM world; she calls those who use their real first and surnames, and include their full postal code "stupid": "Do you want to have visitors, one day, someone who simply googles your names, first names and surnames? Get a nick[name], and no full postal code, please!" In this sense, there is also external structuration of the practices occurring within the social world of BDSM: the expected normative assumptions of the outside world structure disclosure practices within. Still, such privacy practices are not required in the case of Laura and her husband. The latter's profile, for example, features a full body image including the face. The reason that Laura does not consider such relatively easy to disclose pseudonymity risky, is that in her husband's case, the release of the information in question is unlikely to undermine his social position. For, as she states, if her husband was part of upper management, or even on the board of directors, the risk associated with this information would rise from *dangerous* to *deadly*. That is, partaking in the knowledge that Laura's husband was involved in BDSM would allow his rivals to constitute themselves as blackmailers or revelators, and to upgrade their position at the expense of her husband's experiential realm: "I'd say it depends on professional status. Those who make good money perhaps should be a bit more careful than those who have nothing. If somebody has nothing they can't be blackmailed as quickly or the like; or get an invitation: send me this or do that for me." Thus, informational privacy is about social positioning.

Meanwhile, Laura's take on the global declaration of social worlds as public or private—the status of the macro distinction between public authorities and private social worlds—is rather contradictory. For, as a supporter of conspiracy theory (including the *Chemtrail* hypothesis), she does not differentiate between public and private surveillance organizations, such as intelligence services and private enterprises: "It's one and the same pot, just put the lid on it and everything is in there." However, at the same time she calls upon the "Behörden" (authorities) and the police—that is, authorities which are public by definition—to take actions against cyber-crime, as well as right- and left-wing extremism on the internet. Whereas she suspects powerful organizations as such, including public ones, of violating people's privacy in order to more easily lead, guide, irritate, and scare subjects, and to cause "panic," privacy violations by public authorities for the sake of pushing back political extremism and crime seem normatively appropriate to her. In this sense, she acknowledges and disavows the macro-distinction at the same time.

As regards the operational fiction of *totality, the public as such,* Laura has clear ideas regarding the limitation of partaking by others. She claims that it is not possible to know or determine what happens with personal information once it is released on the internet; thus, it is not worth the trouble to be careful: although not trusting anybody, she still disseminates information, for abstaining from doing so would amount to self-limitation:

"I don't trust nobody. But I still do it." Accordingly, the internet is perceived as a kind of *total* public: publishing something there equals a *total* privacy breach. For Laura the only way to keep control is to stay off the internet—not an option for her, but also not necessary, as she deems herself "too marginal" to be of interest. Yet, there is another way to exert minimum control, which is to not release some information at all. In this respect, according to Laura, everybody is personally responsible for exerting self-censorship. In Laura's case, this includes pictures showing her nude; her certificates; the payroll of her husband; and her whereabouts. As to location data, there is only one exception: "Except you are member of the [digital BDSM platform], and you know: ah, there is, say, a party again, next Saturday, there is Laura. There you can find her. *That* doesn't bother me, not a scrap!"

In sum, our ethnographic case demonstrates once again the potential of practices of digital networking to effectively cut across established borders along all of the four modern axes of practicing the public/private distinction, resulting in a massive unsettling of the latter. It is not at all clear by now what the political consequences may be, and which of them should (not) be welcomed. A thorough understanding of the complex transformations currently under way is, however, indispensable if we are to balance all the ontologies in a fair manner. Having said that, it is regrettably plain to see that actual discourses tend to completely confuse the issue by, say, equating the business secrecy of capitalist corporations with the *private sphere* of bourgeois patriarchy, and the latter with *users' lifeworlds* online etc.—as if all these privacies were the same. *They are not.* And if we wish to be able to sort the ontologies that we do from those that we do not want to cultivate in the future, we had better learn to differentiate the plurality of privacies in practice.

KATJA ROTHE

A Media Ecology of the Soul: Play in Child Psychiatry

The first decades of the twentieth century saw an increase in the use of therapeutic play in the practice of psychiatry (Margaret Lowenfeld), psychology (Jakob Moreno), and social work (Charlotte Bühler). Psychoanalysis discovered play (Melanie Klein), as did psychotechnics; for example, elements of play started to be used in the selection process for officers in the German military.

Of course, this expansion can and must be linked to a broader discussion of the theories of play put forward by Walter Benjamin, Georg Simmel, Frederik Jacobus Johannes Buytendijk, and Johan Huizinga. This essay, however, attempts to do something else. In the following, I would like to inquire into whether play, as a situated therapeutic practice, can be helpful in re-conceptualizing the relationship between media theory and practice theory.

My hypothesis is that play, at the beginning of the twentieth century, can be thought of both as a means of self-creation[1] and as an *practice of ecology* within psychiatry; that is, as a research practice. This research practice is media-led or object-led; it is influenced by the specific research environment, play environment, and *toys*. Donald W. Winnicott insists upon practical play for a reason: play therapy is not about testing norms or finding principal psychoanalytical theorems. The practice of play—in which impacts are developed and intensified—is not always controllable; its results are unpredictable and cannot necessarily be translated into discourse or reconnected to research practice. Play therapies are not standardized; in a way, they are *impure*. As practices that cannot be objectified, these practices of knowledge have often not been discussed in the history of psychiatry.

In the following, I examine the relationship between object and ego and object and medium using a theoretical proposal from the early twentieth century: Winnicott's object relations theory. Using the example of Winnicott's therapeutic play with objects, we can ob-

---

[1] The term "self-creation" (*Selbst-Bildung*) shifts the focus from discourses of subjectivization to practices of subjectivization. In this praxeological approach, the subject is "not transcendent, or behind practice, but empirical, that is within practice." Thomas Alkemeyer et al., eds., *Selbst-Bildungen. Soziale und kulturelle Praktiken der Subjektivierung* (Bielefeld: transcript, 2013), p. 18. (All translations by Lee Holt and Laura Radosh unless otherwise noted.) The term "self-creation" furthermore stresses the active "share the individual has in shaping and changing given forms of the subject in practice, and thus in his or her own subjectivization in different concepts, without misunderstanding the individual as a subject that can act absolutely." Ibid., p. 21.

Fig. 22: Winnicott playing the squiggle game.

serve how, in the early twentieth century, play was conceived as both a medium and a practice. From this starting point, I would like to propose that the role of play in psychiatry should receive a more prominent position within academic discourse.

Practices of Play

Play theory was scarcely part of the history of psychology, and remains so to this day because it typically deals with tests that cannot be standardized and that often cannot be assigned clearly to a theoretical tradition. These tests belong to the field of practical knowledge which individual academic disciplines continue to view merely as applications of their theories, bereft of inherent value. Winnicott understood himself as a practitioner, and referred again and again to the importance of his work with patients. In this work, he focused above all on the play between invention and being found, along with non-discursivity and the relation to the transitional object. He connects here to the re-appraisal of creativity that preoccupied psychology and pedagogy at the beginning of the twentieth century.

In Sigmund Freud's psychoanalytic theory, dreams, imagination, and creativity play an important role. The process of artistic imagination and creation was, in Freud's thought and later on in Melanie Klein's view, a process of sublimation or transforming of sexual into non-sexual energies, for example artistic work. Winnicott, however, drew a connection between creativity and play. For Winnicott, a sense of self is found only in being creative and in expressing the power of imagination in play. Playing is—according to Winnicott—the key to emotional and psychological well-being not only for children, but also for adults. He wrote: "Only the true self can be creative and only the true self can feel real."[2] In the *spatula game*, the infant plays with a spatula—a tongue depressor—and the therapist observes

---

[2] Donald W. Winnicott, "Ego Distortion in Terms of True and False Self," in *The Maturational Processes and the Facilitating Environment: Studies in the Theory of Emotional Development*, ed. Donald W. Winnicott (New York: International Universities Press, 1965), pp. 140–152, here p. 147.

Fig. 23: Lowenfeld World Technique. Source: http://lowenfeld.org/the-world-technique/.

the creative metamorphoses of the object (airplane, stick, etc.). In the 1950s, Winnicott developed the *squiggle game* to communicate with children in psychotherapeutic sessions through drawing. The therapist scribbles on a piece of paper, and then the child continues the drawing, which is then taken up by the therapist again, and so on. This play facilitates communication about the transitional area, which is also beyond language.

Winnicott was able to build on the work of the British pediatrician and child psychologist Margaret Lowenfeld. In 1928, Lowenfeld opened the Clinic for Nervous and Difficult Children, which later became the Institute for Child Psychology. It was here in 1929 that she developed the World Technique.

She elaborated her theory of play as a nonverbal diagnostic and therapeutic tool in her book, *Play in Childhood*, published in 1935. Lowenfeld's technique of utilizing play as a tool for the psychoanalysis of children was extremely influential in Europe. For example, Gerdhild von Staabs, senior physician at the neurological psychiatric clinic in Berlin Ruhleben, drew from Margaret Lowenfeld's World Technique in the development of her Sceno Test.

The World Technique was also fundamental for the development of sand play therapy by the Swiss therapist Dora Kalff in the 1950s and Swedish therapist Hanna Bratt in the 1940s. It was also the foundation from which Gösta Harding and others developed the Erica Method in Sweden, and it inspired Charlotte Bühler's World Test in Austria in 1951 as well as the Village Test developed by Henri Arthus and Guy de Beaumont in France in the 1950s. Lowenfeld's play techniques still influence psychotherapeutic tools and practices today, for example systemic constellations or the family sculpting process used in systemic family therapy as well as Kurt Ludewig's Family Board.

It is characteristic of these non-standard techniques that they create the norms they want to *test* through testing. There are no right or wrong scenarios, only arrangements that can be interpreted. The child creates setups and when they are done, a decision is made about whether or not they are in the *normal* range, which is defined as what most children would do.[3] But even the Swiss psychiatrist Hermann Rorschach—the founder of

---

[3] According to Rohrschach, "A good form is then a form that elicits recurring answers from a 'large number of normal subjects'." Quoted in Andreas Reckwitz, *Die Erfindung der Kreativität: Zum Prozess gesellschaftlicher* Ästhetisierung (Berlin: Suhrkamp, 2012), p. 200.

Abb. 10 (S. 56). Adoptivkind

Fig. 24: Sceno Test Adoptivkind (adopted child),
Gerdhild von Staabs, *Der Scenotest, Beitrag zur
Erfassung unbewusster Problematik und Charaktero-
logischer Struktur in Diagnostik und Therapie*
(Stuttgart: Herzel Verlag, 1951), p. 56.

psycho-diagnostics—had already interpreted some deviations from the norm as indicators
of originality. This inadvertently cast doubt upon exactly that which he wished to gauge,
namely the differentiation between psychological normality and abnormality.[4] Andreas
Reckwitz believes that this shift of interest towards *original* behavior is connected to a
theory of personality, the impetus of which is "no longer the healing of the sick, but the
qualitative improvement of the mediocre."[5] Reckwitz diagnosed these tendencies towards
subjectivization, founded on the ideal that each individual should develop to his or her
full potential, in the 1930s and 1940s in the USA. These same tendencies, especially in
the area of play therapy, could be observed in Europe in the field of child psychology as
early as the 1920s.

In contrast to the larger debate on psychological self-government and self-regulation
(Foucault, Reckwitz, Illouz, Rose, etc.), I understand these play therapy techniques not
only as an optimized means of self-government of the human subject's creativity, but
as research practices that recognize the impact of play. For play is only a research practice because it is also understood as a means of self-creation in which objects take on a
central and active role. They stabilize the child's ego and open it to research, including
self-exploration.

Play therapy's object orientation stems from the necessity of not grounding an interpretation of children's play in language. Instead, the interaction of children and objects in
play is comprehended as a process that generates meaning and can thus give insight into
children's psyches. Subconscious re-enactment through figures circumvents language—
their parents' main means of expression—and provides children with their own means
of articulating their position through images. The figurines and mosaic pieces are put in
relation to one another to create individual settings. The setups are not psychoanalytical
tools; they are methods that allow children to explore and communicate their nonverbal

---

4   Ibid., pp. 200–201.
5   "It is not at all necessary to have debilitating psychiatric symptoms or some deviance in order to
     undergo psychological treatment. The aim is rather the qualitative improvement of normal, socially
     acceptable and unobtrusive behavior. This marks a structural transformation in techniques of sub-
     jectivization in psychology. Rather than identifying and eradicating unwanted traits and behavior,
     the goal is to mobilize psychological potential which is, in principle, endless." Ibid., p. 217.

ideas. The value of this method does not lie in the visualization or charting of cognitive processes; instead, the method is seen as a tool to make manifest children's ideas and their approach to the world.

These play sets turn the psychoanalyst into an art critic who must learn to interpret the setups and the mosaics—with the help of the child. The *worlds* simulated by children and adolescents in this type of play therapy are jointly explored by patient and therapist—visually, tactilely, and actively—and this exploration itself is part of the process of self-creation, which can in turn be observed. In play, the therapist or doctor takes a back seat to the techniques and objects and becomes simply an arranger of processes of reception and ways of acting, which they both initiate and research.

It should be stressed that in contrast to mathematical play theories, the child psychology play therapy tools discussed here do not understand play as a rule-based interactive game between multiple agents in which decisions are made, but as an individual child's creative search for expression. It is about *play*, not *games*,[6] about "reduplicating, aimless, continually repeating movement such as that of the play of light on water."[7] As the Dutch biologist, anthropologist, and psychologist Frederik J.J. Buytendijk said as early as 1933 in *Wesen und Sinn des Spiels* (*Essence and Meaning of Play*), a book that has been very influential in games studies, play is an image-led way of exploring the world that is governed not by "logical thinking and reasoning" but "through concrete phenomena" and "sensate givens."[8] Buytendijk suggests that a shift from subject to object takes place in play: "Play is thus not only someone who plays with something, but also something that plays with the player."[9]

Donald W. Winnicott's transitional objects can be understood in just this way. For in play as a form of self-creation, objects have a crucial meaning, as we shall see in the following exploration of Winnicott's object relations theory.

Internal Objects, Transitional Objects, Play

The idea of the object plays a major role in psychoanalysis. In this paper, I concentrate on Donald W. Winnicott's concept of the object, for which Lowenfeld's play therapy provided a critical frame of reference. In the 1920s and 1930s, Winnicott was on the board of Lowenfeld's Clinic for Nervous and Difficult Children. At the time, like most of his fellow psychoanalysts, including Melanie Klein, he was critical of Lowenfeld's work and thought play in particular was irrelevant to analysis. Later he changed his opinion, at

---

[6]   Katie Salen and Eric Zimmerman, *Rules of Play. Game Design Fundamentals* (Cambridge MA and London: MIT Press, 2004), p. 80.

[7]   Astrid Deuber-Mankowsky, "Mediale Anthropologie, Spiel und Anthropozentrismuskritik," *Zeitschrift für Medien- und Kulturforschung: Medienanthropologie* 1/13 (2013): pp. 133–149, here p. 137.

[8]   Frederik J.J. Buytendijks, *Das Spielen des Menschen und der Tiere als Erscheinungsform der Lebenstriebe* (Berlin: Wolff, 1933), p. 146.

[9]   Ibid., p. 116.

least in regard to play.[10] From the 1970s, he believed play with transitional objects to be the first step in the development of creativity.[11]

Returning to his object relations theory, Winnicott follows Melanie Klein's idea of the *internal object*,[12] but takes the idea of the object beyond its psychoanalytic conception. He emphasizes that a *transitional object is not an internal object (which is a mental concept)*, rather, *it is a possession*. Yet for a child, it is also an *external object*. Winnicott is therefore concerned with an object that is neither internal nor solely a mental phenomenon, but is also not only external to the child's perception. The transitional object is an intermediate object. Winnicott summarized his findings in his essay, "Transitional Objects and Transitional Phenomena – A Study of the First Not-Me Possession," writing:

> I have introduced the terms "transitional object" and "transitional phenomena" for designation of the intermediate area of experience, between the thumb and the teddy bear, between the oral erotism and true object-relationship, between primary creative activity and projection of what has already been introjected, between primary unawareness of indebtedness and the acknowledgement of indebtedness.[13]

The transitional object is therefore an object of transition, a descriptor for an "intermediate area of experience" that mediates between "inner reality and external life."[14] The transitional object represents a point in the development of a child at which an object associated with the child is first perceived as standing outside the ego. The "other-than-me objects" are woven "into the personal pattern."[15] In this process, according to Winnicott, the illusion that the mother's breast belongs to the infant, that the breast is its possession, is replaced by the transitional object. In this "intermediate area of experience," the question repeatedly arises as to "what is objectively perceived and what is subjectively conceived of."[16] The child has the illusion that "there is an external reality that corresponds to the infant's own capacity to create."[17] Winnicott argues that the exchange between mother and child is an illusion.

---

[10] Margaret Lowenfeld, "Child Psychotherapy, War and the Normal Child," in Cathy Urwin and John Hood Williams, eds., *Selected Papers of Margaret Lowenfeld* (Eastbourne: Sussex Academic Press, 2013), p. 224.

[11] Donald W. Winnicott, *Playing and Reality* (1971) (London: Routledge, 2005).

[12] Donald W. Winnicott, "Transitional Objects and Transitional Phenomena – a Study of the First Not-Me Possession," *International Journal of Psycho-Analysis* 34 (1953): pp. 89–97; Winnicott, "Ego Distortion in Terms of True and False Self," p. 30.

[13] Winnicott, "Transitional Objects and Transitional Phenomena," p. 89.

[14] Ibid., p. 90.

[15] Ibid., p. 91.

[16] Ibid., p. 94.

[17] Ibid., p. 95.

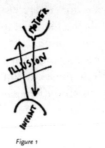
Figure 1

Figure 2

Fig. 25: Illusion and Transitional Object, from Donald W. Winnicott, "Transitional Objects and Transitional Phenomena – a Study of the First Not-Me Possession," *International Journal of Psycho-Analysis* 34 (1953): pp. 94–95.

The main function of the transitional object is to preserve this illusion, and above all not to question it:

> Of the transitional object it can be said that it is a matter of agreement between us and the baby that we will never ask the question "Did you conceive of this or was it presented to you from without?" The important point is that no decision on this point is expected. The question is not to be formulated.[18]

The transitional object is therefore a material object that facilitates the correspondence of an internal and external reality in an "intermediate area."[19] What is interesting here is Winnicott's description of the creation of objects: the infant "creates what is in fact lying around waiting to be found."[20] The object is therefore constructed as something found, which can also elicit aggression if the thing is "in the way."[21] But the "frustrating aspect of object behaviour" (being in the way) has value in educating the infant in respect of the existence of a not-me world. Adaptation failures have value in so far as the infant can hate the object, that is to say, can retain the idea of the object as potentially satisfying while recognizing its failure to behave satisfactorily.[22]

Following Winnicott then, both the object—as a discovered entity that offers resistance—and the environment are actively involved in the formation of the subject, and this process is described as play. Winnicott presents the intermediate area as the "play area of the small child who is 'lost' in play."[23] Playing with objects is therefore an *illusory experience* that can, however, connect entire groups of people in art, religion, and philosophy, as long as no claims must be staked as regards objectivity and subjectivity.[24]

---

[18] Ibid., p. 95.
[19] Ibid., p. 96.
[20] Winnicott, "Ego Distortion in Terms of True and False Self," p. 180.
[21] Ibid.
[22] Ibid.
[23] Donald W. Winnicott, *Playing and Reality*, p. 18.
[24] Ibid.

What is central for Winnicott is that play with transitional objects does not refer solely to an inner or an outer world. For this reason, play does not enable the therapist to look directly into children's souls, nor is it only a field of subjective perceptions. Play with transitional objects is a strategy of ego-organization; it leads to a feeling of omnipotence and thus, Winnicott claims, to greater independence, no matter how illusory. With this, Winnicott makes clear that through play, something that is not currently happening is nevertheless able to have an impact, and that objects do not stand for a concrete figure (such as the bad mother), but are an expression of the ego-organization.[25] Playing is a field in which one loses oneself—experiences the self as not omnipotent, but dependent—only to again find oneself. Play is practicing the illusion of being able to form the world, to have an influence, and to understand the rules. Playing with transitional objects makes it possible to find that which the player invented or to link fantasy and the real world.

Therapeutic play is thus a highly effective medial practice that allows things to appear in the here and now that do not need to be actualized, but are nevertheless constitutive for the subject. Play makes it possible to bring things into the present that cannot yet be experienced (for example, because the child is at a developmental stage where the self is not yet fully formed). The non-actualized, yet experiential character of play is the site of its potential as a medial experience—it brings forth the ungraspable and inaccessible. For Winnicott, play is a transitional area between subject and object, between presence and absence, in which action does take place, but not in the sense of an active subject using a passive object. Rather, play is a gathering place, where subject and object are not separate, but mutually constitute one another. Inaccessibility and silence also play a central role for Winnicott. For him, in play there is no complete access to *the* subject or *the* object, especially not through language. Against the common psychoanalytic assumptions of his times, Winnicott did not deal with transitional objects discursively. He confronted psychological discursive practice—based in the main on language—with the right of "non-communicating" and the "fantasy of being found."[26] His theory of object relationships is based on the realization that it is the non-communicative nature of the human-object relation that allows for the development of the "capacity to communicate."[27] This relationship to objects can, in turn, only mature within a "facilitating environment."[28] In such an environment, the child develops a relationship to objects that is *not* communicated. In summary, it is not language—Winnicott claims—that leads to the inner core of self-creation. Rather, the subject, in a facilitating environment, develops from *holding*, via *handling*, to *object-presenting*.[29] Children move from awareness of objects, to

---

[25]   Donald W. Winnicott, "Fear of Breakdown," in Donald W. Winnicott, *Psycho-Analytic Explorations* (Boston MA: Harvard University Press, 1974), pp. 87–95.
[26]   Donald W. Winnicott, "Communicating and Not Communicating Leading to a Study of Certain Opposites," in Winnicott, ed., *The Maturational Processes*, pp. 179–192, here p. 179.
[27]   Ibid.
[28]   Ibid., p. 180.
[29]   Winnicott, "Fear of Breakdown," p. 89.

playing with them, and, finally, to language.[30] This shift to non-discursiveness has grave consequences, as Félix Guattari has made clear. It is a turn from a "logic of discursive sets" to a "logic of intensities."[31] Guattari refers to Winnicott's transitional objects to make clear that subjectivity is first a "bringing-into-existence, that authorizes, *secondarily*, a discursive intelligibility."[32]

An Ecology of Practices

A practice of play is necessary to bring something into existence in a logic of intensities. Winnicott himself described his therapeutic practice as play and said that the therapist must be someone who likes to play, otherwise "he is not suitable for the work."[33] That which seems like a medium when playing, becomes real within the context of therapy as a practice of play. In such practice, the medium of play allows the child's fantasies of omnipotence to develop an ego. To become existent in this way, Guattari added, a logic of intensities is necessary. To this aim, Deleuze proposed a correlating method of dramatization.[34] Didier Debaise describes this method as "a construction, an artificial attitude, something non-intuitive engaging thought," aimed at intensifying the importance of a concept or event.[35]

Dramatization emphasizes those moments of practice that understand actions not only as representations of intentions, social norms, etc., but as a performance of actions in order to test their functions. In play, children can perform their self-creation through their relations with objects without having to *be* the plaything or the role. After all, they are *only* playing. All players can explore and shape possibilities, even when inaccessible elements are present.

---

[30] It should be mentioned that Winnicott's theory of transitional objects engendered much controversy. In particular his corollary—that the lack of a transitional object leads to mental disorder—remains unproven. Studies of other cultures suggest that attachment to objects might be related to an active mother, who separates from her child at an early stage. Transitional objects are found less often in cultures in which children are breast-fed longer or spend a longer period close to their primary care-takers. There are many indications that the self-creation processes described here are culturally and historically coded and transport a particular picture of families and of women. Thus, this process of object-led self-creation is not an anthropological constant. On this, see Tilmann Habermas, *Geliebte Objekte. Symbole und Instrumente der Identitätsbildung* (Berlin: de Gruyter, 1999), pp. 355–360.

[31] Félix Guattari, *Three Ecologies*, trans. Ian Pindar and Paul Sutton (London: Athlone Press, 2000), p. 44.

[32] Ibid., p. 37.

[33] Donald W. Winnicott, "Playing and Reality," p. 72.

[34] Gilles Deleuze, "The Method of Dramatization," in *Desert Islands and Other Texts, 1953-1974*, ed. Gilles Deleuze, trans. Michael Taormina (Los Angeles: Semiotext(e), 2004), pp. 94–116.

[35] Didier Debaise, "The Dramatic Power of Events: The Function of Method in Deleuze's Philosophy," *Deleuze Studies* 10/1 (2016): pp. 5–18, here p. 6.

Wolfgang Lipp uses the term *dramatology* to describe Erving Goffman's sociological theory,[36] which underlines the aspect of acting. Drama, (from the Old Greek δρμα) means deed or action and was, following Aristotle's poetics, often understood as a causal series of events with an endpoint and a goal. For Goffman, the term *drama* stresses the activating, interactive aspect of theater.[37] Rather than focusing on logically connected series of events in time, Goffman emphasizes observation in a situation in which participants act and interact simultaneously. The spatial relation of actors is at the fore, rather than the temporal order of events. The self is an acting agent which interacts with other acting agents,[38] and this structure also holds true for play with objects. Dramatology denotes the relational generation of knowledge on the basis of actors' or agents' (mutual) observations of situational actions. The objects of dramatology are found in enacted actions, in the observation of practices (praxis—from the Greek πράξις, practice, action, doing) which I call theatrical. The observation of enacted actions becomes in part a "research strategy."[39] Dramatology thus refers not to a philosophy of human nature or to an anthropology of the theater, but to the way in which knowledge is organized, an ordering of knowledge which makes a *self* observable and, in doing so, first constitutes this self.

Dramatology of play therapy denotes the relational generation of knowledge about children on the basis of actors' (mutual) observations of situational actions. In this case, play therapy practices must be endowed with efficaciousness. After all, an ego can evolve in this process of spatial-theatrical performance of scenes. To this end, Winnicott calls upon therapists to concentrate not on the internal structure of the psyche (psycho-analysis), but on the performative process or intensive practices of ego-creation.[40] Subjectivization is no longer only a process within the subject, but the result of an insoluble interplay of practices and their subjects.[41]

In Conclusion

Winnicott's play therapy describes play as both medium and practice. As a medium, it brings to light a result of transference: a possible, omnipotent ego that has power over objects. As a practice, it is a method of intensification that tests efficacy and stabilizes the

---

[36] Wolfgang Lipp, "Kultur, dramatologisch," Österreichische *Zeitschrift für Soziologie* 9 (1984): pp. 8–25.

[37] Hitzler points out that one cannot call Goffman's dramatology a philosophy or anthropology, but rather a research strategy, which Hitzler terms "methodological behaviorism." Ronald Hitzler, "Goffmans Perspektive. Notizen zum dramatologischen Ansatz," *Sozialwissenschaftliche Informationen* 20/4 (1991): pp. 276–281, here p. 277.

[38] "Which characters deal with one another under which conditions and in which settings, how well do those who are interacting play their roles, which scripts they are using and which audience do they speak to." Ronald Hitzler, "Der Goffmensch. Überlegungen zu einer dramatologischen Anthropologie," *Soziale Welt* 43/4 (1992): pp. 449–461, here p. 458.

[39] Hitzler "Goffmans Perspektive," p. 277.

[40] Thomas Alkemeyer et al., *Selbst-Bildungen.*

[41] Thomas Alkemeyer et al., "Einleitung," in *Selbst-Bildungen*, pp. 9–30, here p. 21.

ego. Media theory and practice theory converge in play. A media theory description of play would stress the object-led appearance of the absent in the medium of play. Practice theory would focus on the routines and norms within the action, or the self-creation in the sense of a psychologization of an ego that observes and regulates itself. Both can be found in Winnicott's play with objects. For this reason, I would like to end with a first attempt to connect media theory and practice theory in play therapy by looking at it as an "ecology of practice" as put forth by Isabelle Stengers. Stengers defines an ecology of practice as "a tool for thinking through what is happening."[42] Starting from concrete practices, specific impacts or efficacies should be analyzed.[43] There is no universal method; every situation and every material suggests a different use, which in turn depends upon both the situation and the material.[44] Stengers describes this "thinking par le milieu" in the Deleuzean sense as particular, situated involvement.[45] In Stengers' ecology of practice, responsibility does not mean obeying principles, but recognizing the "matter of concern" within a specific situation: "That is, you need to decide in this particular case and not to obey the power of some more general reason."[46]

Similarly, Winnicott describes the work of the therapist as responsible play with objects—found and fantasized—and with the possible permutations thereof. It is a concrete practice that opens new possibilities, which, in turn, cannot be imagined as divorced from their milieu. The therapeutic work makes efficaciousness probable and tries to support its coming into existence, but not outside the field of play. The therapist must also play and cannot suddenly begin to lecture or deliver a distanced diagnosis. Therapeutic practice is a dramatology in which efficacious scenes are set up and stabilized in specific situations. Play is a powerful medium of therapy because it aids the exploration of object-led images of the self. Because it is so effective, the practice of play therapy is a delicate matter that must be accompanied by a therapist in play, adding another practice of play. Therapeutic play thus never leaves the level of practice in which, depending upon the setting, varying dramatologies intensify efficaciousness.

---

[42] Isabelle Stengers, "Introductory Notes on an Ecology of Practices," *Cultural Studies Review* 11 (2005): pp. 183–196, here p. 185.

[43] On this, see also Karin Harrasser and Kathrin Solhdju, "Wirksamkeit verpflichtet," *Zeitschrift für Medienwissenschaft* 14 (2016): pp. 72–86, here p. 82.

[44] Stengers, "Introductory Notes on an Ecology of Practices," p. 185.

[45] Ibid., p. 187.

[46] Ibid., p. 188.

Practice in the History of Computing

INTERVIEW WITH THOMAS HAIGH, BY ERHARD SCHÜTTPELZ

ES: How would you characterize your own work concerning media practices and/or practice theory?

TH: My initial university training, through my first master's degree, was in computer science at the University of Manchester. Then, for my Ph.D. from the University of Pennsylvania, I shifted disciplines to become a historian of computing and information technology. Although my degree was from the History and Sociology of Science department, my primary advisor, Walter Licht, was in the History department and worked at the intersection of business history, labor history, and social history. I quickly realized that my interest was not so much in technology itself but in how technology was used to change practice. During grad school, I worked as an IT contractor to supplement my fellowships, which gave me a bottom-up interest in the specifics of ordinary IT work practice.

The focus of the History and Sociology of Science department was very much on social history rather than actual sociology of science. However, the ideas of science and technology studies shaped the way we learned to think about history. That was particularly true for those of us working on the history of technology. Penn professor Thomas Hughes, recently retired when I arrived, had been one of the editors of the famous *Social Construction of Technological Systems* volume. Steven Shapin, the program's most famous graduate, had integrated science and technology studies sensibilities into historical work.

Starting out my research in the late 1990s, it seemed natural to focus on the use of IT within large organizations. That was where computing had built up the longest history, and where its effects seemed most fundamental. Enthusiasts had been using personal computers for more than twenty years, but they had still played only a minor part in most people's domestic or social practices. In contrast, work practices and organizational structures had already been comprehensively remade around the affordances of computer technology. My dissertation explored the practices of administrative work and the ways it was reorganized and systematized over the twentieth century, from the scientific office management movement of the 1910s onward. I concluded that the rhetoric used by different waves of self-proclaimed experts to assert control over the organization of work had changed remarkably little, but that shifts in technology from files and forms to databases and computer networks had transformed the material resources available to legitimate that claim. Organizations delegated enormous power to information technology departments without ever quite working out how to align their culture and expertise with that of the broader organization.

ES: Would you say that this historical focus on information *technology* or on office *media* was part of a practice turn in the 1990s?

TH: History was my dominant discipline, and historians are for the most part reluctant to engage explicitly with theory. We like to get to the narrative quickly, relegating the discussion of methodology and inspirations to a footnote. We introduce big ideas at the point in the narrative where they help us frame something specific, rather than presenting our narratives as case studies that prove some abstract point. Although I sometimes find those aesthetics constraining, that way of working and thinking has become congenial to me. As a result, there's still something that sounds slightly paradoxical to me about *practice theory*—it's as if academics have recognized the abstract importance of practice as an area of study, but continue to privilege theory over practice in their own realm. Having come to think of my own research as a craft practice, rather than a theoretical enterprise, if anything I engage in *practice practice* rather than practice theory.

To put that less provocatively, I am a consumer of theory rather than a producer. One of the things that attracted me to a Ph.D. in the United States was the chance to do several years of coursework to ground myself in the humanities and social sciences more generally. We had few restrictions on what courses we could take, so I read through the course catalog looking for things that might be useful or interesting. This included two courses in advanced statistics, a course on the sociology of mass communication, and the two core courses in the comparative literature program *Introduction to Literary Theory* which were taught by the aptly named James English. We read and discussed a couple of famous theorists a week for an academic year. Those naturally included Bourdieu, Foucault, de Certeau, and many of the others who you probably associate with *practice theory* as well as Butler, Derrida, and others who focused on performativity. I'm sure the experience shaped me by broadening the range of things I noticed when looking at historical cases, though I've rarely explicitly cited such theorists. One direct result was that I've been less intimidated in dealing with humanities cultures where theorists are prominently cited. Taking the course made me realize that many scholars who flitted from theorist to theorist in their remarks had probably read only a single famous paper or chapter by each theorist during a similar course! For example, I suspect that Geertz's analysis of cockfights has been invoked a hundred times more than anything else he touched on in a long and rich career.

With the obvious exception of Marx (who uniquely received a whole week of the course to himself) few of those brand name literary/cultural theorists were particularly interested in work practices. That may be why the conceptual works I have cited in my own work are mostly those I was exposed to when putting together a Ph.D. examination field on the *Social Study of Business Organizations*. To do this I worked with six of the more ethnographically minded members of the Wharton Business School, getting maybe twenty books from each one. Karl E. Weick's wonderful book *Sensemaking in Organizations* was a particular inspiration. His work parallels science and technology studies scholarship but is indigenous to the study of business. He makes the case for putting cognition and enactment at the center of understanding what people do in organizations. Powell and DiMaggio's work, collected in *The New Institutionalism in Organizational Analysis,* was another major influence. When I looked at historical documents, I got the sense that the would-be technocrats I was studying were trying to reshape collective understandings of what an organization chart should look like. Powell and DiMaggio argue that cultural labor of this kind is exactly what drives changes in the dominant structure of organizations within a particular field. I also love a book by Robert J. Thomas, *What Machines Can't Do*, a collection of sharply observed ethnographic studies around the introduction of new technology in manufacturing. He had some theory too, but what stuck with me were the narratives. The work of Stephen R. Barley on the technical work within organizations was another huge influence on the kinds of stories I looked for in my historical sources. I was also partial to the old-fashioned sociology of Everett Hughes, who looked at the ways in which occupational groups constructed *mandates* for themselves, a concept that resonated with the emphasis of newer science and technology studies work on the politics of expertise. None of that is media theory as conventionally understood, and scholars in the humanities and cultural studies have generally ignored work coming from the management field.

ES: I suppose it would have been a surprise if media theory had been a direct inspiration for focusing on work practices or on organizational practices. After all, in classical media theory, a change of media is supposed to determine or at least to redirect practices. Apart from that, it still sounds unfamiliar to call office technology *media*, and it must have been unusual in history departments and computer science alike.

TH: Understanding the current era of smartphones and social media will inevitably force us to address the convergence of all media devices and practices around computer technology. Teaching briefly in the information schools at Drexel and Indiana and, for thirteen years, in Milwaukee, gave me a direct interest in relating my work to another keyword: *information*. I'm fascinated by its power, which in the second half of the twentieth century drew many different occupational groups to attempt to mobilize it as a label for their products and work practices: data processing workers, librarians, scientific publishers, computer manufacturers and so on. *Information* is one of the most powerful words of the late twentieth century, and that history hasn't really been told. But its power comes in large part from its vagueness, or as science and technology studies scholars would term this, its *interpretative flexibility* or role as a *boundary object* between communities. This lack of specific meaning has made me reluctant to embrace *information* as part of my own scholarly identity even as I find it a vital phenomenon to study. In contrast, media seem relatively coherently defined as an area of study.

Was I a scholar of media practice all along? If so, you might liken me to Molière's bourgeois gentleman, who had been speaking prose for decades before realizing it. I was interested in the use of computers as a communications medium, in as much as I was interested in the historical use of information technology to organize work processes. Work was structured as profoundly by media such as file cabinets and written work procedures as it was later by computer technology, an idea captured in JoAnne Yates' historical study *Control through Communication*, which is actually about the coordination of work. Within a few years of earning my Ph.D. in 2003, I tackled new projects on the history of database management systems and word processing, looking in both cases at the materiality and capabilities of these technologies as well as their role in the transformation of work practices.

ES: Maybe this is where the historical convergence of information technologies and media devices meets a parallel convergence, or inspires the idea of a partial convergence between science and technology studies, media studies, and the history of computing. And because the theoretical keywords of those fields have only partly converged, the question of practices is more pertinent to this convergence than the terminology of *media*, at least for the moment. Do you think the history of computing has already gone through or is already going through some kind of *practice turn*?

TH: Yes. Though participants have tended to call this a turn towards use and users. That reflects the intellectual prominence of the history of technology within the history of computing community during the 1990s and early 2000s. When the history of technology was getting established as a separate field from the 1950s onward its early practitioners were primarily engineers with an interest in history, industrial archaeologists, and museum curators. This naturally put a focus on artifacts themselves and the processes by which they were produced. By the 1980s the field was broadening out, and excitement grew about the possibility of looking at the users of technologies and the uses made of them, that is, practices. This accompanied a broadening of the range of technologies studied, in particular to cover everyday technologies such as those used by women in the home. The work of two Ruths captures this shift: Ruth Schwartz Cowan in the US and Ruth Oldenziel in the Netherlands.

Historians of computing with Ph.Ds in history have tended to assume that, as a sub-field of the history of technology, the history of computing is following a similar arc but a couple of decades later. Back in the 1970s it got started by computer pioneers and museum curators and was focused on artifacts and inventions. Scholars trained in the history of technology viewed this emphasis as evidence of its backward nature, and pushed to advance it by applying the focus on social history, class, and gender that distinguished the most acclaimed work in the history of technology. More recently, again with a lag, the history of technology has begun to mirror the 1990s rise of cultural history. That also draws attention to practice, though compared with social or labor history it has less of an emphasis on work practices and more on the activities of consumers in their personal time.

A lot of what I've tried to do is simply to produce work that can stand up with the best scholarship in other areas of the history of technology, and with the social and labor history papers I read back in graduate school. The same is probably true of other scholars from similar backgrounds, like Andrew Russell, Nathan Ensmenger, and Corinna Schlombs.

Similarly, for the smaller group of historians of computing who identify primarily with the history of science (rather than technology) their parent field has provided its own track of thinking about practice. That group includes scholars such as Joe November, Stephanie Dick, Ksenia Tatarchenko, and Matthew Jones. The increased visibility of practice in the history of science was influenced by the rise of science studies in the 1980s, particularly the ethnographic kind pioneered by Bruno Latour and Steve Woolgar. Many historians of science were always interested in what went on in laboratories, but by the 1990s the influence of science and technology studies broadened the kinds of practices that were considered worthy of study. The study of field science became a hot area. Historians of science looked more at materiality and practices under the rubric of *instrumentation*, which is a way for them to acknowledge the importance of technology. Historians looked to uncover hidden kinds of labor, such as that performed by the women or servants who often did most of the experimental work but were not named in the resulting publications. Historians paid more attention to the *big science* that emerged during the Cold War, which meant looking at funding practices, management practices, and scientific entrepreneurship.

So, to return to the first question's emphasis on my own work, the attention to practice that runs through my recent book *ENIAC In Action* (with Priestley and Rope) is not theorized in any particular way. Indeed, much of what we do there reflects impulses that are common across several of the fields I'm grounded in. For example, rediscovering the work of the blue-collar women who actually built ENIAC mimics Steven Shapin's gambit in exposing the work of *invisible technicians* but also follows the long-established impulse in social and labor history to probe gendered hierarchies and the intersectionality of class and gender. Overall our exploration of practice means paying attention to the machine's use and users: something that might seem obvious, indeed long overdue, to anyone keeping up with the past twenty years of work in the history of technology.

ES: I think it's best to give one example. Concerning your collective work on ENIAC and early computing, which difference does it make to follow the threads of practice?

TH: ENIAC's been written about a lot, both by technically-oriented historians of computing and by people looking to make points about broader subjects such as the role of women's work in computing. What surprised us, as we began to dig into the relevant archival collections, was how inaccurate much of this literature was. Some basic factual errors in things like dates made by early writers like Herman Goldstine have been widely reproduced. Many scholars had relied on oral histories, which are terrible sources of factual detail, without cross-referencing them with the archival record. Some of this might seem like nitpicking, but cumulatively our efforts to rebuild the history of ENIAC on archival foundations led to some important revisions. On the technical side, we discovered that conditional branching, perhaps the most crucial capability of the modern computer, had been a central design goal from early on in the project and not something added at the last minute. More broadly, we discovered that the work of configuring ENIAC to producing firing tables, which previous authors had believed was first thought about by the machine's operators shortly before its public launch in February 1946, had actually been outlined in detail by the engineering team at the beginning of the project in late 1943 and used to shape the machine's basic capabilities. So, for me our commitment to the reconstruction of practice was inseparable from a commitment to the exhaustive exploration of archival sources. Theorizing about practice without digging into sources would not have accomplished much.

Our commitment to practice also shaped the scope of the book. Previous work on ENIAC had focused almost exclusively on its development and experimental use in 1943–1946. The story stopped as soon as the machine was working and ready for delivery to the Ballistics Research Laboratory which had commissioned it. The conventional narrative then moves on to newer computer designs, and is concerned with conceptual and architectural innovations rather than use. Our commitment to the study of users and use led us to place equal weight on ENIAC's career as a scientific tool from 1947–1955, which is after all why it was constructed. We found that work continued to literally and metaphorically reconstruct ENIAC in ways that completely changed its programming method and substantially modified its capabilities. We also discovered that ENIAC was barely working in 1947, and that it took years of careful attention, repair work, and the buildup of tacit knowledge around its operation to make it a fully practical tool. ENIAC didn't run any calculations after 1955, but considering practice more broadly led us to follow it forward in time to the present day by looking at how its memory has been shaped to serve particular purposes.

ENIAC's users in the laboratory regarded it as one tool among many. We respected that perspective, rather than assuming that ENIAC's electronic speed instantly made other kinds of computational practice centered on desk calculators or relay computers obsolete. Understanding ENIAC practice from the ground up helped us to see that the machine's actual speed was determined far more by the capabilities of its punched card devices, and by the ability of human operators to manually process its input and output cards between steps in the automatic computation, than by the speed of its circuits.

One of my favorite gambits is to intertwine the history of practice with the history of categories. Like other producers of narrative, historians rely on analytical categories like *computer*, *information* or *software* to define what our stories are about and guide us in knowing when to start, when to stop, and what to include. The problem is that these categories appear, change, and disappear over time. They are often contested by the historical actors we write about, and implicitly endorsing any definition of them in the stories we tell can mean siding with one historical position in a way that systematically undermines the visibility of other positions in our narrative. One of the most exciting things that historians can do is to show that the categories we use to structure our own view of the world are historically contingent rather than universal. Historians of computing haven't always been as careful as I'd like in distinguishing between actor's categories and analytical categories. To me, one of the most important things our focus on practice in *ENIAC in Action* provides is a solid basis on which to historicize concepts such as *stored program*, *programing*, and *program* so that others will be able to deploy them more carefully.

There are places in the book where a single line or fact reported in the text reflects days of technical work and discussion. Most of this comes from my coauthor Mark Priestley, who made a remarkable commitment to diving into the details of what was going on inside ENIAC and also inside the minds of its designers. He produced a fully functional ENIAC emulator, which he used to set up the *converter code* configuration we discovered in the original ENIAC binder that sat next to the machine in the 1950s. He also produced a fully annotated edition of the Monte Carlo simulation code run for Los Alamos in 1948, and compared this with several flow diagrams to get a sense of how things had changed as the problem moved from initial planning through several detailed designs and into operational code.

In the introduction of the book we call this an experiment in the reintegration of technical detail into the history of computing. As I mentioned, the core project of the scholarly history of computing community from the 1980s to the early 2000s was to professionalize the field by shifting from the technical and personal focus of writing by old computer pioneers to work that adopted the dominant concerns of more respectable subfields of the history of technology. This has led to some self-identified historians of computing to look down on engagement with technological specifics as a sign of intellectual backwardness because of its association with the retired computer specialists who dominated the field in its early years. Historically minded computer scientists, admittedly a rather small group, have been sad about this—something I explored in a column called *The Tears of Donald Knuth*. I recently met Knuth for the first time, and was very pleased when he told me that he "wasn't crying anymore" because of our book on ENIAC.

In contrast, there's been a lot of interest in media studies and allied fields in the idea of reading old code and discussing it critically. Most notably an entire MIT Press book was devoted to a single line of code (*10 PRINT CHR$(205.5+RND(1)); : GOTO 10*). That works well as proof that scholars can find interesting things to say about a program, but doesn't necessarily provide a scalable model for reading and writing about programs that are significantly more than one line long. We found that it can be done, but that it requires specific skills, a lot of time, and a deep commitment to understanding both the domain area of the program and the platform for which it was written. From a history of science viewpoint this makes the computer a particularly hard tool to engage with, as a single artifact like ENIAC was used for many different kinds of problems. The work we did in understanding how Monte Carlo techniques were applied to nuclear fission would have been only partially transferable to understanding the code of another ENIAC problem (say the supersonic flow of air around a wing).

ES: How does that change the *theory of early computing*, if there is such a thing?

TH: If there is a *theory of early computing* guiding historians then it is probably some-thing implicit in the practice of the people writing about it—you would have to reverse engineer it by looking at what we do. That, I think, is how new historical methods spread. I don't know of any cases in which proposing a manifesto or writing an article with bul-let points about what topics and methods historians should research has been a primary cause of changes in historical practice. That's perhaps a difference between history and cultural/media studies, in which telling other people what they should be doing seems to be what establishes one as a *theorist*. Instead, historians respond to a book or article that implicitly makes the case for a new method by serving as an exemplary new narrative, telling a story in exciting new ways by taking novel perspectives, using unfamiliar sources, interpreting evidence in a different way, etc. In a way, this means that when it comes to methods historians follow the advice given to novelists, "show, not tell." When a few of those works come along it can transform historical practice.

Early in my graduate studies a friend noted that those of us coming from science some-times had a hard time adjusting to history because we assumed that creating theory was the most visible, highest status kind of work. Historians do produce articles that review areas of research or make methodological arguments, something we call historiography. It's a valuable activity, and I've done more of it than most (including the first and last chapters of *ENIAC in Action*). But I can only think of one historian in the fields with which I am familiar who is known primarily for historiography (John Staudenmaier, if you are curious). History is like art, in that fashion. Someone with a new artistic technique is more likely to spread it by using it to produce impressive artworks than by writing about its potential. Some artists did produce manifestos, but most leave analysis and theory to critics. Even conceptual artists are remembered for tangible works, like Marcel Duchamp's urinal or Warhol's giant Brillo boxes, rather than for abstract statements.

For example, the history of computing and environmental history both deal with areas that became hugely important in the second half of the twentieth century. But thanks to works like William Cronon's *Nature's Metropolis* and Richard F. White's *The Middle Ground* environmental history legitimated itself within history departments. Scholars like White and Cronon are among the most respected historians working today, and environ-mental historians have had relatively good employment prospects. Other scholars who influenced me, and many others, by producing hugely influential work that legitimated new kinds of historical practice included Alfred Chandler (*Strategy and Structure*—at-tention to organizational forms), Liesbeth Cohen (*Making a New Deal*) and Sean Wilentz (whose attention to contested ideas like *democracy* in *Chants Democratic* shaped my own determination to intertwine the history of concepts like information with the social his-tory of groups trying to mobilize them). Laurel Thatcher Ulrich's *A Midwife's Tale* was a spectacular demonstration of the possibility of piecing together sources to reconstruct the everyday life and work practices of a woman and her part in the larger community.

So, the biggest problem for the history of computing in establishing itself in history departments is not a lack of theory but the fact that we haven't yet produced outstanding books that are (1) obviously relevant to the issues that historians already care about and

(2) use engagement with the past of computing to tell some kind of story that could not otherwise be told. Work of that kind would speak even to people who didn't realize that they cared about computing. While I'm not good at false modesty, let me be clear that I don't aspire to achieve that kind of impact for *ENIAC In Action*—it's too quirky, points in too many different methodological directions at once, and is too engaged with technical detail that will put off most historians. The best case is probably that it becomes a cult favorite, discovered and loved by a few people precisely because of its difference from more conventional and accessible work. Not unlike some of your beloved Krautrock bands. I will admit that as a young scholar I once aspired to follow the path of my dissertation towards work that was compelling enough to convince historians to take the study of information technology work seriously.

There is, as you know, a European community centered on the *History and Philosophy of Computing* which probably accounts for most of the people working on early computing topics at present. Much of this work comes from a history of mathematics perspective, and many of its members are computer scientists or seek to engage with computer scientists working on the theory of computation. History and philosophy of science is the once-dominant tradition, popular in the 1950s and 1960s, that the History and Sociology of Science department that trained me was named in opposition to. Some of the most active scholars in that group are interested in questions of practice, but I think their methodological approach makes it hard to get to grips with practice in the ways that seem natural to me. In particular, they seem reluctant to engage with archival sources, which are at the heart of conventional historical practice. So, in as much as you will find people working on early computing who seek to affiliate themselves with theory, the theory in question is probably computational logic or philosophy rather than media, cultural, or social theory.

ES: So, it seems your answer concerning a *practice turn* in the history of computing is positive on the practical side, and negative on the side of theory.

TH: In answering this question, it makes a difference whether one considers the field of the history of computing as consisting (1) of people who would identify themselves spontaneously as working on this topic, or (2) of people who work on things involving computers and the past. My comments above primarily concern group 1, which is a fairly small and stable community that's grown and evolved slowly over decades.

There's been a huge expansion in group 2 in the past decade, but the people involved identify themselves with a range of new identities: digital humanities, software studies, platform studies, critical code studies, demo scene studies, video game studies, web history, media archaeology, and so on. Also, more generally, with cultural studies, English literature, or gender studies. My impression is that people in these fields often talk about practice, but often are more concerned with discursive practices than work practices.

That said, as I mentioned earlier, some self-identified historians of computing have also looked down on engagement with technological specifics as a sign of intellectual backwardness. And some of the recent work that's most deeply engaged with practice and materiality has come from individuals, like Matthew Kirschenbaum, who is an English professor, or Paul Edwards, who was trained in the history of consciousness.

Some individuals within these communities have engaged with the history of computing, for example by participating in the series of SIGCIS workshops I founded back in 2009 or by publishing in *IEEE Annals of the History of Computing*. The disciplinary scope of SIGCIS has certainly broadened beyond that of its parent group, the Society for the History of Technology. As a whole, however, these communities have not engaged with the history of computing community and our literature—to the detriment of both sides. The established history of computing community has a depth of knowledge and a grounding in the context of computing practice that could and should be of more general interest. That's one reason I have recently been promoting the *early digital* as a broadening identity, rather than the *history of computing*, for interdisciplinary engagement.

List of Figures